Not Easily Broken

Brian S. Chan

Copyright © 2015 Brian S. Chan

All rights reserved. In accordance with the U.S. Copyright Act of 1976, no part of this book may be reproduced in any form or by any electronic or mechanical means, including information storage and retrieval systems, without permission in writing from the publisher, except by a reviewer, who may quote brief passages in a review. Prior written permission must be obtained by contacting the publisher at brianschan@luminarywarrior.com.

First Paperback Edition: 2015

Published by Brian Shee Yuen Chan
Printed in the United States of America
by Lightning Source, Inc.

This is a work of fiction. Names, characters, places, and incidents either are the product of the author's imagination or are used fictitiously, and any resemblance to actual persons, living or dead, businesses, companies, events, or locales is entirely coincidental.

ISBN 978-0-57894-813-3

www.luminarywarrior.com

*Dedicated to God, the source of my life;
Ellen, the love of my life;
and Josiah, the joy of my life.*

Not Easily Broken

Acknowledgements:

Thank you to God for the inspiration to be creative, to my wife Ellen for being my very first supportive and critical reader, to Reg Grant for mentoring me in creative writing and to my parents, Randy & Mariana, who fought for me.

Not Easily Broken

Chapter 1
Close

"Allow your enemies to get close to you," Ray Lee said to his students encircled around him as he demonstrated a Wing Chun kung fu technique. He performed an effortless wrist twirl to escape a grab while simultaneously flashing a straight punch that stopped a quarter of an inch from a student's nose.

Ray had been running his Wing Chun studio out of a converted storage space for the last ten years. It provided a community he needed, especially since his tragic loss two years ago. People kept encouraging him to stay in the grief support group, but he was tired of the same, constant sympathetic question, "How are you doing?" He never knew how to answer. He was tired of hearing he needed to heal, which felt like added pressure to accomplish something he didn't know how to do. Heal?

In his Wing Chun community, they focused on overcoming opposition and taking control of obstacles. Through this endeavor, he and his thirty students bonded.

"Be confident that you are deadlier when your enemy is closer." Ray motioned for a five-foot-eleven-inch tall Caucasian student to attack him. The student put up his fists, assumed a fighting posture, and fixed his stare on Ray, who was a 38-year-old, 153-pound, five-foot-seven-inch, Chinese man. The student stepped forward with his right foot and thrust a hard right punch, but Ray simultaneously stepped forward to intercept the punch with a soft left deflection that absorbed the force of the powerful arm. The student's body continued to lunge past Ray within two feet of him. Ray executed five punches and chops throughout the student's body and face before the student regained his composure from his failed attempt.

"Stay calm, maintain composure, and get close," Ray instructed. "Wing Chun is a close range fighting style that relies on speed, sensitivity to your opponent's movements, aggressive offense, and use of your opponent's energy to your advantage." The students watched intently with raised eyebrows. Some cocked their heads to one side and squinted their eyes.

"I know it's uncomfortable to be close to an opponent while being calm and relaxed at the same time," he continued. "It's against our nature." They nodded. "But keep in mind that before you can learn to overcome your opponent, you have to learn to overcome yourself. Overcome your habit, fear, and inclination. Wing Chun means first changing your mind before changing your actions."

But Deon, a six-foot-one tall, muscular African-American college athlete, was unconvinced. This was only his second session. Ray had the impression this kid could be trouble when he walked in the studio for the first time with his skeptical, defiant attitude. He acted like he had to prove Ray wrong. There were students who came in not genuinely wanting to learn but only to prove they were better than the teacher. Still, Ray admitted everyone.

Deon interjected, "But doesn't size matter?" The crowd turned their heads toward him, taken aback by his challenging tone. Ray noticed his confronting poise as he stood in his tank top with his feet squared off, like a boxer, and his tattooed arms rippling with muscles.

"If you let me get close enough to you," Deon said with a half smirk, "I'll grab you and slam you to the ground." He made squeezing motions with his hands in front of his chest. His biceps swelled as he did so. His reputation for hitting hard as a star football player at his junior college was no secret. Even his brutish figure reflected the reputation. Ray was half the size of Deon, whose frame alone overshadowed Ray. The students looked to Ray for an answer, and he knew he had to give one.

In a respectful and relaxed tone, he said, "Well, let's see how I would respond to an attack from you."

He felt a knot tighten in his stomach and a glaze of sweat on his back. He knew there were no guarantees in altercations, and he worried about losing respect from his students if he faltered. He knew he was skilled, but his insecurities lurked in his heart.

But this was kung fu, and kung fu was about overcoming.

Deon hunched into a ramming posture. He lurched forward and charged at Ray with his massive shoulders driving forward like the bumper of a Chevy pick-up.

Ray stood in a gentlemanly stance with his feet shoulder-width apart and his knees just slightly bent. When Deon's head was three feet from Ray's chest, Ray swiftly slipped his right palm into the groove of the goliath's neck and jawline and smoothly rotated to the left, moving in accord with Deon's forward motion, and sending him hurtling to the mat. Ray followed the falling giant like a butterfly gliding over grass and delivered three straight punches to his face, contacting the nose and cheek. His punches didn't penetrate beyond Deon's skin, showing his superior self-control.

Deon flailed his arm, rolled on his back, and scrambled to his feet. He pulled away from Ray, who remained in his relaxed posture with his hands in guard.

Deon shuffled his feet and bounced up and down like a boxer. His reddened face revealed his frustrated determination to redeem himself. He swung his left arm in a wide arc, like a baseball bat. Ray leaned back just enough to let the colossal fist pass inches in front of his eyes.

Deon followed the punch by grabbing Ray's arm. He shoved his body weight forward to overtake Ray with his sheer size. But as his massive body moved in, Ray fired out two strikes with his free hand and simultaneously freed his restrained hand with an arm twirling technique. As his arm slipped out of Deon's grip, he pressed Deon's arm against his body to trap it and followed with repeated punches from his other hand. Ray's punches fired incessantly, like an automatic rifle, while he pushed forward against Deon's trapped arm. The football star stumbled backwards and became a free-falling, 310-pound mass. Ray was in control. He stopped the pressing assault when Deon hit the wall.

Ray paused to watch Deon process what happened. He helped his student off the wall and respectfully invited him to rejoin the observing students.

"Get over thinking that size will overpower skill," he said to them. "Don't throw your weight around. Wing Chun doesn't work that way. Life doesn't work that way."

He was relieved the ordeal was over, or at least he thought it was over.

"Man, what was all of that?" Deon stubbornly challenged again.

With gaping mouths, the crowd of students watched Deon sweat through his tank top. Ray was also surprised by Deon's persistence.

"All you did was hit me with these short jabs that probably couldn't hurt anything," the defiant football star mocked, mimicking Ray's movements. "Where's the power in that? This is how you punch!" He took three steps over to a 200-pound punching bag hanging from the ceiling. He drew his massive arm as far back as he could, swung with impressive force, and slammed his boulder-like fist into the bag. The bag concaved and swung side-to-side like a wrecking ball. Then Deon stood there without saying a word, but his cocky, imposing posture screamed, "Now what?"

Ray merely locked into his gaze for a few of seconds, the longest and most awkward few seconds ever experienced in the studio. The students looked back and forth between the two gladiators with wondering expressions of what-will-happen-next.

"Miguel, please grab those for me," Ray requested, pointing to a stack of three yellow phonebooks on a shelf.

Miguel brought them to Ray.

Ray took the phonebooks. "Stand over there," he told Deon.

Deon arrogantly strutted to the spot Ray pointed, which was in front of a thick mat. Ray handed the phonebooks to Deon and asked, "How much do you weigh?"

"A proud 310," Deon said with his chin up.

"Good," Ray replied. He made Deon hold the three phone books vertically against his chest. Ray stood two feet from the phonebooks and gently placed the fingertips of his right hand on the surface of the phonebook like he was pointing at them with all four fingers. He looked up at Deon as if silently asking him, "Are you ready?"

Deon kept his chin up and looked down at Ray.

Without drawing his hand back, Ray punched with explosive force, like a bullet suddenly ignited by a gun's hammer and blasting through the barrel. Deon's body flew five feet backwards onto the mat.

Deon lay on his back looking up at Ray with wide eyes for a few seconds before pushing the phonebooks off of his chest and coughing a couple times. He didn't get up yet. Ray looked at him to see if he had a comeback. He didn't. Ray knew the lesson was over.

Ray sighed discreetly, relieved that the challenge was said and done. He knew he should be more confident about his ability to handle a situation. The many trophies and medals on the walls attested to his formidableness. But those awards were in the past, and things were different now. Ever since his wife Melanie died, he was haunted by the realization that no matter how hard one tried or how good one was, life promised no guarantees. Things don't always go according to plan.

He looked around at the room of students mentally chewing on the impromptu demonstration. "Okay, show's over. Partner up with someone for sparring. Now that you've heard and seen it, it's time to do it. Otherwise, you'll never get it."

All the students naturally paired off with each other and began sparring while Deon slowly got up off the mat. Ray approached Abigail, who was practicing with a much taller male student, and observed her struggling to get out of his grip.

"Relax, Abigail," he instructed. "Don't tense up."

"You'd think that after two years of training here I would get that by now," she replied "He's just so darn strong, Sifu Ray."

"All the more reason for you to relax. You can't beat him by sheer strength. The tension is all in your mind. Train your mind to relax, and your muscles will follow."

"I know. You keep telling me that."

"Yes, and I'll keep saying it. At some point, Abigail, it's going to stick."

"And for two years, I keep telling you to call me Abby," she said with a sweet smile while her practice partner grabbed her arm again. "Abigail is too formal."

"OK," he agreed, "I'll remember that if you remember to relax."

"Deal," she said through a warm smile.

"Can you show me that move again?" asked an elderly lady.

Mrs. Swanson was one of Ray's favorite students. Although she was 74 years old, she had the heart of a 17-year-old and the alertness of a 25-year-old. Not many elderly people trained in martial arts, but when Mrs. Swanson heard Ray say Wing Chun suited women and the elderly, she signed up right away.

"Let me show you, Mrs. Swanson," he offered kindly. He adjusted her hand position. When she tried the move herself, he gently corrected her hand position again. It wasn't until the sixth try that she executed the move properly.

"That was perfect," Ray said to her, "Now follow it up with a punch to complete the sequence. Always have a ready counterattack."

She executed the move and made a swift punch to her sparring partner's face, stopping just short of hitting his nose. The young man was startled by her white, boney fist with varicose veins and wrinkly skin.

"I think he looks scared," Ray said with a chuckle.

She replied. "You make an old lady feel like a butt-kicker!"

As Ray opened his mouth to respond, two men almost rammed into Mrs. Swanson as they wrestled each other. He reflexively stood between her and the men barreling toward her, blocking one of their elbows from flying into her face. One of the men slipped and fell at Ray's feet.

When the man looked up, Ray said, "Miguel, what is going on?"

"That guy's crazy, man," Miguel said with a stressed look.

"I just want to test how good his wang chung was, that's all," Deon said, standing over Miguel. Once again, all eyes were on him.

"Punk!" Miguel sprang up. "I didn't want to hurt you. We're just practicing. This ain't for real. What's wrong with you?"

"On the streets in L.A., it's always for real," Deon said. Though his words and demeanor were pompous, Ray strangely heard honest realism beneath the hard exterior and arrogance. "This homeboy said he's been learning wang chung for four years, but all I see is him getting knocked around."

"Martial arts is about technique and self-control, fool," Miguel retorted. "But if you really want to see what's up, I'll show you. And it's Wing Chun, fool! Not wang chung."

"Wang ching chong. Whatever," Deon mocked. "I jus wanna know. Can you fight?"

"You wanna see the real deal?" Miguel put up his guard.

"Guys," Ray intervened.

"Come on, then, little man," Deon taunted.

Ray placed his hand on Miguel's shoulder, but Miguel advanced forward.

"Now we're talking," Deon egged. He moved forward with both fists up, like a boxer.

"Miguel," Ray addressed, "I want you to—"

Deon swung his fist. Miguel evaded and responded with a kick to Deon's stomach, but that didn't phase Deon. As Deon stepped in and threw another punch, Ray blocked it.

"Enough," he demanded as he stepped between them. But Deon reached over Ray's shoulder to grab Miguel. Ray deflected the arm and spun Deon around. Grappling Deon's wrist and grabbing him by the back of the neck, he said again, this time in Deon's ear, "Enough."

As soon as Ray released him, Deon turned around, but he was not confrontational. By his submissive posture before Ray after the previous four exchanges, it seemed Deon was persuaded that Ray was the superior one.

"Hey, man," Deon said with agitation, "he was the one who wanted to show me up."

"It's Sifu," Miguel corrected, "not 'Hey, man.'"

"Whatever. You're taking this too seriously." Deon looked at Sifu Ray and said, "Look, man, we're just screwing around. I wanted to see how good he was, and he got all sensitive."

"Deon," Ray spoke in a judicious manner, "you're done for tonight. It's time for you to go. I'm going to say this very clearly: only come back if you come with respect and humility. If you can't do that, I'll mail your tuition check back to you." He pointed at the door with an open hand.

Deon hesitated to see if Ray was serious, but Ray insistently pointed at the door. Deon fumed from embarrassment. After a quick glance at the faces watching him, Deon stomped toward the door. "Wang chung's a joke," he shouted, grabbed his jacket and exited.

Ray exhaled and said, "Everyone, back to training." He glanced back at the door, where Deon just exited, and felt some remorse for kicking the young man out.

The rest of the class time passed quickly. People dismissed the earlier disruption and resumed what they loved doing. Abby trained on her own in front of the mirror to scrutinize her moves. Miguel sparred with a girl. Mrs. Swanson practiced with another partner who was larger and younger than the previous one.

"Hey, it's time," Jeremy announced to Ray. His fifteen-year-old son pointed at the clock on the wall. He had been doing Wing Chun with his father since he was five. But since the death of his mother two years ago, he had lost motivation and reluctantly accompanied his dad to most of the classes out of a bitter sense of tradition. Lately, he attended the classes less and less.

"Okay," Ray said with a smile, "that's it for tonight. Remember to go home and practice. Pay attention to the details. I'll see you next time." Ray walked to Jeremy to put his hand on the back of his neck in a chummy sort of way, but Jeremy slightly shirked away and tensed.

"Sifu Ray," Miguel, said, "thanks for another great lesson." Then he whispered, "Not trying to be mean, but that Deon was a punk. You gave him what he deserved."

Ray carefully thought about his response before saying, "Thanks, Miguel. We're all going through a learning process."

"Oh, I know," Miguel replied. "I don't know if that fool can learn anything, but you're a good man. Appreciate what you're teaching us." He patted Ray's shoulder and walked out the door.

Ray hated to admit that students like Deon were disruptive to the camaraderie he enjoyed in his school.

"Sifu Ray," Abby said, "A few of us are going to catch a movie. You and Jeremy want to come?" A sweet smile and wide, anticipating eyes accompanied her invitation. She was thirty years old with dirty-blonde hair and blue eyes.

Ray smiled back, "Thank you, Abigail. Normally, I'd love to join you guys, but I think we should get back. We have church tomorrow morning, and I should probably rescue Jamie from her sitter. I think three hours are all the sitter can handle of my six-year-old princess. Plus, I have a bit of work to catch up on."

"All right," Abby replied with a smaller smile. "I understand. All that you do is amazing," she said with expressiveness. "Computer engineer by day, Wing Chun master by night," she said with a giggle, "and father all the time. Any secret identities you have?"

Ray said, "I couldn't handle anymore."

"And like I said, call me 'Abby.'"

"I'll remember. Thank you, Abi – Abby."

"Okay. Next time then."

"Yes, next time. Have a good night."

"Come on," Jeremy said impatiently, while rolling his eyes. "Let's go already, Mr. Multiple Identity Man."

. . . .

The drive home from the studio was a short fifteen minutes, which was just the right amount of time for the awkwardness to not last too long in the confined space of the car. "So how was it for you tonight?" Ray asked Jeremy, which was the typical question after each Wing Chun class Jeremy attended. He was hoping to strike up a father-son talk.

"It's fine," Jeremy replied blandly.

"Well, what do you think you learned tonight?" Ray asked. He attempted to kindle Jeremy's fading interest in Wing Chun. It had been a common interest that bonded them for years until recently. "What did you think about that little sparring match between Deon and me?"

"I've seen you do it before," Jeremy said.

"Oh, come on! This was different," Ray dug deeper. "Did you see his hard-up attitude, like he was set on pummeling me? And you have to admit he was a really big guy," he said with a light chuckle.

"Some could say you were showing off," the teenager responded without looking at his dad.

"What do you mean? It was an important teaching moment. Did you see the change in his face afterwards?"

"What's the point?" Jeremy asked, looking out his passenger window into the dark.

A little surprised by the critical question to which he expected Jeremy to know the answer. "It was pretty important for me to address Deon's challenge in front of everyone, don't you think?"

"No," Jeremy replied abruptly, "What's the point of all of this?" The frustration in his voice climbed. "We've done this three times a week for the last ten years. What's the point?"

Taken aback, Ray took it in and thought about his response; he knew there was more going on inside his son—something beneath the hostile attitude that he couldn't reach. But losing this one thing they shared for a decade felt like he was losing the last connection he has to his estranged son. Without trying to make it into an emotional discussion, he kept the topic on Wing Chun, "You know Wing Chun is good for your health and your mind. Someday you may need to use it."

"These days, people just pull out guns and shoot you. You're dead before you can get *close enough* to your enemy." Jeremy's sarcasm cut.

"You always liked Wing Chun, Jer," Ray's voice softened to a tender plea. "Why this attitude?"

"I was little and stupid," Jeremy answered. "Now I know all of it is pointless."

"Jeremy," Ray said, trying to make eye contact and deciding to get to the bottom of the issue, "let's talk. What's going on?"

"Nothing." Jeremy's response was short.

Ray watched the road, unsure of what to say. Was there a *right* thing to say? Was there something he should ask his son? Or maybe that was the problem: he asked and shouldn't have. "Jeremy," Ray said his name again, but only a pause followed, as the only thing he could think to do was to call out to him. But he decided to take a stab at saying, "I can understand if you're still hurting about your mom."

"I don't want to talk about Mom," Jeremy declined sharply.

"I just want to say that it's okay to talk about it," Ray said in a caring tone. "It would be good to talk about it. It's been two years, and we've hardly talked about it. Look, I understand you're –"

"You don't understand anything!" Jeremy fired. "You don't know me. You think you do, but you don't! You don't know anything." He made eye contact now through the narrowed corners of his eyes.

Ray was quiet, feeling slammed on the floor by a large opponent. The silence lasted for several seconds, but it felt like an eternity of searching for words. The space between them felt like the cosmos, while the space enclosing them in the car felt like a closet.

The loss of his wife was exacerbated by the increasing estrangement of his son.

"Forget it," Jeremy replied before his dad could form a sentence. "Let's just rescue Jamie." Then it was over.

. . . .

As they pulled into the garage, Jeremy opened the door before the vehicle came to a complete stop. He made a beeline for the front door. Ray got out of the car and followed behind with a defeated sigh.

"Hello, Tracy," Ray called out to the sitter. "We're back."

Jamie ran out of the bedroom and down the hallway. "Daddy, you're home!" she cried and ran into Ray's arms. Ray lived for her tiny and warm embraces. "Look at what I drew," she said, holding up a picture drawn with markers. It was a portrait of their family with her mom and dad standing in the middle. A green landscape with an orange sunset spread over the background.

"She really likes art," Tracy said as she walked down the hall.

"Take a look at this, Jeremy," Ray said as Jeremy came out of the kitchen with a drink in his hand.

"Later," Jeremy responded curtly without looking at Ray. "I'm tired."

As Jeremy walked past Tracy in the hallway, she asked pleasantly, "Hi Jeremy, how was Wing Chun?"

"Same," he said, disappearing into his room and shutting the door.

"It was fine," Ray said to Tracy, who had a forced smile on one side of her mouth. "He's just tired," he remarked to make an excuse for his son so Tracy wouldn't feel bad. Then quickly switching the focus, he asked, "How was Jamie tonight?"

Tracy opened her mouth, but before she could answer, Jamie said, "I was good."

"She was an angel," Tracy added. "We watched a movie and did artwork. Jamie's a talented girl."

"Maybe we should get you some paint to try," Ray said, stroking Jamie's back.

Her eyes grew big as she exclaimed, "Yeah! That would be cool!"

"Okay, we'll get you some," Ray said, "Right now, it's time for you to get ready for bed. Go wash up." Jamie ran back down the hallway and into the bathroom. "Thanks again for taking care of Jamie tonight. Hopefully she's not too much of a handful," he said to Tracy.

"Oh, it's no problem," she said pleasantly with a wave of her hand. "She has a lot of energy, and she keeps me on my toes, but it's good. I like spending time with her."

"That's good to hear," Ray said as he pulled some cash from his wallet. "Here you go. I really do appreciate you babysitting. You've been a big help to my family these past two years, especially to Jamie. I think she's needed an older woman in her life."

"Thanks. I'm really glad to be here," she said again. "Jamie is pretty special."

"That she is," Ray affirmed.

"I was thinking," Tracy suggested, "Since Jamie likes art so much, I could take her to this after school program at the community center one day. On Tuesdays, they have an art class for kids. It might be neat for her to learn some art techniques, if you're comfortable with me doing that."

"That's a great idea," Ray responded. "I think Jamie would like that."

"Cool," Tracy said. "It's only an hour long, and I'll stay with her the whole time. You don't have to worry."

"I'm not worried, Tracy," he said. "I trust how responsible you are."

"Thanks. Okay, Mr. Lee. I should let you all get some sleep," she said. "So I'll pick up Jamie on Tuesday from school, and we'll try out the art class."

"Yes, Tuesday."

"All righty, good night," she said while walking towards the door. "Good night, Jeremy," she called out toward his bedroom, but she was met with silence. She said softly, "He must be pretty tired."

"Good night, and have a safe drive home," Ray said as he saw her out the door. He closed the door and turned the deadbolt.

He let out a small sigh and walked to the bathroom to find Jamie standing in front of the sink motionless, with one of the drawers opened. "Jamie?" he asked with concern. "You okay?" He heard her sniffle. As he walked up to her, he saw her in the mirror, crying. She wasn't crying hard, but softly whimpering. He bent over her, trying to look directly at her face, and asked, "What's wrong? What happened? Did you hurt yourself?" He squatted down beside her and gently turned her towards him. He examined her face and hands.

She opened her right hand. She held a butterfly barrette with pink and green stones on the wings. "This was Mommy's," she said through the sniffling. "I didn't know it was in there," she said, looking at the opened drawer. "I didn't mean to find it. I was looking for the toothpaste, and this was in the back under… under…"

"It's okay. It's okay." Ray stroked her facing, wiping her tears.

She looked at the barrette. "Butterflies were her favorite. I remember."

Ray suppressed his own tears. He gently took the barrette out of her hand. "It's okay, princess," he said softly. He had difficulty looking into her pink, teary eyes and so he pulled her in and embraced her so he wouldn't have to. "It's okay," he said again, but his hand that held the barrette trembled. Jamie muttered something through her runny nose and tears, but Ray couldn't make out what she said. "Hey," Ray spoke softly, "do you know how much I love you?"

She took a breath. "How much?" she asked, slowing her whimpering and bracing herself for her dad's usual response.

"This much," he said and squeezed her tightly in his firm arms, securing her against his warm chest.

After ten minutes of drying Jamie's eyes and helping her get washed up, he tucked her in bed.

Jamie looked up at Ray, saying, "Daddy, what happened to Mommy wasn't fair."

He caressed her cheek with his thumb. "No, it wasn't, sweetheart." He wanted to offer some comforting words, but none came.

He returned to his own room and was about to close his bedroom door like usual, but he swung it back open this time just in case Jamie needed him.

He had thought about exchanging the daunting king-size bed for a simple full-size, but he never got around to it. He set the barrette on the nightstand next to a photo of him and Melanie in Maui, where they honeymooned. He was about to head towards his bathroom, but he felt the strength in his legs give out. He sat down on the bed and looked again at the photo with the butterfly barrette next to it.

Hunched over with his elbows on his knees, he quietly said, "I don't know how to do this."

He wasn't sure if he was speaking to himself, his late wife, or God. He had thought about praying but the words never developed, because he didn't know what to ask for. Strength? Guidance? Peace? Relief? *I don't know how to do this* seemed to be the only comprehensible, complete sentence he could form whenever he tried praying. Beyond this, he had not prayed on his own for the last two years. He knew, though, the statement wasn't a request. It was simply an expression of his condition. *I don't know how to do this.* Sometimes he felt relief from saying this; sometimes he felt confinement.

The tears at last won the fight and rolled down his cheeks and along the edges of his nose. The teardrops fell off his chin and onto the carpet—one after the other. Though, he couldn't tell what he was hurting from. Being a single father? His son's distance? His loneliness? Not having said good-bye to Melanie? Or missing Melanie? He felt he was facing the most difficult challenge he could bear—one that trapped him, weighed on him, and repeatedly broke him. All the while, he couldn't see a remedy.

At times he felt he was losing control, so he tried to hold on tighter to what he had. At other times, he felt he needed to let go. *If only I could…* He would begin such a statement from time to time, thinking that if he had or did a certain something then everything would be fine; the pain would go away and peace would return. But he was never able to finish that conditional statement, because he knew that nothing could replace his Melanie. Nothing would suffice. Nothing seemed like the "right" answer.

There could not be a pain or struggle greater than what he had faced these last two years and continued to face day after day. But he was wrong. Another loss was coming. If only he knew…

Chapter 2
Noise

"You have to be kidding me," Fred Carlton said. His five-foot-eight-inch, middle-aged Caucasian frame blocked the doorway of Ray's office. His tie drooped over his sloped belly. "They expect us to have this vector project done by the end of the week. That's the problem with these executive guys in corporate; they don't realize how much work goes into these projects. It's only Monday. Man, aren't you ready for the weekend?"

Ray affixed his eyes to his computer screen, furrowing his brows while furiously typing away. His wedding ring on his finger glistened in the light as he typed. His white desk was immaculate, organized, and clear of any stacks of paper. He had his computer engineering books and binders on the bookcase to his left and his nine framed diplomas and certificates hanging on the white, glossy wall behind him. There were awards for specific engineering achievements, certifications for special technical skills, a diploma from CalTech, and above them all was his diploma from M.I.T., where he considered his most formidable years took place.

Beneath the plaques hung a family photo of him, Melanie, Jeremy, and Jamie. The natural light, which Ray routinely welcomed, brightened the plain white décor of the room. Another photo of him and Melanie rested on the corner of his desk where a ray of sunlight illuminated the picture for an hour every morning. Next to that photo was an odd-looking device, like it could be a geeky, sci-fi ornament.

Fred stood in the doorway of Ray's office waiting for a response. "Hey, Ray, you there?"

"Yes, sure," he said nonchalantly with his eyes anchored to his monitor. "Just trying to get this project done. Like you said, it's already Monday."

"That's not what I said," Fred sounded exasperated with his friend's disconnectedness. He walked in and dropped on the chair in front of Ray's desk. "What is up with you lately?"

"What do you mean?" Ray asked through the rapid pecking of his fingers on the keyboard.

"Look, man," Fred leaned forward on his desk, attempting to achieve eye contact with his friend. "Hey. Could you just stop for a minute?"

Ray paused and turned his face toward Fred. "Sorry. What?"

Fred sat back and let out a sigh of frustration. "Look at you. It's like you're not here. What's with you? You've been checked out and buried in your work."

"Well, Fred," Ray responded, "in case you forgot, we are here to work."

"Don't give me your whole work-ethic thing." Fred would not allow Ray to dodge him. "I talk to you, and it's like you're spaced out. Yesterday, at lunch you accidentally put ketchup in your salad."

"I really do like ketchup," Ray jested.

"I'm not playing," Fred persisted. "I know you too well. Something's up."

Ray looked down. "Got a lot on my mind."

"I can see *that*," Fred said. "Tell me."

Ray felt reluctant to share, especially since he'd rather immerse himself into his computer. It was safer that way. He was good at what he did, and it allowed his mind to easily be lost in an automated train of thought. His work was all numbers, codes, and algorithms to him. The algorithms and programs served specific purposes. You input the right commands or data, and you get an expected output. What he loved most about his work was that he got the results he intended. Formulas were easy; two plus two always equaled four. There was no other possibility. It was predictable, straightforward, and dependable. He loved formulas.

But he conceded to let his friend unearth him from his work for a minute. "Things have been tough with the kids lately."

Fred nodded his head sympathetically as he looked out the window. Biting his lip, he looked back at Ray, his expression communicating clearly that he was familiar with this tune.

"I know it's the same old story, but I don't know what to do." Ray tried not to sound desperate. "It's been two years, and not much has changed." As he said that, Fred casually glanced at the photo of him and Melanie on the desk. His eyes were then drawn to the metallic, sci-fi looking device beside the photo. "If anything," Ray continued, "it feels like things are getting worse. Jamie's sadness comes out of nowhere. Lately, she's had a string of reminders about her mom. Jeremy's anger is becoming irrational. I don't know what to do for either of them." He stuttered and then stopped to turn his emotional faucet off before there was no halting his heart from pouring out.

Fred offered, "There's no easy way about this, Ray. It's going to take time."

"How much time?" Ray slightly snapped back, annoyed at Fred's cliché, which he heard too many times from others. *Time? I'm sick of time and even sicker of hearing about it. Two years was enough.* He shook his head. "With Jeremy..." he paused, at a loss for words. "He's hurting, but he won't talk. I can't get past his anger. Lately it's gotten exponentially worse. He stays out after school on most days. He tells me he's studying with a friend, but I don't believe him. When we're together, he's checked out."

"Oh, that doesn't sound familiar, does it?" Fred said sarcastically.

"Yesterday at church service," Ray continued, "he just stared at his shoes during the singing."

"You're still doing the church thing?"

"We go once in a while," Ray specified.

"So he's not comfortable singing in front of others," Fred minimized.

Ray continued as if Fred had not spoken, "During the prayer time, I peeked at Jeremy. He scowled while he stared at the crucifix. I think he's heading to a dark place. I..." He stopped himself again, but he decided to finish the statement. "I feel like I'm losing him. I can't lose anymore." His eyes turned red, but he looked away and blinked rapidly to turn off the faucet.

Fred shifted in his seat and interjected hastily. "Okay, okay," he put up his hands like he was trying to halt a moving vehicle. "You know what you need? You need an outlet."

"I do Wing Chun," Ray replied.

"No. I know you do. You need something else."

Ray could tell he had an agenda.

Fred went on. "Wing Chun was a good thing for you and all, but it's too loaded now because it was a father-son thing. With Jeremy's funk, Wing Chun is a sore reminder of your troubles. Church isn't helping either. The whole God-thing is too complicated. I think that was Melanie's thing, anyways. You weren't into church."

"It's not like I don't believe," Ray defended himself. "I mean I try."

"Yeah, but are you doing church for Melanie or for yourself?" Fred probed.

Ray was surprised by the depth of Fred's question. "Ever since Melanie's passing, we needed *something*. You know honestly, I've been questioning if there is a God. If there is, then how could he allow us to suffer like this? Isn't he supposed to be a God of love, peace... order? Melanie never hurt anyone. You knew her. She was compassionate and charitable. Why would this happen to her? It doesn't make sense."

Fred looked away from Ray. "I really don't know, buddy. You know me. I've never been a religious guy. I don't know what to tell you."

"Ah, it's too early for religious discussions, anyways," Ray said to relieve the tension brought about by his rhetorical questions.

"You know what you need?" Fred said in a spirited way.

"What?"

"You need something that will help ease your mind and lighten your heart. Your mind is too weighed down." Fred sounded like a therapist, sensitive and insightful, until he said, "You need to check out other women. Seriously."

Ray slumped his head back, looking up at the ceiling with his mouth open.

"I know what you're thinking," Fred said, patting the air with his hand to settle Ray down. "No one will replace Melanie, but it's been a while, and you need company. You shouldn't be alone. Ray, you still wear your wedding ring."

"Fred, I can't go there," Ray stated. "I don't even notice other women."

"I know that. That's the problem. Like last Friday at lunch, you didn't even check out the hot waitress that was serving us."

"You're married with three kids," Ray reminded him. "Why were you checking out the waitress?"

"Hey, I can look as long as I don't touch," Fred defended with a squeak in his voice, but Ray shook his head in disapproval. "But we're not talking about me. We're talking about you. Let me introduce you to some single ladies I met at the gym." He motioned for Ray to hand him the keyboard. "I can show you their Facebook profiles."

"You're meeting single women at the gym?" Ray asked, but he shook it off, realizing he actually didn't want to hear anymore.

"Yes and you're lucky that I am for your sake. Come on, Ray, you're widowed, not unwanted. Besides, chicks dig the whole widowed profile. It makes them all sympathetic and vulnerable."

"No. The last thing I want to add to my life are blind dates with women you randomly met on a treadmill."

"All right. Hooking up with strangers could be too far-fetched," Fred acknowledged. "But you're going to need someone in your life again, if not for you, then at least for your kids. Jamie could use a mother figure again, right?"

Ray considered that statement. "Yeah. So could Jeremy, actually."

"See? I mean, come on," Fred pressed on. "You're a good-looking guy. You're a smart and successful engineer. You're a martial arts instructor. You can kick anyone's butt, and you're sensitive. You're like the Asian version of *The Officer and the Gentleman*. I could think of a dozen women who would go for you. Women dig Asian guys nowadays. Plus, you're in the City of Angels where people hook up!"

"It's not that easy."

"I get it. You need to start with someone familiar and close to home to get you back on the saddle." After thinking for a second, he looked up with a glint in his eye, "What about your sitter, Tracy?" he said in a slight whisper. "She's super cute."

"What?" Ray reacted with immediate incredulity, "She's our babysitter!"

"So? It makes perfect sense. She knows your family. She already has the mother-figure pretty much down. She's sweet and attractive."

"And she's twenty years old!" Ray stated. "She could be Jeremy's older sister!"

"What's your point? I know young girls are into you. Wouldn't it be awesome if you scored a college girl? How many middle-aged men fantasize about that? And besides, she's twenty-one. I asked her the last time I was over."

"You're unbelievable." Ray waved at Fred to motion for the conversation to end. "I have work to do. *You* have work to do."

"I'm just looking out for my best friend," Fred commented. "This wallowing in misery you do is self-destructive, and it makes you boring to be around."

As much as Ray and Fred were contrasting people with differing opinions on most everything, they became best friends not by commonality, but by camaraderie. Ever since they were thrown together as roommates at M.I.T. they found camaraderie through calculus classes, ultimate Frisbee leagues, work projects, and, most of all, hard times. They liked each other because, for years, they had stood by each other.

"Fine," Fred yielded. "But when you're ready to stop meandering in loneliness, let me know, and I'll have at least three names for you."

A blonde-haired female co-worker with a white, silky blouse and a knee-high, fitted black skirt walked in and said, "Sorry to interrupt, gentlemen."

"Not at all," Ray welcomed her, "Come in, *please*."

She said to Ray, "Miranda needs you to check out this glitch on one of our radars in New Mexico. The radar's not responding one hundred percent, and it is picking up more static than usual." She placed a file on his desk. "Here's a description of the problem, but we have no diagnosis," she said as she opened the file. "It's nothing major. It could be just normal wear and tear, but Miranda wants your eyes on it."

Fred repeatedly pointed at the female co-worker with his eyes until he acted so emphatically that he started pointing with the corner of his head. His twitching motion caught the woman's attention. He straightened up and looked attentively at the file, but his attempt to appear innocent was futile as she gave him a disgusted look.

"Sounds complicated," Fred commented, "but it's not too much for my boy. He's intelligent. And handsome."

"Thank you," Ray abruptly interjected. "I'll get on it."

After she left the office, Ray held the file up in front of him and said, "Well, looks like Thunder Queen Miranda summons."

"Fine, but before I go, I have to ask," Fred said anxiously as he picked up the metallic, sci-fi looking device next to the photo of Ray and Melanie. "What in the world is this? I've seen this on your desk for the past two years. It just appeared one day. I never bothered to ask because I thought it was just some silly ornament. But it's been driving me crazy. I'm an engineer, and I have no idea what this is. What is it? Looks like a Star Trek tricorder or a Ghostbusters' P.K.E. meter!" Fred examined it.

The device consisted of a metallic, chrome casing about the size of two VHS tapes stacked on top of each other. On the top face of it, there was an electric meter, a large dial below the meter, five grey buttons below the dial, three small knobs below the buttons, and a red power switch below the knobs. To the left of it was a glass tube with a lot of copper wires, a coil, and some circuitry inside. The tube was attached to the box by three silvery, metallic strips. On the front end of the box were a red and a blue LED light, two retractable antennas on opposite sides, and two metallic, thimble-sized cylinders in the middle. Inside the little cylinders were a bunch of copper prongs. In between the cylinders appeared to be a green laser pointer. On the right-hand side of the device was a thick, red plastic lever that flipped up.

"It's something that doesn't work," Ray said dryly.

"Then why do you keep it around?" Fred asked.

"Because…" Ray paused and reached over his desk to take the device back. "Because it's something Melanie and I worked on together back at M.I.T. It was a crazy, experimental thing that she and I dreamt up. We always dreamed big. It was our little project, but it never quite worked. I can't seem to get rid of it. It reminds me of what we had together."

"All this time, I never knew about this," Fred said. "I always thought it was some goofy gizmo you picked up at a geeky convention." He paused. "I'm sorry, I shouldn't have said it like that, especially now that I know it means a lot to you. Sorry it doesn't work. Well, it's a cool looking sci-fi device!"

"Anyway. Work calls. I have this special project of figuring out this glitch!"

"Oh, yes. The glitch. Fun for you," Fred commented. "That's what you get for being so good at what you do; you get more work. If there's one thing about this job that suits you, it's that it gives you plenty of opportunities to bury yourself. Better let you get to your glitch before The Thunder Queen rains down on you." Fred got up, and, as he walked out, said, "See you at lunch."

"See you later, Fred."

. . . .

The late afternoon sun hid behind the tall downtown buildings, and the shadow cast a dim dreariness over Ray's office. His office became stuffy after he labored for the last five hours over the radar glitch. It appeared to be a trivial matter that wouldn't normally require much attention, but something strange about it arrested his attention.

Wearing earphones that looked like oversized earmuffs, he keenly watched a set of lines bouncing across his computer screen. They were the beating patterns of signals from the radar. He listened to the sounds of the beating signals. One of the signals sounded like random static represented by erratically jumping lines on the screen. The beating lines mesmerized him, until a voice broke his trance.

"Yo, Ray!" Fred shouted from the doorway, startling Ray. "What happened?" he interrogated. "You stood me up for lunch. We always have Cafeteria Monday to remind us of our long, arduous week ahead. Remember?"

Ray apologized, taking off the earmuffs. "I completely lost track of time," he said as he looked at the clock on the wall.

"I had to eat with Sour Susie," Fred complained. "She saw the open chair in front of me, which wouldn't have been open if you were there. I got to hear all about her nine cats and their distinct 'meows'."

"Sorry." Ray packed up the scattered paper on his desk and grabbed his laptop. "We can do cafeteria lunch twice this week to make it up to you. Sound good?"

"No," Fred whined, "that would mess everything up, because it's supposed to be Cafeteria Monday on Mondays!"

"Then we'll have cafeteria lunch twice next Monday," Ray said, as he hurried to leave his office, "but for now, you're just in time. Come with me to Miranda's office. I have something to show her and it would be good if you could look at this too."

"You know I hate going to see Miranda."

"I found an anomaly," Ray said as he dragged Fred by the arm out the door.

Ray knocked on Miranda's closed door and entered before he was invited in. The men found a balding gentleman with a pitiful comb-over. He wore an expensive suit and a burgundy silk tie sitting on the chair across from Miranda. She was a white-haired woman in her mid-50s with a perfectly fitted grey suit. Her white hair gleamed even in the low lighting. She sat enthroned on a tall and thick black leather chair.

"I'm sorry. I didn't know you were in a meeting," Ray said as he took a step back out the door.

"It's okay, Ray," Miranda said, motioning for Ray to enter. "It must be urgent for you to come in unannounced. Judging by the look on your face, I must be right."

Ray approached her black desk, which looked like a massive altar. He made eye contact with the gentleman and smiled. "This is Mr. Thornton," Miranda introduced. "He is one of the newest corporate executives here at Miracom Systems. He's here to observe *how* we operate." She widened her eyes at Ray as she said that. She said to the comb-over gentleman, "Mr. Thornton, an urgent matter demands my audience. I'll spare you the boredom of our engineering jargon. We should reschedule your visit."

"Nonsense. This is perfect," Mr. Thornton responded, to Miranda's disappointment. "This is a timely opportunity for me to observe Miracom in action. Besides, I'm not threatened by technological mumbo-jumbo, as long as you explain it to me in layman's terms. Just think of me as a fly on the wall that needs an interpreter," he said with a cheesy smile as he reclined in the leather chair. "Carry on."

Miranda's eyes twitched, which indicated to Ray and Fred she was rolling them in her head. "Fine," she agreed with obvious annoyance. "Mr. Thornton, this is Ray Lee. He's one of our lead creative engineers in our research and development department. Many of our systems and devices have Ray's fingerprint on them."

"Well," Mr. Thornton said with enthusiasm as he shifted in his seat, "it's an honor to meet one of the men responsible for Miracom's leading success in advance communications." The two shook hands.

"Go ahead, Ray," Miranda invited. "What do you have for me?"

He laid a series of papers sequentially on her desk and opened his laptop. "As you asked, I worked on the signal glitch affecting one of our radars in New Mexico."

"There's a glitch with one of our radars?" Mr. Thornton queried. His positive enthusiasm schizophrenically switched to alarm.

"Not to worry. It sounds bigger than it is," she attempted to diffuse his overly dramatic reaction. "It was picking up a bit more static than usual, so I had Ray take a look at it to clean it up." Turning back to Ray, she asked, "So what did you find? A pigeon on the dish?"

"At first glance, it looked like it was probably nothing, maybe just a pigeon. But I started listening to the pulses and echoes in the frequencies."

"You actually listened to the frequencies?" Fred asked. "You really need to get out more. We have programs that map out the frequencies for us. Can't believe you missed lunch to listen to a score of beeps."

"The programs wouldn't pick up on this anomaly," Ray answered.

"What anomaly?" Miranda asked.

"Yes," Mr. Thornton annoyingly echoed, "what anomaly? Spell it out already."

"Here is the map of the pulse frequencies emitting from the radar," he replied as he brought up the window with the pulsating lines on his laptop. They appear to be random, erratic lines zig-zagging up and down across his screen. "By listening to them, I noticed an anomaly in the pulse frequencies. Listen to this." Ray turned up the volume.

The laptop emitted loud beeps, buzzes, and hums.

"I don't hear anything. I hear what pulses and echoes should sound like," Fred said.

"No, listen to the clutter and noise in between the pulses and echoes." Ray rapped on his keyboard to isolate the noise. "Keep listening." They listened, and after a moment they tilted their ears toward the speakers, as if they were honing their hearing to something identifiable in the jumble of snowy static. "There is a patterned modulation hidden in the static and noise that resembles an algorithm."

"Yeah, I think I hear that too. Weird. What is that?" Fred asked.

"Hold on," Mr. Thornton interrupted. "Catch me up. What are we talking about?"

"What we're listening to are the messages sent on our radar," Miranda explained in a stoic manner. "The messages are carried on these pulse frequencies. The pulses are the actual content, that is the intelligible and intentional signals we send and receive."

"The noise and clutter, or static as you may understand it," Fred continued, "are interferences, generally from planes, hills, passing clouds, pigeons. Noise is normally inconsequential. But *this* is strange."

"What is?" Mr. Thornton asked impatiently. "What's strange?"

Fred and Miranda now looked to Ray to explain.

He took their cue. "There seems to be an intelligible pattern in the noise. It's not just jumbled static. I mean, off-hand it looks and sounds like static. But when you listen closely enough and long enough, you can discern an obvious pattern."

"So what does that mean?" Mr. Thornton's impatient curiosity turned into annoyed perplexity.

Ray continued, "It means the noise is an intelligible, intentionally embedded sequence of information that we did not put there. Someone else did, and they deliberately masked it; the virus is pretending to be a noise."

"You said, 'virus.'" Mr. Thornton said now with aggravated alarm.

"Someone is purposefully trying to hide this from us," Ray said. The four were silent, and only the buzzing static was heard. He continued, "I think we have a Trojan horse in our system."

"A what horse?" Mr. Thornton inquired.

"You're saying we have a virus that's hiding in another program?" Fred clarified. "That's impossible."

"Well, sort of," Ray added. It's hiding in the static, but it's also mimicking static to blend in. This is not just *a* virus, but a very smart one. We bypass noise as normal junk all the time. By camouflaging itself as noise, our filters would easily dismiss it."

"This is a problem, isn't it?" the comb-over man asked.

"Yes, it might be," Miranda concurred irritably.

"How big of a problem?" Thornton demanded in a higher pitch.

"You know how powerful our radars are," Miranda said matter-of-factly. "They relay military messages to aircraft carriers and can detect a person using a cell phone five-thousand miles away. Plus, you know we have three satellites in orbit. Controlling our systems means controlling our radars and satellites."

"But come on. This is impossible," Fred repeated again. "Right? We're saying some hacker, probably a college kid, got into our system and infected one of our radars? Nobody can do that! Our systems are military grade with a dozen firewalls. How could anyone hack in? We're the Fort Knox of computer systems."

"Well," Comb-over Thornton said, "it's a good thing you have Mr. Ray Lee on this then. What's the solution?"

"This is not all there is to it," Ray replied.

"There's more?" Comb-over Thornton asked.

"I graphed the modulation pattern and tried to identify its algorithm to find some coding and understand what the virus was actually doing. I couldn't find much but, in the course of researching it, I found another modulation pattern masked in other noises that weren't there three hours ago."

"Oh, no," Fred exclaimed.

"What?" Comb-over Thornton asked, looking at each of them.

"It had a baby," Fred said in a frozen manner.

"What?" Comb-over Thornton repeated with distinct annoyance.

"It's self-replicating," Miranda clarified.

"Just like a virus would do," Fred said.

"The virus we're dealing with is a polymorphic virus," Ray specified.

Mr. Thornton's brows and cheeks squished together toward his nose, pruning his face, as he asked in a higher pitch, "A power-morphing what?"

"Actually to be more specific, it's a metamorphic virus with a polymorphic encryption code," Ray added.

A burdening alarm sunk on everyone in the room. Except Comb-over Thornton simply looked around at them in dismay. "Somebody! Speak English!"

"Okay. As a metamorphic virus," Fred explained to him, "it mutates with each file it infects, so it reproduces itself but into an entirely different virus. It has an encryption code that conceals the algorithm of the virus, which means even if we locate the virus we would need to decode the encryption before we can purge the virus. The added problem is that the encryption is polymorphic, and that means it self-modifies its encryption code each time it infects a new file. Got it?"

"Mutations and modifications? We're dealing with a piece of software, aren't we?" Mr. Thornton asked incredulously.

"We have a mutating virus with a self-modifying encryption," Fred asserted.

"So the bottom line is?" Mr. Thornton asked impatiently.

"The bottom line: this is a very complex virus that's spreading through our system," Ray stated, "and right now, we don't know what its intent is."

"Intent? It's a program. How could it have an intent? I'm starting to think this virus is organic!" Mr. Thornton asked.

"It's like any created thing," Ray said. "It has a purpose because its creator had an intent in making it. So the question is what is its purpose?"

"Hold on before we blow this out of proportion. For all we know this could be a hoax," Miranda interjected, taking charge as she stood up with her arms and hands propped, like stilts, on her monumental, black desk. "It could be a prank of some nineteen-year-old genius from M.I.T., who's going to invent the next social network. He's probably bored and he's trying to flex his skills."

"So, Mr. Ray Lee," Comb-over Thornton interrogated, "What is the solution?"

"I'm afraid I don't know yet," Ray confessed.

Thornton turned to Miranda with judging eyes, "So we have a massive problem that could compromise our military-level communications system. We're possibly being made to look like fools by a college student. *And* your lead research and development engineer has no answers?"

"Don't lose your hair over this," Thunder Queen Miranda fired at Thornton. "You're overreacting. We have a process for how we deal with these matters."

Thornton's face turned red, boiling with anger at Miranda's condescension.

"I need to get Marvin and his security team on this. We need to identify all of the infected parts of our system and expunge this virus before it does any real damage, which it hasn't yet." She said that last phrase with a glance at Thornton.

"Who is Marvin?" Comb-over Thornton demanded to know. "You believe he's the man to rectify the catastrophe? I thought Ray Lee here was the man," he belittled.

"Yes, I do. And this is *not* a catastrophe," she said definitively without looking at him, trying to dismiss his insinuation. "He is the head of our security, and if anyone can handle this, it's him and his team." Having kept her eyes on Ray, she spoke to him, "I want you to brief Marvin on this. He needs to know everything you know. He needs to stop this ASAP."

"Perhaps, Miranda, I need to remind you," Thornton drilled in, "that we are the world's leading organization in communications, and communication holds this world together. We are supposed to be the very top of the line. There is nobody else above us. I like to see that we are running a top-of-the-line organization. Being breached by a sneaky virus doesn't seem characteristic for our level, does it?"

She looked down at the paperwork on her desk and let out a brief sigh, then raised her eyes to Thornton. "The virus hasn't actually done any harm yet except for creating some extra static. That may be all there is to this. For now, there is no reason for alarm. I recommend that this matter not be reported to the executive board for the time-being."

Comb-over Thornton pierced Miranda with his glare and

said, "That I cannot do. I've been privy to this discussion. I have a responsibility as an executive member to relay critical information about this company to the board."

Ray had seen Miranda's stone-cold expression before; it occurred when she was fortifying the concealment of her boiling frustration. She pressed a button on her phone intercom and ordered, "Call Marvin. I need him in here, now."

Minutes later, Marvin, a thin Caucasian man with curly, light-brown hair and in his late twenties appeared at the door within seconds. "Yes, Ms. Miranda."

"I have an urgent job for you. Drop whatever you are doing. I need you to meet with Ray. He'll brief you on the problem for which we needed answers yesterday."

"Yes, Ms. Miranda," he squeaked.

The men stood waiting for further instructions.

"Well," she yelled, "get to it!"

Ray packed up the paperwork and laptop. They scurried out of her office, leaving the white-haired Thunder Queen and Comb-over Thornton to themselves.

Ray met with Marvin in his office, sharing his findings and suspicions on the problem. The briefing was short since there was not much to go on, but that was where Marvin would come in as the security guru. Stonewalling hackers and expelling viruses were his specialty.

"Don't worry, Ray," Marvin assured, "My team and I will figure this out. There isn't a virus I haven't been able to resolve."

"I know, Marvin. That's why Miranda calls on you."

. . . .

After an eventful day of unwanted conversations, stuffy meetings with stiff-necks and system breaches, Ray was glad to pull up to the driveway of his house. Instead of parking in the garage and entering his house through the garage as usual, he parked on the driveway. The conversation with Fred lingered in his mind, and so he felt like doing something different for a change. It's small, but it's a start. He thought, *I'll walk through the front door tonight!*

When he got out of his car, he took note of the neighborhood during the sunset hour. It felt and smelled new to him. He had not noticed the colors of the sky, the coolness of the air, and the rustling of the leaves during this hour of dusk on a weekday.

He also had never noticed the large, grey, four-door sedan parked a quarter of a block down the perpendicular street in the shadow of a large tree, with the driver sitting inside. The driver appeared to be watching Ray, but Ray couldn't tell what he was doing or what he looked like through the shadows and distance. Ray tried to brush off the eerie feeling of being watched by a stranger and walked to his porch. Maybe that car was always there, a neighbor's friend perhaps, and Ray had never noticed since he didn't normally enter through the front door.

He was about to put the key into the keyhole when heavy footsteps approached him from behind and the shadow of a figure was cast on the door. He instinctively dropped his keys and spun around with one hand raised in a guard position.

"Whoa!" a man in a dress shirt and slacks said with his hands up in surrender. "Didn't mean to startle you."

"Oh, hi," Ray greeted. "Sorry, I didn't mean to scare you either." He took a harder look at the familiar face and jogged his memory. "Do I know you from church?"

"Yes," the man concurred. "But we only spoke twice in passing. I'm Nathan."

"Oh! Elder Nathan! I'm so sorry I didn't recognize you."

"No, it's okay. It was a long time ago," Nathan said with a cordial smile.

"What brings you to my home?"

"Just want to see how you're doing."

"The church didn't discover a particular sin in my life, right?" Ray jested.

"No, no. It's been a long time, over a year actually, since we last talked. I thought of you this week and told myself that I need to visit you to see how you're doing."

"Thank you." Ray sounded surprised. "I didn't know you knew where I lived."

"Fear not," Nathan said light-heartedly. "I know from Melanie."

Hearing him say that, especially in the present tense, made him uneasy. "From Melanie?"

"Yes, when she became an official member of the church, she gave us all her contact information. Anyway, I won't keep you. I hadn't seen you in church for a while, and I wanted to make sure you, Jeremy, and Jamie are fine. Your family went through a tough loss."

"We've been attending church still. I mean on and off. But we leave right after the service, so we probably miss you. We're fine."

"If you ever want to talk…"

"I appreciate that. I think we're fine though. We're getting through it."

"Okay. I'm glad to hear you're doing well. A loss is a difficult thing to get through on your own. Don't do it by yourself."

"Thanks for your concern."

"Here." Nathan took out a business card from his pants pocket. "If there's anything I can do for you, this is my card. You've been on my mind lately, so I just want to make myself available to you."

"Thanks, Elder Nathan." He took the card.

"Please, call me Nathan. Could I just say a quick prayer for you and your family right now?"

"Oh, no. That won't be necessary."

"Very well. I won't keep you from your family. Have a good night."

"You too. Thanks for dropping by."

He saw Nathan walk down the driveway. He looked at the business card that read: *Nathan Miles, church elder*. He placed the card in the small pocket of his red backpack, where most of his random items went, before turning to pick up his keys.

He entered and the house appeared deserted with only the TV running. "Hello," he called out. There was no response. He called out again, "Hello," this time trying to project his voice down the hallway. No response. He looked around as he placed his keys back in his pocket. "Anyone here?" he tried again.

"Boo!" Jamie jumped out from behind the couch.

Ray reacted with surprise. "There's my princess," he said as he set his backpack down and squatted.

She ran to him with a mischievous laugh and hugged him. Pulling back to look at his face with her hands resting on his neck, she asked with delight, "Were you scared? We saw your car in the driveway and then heard you unlocking the door."

"Hello, Ray," Tracy said standing in the middle of the living room. "She said she wanted to surprise you."

"Well, I *was* surprised," he said playfully, "especially, when I couldn't see you. I thought aliens got you." He riddled her ribs with tickling fingers.

"No," Jamie squirmed with uncontrollable laughter.

Ray looked up and asked, "Jeremy isn't home yet?"

"No," Tracy responded regretfully. "He hasn't come home."

Just then, Ray received a text message. He read it and said, "It's Jeremy. He says he will be at his friend, Louie's, for a study group." There was an awkward silence as their minds wandered and wondered.

"Well, I suppose it's good that Jeremy is studying," Tracy said. "He seems to be out studying a lot these days."

"Yeah," Ray responded insincerely, as he tried not to dwell on his suspicions of his son's lies since he didn't have evidence. He never called him out on lying for fear of Jeremy's reaction if he wrongly accused his son.

He hated to admit that he found himself afraid of his fifteen year old. He treaded lightly to not cause the teenager to erupt. But he also condemned himself for his poor parenting. His son was out late, defiant, lying, and out of control, and what was he doing about it? Nothing. He badgered himself with this question every time Jeremy didn't come home at a proper hour, which was becoming increasingly frequent. Why didn't any of those parenting books he read help him understand what was going on? If only his son could be more like an algorithm. He would plug in the right formula and get the right results. *Leave him be*, he thought to himself, *Jeremy is a grown young man now; he'll have to grow up by making his own choices and dealing with the consequences. Tough love, wasn't that what it was called?*

"So," Tracy said, breaking the silence, "I want to ask if I could bring an extra snack for Jamie tomorrow when I take her to the art class, since it would be a longer day for her than usual."

"Of course, Tracy," he replied. "Thank you for thinking of that."

"All right, I'll make sure to pack her favorite – animal crackers."

Jamie's eyes beamed. "Oo!"

Tracy said to Jamie, "I know! I'll see you tomorrow after school, and I'll see you, Mr. Lee, tomorrow night after your Wing Chun class."

"Yes. Thank you."

"Bye, Tracy," Jamie said, hugging her before she went out the door.

"No Jer tonight?" the little girl asked.

"No, princess," Ray said. "It's just you and me." He looked at her endearingly. "What do you want for dinner? How about pepperoni pizza with extra sauce?"

"Yes!"

"What did you do this afternoon?"

"Tracy and I played games, and we watched TV together."

"That sounds nice," Ray said as he dialed the number for the pizza place.

"I wish you would watch TV with me, Daddy."

"You know I don't watch TV, princess," he replied while listening to the ringing on his phone.

"You used to."

"Yes, I used to, but that was a long time ago. I don't anymore."

"I wish you still did."

Chapter 3
Gone

Ray accidentally inhaled a putrid odor on his way to his office when the men's restroom door swung open. He gagged on the fecal smell. For some reason, the day started in this ill-mannered way. Moods felt tense.

Marvin stumbled out of the restroom.

"Ray, you're here," he said with a shortness of breath, as if he had been holding his breath while in the restroom. "I need your help."

"Sure," Ray said, scanning Marvin from head to toe and noticing his unkempt appearance. "Don't mind me saying, you look horrible," he said, looking at his wrinkly white shirt, half tucked and half draped over his belt. Parts of Marvin's hair stuck out, and the other parts were matted down. "Have you been here all night?"

"Yes," Marvin said with little energy, "I haven't gone home or slept or eaten."

"Or showered or brushed your teeth," Ray added.

"I've been working on this virus problem."

"What's the news? Is it contained?"

"No. It's bad."

"Okay," Ray said, trying not to sound too concerned, but he didn't know what to make of Marvin's brief report. "Let's take a look at this. Your office or mine?"

"No. We have to go to Ms. Miranda," he said, pulling Ray's arm just in time to make a left turn toward the Thunder Queen's office.

"Wait. Are you sure?" Ray protested. "Let me settle into my office. Then we can take a look at it together, first."

"No." This seemed to be Marvin's preferred word for the morning. "We should see Ms. Miranda. You need to come too. Please." He continued his brisk pace.

"Okay, okay." Ray submitted. He had worked with Marvin long enough to know he was a socially awkward genius with a fixated personality. When his mind was set, there was no swaying him. Ray wondered out loud, "This must be bad."

"It's bad," Marvin repeated.

The two men knocked on Miranda's door and entered upon her

permission.

"Marvin," she said. "Just the man I want to see, and you brought a friend with you. So report."

"Ms. Miranda," he addressed her with a slight tremor, "I'm afraid I don't have good news yet."

Just then, Fred walked past the office and doubled back to poke his head through the doorway. "Hey, any word on the virus?"

"Come in, Fred, and close the door behind you," she told him. "Marvin, what is going on? If the virus is not eliminated, is it contained?"

"No, ma'am," Marvin responded plainly. Sweat beads formed on his temples and curly, brown sideburns.

"Well," Miranda said impatiently, "go on. Tell me what's happening."

"Yes, ma'am. The virus has multiplied into more than fifty viruses," he said. He paused. There was an anticipatory silence in the dim room, as they waited for Marvin to say more. He swallowed and continued. "The rate of replication increased. Each virus reproduces itself currently at a rate of five per hour."

"Marvin, why are we not able to eliminate this problem?" Miranda questioned.

"Well, ma'am —"

"Don't 'ma'am' me, Marvin! Just tell me what is going on." Miranda's tone grew louder and harsher. "What is the issue?"

"My team and I worked all day yesterday and all through the night. We're still working on it now, but the virus morphs. As we work on it, it actually changes itself, like it's rewriting its own algorithm and reproducing itself."

"What?" Fred intervened, "That's insane."

"So," Marvin said while rubbing his long, pale fingers together, "the viruses are affecting twelve of our radars… in New Mexico and a few in Alaska."

"Oh, for the love of—," Miranda exclaimed, throwing her pen on her desk with such a snap that the pen bounced onto Ray's feet. "What's next? Our satellites?"

Picking up the pen, Ray asked, "Have you run all the safety filters you've created to isolate and flush out the virus?"

"None of the anti-virus programs we have work," Marvin replied with a stressed demeanor. Fresh sweat marks appeared under his armpits. "Between its fast rate of reproduction and its ability to rewrite itself, it either eludes our anti-viruses or deletes them. It's very aggressive." He paused, looking as if he was allowing himself to hear what he just said. He breathed out and continued, "I'm very sorry. I'm trying. But this hacker—maybe a team of hackers—is really, really smart. I'm sorry. I—my whole team—we're trying, Ms. Miranda." After he concluded his apology, he fidgeted in place.

Ray felt sympathy for Marvin. He was an expert but still just a kid. He was proud of him for standing before the Thunder Queen and coming clean.

"Okay, Marvin," she said, grabbing his attention. "Calm down. You are our best, and we kept you in this company for the last five years for a reason. I need you to get a grip and tell me what is being done now."

He took a deep breath and answered, "Right now, Ms. Miranda, our team is working on writing a customized anti-virus program that can directly attack this thing."

"That's going to take too long," said Fred. "By the time you finish, the virus will have already morphed a dozen more times or have spread throughout our entire system."

"How is the virus exactly affecting our system?" Ray inquired.

"As of right now," Marvin said with child-like eyes of curiosity, "nothing, really."

"Nothing?" Ray clarified.

"Yes, it's curious. Aside from causing some minor interferences with the mechanical functions of the radars and increasing a bit of static, it's actually not harming our systems in any substantial way," Marvin specified. "The radars rotate a little slower and jerkier, and the extra static is annoying, but that's all."

"That doesn't make sense," Ray pondered. "Why go through all the trouble?"

"College kid prank," Fred said. "That's what this is! It's what we thought from the beginning. Some spoiled, bored genius at an Ivy League is messing around because he can't get a date on Friday nights."

"But Marvin," Miranda asked, "it's not possible for some college kid to hack through all the firewalls you and your team implemented, is it?"

"It's virtually impossible," Marvin said emphatically, "but I suppose… in theory, anything can be hacked given the time and the right person."

"I'm just throwing this out there," Ray said, "but is it probable the virus was introduced from the inside?"

"An employee from Miracom Systems?" Fred added, "Why would anyone risk their job over a prankish virus that doesn't do anything?"

"Why does anyone invent viruses," Marvin said with annoyance, "other than to fulfill some sick need in them for attention?"

Everyone was surprised by Marvin's sudden fieriness, but his passion for excellence in his work was always known.

"Well, how about that girl on your team, Rachel?" Fred suggested. "She's new. She's only been on your team for a year. How well do you really know her?"

"No," Marvin said defensively. "Not possible. No one on my team would do this. You should see how hard they are working right now."

"I'm just saying," Fred pressed, "Rachel seems suspicious to me. She has that look. You know? With her bushy eyebrows and quiet, sulky personality."

Ray ran through some names in his mind, but he didn't want to fuel a witch-hunt without evidence. Although he knew if a mole were present, it would drastically change their situation.

"Everyone at Miracom," Miranda affirmed, "has been meticulously screened, especially those handling systems security."

She rose from her chair. They waited for Miranda's next words, but all they could see was the top of her white head.

Finally, she looked up and said, "We need to call on outside assistance. Marvin, contact our two major partnering agencies and ask them for whatever resources they can offer your team. Brief them. Tell them we are desperate. Ray. Fred. Work with Marvin. Do nothing else."

Miranda squinted her eyes at them, like a snake fixed on a prey, and said sternly, "Maybe this virus is nothing more than a juvenile irritation. Prank or not, it is an embarrassment. I need this resolved, gentlemen. In the meantime, Thornton is expecting *me* to give him an update on the matter. So if you'll excuse me, I need to get on the phone with this hardnosed reprobate to give him the bad news. Now, get out and fix this!"

She sat down in her black, high-back chair and spoke a voice command to her phone to call Thornton while the men shuffled out the door.

Ray had been at this job for twelve years, longer than the other two men, and he had never witnessed a dilemma of this sort. Marvin might be right—it was just a matter of time before something like this happened. However, the whole matter seemed skewed. Logically, they were missing a critical element, but he didn't know what.

He spent the next hour with Marvin and Fred specifying their plan of assault on the virus. Afterwards, while Marvin directed his attention to soliciting help from outside resources and Fred assisted the systems security team, Ray decided to do something extracurricular on his own. He dug up an old project he developed six years ago, an encrypted firewall that would act as a fortified hedge around a main server, blocking unwanted access to vital data and command controls.

Pulling out the files, charts, and external hard drives for the old project was an emotional undertaking, because this was the first time he looked at it since Melanie died. Most of his creative feats paused or died when he lost her. But the eerie oddness of their viral problem was enough to compel his rational mind to tear through the emotional barrier and resurrect this project. While the files loaded, he fiddled with the metallic, sci-fi device on his desk and looked at it reminiscently. Memories of him and Melanie working on it floated across his mind. He became lost in the device, until his computer sounded upon the completion of the upload. He spent the rest of the workday building the encrypted firewall.

After Ray set up the mats in the training studio, swept the hardwood floor, and wiped down the wooden dummies and mirrors, he was pleased to receive Tracy's text that read: "Jamie had an awesome time in art class. Will get ice cream. See you later." But the delight dissipated into disappointment when he looked at the clock and saw Jeremy hadn't arrived. He looked to the door with expectation when he heard it open.

Miguel entered. "How's it going, Sifu Ray?" he asked, giving the proper kung fu salutation with one hand cupped over a closed fist.

"Miguel," Ray responded with a half smile, "glad to see you."

Abby and several other students entered. She offered Ray a warm smile, showing her dimples, and handed him an iced mocha, a drink she knew he favored. He smiled cordially in return and thanked her.

"What?" Miguel asked her with palms facing up. "No love for me too?"

She smiled with embarrassment and went to set her workout bag in one of the cubbies.

The door opened again.

"Well, look who it is," Miguel teased.

Deon entered followed closely by a black, elderly lady half his height, who appeared to be in her eighties.

"Was wondering if you were coming back for another whooping."

"Shut up, Miguel," Deon said. "I can still crush you, fool."

The black, elderly lady cleared her throat with authority and pinched the thick skin under Deon's arm.

"Ow! OK! All right." Deon approached Ray and saluted him. "Sifu."

"Deon. You're back," Ray said with skeptical curiosity.

"Yes, sir. I'm here to learn," he responded.

The lady cleared her throat again and pinched his love handle.

"OK! Grandma, OK! I also want to say that, well, I want to apologize for my attitude last time, and, I mean—"

"What my little D means," the lady interjected, "is that he is sorry for being a prideful hothead, and he's sorry. If y'all will accept him, he will change."

"Sifu, this is my grandma."

"Oh, I think he knew that already after you addressed me by 'Grandma!' Don't insult your teacher."

"Sifu, may I be welcomed back to learn?"

"Of course," Ray said with a smile.

The grandma pinched Deon again. "Say 'thank you' to your seafood. Go on."

"Thank you, Sifu."

Ray nodded with the same smile.

"I'm going to leave now," the grandma said to Deon. "Play nice with the others."

"Yes, Grandma."

"You have your water?"

"Yes, I have it right here."

"You have your snack?"

"Grandma," Deon spoke in a softer, stressed tone. "I have everything. I'm fine."

"Good. You don't come back until you learn something," she said, pulling him down by his shirt, and kissed him on his big, round cheek. Then she exited.

Deon turned around to see the others watching and smiling. He shook his head and walked to the cubbies to stow his belongings.

. . . .

After going through some warm-ups and instructions in basic forms, Ray gathered them in a circle to explain an essential principle of Wing Chun.

"When you execute your forms, be relaxed, calm, and fluid," he said as he demonstrated a few movements. "Some of you are trying too hard. Wing Chun is aggressive but soft. Your calmness is your means to control your opposition."

"But," Deon asked, "how do you get power if you're relaxed?"

"Good question," Ray affirmed, hearing his doubtfulness. "We generate power from a posture of calmness. Watch." He had Deon hold a hitting pad in front of him. He whipped out a short, straight punch from the center of his chest to the pad, which was only the distance of a couple feet. Deon's whole body trembled from the impact. Ray fired a series of the same punches, each one sounded like firecrackers as his knuckles contacted the vinyl. He delivered ten punches into the pad in less than two seconds, creating an indentation in the pad. All the while, his body appeared completely relaxed and his movements flowed through the air, like a soaring bird. "Our power comes from a place of peace."

For the rest of the evening, the students practiced this foreign concept in pairs. He further explained that Wing Chun was a matter of developing one's mind to have control over one's body—calmness was not in the muscles but in the mind.

At the end of the class, Abby asked Ray, "Sifu Ray, I don't see Jeremy tonight. How is he?"

He could tell she asked out of courtesy, but it was not a subject he particularly wanted to entertain, especially when the explanation was negative at worse and confusing at best. "He's fine," he said. "Thanks for asking, Abigail."

"I said you can call me Abby," she said, almost pleading.

"That's right," he said with gratitude, remembering that the little graces he received from people like Tracy and Abby actually add to his life. "Thank you again for the drink. I'll see you on Thursday night."

. . . .

Ray decided to park in the driveway again. He noticed the grey four-door sedan was still in the same spot, almost completely hidden in the darkness. He tried to see if the driver was in it but did not want to be conspicuous. He hurried to the door, eager to come home to his princess, and hoping to see his son.

"Hello," he called out. The house was quiet except for the television.

"Hello," he called again in a more playful manner with a grin. "I wonder where Jamie is. Did she get abducted by aliens?" He listened and waited for a little girl to jump out screaming from behind a door or the couch. He only heard the background laughter coming from a sitcom playing on the television.

He removed his shoes and slowly took a few steps into the living room.

"Hello?" he called again as he quickly looked behind the couch. "Wow, this is a tough one. Where could Jamie be? I'm a little scared," he said light-heartedly.

He walked through the unlit dining room, scanned the kitchen, and started down the hallway when he noticed a light peering through the doorway of Jamie's room. "I wonder where Jamie could be. When I find her, I bet she deserves a good tickling!"

He gradually proceeded down the hallway, stepping lightly on the carpet and trying to minimize the squeaks, until he came to the doorway of her room then spun around the wall and stepped inside, saying, "Where's my princess?"

To his surprise, he didn't see anyone in the room. He walked to the bed, where there was a large lump under the blanket. One hand removed the covers while his other hand was in tickling attack mode, but he only uncovered a bunch of stuffed animals. He used the same tactic in opening the closet door, but again, no six-year-old girl.

He went down the rest of the hallway into his bedroom, calling her name and using the same open-and-ready-to-tickle tactic. He then poked his head into Jeremy's room, where he thought would be odd for her to hide in since she and Tracy knew that trespassing in his room risked erupting a teenage fury. He went to the laundry room and garage. When no one was to be found, he revisited Jamie's room again to search under her bed and inside her cabinet. His search turned out empty.

"Jamie?" he stepped back into the hallway and called in a loud voice. He hurried back to the living room and called, "Tracy?" Anxiety stirred in his chest. "Hello? Where are you?" But no one answered. "Okay, it's time to come out now."

He picked up the remote control to turn off the television, allowing the dead silence to take over. He pulled his phone out of his pocket to check it, but there were no new messages. Perhaps they were still out for ice cream, but that would be uncharacteristic of her to keep Jamie out this late and without him knowing about it. Maybe they were hiding in some unusual space in the house, but carrying out a joke for this long would be going too far, even for Tracy. Did he mishear Tracy? Was he missing some important information she told him? He has been aloof lately. Did she say she was taking Jamie back to her place for ice cream? But a sleepover wouldn't make any sense on a school night.

He dialed Tracy's number, but to his shock, he received the standard, automated operator recording: *The number you dialed is not a working number or is no longer in service; if you believe you have received this recording in error, please check the number you dialed, then dial again.* He double checked her number, dialed it again, and received the same recording.

His eyes were dry from not blinking. He stood frozen, confused, and growing worried. *What is going on?* He received a text message from her earlier that evening from this same number. This didn't make sense, unless something terrible happened after the art class.

He broke into a frantic search around the house, shouting their names while dialing the community center where the art class was held. He expected to get an answering machine, but he had to try. Surprisingly, a young man answered the phone.

"Hello?" Ray said.

"Yes, how can I help you?" the young man asked.

"I'm so glad you answered. I didn't expect to get anyone this late."

"I'm just about to lock up. I'm the youth basketball coach, and we have a league practice on Tuesday nights. What can I do for you?"

"This is going to sound crazy, but I'm looking for my daughter," Ray said with extreme nervousness. "She attended your art class for the first time this afternoon. I was wondering if she might still be there for some reason."

"Let me see. What's her name?"

"Jamie."

"What's your name?"

"I'm Ray Lee, her father. Her name is Jamie Lee."

There was a rustling sound.

"Uh, Mr. Lee, I'm looking at the sign-up sheet here for today's class, and it doesn't show a Jamie Lee on it."

"What? No, that's incorrect," Ray argued. "Yes, she was. She attended the art class this afternoon with her sitter, Tracy. I received a text from Tracy saying that Jamie was in the class and had a great time. Jamie has long, brown hair and looks partly Asian. She was there. Her last name is spelled L-E-E not L-I. Please check again."

There was a pause with the sound of papers rustling in the background before Ray heard the young man say, "No, Mr. Lee. I'm checking today's sign up sheet, last week's, and the week before. We have no Jamie Lee here."

"Maybe she attended the class without signing in," Ray reasoned.

"Not likely. Everyone has to pass by the security desk, sign in, and get a name badge before they are allowed inside to attend any classes or activities. I'm sorry."

"Wait, just wait, please." Ray tried to steal a moment to think. "Is there another community center?" he asked.

"Yes, there are many, but we're the only one in this neighborhood. And if you're saying she went to an art class on Tuesday, we are the only community center that offers a children's art class on Tuesdays. So I think you got the right center. We just don't have a Jamie."

"All right, you can stop repeating that!" Ray snapped. He gathered himself. "My apologies. Thanks for your help."

The young man said again, "Sorry," before Ray hung up.

Ray went to the kitchen counter and turned on his laptop to look up every hospital listed in L.A. He called each one as his mind raced through the worst-case scenarios. But neither Jamie nor Tracy turned up at any of the hospitals. He was both relieved and troubled. He then called the police, but while the officer wrote a report, he informed Ray that an actual search for a missing person could not begin until the person was missing for twenty-four hours.

Ray wasn't sure what his plan was yet, but securing his son was the next critical step. He called Jeremy but didn't get an answer. So Ray texted his son, writing, "Where are you? I need you to come home." He kept it short and direct to avoid causing Jeremy to panic.

"I'm out studying at Louie's. Be back late," read Jeremy's text message reply.

Ray sent a text message back to him, begging, "Please. This is urgent. Tell me where you are. I'll come get you."

Jeremy's text message back to his father was stern: "No. Be back later."

Ray texted again, but Jeremy stopped responding.

After standing over the kitchen counter with his hands firmly pressed against the countertop for a moment, he did what he knew was forbidden. He went into Jeremy's room, booted up his computer, bypassed his teenage son's computer password, and looked up Louie's contact information. When he called Louie, he heard someone answer the phone without saying anything and then hang up. This happened twice. So Ray grabbed his car keys and drove to Louie's house.

. . . .

After a seven-minute drive, Ray stood on Louie's porch, ringing his doorbell and pounding on his door. The door unlocked and opened.

"You?" Louie said, falling speechless upon recognizing Ray. "What are you doing here?"

"Where's Jeremy?" Ray demanded. "I need to see him."

"He ain't here. Go away."

"What? He said he was here. Where is he?"

"Look, man, I can't tell you," he stated, "This deal with you and Jer ain't my problem. Just get out of here." He tried to shut the door, but Ray stuck his heel in the doorway with the ball of his foot pointing up, making his foot a doorstop. "Dude, you can't do this." Louie tried to force the door to shut.

"Come here!" Ray reached in and grabbed the back of Louie's neck.

He pulled Louie forward and wedged his torso between the door and the doorframe. The pressure from Ray's heavy-handed grip caused Louie to wince. "I need to find my son."

"You're hurting me," Louie complained. "Let go. This ain't right, man."

"Tell me. Where is Jeremy? Now."

After an unsuccessful attempt to budge loose, Louie disclosed, "All right! He's at Craig's. 65 Los Alamo Street."

"You're not lying, are you?"

"No, man. I ain't lying. Now let me go."

Ray let him go and turned toward his car.

"You're freaking crazy," Louie shouted at Ray's back. "It's no wonder Jer stays away from you. I hope you go to Craig's and get stomped!" With that last parting word, Ray peeled out of the driveway and went after his son.

. . . .

Ray didn't have any trouble walking into Craig's house, since the door was unlocked. High schoolers and college students loitered in the hallway, bathroom, living room, and closets. The smoke fumes and alcohol odor were intoxicating. The home was filled with wild laughter, shouting, cursing, and music with heavy bass, amounting chaotic commotion. As he weaved through the partiers, people gradually noticed his presence. Strange looks displayed their disapproval of this older Asian man who didn't belong. There was Jeremy sitting on the couch in the middle of the living room with a girl in a short, tight dress cuddled up to him on one side and a large fellow sitting next to him on his other side. He approached his son.

Before Ray could say anything, Jeremy exclaimed in shock and disgust, "What? Are you kidding me?"

"Jeremy, come home with me." Ray felt he said the worst words a dad barging into a party could say to a rebelling teenager in front of his peers.

"What are you doing? I can't believe you're here! How did you find me?" The surrounding faces mirrored Jeremy's disgust as they observed the unwanted intrusion.

"Jer, something's happened with Jamie. Please come home with me," Ray insisted. He held out his hand but noticed the red cup in Jeremy's hand and his red eyes. "Are you drinking?"

Jeremy's obvious embarrassment led to an eruption. "This is none of your business. Just get out of here!"

Ray could not squelch his escalating anger. "Jeremy, you need to—"

"You need to get out!" Jeremy screamed.

"Ay!" A large Asian man in a muscle shirt, maybe a college student, approached Ray from the side. "He said get out, old fart."

The African-American man sitting beside Jeremy stood up and faced Ray in a confrontational manner that told him to leave.

"Guys," Ray said sternly, "I'm here for my son. Back off, and let me—"

The Asian male grabbed Ray by the shirt and said, "But he told you to get out, deadbeat dad."

He jerked Ray backwards. Ray didn't resist the Asian thug's shove but stepped backwards, simultaneously grabbing the back of the guy's hand and twisting his wrist. The Asian guy cried out in pain, and Ray pushed him away. Just then, the African-American man swung at Ray, his knuckles barely brushing Ray's upper lip as Ray leaned back. Ray trapped his attacker's swinging arm by immediately stepping forward and pressing his palm against his opponent's tricep. He followed the trap with a short, straight punch to the guy's face. The punch and pressure of the trapping hand knocked the African-American man over the couch. The young man landed with a thud.

The Asian guy charged with his head hunched down at Ray's hips, like a football tackler. Ray took one step back and slightly rotated his hips to absorb the initial force of the charge. Before the Asian man could wrap his arms around Ray's waist, Ray struck downward with the back of his fist onto the back of his attacker's head, nullifying the force of the charge. With his other hand, he pressed down on the back of the Asian man's neck while kneeing him in the gut. With both hands, he shoved the Asian man down into the coffee table. His attacker fell through the table with a shattering crash.

The African-American man rose from behind the couch. Blood ran out of his nose. He examined his Asian friend on the floor and reconsidered attacking again.

Jeremy threw his drink at Ray's face with a cry of outrage. Ray dodged it but beer splashed onto his jacket. The flying cup distracted him from Jeremy's series of straight Wing Chun punches. Ray blocked each one effortlessly, since Jeremy was too intoxicated to be coordinated. Ray caught the last punch by Jeremy's wrist, spun him around so Ray had his backside. He wrapped Jeremy's arm around his own body and escorted him to the front door.

"Let us pass, please," Ray told the onlookers.

They got to the car and Ray shoved Jeremy into the passenger seat before taking his place in the driver's side.

"What the hell?" Jeremy screamed as he pounded the dashboard. "What is wrong with you? You freak!" He shouted and cursed during the whole ride.

Ray didn't respond. He focused on getting them home. Once they parked on the driveway, Jeremy fell out of the car and fumbled his way to the front door with his house keys jingling in his hand. Ray followed at the same pace and slowed a few steps when he noticed the black sedan still parked in the same spot.

Jeremy darted for his bedroom.

"Jeremy!" Ray called as his son disappeared into his room. "Jeremy, stop!"

But the fifteen-year-old slammed the door furiously and locked it behind him.

Ray jiggled the knob and commanded, "Jeremy, open this door!"

"No!" Jeremy shouted through the door. "You're a jerk!"

"Listen to me."

"I'm done listening to you. You have nothing to say to me."

"I don't have time for this. Open it, right now!"

After a moment of hesitation, Ray sensed the mixture of anger, frustration, urgency, and desperation exploding in him. He worried about Jamie, and he fumed at his drunken son barricading himself to shut out his father. He was tired of being called a jerk, but more importantly he needed his son right now for the sake of his daughter.

He kicked the door open, bursting splinters of wood from the doorframe into the room. He stepped inside.

Jeremy, wide-eyed and stunned in silence, lay frozen on his bed, as if a blast from the door had knocked him back. Ray stood there staring at his son, who offered his quiet attention. But Ray didn't say anything, allowing the silence to calm both of them.

"Jeremy, please," he spoke with an ache in his voice. "Listen to me." He panted from the adrenaline and then his eyebrows drooped slightly as he felt the remorse for his destructive outburst. His volume lowered to a speaking level when he said, "Jamie is missing. Jamie... is missing. You understand?"

Chapter 4
Clue

Ray sat on the floor before Jeremy, who was on his bed, as he explained what happened that evening before he tracked Jeremy down at the party house. When he finished speaking, he noticed how foreign the room was to him. He was not allowed in his son's room, and he respected the personal space Jeremy needed to deal with his grief in his own way.

But he realized he sat in a cave of chaos. Empty coke cans were scattered on the floor by the desk, crumpled paper and candy bar wrappers overwhelmed the trashcan, stained socks were littered around the bed, and soiled laundry huddled in front of the closet. He felt crumbs on the carpet beneath one hand and a crusty film beneath the other. The walls were plastered with posters of violent Tarantino movies, like *Pulp Fiction*, *Kill Bill*, *Death Race*, and *Inglorious Basterds*, and dark drawings of figures in agony or anger. Some of the drawings were of science-fiction warships and creatures in battle. They were surprisingly good, good enough to be viscerally disturbing.

"So what are we going to do?" Jeremy asked with a tempered demeanor. "It's 10:20 PM," he said, looking at his clock on the desk. "It's getting late."

"I'm worried. This has never happened. I'm afraid Tracy got into an accident on her way to the community center. But I checked all of the hospitals, and they weren't at any of them. And she did text me saying Jamie had a great time at the art class." He showed Jeremy the text message he received from her. "This isn't adding up."

Jeremy speculated, "Maybe they were kidnapped or something."

Ray pondered that possibility for a couple of seconds but did not want to assume that yet.

Jeremy said, "I'm just saying, since it seems like they vanished."

Ray stood up. "They didn't vanish. There's an explanation. Here's what we'll do," he said, shifting into action mode. "The police aren't going to search until tomorrow, but we can't wait. We need to do our own search tonight. First, let's get you a large mug of tea to wake you up from the alcohol." He tried to say that without condescension.

"Then," he continued as he led the way to the kitchen, "we'll drive around, stopping by the school and the community center and tracing the routes that Tracy would've taken. While I drive, you'll call up a few friends to help us search. Okay?"

"Fine. Sounds like a plan," Jeremy said as Ray poured him a hot mug of tea.

"Jeremy," Ray said, handing him the tea, "I'm sorry about your door. I—" He scanned for the right phrase that didn't sound like an excuse. "I needed you to listen. I'm worried." He fumbled over his words. "Look, I'll fix it, but right now we have to—"

"It's fine. Let's just find Jamie."

With that, he took his mug and went toward the door.

On the way to the car, Ray noticed the black, four-door sedan again, and he saw a silhouette of a man sitting inside. He shook off the perturbed feeling and returned his concentration to his missing daughter.

Ray drove slowly to Jamie's school while Jeremy sipped his tea and used his dad's cell phone to call Fred, Miguel, and Abby. He explained the situation to them. They were sympathetic and motivated to help with the search. They knew what Jamie looked like, and Jeremy described to them the appearance of Tracy and her car.

The main streets were semi-active with cars, loiterers, and pedestrians. The residential streets were empty.

After scoping the school perimeters and peering through the schoolyard fences, Ray and Jeremy searched the premises of the community center. The ground around the center was well lit, but all was quiet. Ray peeked through the locked, glass doors. He saw Jeremy looking behind the bushes and shrubs, which made Ray nervous. He wasn't ready to consider the possibility of Jamie falling victim to an act of violence yet.

They left the community center and drove on three possible routes that Tracy could've taken. The first was the most direct by taking streets, which took them through an uneventful neighborhood. The second was on the freeway with moderately active traffic but no broken down cars along the side of the highway that they recognized. The third was through dark backstreets lined with 24-hour liquor stores, adult video shops, and drunkards on street corners. They slowly scanned the areas and met the eyes of street inhabitants who glared back. But there were no signs of a college-aged, blond female with a six-year-old girl.

After an hour and a half of driving around, the entire search crew convened at Ray's house.

Ray and Jeremy walked into their living room with their chins dragging and their eyes clouded with befuddlement. Shortly after, Fred and Abby walked through the door.

Abby gave both Ray and Jeremy an empathetic hug, which Ray welcomed with reciprocation but Jeremy tolerated with a stiff poise. "I'm so sorry," she said.

"This is bizarre," Fred added.

Then Miguel walked in with an additional person behind him. "Hey, Sifu," he greeted with a smile. "Look who I brought with me."

Deon walked in behind him, dressed in his college school tanktop.

"I was instant messaging with this guy online when you called, and he said he wanted to help," Miguel said. "Don't ask how we got started instant messaging each other. Long story. But it ain't like we're BFF."

Deon walked up to Ray and offered the respectful Wing Chun salute with one hand cupped over a closed fist. "Sifu," he said, "I want to help find your daughter."

"Thank you, Deon," Ray said gratefully as he shook his hand. "Thank you, everyone. I'm very appreciative of your help."

"The more eyes the better," Miguel said.

"You must be so worried," Abby said to Ray.

"What do you think could've happened?" Fred questioned.

"I have no idea!" Ray said with frustration. He looked up and slowly sat down on the easy chair. They followed and sat around the living room. Ray felt the cold leather of the easy chair against his warm, sweaty hands. "I have a text from Tracy about Jamie having a great time at the art class, but the community center said Jamie never showed up there. Tracy's cell number isn't working. No hospitals report admitting them. I can't contact the school since it's closed. The police aren't able to help yet, and we've searched everywhere for them." As he reviewed the facts, it only magnified the puzzle.

"Could Tracy have brought Jamie back to her place?" Fred conjectured.

"She wouldn't do something like that," Ray responded with certainty. "I know her. She wouldn't do that without asking me. Even if she did, she would call me to let me know they were okay. She's always been good at checking in."

"Maybe they ran into some bad people," Jeremy suggested a darker possibility.

"Have you done a background check on Tracy?" Miguel asked suspiciously.

"Did Ray do a background check?" Fred said. "Do you know this man? He probably did a background check on all of us!"

"Yes," Ray replied, "I did a whole background check on her before we hired her. I was very careful," he reinforced and sounded almost defensive toward what Miguel insinuated by his question. "I wouldn't leave my daughter with someone I didn't know. I went through Live Scan and checked her references. I'm telling you, she wouldn't do something irresponsible. She's practically been part of our family for the last two years. We know her well." He looked at Jeremy for an affirmation of that statement, but his son gave no response.

Deon said matter-of-factly, "We should go to Tracy's home, Sifu."

"I'm with Deon," Jeremy concurred as he looked at Deon and then at his dad. "We need to go over there. Where else could she be?"

Ray looked off to the side, searching for another alternative. Going to her home seemed invasive and accusatory, but he knew logically that was the best thing to do. "I have her address on her application," he said as he got up and went to his bedroom. He came back with a manila folder. "She lives near her campus."

"It's 12:05 AM now," Abby said. "Do you think it's too late to go over there?"

"I say we go there now," Jeremy said commandingly. "It doesn't matter how late it is. If she has Jamie, we should find out."

"I'm with Jeremy," Deon concurred. "It can't wait."

"I've met Tracy too. She's a nice girl. Maybe there was a miscommunication between you two, Ray," Fred postulated. "Maybe she brought Jamie to her home for a sleepover or something. Did she ever mention that?"

Ray thought hard, considering the possibility that he may have dropped the ball. "I have had a lot on my mind lately," he confessed and tried not to look at Jeremy. But he looked at Fred, who affirmed his abnormal stress lately. He tried recalling the exact conversations he had with Tracy. "It's possible she mentioned something to me and I missed it with all that's been going on." Then he thought again. "It's still strange that the community center doesn't show that Jamie was there for the art class." He rubbed his forehead. "Something's missing."

"Let's just go to Tracy's," Jeremy said, "and find out for sure."

"I agree," Deon said. "Let's go bust down her door and see what's up."

Abby turned to Deon with annoyance. "You can't go busting down some college girl's door in the middle of the night. Let's think about this."

"What's there to think about?" Jeremy retorted somewhat angrily. "This isn't *your* sister we're talking about."

Abby said with an objecting tone, "I'm just saying, it's midnight, we don't want to treat Tracy like she's a fugitive and freak her out in the middle of the night."

"What do you think, Ray?" Fred asked.

Evaluating the events of the night, his reactions, and all they had done in the search, at least he believed he could somewhat rule out any tragic probabilities. The thought of something negative happening to Jamie was horrific, but there were no real evidences of that being the case. No hospital reports. No police reports. No citing of accidents during their searches. There could be a number of good reasons for her cell number not working—she forgot to pay the bill on time, or she changed her number today but forgot to tell him. With all the stressors lately sending him into a mental tailspin, it wasn't unlikely he missed something in a conversation with Tracy. He felt strained from trying to recall the details of his past conversations with her. He felt his temple pulsating.

From him beating up a couple of high school and college boys at a party to breaking down his son's bedroom door, he had already gotten out of hand. But he couldn't do nothing. Jeremy was right. If Jamie was at Tracy's, he had to find out tonight.

"Jer and I will go over to Tracy's tonight," Ray finally answered. "It is late, but I can't wait 'til morning. I have to know where Jamie is."

"I could go with you," Abby offered. "I don't start work until later in the morning, so I have some time."

"Thanks, Abby," Ray said.

Jeremy released a sigh with attitude.

"You want us to come too?" Deon asked, pointing at himself and Miguel.

"No, no," Ray replied. "Thank you, but I don't want a big gang showing up at her door after midnight and frightening her. The three of us will be good. It'll be good to have a female presence there," he said looking at Abby with gratitude. "I'm sure there's some reasonable explanation for all of this. They probably did have a sleepover planned, but somehow I forgot about it or didn't catch it when she told me."

He fought back the looming possibility that the situation might not be so innocent, but he restrained his thoughts from wandering into that disorderly realm until there was concrete evidence. He was worried, like a father ought to be, but rationally there was no reason to start imagining the worst.

"I should get back home anyway," Deon said. "My grandma will whoop my hide if I'm out too late, and she doesn't know where I am."

"Funny," Miguel teased, "that a big, tough guy like you is scared of his granny."

"Man, don't even get started with me," Deon replied.

"Thank you to you all. I mean it," Ray said to them. "I'll keep you posted." He looked to Jeremy and Abby, saying, "The three of us will head out right now."

. . . .

They arrived at a well-lit, three-story apartment building painted deep green and surrounded by a lush, green lawn. As they walked up the brick path to the main double-glass doors, a college student came out and took off on his skateboard. Jeremy ran up to catch the door before it closed. They walked into an elegant foyer with dark wood flooring. In the center was a round table with a large vase of flowers.

"She's in apartment 28," Jeremy read off the application in his hand.

They took the elevator up to the second floor and stepped onto a plush, brown carpet in a narrow hallway. It smelled more hotel-like than college apartment-like. They saw number 23 in front of them. The hall was dormant with no sign of life.

"It's this way," Abby pointed to the right toward apartment 24.

They walked past apartment 25 on the left, 26, and then 27. Apartment 28 was on their right. Ray glanced at Jeremy, then stepped up to knock on the door lightly. They waited. No answer yet. Thinking he knocked too lightly, he knocked again but harder. Still no answer. Jeremy stepped up and hammered on the door, shaking the walls and rupturing the hallway's sleepy silence.

Then the door to apartment 27 behind them opened, and there stood a short, curly-brown-haired girl putting her glasses on.

"Hi," she greeted with a slight smile. Her eyes were half open, her hair was in a frizzle, and her voice sounded groggy. She observed them standing in front of the door to apartment 28. "Can I help you? Are you looking for someone?"

"We're sorry for waking you," Ray said. "We're looking for Tracy. It's very important. Do you know her or if she's in?" He pointed behind him with his thumb at the door of apartment 28.

"Do I know her?" she repeated with a fuller smile. "We've only been neighbors for the last three years. Isn't she awesome?" She gave a bounce on the balls of her feet.

Jeremy shook his head, annoyed and antsy.

Ray returned the smile while holding back his anxiousness to not scare away the short, bubbly girl. "Yes, she is pretty awesome. She's my babysitter. I mean she babysits my daughter."

"Oh, that's so good," she responded immediately with excitement.

"She must be *so* good with kids."

"Yes," Ray replied, "she's great. Could you tell me—"

"She's just *so* nice! I really loved being her neighbor."

"Yes, okay. Look, we really need to find her. Do you know if she's home?"

"Home? In there?" she said with a higher pitched tone.

Jeremy jutted his face at her in a demeaning way with a gaping mouth and widened eyes.

"Uh, no," she responded with a puzzled look while trying not to look at Jeremy.

Feeling the sweat develop under his collar, Ray asked, "Do you know when she will be home?"

The girl replied, "I'm sorry, she moved out."

"What?" Jeremy said, taking a step toward her.

She flinched and backed up behind her doorway.

Ray placed a firm hand against Jeremy's chest as Ray turned his face slightly left and looked at her intently through the corner of his eyes. "Please explain. What do you mean? She doesn't live here anymore? When did she move?"

"She just moved out this afternoon," the girl replied with her hand on her door as if she were getting ready to slam it shut. "I don't know if she moved everything yet. She might still have some furniture in there. But I don't think she was planning to come back." She tried to force a smile from one corner of her mouth.

"I know this seems very strange to you with us asking these questions," Abby said in a comforting tone. "But could you tell us where she moved to?"

"No. She just said somewhere out of town." The girl smiled big again and gave a little in-place bounce as she said, "I tried calling her too. She said she was going to leave her new number for me, but I think she forgot in the frantic move. That girl. She gets so busy sometimes and forgets the important things. I sure will miss her. Won't you?"

Jeremy turned and pounded on the apartment 28 door again. That startled the girl and wiped her smile away.

Abby and Ray looked at each other with desperate concern.

Ray looked down both ends of the hallway, thinking hastily in his mind of what to do next and what else he could ask this girl since she may be the only lead to what's happened today. "Did she say anything about how you can contact her?"

"No, I'm sorry," the girl said, appearing nervous and scared as she closed her door halfway so she was behind it. "Who did you say you all were again?"

"She babysits my little sister," Jeremy shouted, "and Tracy has her!"

"I don't know. I can't help," the girl said. "Hope you find her."

"Thank you for sharing what you know," Abby said.

The girl retreated back inside her apartment like a gopher into its hole.

"Oh my goodness," Abby said through her hand covering her mouth. "Sifu Ray, what now?"

Ray pressed his hand against the number 28 on the door. He tried turning the doorknob and jiggling it. "We need to get inside," he said as he examined the deadbolt lock and contemplated kicking the door down. But that would most certainly draw too much attention from all the students and likely alert the campus police.

"Here, move away," Jeremy told his Dad. He drew a mechanical pen from his pocket and removed its insides. Then he took a paperclip and unraveled it. Lastly, he pulled out a small flathead screwdriver from his back pocket. He inserted the paperclip into the top notch of the keyhole for the deadbolt. With the pen and screwdriver in either hand, he simultaneously used them to tweak the keyhole. Ten seconds later, he unlocked the deadbolt.

Ray and Abby looked at each other with surprise, then Ray looked back at Jeremy who was now working on the lock for the doorknob. "You're really familiar with this."

"Yes, it's not my first time."

"And you just happen to have these three items in your pocket?"

"That's right," Jeremy said nonchalantly. "Never know if you might need them, but now is not the time to question me about this. Right?"

Another ten seconds later, he unlocked the doorknob.

The instant Jeremy rotated the doorknob Ray stepped in front of him and pushed the door open.

The place was empty, except for a small couch, a TV stand with no TV, an empty bookcase with some scraps of paper on it, an empty box, and several random items, like pens and pennies on the kitchen counter. The coat of dust on the edges of the wood floor revealed no sweeping or vacuuming had been done. But the smell of ammonia confirmed that the appliances, windows, counters, and walls were wiped down.

"This wasn't a clean move-out," Ray commented. "It's pretty apparent she left in a hurry."

"When I find her," Jeremy said, "I'm going to beat the lights out of her. I don't care if she's a girl."

Ray tried to dismiss his comment, though identifying with the feeling of anger welling up. "Let's search the place thoroughly and see what we can find. Maybe she left something behind that will help us track her down."

The three of them only found more emptiness and the evidence of someone moving out in a hurry. There was not a piece of hair in the bathroom or a scrap in the trashcan. The bedroom was the emptiest and cleanest.

Ray's worst fear since the death of his wife streamed through every part of him to his very fingertips. Petrified, the evidence was now confirming his worse nightmare, and the truth that he didn't want to accept settled into his mind—*my daughter was kidnapped.*

"She took her!" Jeremy snapped. "That lying, two-faced wench. Now what?" he said looking at his father intensely for an answer. "What are we going to do now?" he asked with tears in his eyes and redness in his face.

Ray screamed in his head, overwhelmed with shock, anger, worry, and fear. *No,* he said to himself. *Why would she do this? It doesn't make sense. How could this happen?* He fought off the self-defeating thoughts of how the same guy could lose both his wife and his daughter to crime. How could he have allowed this to happen to his daughter? Was he that incompetent of a father that he couldn't protect his children?

He strained to focus on what to do next. "Clues. We need to find some clues of where Tracy went. Anything."

"There's nothing here," Jeremy stated.

"We have to call the police," Abby said.

"I will, but let's look one more time to make sure we didn't miss anything."

Ray called the police to explain what they uncovered, having to also admit that they broke into Tracy's former apartment. But he figured in light of the situation, they would not charge him for this infraction. However, the police told him they still needed to wait a whole twenty-four hours, until after school when Jamie would normally return home from the day. They told him he needed to vacate the apartment immediately and warned him he could be charged with breaking and entering. Incredibly frustrated, he hung up the phone. *This didn't make sense!*

"Nothing," Jeremy said as he came out of the kitchen. "Not even a receipt."

"I only found this on the closet floor," Abby said, "but I'm sorry it's not going to help much. It's just a handwritten reminder for herself to buy a Fastrak Pass but it's not an actual receipt."

"Wait, let me see," Ray said. He looked at the little memo paper torn at the top edge. "She uses a Fastrak Pass."

"Yeah, so?" Jeremy asked.

"I think I have a way of tracking her," Ray said with a gleam in his eye while holding the paper in front of him. "Let's go to my office."

. . . .

The three of them arrived at Miracom. It was a cold, dreary night. Ray used his key card to unlock the front door. The night guard at the security booth admitted them in once Ray showed his ID badge, provided fingerprint verification on an electronic scanner, and signed in for Jeremy and Abby to receive guest badges.

Ray took them up the elevator to the 37th floor where they entered a wide, dimly lit hall with dozens of empty cubicles extending for twenty-five yards in the center. Office rooms lined the sidewalls. The place was empty, as was expected. The vacant chairs and blank computer screens created a ghostly atmosphere.

They walked on the well-padded carpet to Ray's office.

Jeremy walked inside, looking about as if it were his first time visiting his father's workplace. It had been at least two years since he was here. He plopped himself onto the chair in front of the desk. He picked up the metallic, sci-fi looking device on the desk. "What is this thing?" he asked.

"Nothing," Ray replied. "It doesn't work."

"Then why do you keep it?" He tapped on the glass tube on the left-hand side of the device with the copper wiring and circuitry inside. He flipped the device right-side up and upside down to examine it and pressed the on/off switch a couple of times.

"It was something your mother and I worked on together."

Jeremy put it back. He picked up the photograph of his father and mother next to the device and looked at the picture with solemn eyes. He put that back as well. He watched his father boot up his computer behind his orderly, pristine desk. "Why are we here? How are we going to find Tracy?"

"Jeremy, we'll find her and get to the bottom of this," Ray said trying to calm him as he logged into his computer. "There's an explanation for this. There has to be." The questions in Ray's mind whirled like a tempest; every conjecture collided with the other so that it was difficult to make sense of anything. The only way he kept his mind from running out of control was to focus on the task at hand.

"So how can you find Tracy with just this note?" Abby asked as she sat down in a chair next to Jeremy. "It's just a reminder to herself to buy a toll pass."

Ray typed industriously, pulling up one window after another. "I have an idea. I'm banking on the fact that she actually bought the Fastrak Pass. Knowing how detailed and responsible she was, I bet she followed through." Ray typed some more and another window opened on the screen, asking for a security PIN and password.

"Fastraks and all toll passes are RFID cards—Radio Frequency Identification cards," he continued to explain while he typed. "A RFID card contains a microchip inside of it that contains a host of identifying information on the driver, including photo, full name, telephone number, address, driver's license, license plate number, and car model. The microchip is dormant. When Tracy's car passes under a toll station, the microchip will activate and send all that information by radio frequency to that station's scanning antenna. I can access one of our nearest radars to intercept the radio frequencies emitted from all Fastraks within a seven hundred mile radius from here. I'm programming the system to flag for any person by the name of Tracy R. Pendleton, assuming she actually goes by that name. Then we'll get all her identifying information, and her activated RFID will give us her location at that very moment. I just hope that the virus we've been battling here isn't inhibiting the major functions of the radar."

"That's amazing," Abby said with admiration. "Really!"

"Thanks, but it's still not a sure plan because we need to wait for her to actually cross a toll station," Ray said.

"Why can't we just intercept her Fastrak frequency, or whatever, right now?" Jeremy asked. "Isn't there a billion dollar radar that could track anything?"

"Well, it's not that simple," Ray explained while not breaking his rhythm in typing. "The Fastrak is a passive RFID, meaning the microchip has no energy or battery powering it. So it's not emitting any radio frequencies until it is charged. When she passes one of the toll stations, the scanner's electromagnetic field charges the chip just enough to send a signal. The scanner is basically a local power source that activates the RFID's microchip."

As he finished speaking, he typed the last command. "I set up the radar to stream information to my personal laptop on an encrypted frequency," he said, looking at them. "My laptop will alert me when she is flagged. Now we wait," he said with exasperation. He knew this wasn't a foolproof plan, but at least they were going off of something.

As he was about to shut down his computer, he worried the virus would interfere with his operation to track down Tracy. The virues could be a prankish malware toying with the trivial functions of the system or a spyware to siphon unimportant data. But he needed to ensure that his attempt to track Tracy would work. He decided to take one extra step since he was already logged into the system.

He began typing again, pulling up windows that required several more layers of login information. He accessed Miracom's main server, the central brain within the company that was already protected by a specialized firewall designed by its own in-house security team.

"What are you doing now?" Jeremy asked.

"Just one second," Ray said. "Our company is fighting a virus. I'm going to upload a firewall I created, kind of a personal recipe."

Jeremy said with incredulity, "Seriously? Are you doing work right now? Can't you give it a break for one second while your daughter is missing?"

"Jeremy," Abby intervened with a consoling tone.

"Shut up," Jeremy lashed out at her. "This is none of your business."

Ray scolded, "Jeremy, you're not going to disrespect Abby. Just wait a minute! I can't risk having this virus interrupt our attempt to track Tracy."

Ray took out his keys to unlock the bottom drawer of his desk. He pulled out an external hard drive with the encrypted firewall he had been developing for the last six years. He plugged the drive into his computer. Through several clicks of accessing files and typing several more commands, the external drive sounded like a small, motorized radio-controlled car and the power light on it flickered green. A bar on the screen displayed the downloading time of the personally customized encrypted firewall.

"What is that?" Abby asked.

"An extra protective measure I'm giving to the company. Just in case. This'll upload through the night."

He zipped up his bag to leave, and they followed him out the door. As soon as Ray locked the door to his office, Marvin approached.

"Ray," Marvin said with surprise.

Ray started. "Marvin! What are you doing here? It's 2:00 AM."

"I was going to ask you the same thing," Marvin said with an awkward chuckle. Then he looked at Jeremy and his chuckling demeanor soured into an investigative suspicion. "This is your son, right?"

"Oh, yes."

"What's going on?" Marvin asked, examining the unfamiliar woman.

Ray didn't want to disclose what he was doing for he knew he violated at least two rules of the company, using the company's billion-dollar equipment to pirate information, which was invasive and illegal, and installing an unauthorized encrypted firewall onto the main server. "Nothing really. Just picking up a few things."

"At 2:00 AM?"

"Yeah," Ray said, looking down with a diffusing smile as he rubbed the back of his head. He noticed from the corner of his eye Jeremy's expression of disbelief at his father's attempt to lie. "Well, you know, I wanted to show these kids this home video," he said gesturing at them. Abby looked uncomfortable being referred to by Ray as a 'kid.' "I had the video on a USB drive here at the office. I kept talking it up and finally decided to come out here and grab the drive to show them."

Marvin still appeared to be struggling to comprehend.

"I know it's late, but we were wired from coffee anyways, so I thought: Why not? Right?"

"Yeah," Marvin agreed weakly, "Why not?"

"Well, what are you doing here at this hour?" said Ray, deflecting the attention from himself. "Don't tell me you're working on that virus problem still."

Marvin slouched, shook his head, and blew out a stream of air through his lips. "Uh, yeah." He ran his hand back and forth over his wavy hair. "I'm afraid so. We contained some of it and caught up to some of its latter parts that morphed. But it has a life of its own. I tell you, I'd like to find this hacker to shake his hand. Or her hand. You know. Don't want to sound sexist like only a man could've done this."

"You think you'll be able to nail this soon?"

"Ms. Miranda wanted this taken care of two days ago. I'm worried for my job if I don't get this canned by tomorrow. So my team and I are working through the night again."

Ray placed his hand on Marvin's shoulder. "You're doing your best and I know you'll beat this. I don't want to keep you, so hopefully you can get some sleep tonight."

"Thanks. Enjoy your video. See you tomorrow morning, or rather, later this morning." He nodded his head at them and continued on his way toward the bathroom.

"Let's get out of here."

. . . .

"How long do you think we need to wait?" Jeremy asked with his head propped up on the dining table.

The three of them stared at the laptop screen with squiggly lines bouncing up and down that represented radio frequencies being picked up by the radar.

"I mean," he asked, "what if she never crosses a toll station?"

"If she bought a toll pass," Abby reasoned, "she must have to cross it sometime."

"But what if she already crossed it and she won't need to cross it again for a while?" Jeremy speculated pessimistically. "Or what if she never actually bought the toll pass? We could be sitting here for days looking at this for nothing!"

"For now, this is all we have to go on," Ray responded. "We'll just need to keep this program running and nearby one of us at all times."

Jeremy dropped his forehead onto the table and said, "Unbelievable!"

"I can't believe the police have not been responsive," Abby commented.

"They say it's their policy on missing persons," Ray said.

"A dumb one," Jeremy added.

"We should have their help by the afternoon," Ray said, rubbing his face. "This is a nightmare. I just want someone to tell me this isn't happening."

"We have to find her," Jeremy stated with a glare at his father.

"I know," Ray said with a stubborn resolve showing in his body language. "We will. Whatever it takes, we'll get her back."

Chapter 5
Searching

3:00 AM. The laptop sat in the middle of the dining table, tracking Tracy's Fastrak Pass. Jeremy was snoring with his head on top of the dining table while Abby slept curled in the easy chair in the living room. Ray sat upright at the head of the dining table, staring out the living room window into the black night. His mannequin-likeness was no representation of his mental stirrings, for his mind could not rest.

Where was she? He repeatedly recounted the events and conversations with Tracy and Jamie for the past several days, struggling to recall any details he may have overlooked. What about scouring the house for clues? He has been on such a constant move since Jamie's disappearance that he had not thoroughly searched his own house yet.

He robotically rose from his chair to go to Jamie's room. Deep in thought and focused, he knew that was the place to start. Perhaps Jamie left a scribbled note. She must've dropped a breadcrumb for her dad to follow. She was a smart girl. That's something she would do if she knew she was in trouble. He felt a surge of confidence in finding something significant.

He entered her room. The scent of fabric softener and shampoo reminded him of what it was like to embrace his daughter. Her bed was neatly made with the light-green, turtle-pattern comforter evenly spread over the top. There was a Winnie-the-Pooh poster next to a Selena Gomez poster on the wall above the bed. The bookcase by the window was adorned with storybooks, books on astronomy, and stuffed animals. All her toys were piled in the toy chest—dolls, dollhouses, puppets, a bucket of Legos, Happy Meal toys, some Lincoln Logs, and more.

He started his inspection at one corner of the room.

He slid the closet door open, flipped through the hanging clothes, checked the pockets, and dug through the bins on the floor. He got on his knees to look underneath her bed, but found there was not even a stray Cheeto under there. He worked his way around to survey the top of her pink dresser, and then rummaged through the folded clothes inside but was careful to place everything back exactly the way it was. He removed the first layer of toys in the toy chest but only found more toys. He replaced the toys in the arrangement he found them.

He opened the drawer to her pink desk and shuffled through her perfectly arranged pens, erasers, Hello Kitty notepads, and coloring books. Again, he made sure to put everything back the way it was originally. Even if a pen was slanted, he ensured it returned to that same slant. He did not want to disturb anything, not that Jamie would've cared. But for him, it was important that everything remained as it was before she left.

On the desk was a pile of several pieces of loose Hello Kitty notes. He shuffled through them, hoping that one of them might be a secret message to him. But they were notes to her two best friends in her first grade class. Reading the notes of encouragements and jokes she shared with her friends made him smile. One read, "You're an awesome best dancer! Teach me the shuffle dance," and another read, "Boys are so annoying. Girl power!" Finally, he saw the last note was addressed to him. It was not a clue or a distress note; it simply read, "I'm glad you're my daddy. Thank you for loving me and taking care of me." He realized that these notes were yet to be given out. With trembling hands, he placed them back in the same way he found them.

On the corner of the desk, he saw a picture frame made of colored popsicle-sticks. The frame was decorated with cutout flowers and hearts. Inside the frame was a picture of Melanie kissing Jamie on the cheek while Jamie grinned, bearing her teeth and crinkling her nose. Ray could tell it was less a smile and more an uncontrolled laugh in reaction to the wet kiss. He remembered that day, because it was her first visit to Disneyland. The photo was taken two months before Melanie's death.

The framed picture trembled in his hand. Staring at Melanie's loving interaction with Jamie in the photo, he realized he didn't just miss her. He missed his family. The robbing of a wife and a mother left his family less than whole. A group's dynamic changes when someone vital is gone. That group is never quite the same again. He knew that, but he never really knew how to adjust to what they had become. He longed for the intimacy of his soul mate; he yearned to see her motherly interactions with her children. He missed the relationships she provided to them. But he couldn't allow himself to sink into that sorrow, so he peeled his eyes away from the photo.

He looked up from the desk to a Winnie-the-Pooh lamp with a yellow shade. It was left on. This grabbed his attention. He couldn't remember if the lamp was on in the morning when they left the house. This could be significant, he thought. If it wasn't on from the morning, then Tracy and Jamie came back to the house before Jamie disappeared. In which case, that meant there was a reason for them to return here before Tracy finally took Jamie. Did Jamie leave this on deliberately for him to notice? He examined the possibility of this lit lamp being a clue to Tracy's plan and Jamie's where about. He peeked under the lampshade for a hidden note. Nothing.

He strained to recall if the light was left on from this morning or not. He didn't usually enter Jamie's room in the morning to help dress or prepare her for school. She put on her own clothes and packed her own backpack. He had his own routine in the morning that involved a checklist of things to do—double check the contents of his briefcase, double check his paperwork, grab his phone, make sure he had his tablet, pack Jamie's lunch, get his jacket from the closet, get his car keys… but none of the to-dos included taking notice of Jamie's lamp!

He knew he was a detailed person, but it dawned on him as he looked at the lamp that he was only detailed about certain things. He was detailed about his job, the tech projects he works on, his children's safety, and his children's school needs.

He walked by Jamie's room every morning. Had he noticed from the corner of his eye the light being left on? He couldn't remember. Did she normally turn this lamp on in the morning? Was that her routine? What other daily, lifestyle things did his six-year-old girl do that he never took note of? What else about her was he missing? He felt unconfident in being able to distinguish what were normal activities of his daughter and what were exceptional.

Feelings of failure attacked him. *What was I so caught up with that I wouldn't notice whether my daughter left her lamp on in the mornings?* The details eluded him no matter how hard he reached for them, and the condemning thoughts badgered him, until he felt he would either break apart or he would break something apart.

He oscillated between being angry at his fake babysitter and despising himself for letting this happen. *His motherless daughter was forcefully taken and now she is without her father,* he thought. *I'm so sorry, Jamie,* he whimpered in his mind, *I should have done better.*

He evaluated and blamed himself. Was he not careful enough? How could this have been brewing for two years beneath his nose and he didn't see any evidences of it? The reality of having a child-abducting criminal in his home working with his daughter for two years disgusted him! She befriended Jamie, watched movies alone with Jamie, held Jamie, and kissed Jamie. He was the father, the only parent Jamie had. He was her protector, and he failed.

"Is that your wife?"

Abby stood at the doorway. Random strands of hair waved and looped outward, and her left eye was still only half-opened.

Ray snapped out of his matrix of thoughts and emotions to notice Abby looking at his right hand. He then realized he was still holding the popsicle picture frame.

"Oh, this. Something Jamie made," he said nonchalantly as he placed it back on the desk.

Abby asked, "How did she die?"

An awkward silence lingered while Ray searched his myriad of thoughts and emotions for a response.

"I'm sorry," Abby injected abruptly. "It's probably not the right topic."

"Yeah, I'd rather not talk about that right now."

"Of course, I understand. Sorry, wrong place and time for me to ask."

"No, you're fine. I just need to deal with this right now."

"Are you okay?" Abby asked. "It's 3:30 in the morning."

"I was just looking for clues that Jamie may have left."

"Anything?"

Ray shook his head in defeat.

"Maybe you should get some rest," she suggested. "I'm sure you'll be more alert if you allow yourself some sleep."

Her tone was soft, concerned, and genuine. It soothed him a bit, but internally he fought against being soothed. The compelling urge that drilled in him resisted soothing, rest, or pause. He felt he needed to remain urgent. Being soothed felt like giving up.

"I need to do something," he said plainly.

Abby stepped into the room with a sympathetic gaze, but he didn't want to make eye contact. He feared the comfort she offered.

"I can't imagine how hard this is for you," she said. "It must be tearing you up inside, but this isn't your fault."

"I'm her father." To him those three words bore the weight of the universe and validated his burden.

"Yes, you are," she affirmed. "And if anyone will find her, her father will. I'm sure of it. Not the police. Not the school. You will."

"I keep reviewing where I went wrong." She was his student, he knew, but in this moment she was also a woman standing with him in his daughter's room in search of his daughter. "I keep thinking about what I missed—what I'm *still* missing."

"I think the idea of tracking her with the Fastrak was brilliant, something that no ordinary person would've thought of. You gave us something to go on."

"I know you're trying to console me and give me a positive outlook," Ray said, "but that's not what I need. I need to keep thinking. Searching. Doing."

Abby listened to him without disconnecting her engaging eyes, although he only met her gaze now and then. "I'm not trying to give you a positive outlook. I'm trying to relieve you of unnecessary blame."

"You only met her a few times," he said, "but if you knew her, you would know that she didn't deserve this."

"No child does."

"I know that. What I mean is there's no reason why *she* should suffer this." He put his palms up and looked around the room. "What does Tracy want with her? What kind of a sick person poses as a babysitter for two years and steals a six year old girl?"

"She won't get away with this."

"Do you know that for sure?" Ray challenged. "How many children go missing and are never found? A lot! There's a reality to this problem."

"But that's a reality we don't know yet, because it hasn't come to that. What I do know is you're going to fight this. That I know, and if Tracy really knew you, she would know she doesn't stand much of a chance against you."

"You're kind," Ray minimized.

"I'm not trying to blow sunshine up your you-know-what. Excuse me, Sifu. Since I met you a couple of years ago, I've known you to be a fighter and it's not easy to beat you. Now that this is about your daughter, I know you'll fight this harder than anything else you've ever fought."

"You're right. I'll fight this. I wish I knew what she wanted with Jamie."

"Do you think this is about money?"

"Maybe. Or she could be crazy and wants Jamie for herself. She might be trying to make a run for Mexico for all we know. I should steer one of our satellites to watch the border," Ray said with a slight factitiousness.

Then Abby perked up and said, "What if this has something to do with you working at Miracom? You have access to a lot of high level communications systems."

"Tracy doesn't seem that sophisticated to want something from Miracom, unless all she wanted was to get more bars on her cell phone." Again, factitious.

"You could be right in that this is probably some passionate crime to have Jamie for herself. If that's the case, she won't get very far running around on her own with a child. Plus, it's not like she has a ton of resources as a college student."

"But you also saw how cleaned out her apartment was. This was meticulously planned and timed," Ray observed with concern. "This was too calculated for it to be a crazy act—posing for two years, the elaborate escape plan."

"That's a different level of crazy," Abby commented. "It's like an intelligent, purposeful crazy."

"Which is an oxymoron, but that's what this is turning into. I worry that if Tracy is crazy enough to do something like this could she be crazy enough to hurt Jamie?" he asked with furrowed brows. He unconsciously clenched his hands.

"Sifu Ray, don't torture yourself with that kind of speculation. We'll find her, and she will be fine. Even if the police won't help us, I know you have the skills and resources to find her. And you have friends—me, Miguel, Fred, and I'm sure even Deon will help."

"I'm very grateful for all your help. I'm not showing it much, but I am. As her father, this is still primarily on me."

"You always said that when we train together our Wing Chun group becomes family. So we'll get through this with you."

"I never thought this would happen to my family. You see the pictures of missing children on the back of milk cartons, the Amber Alerts and news reports of abductions, but you don't think this would actually happen to you, because you take every precaution to prevent it. You know, honestly, I used to think this happened to *other* people—*those* people, because they weren't as careful as me. They didn't pay the extra money to do the most expensive background checks, they didn't actually call up the references listed by the applicant, and they didn't Google their names to find out everything about them on the web. I did! So how could this happen to my daughter?"

Ray's breathing became visibly heavy. He shook his head. His shoulders rose and fell with each inhale and exhale.

"Okay, no more self-pitying," Abby said. "Please, sit down for a minute." She walked over to the bed and was about to sit.

He motioned for her to halt. "No, don't!"

She paused with her knees and back half bent.

"Please," he said more gently, "don't sit on it. I know it's stupid, but I want everything in her room just the way it was."

"Okay," she said softly.

"I know it's irrational."

"No, I understand," she said as she glanced at the items in the room.

"I don't know what to make of this whole situation. I'm just trying to get things back under control. I thought I did everything to protect her."

"You did everything you could do. Tracy was a very good liar. You couldn't account for every factor. No father is infallible."

"That's not good enough! Not for Jamie. Not for me." Ray's response silenced their dialogue until he added, "This is like… like losing my wife again."

Abby's engaging eyes finally retreated and floated to the floor.

"You'll find her," she repeated.

"She didn't deserve this," he repeated.

"I know."

"I'm sure any father would say that."

"Even if I never met Jamie, I can tell how special she is by the way you love her."

He wrestled back the tears. The further his pain dug into his heart, the more his anger increased. "Thank you for talking with me, but I need to do something. I'm going to look for clues outside. If they came back to the house, then maybe Jamie dropped something in the driveway. I need to check."

"Why don't I look, and you get some rest," Abby suggested.

"No, I don't want rest. I'll handle it."

With that said, he walked out of the room and into the kitchen. He pulled out a large Mag-light from one of the drawers under the counter. Jeremy remained motionlessly asleep on the dining table. Ray went out the front door as Abby came out into the hallway to see him exit.

. . . .

There were not enough streetlamps on his block, he always thought. He sent repeated complaints to the city that went unanswered. He could've used more lighting right now.

He shone the flashlight into the darkness and searched the grassy area and flowerbed next to the driveway. He looked for a note or a shoe, anything. He scanned the driveway, thinking perhaps Jamie may have inscribed something onto the concrete with a pencil or marker. Nothing. No trace of his daughter.

He looked out into the street. All was still and dark. Then he suddenly saw a tiny, reddish light appear halfway down the block on the perpendicular street leading up to his house. It came from inside a vehicle parked beneath the canopy of a large tree, which shielded it from the scarce streetlight.

He pointed the beam of his Mag-lite at the car. There was a man sitting inside smoking a cigarette. This was the same stranger and vehicle he had noticed before, and he was there at 3:45 in the morning! *Has he been watching my family?* Ray thought.

Ray started to walk towards the vehicle. The engine of the grey, four-door sedan turned on.

"Hey," Ray yelled at the stalker and broke out into a sprint towards him, keeping the beam fixed on the grey car. He tried to make out the face; he saw a grey-haired man, perhaps Caucasian.

The cigarette light appeared again, as the vehicle went several feet in reverse.

"Who are you?" Ray shouted as the car pulled out of the parking space with a roar of its engine.

"Sifu, what's going on?" Abby called out from the front door of the house.

"What are you doing?" Jeremy yelled from behind Abby.

Ray was almost upon the car when the stranger made a U-turn. "Stop!"

The car completed its turn.

As the car began to accelerate, Ray swung the Mag-lite down, slamming it on the trunk, shattering the glass of the flashlight and igniting sparks from the bursting bulb. "Stop! Do you have something to do with my daughter?" He shouted as the grey car sped away down the street.

"Come back!" he yelled at the fading red taillights.

Abby approached Ray from behind. "Who was that?"

Lights from two of the neighboring houses came on, and a dog barked.

"Come on," she said, tugging him by the arm. "We should go back inside."

They jogged back to the house, while Ray repeatedly turned his head to look down the dark, empty street.

"What was that all about?" Jeremy asked.

"That man. I noticed him sitting in the same spot in that car for the last few nights. He's been watching us."

"Are you sure?" Abby asked.

"I'm sure." He ordered, "Jeremy, write this down." He recited a license plate number.

"You got his license plate in the dark while he sped away? And while you were shouting and busting up his car?" Jeremy asked with amazement as he wrote down the number. "Dang, you should be a cop!"

Then he muttered under his breath, "You practically are most of the time."

"We have to find out who this stalker is. It can't be a coincidence I started noticing him a few days before Jamie went missing."

"You think he's an accomplice?" Abby asked.

"I don't know. If he were, it wouldn't make sense for him to sit outside our house and watch us after Jamie's been taken. If he were in this with Tracy, they would be trying to get as far from here as possible. I'm not sure who he is or why he's here, but these events are too coincidental to be random."

"I'll research these digits online and see what I find," Jeremy said.

"Good. Let's stay on top of everything," Ray said with adrenaline coursing through him. "We're already a few steps behind. We need to catch up. We can't wait for the police to help. This is on us."

"What can I do?" Abby asked.

"Help me put this on Amber Alert. I'll give you the information on Tracy's car."

"Sure, Sifu Ray. I'll get on this," she replied.

"Thank you," was all he said before setting the broken Mag-lite on the dining table and turning to head down the hallway. The short walk to Jamie's room helped his adrenaline subside. He felt the need to return to her room one last time. Perhaps it had to do with being a little neurotic about checking for clues. Perhaps it had to do with the way he darted out of her room earlier that didn't suffice as a proper closure. When he walked in, the first thing he noticed was that the Winnie-the-Pooh lamp was still on.

He motioned to turn it off as his engineering mindset would normally prompt him to do—shouldn't waste energy when no one was using it. He reached for the switch beneath the shade but stopped. He couldn't turn it off. His eyes watered, and his nose ran. He looked at the illuminated characters on the shade and how the soft light fell on the desktop, brightening her spiral-bound Hello Kitty notebook, Hello Kitty pen and the picture in the popsicle frame. Somehow this lamp that was impractically wasting energy was significant to him. It didn't tell him where Jamie was. Leaving it on obviously didn't provide any information. But it was significant in telling him that she was still out there. It held out hope in finding her. Jamie left this on. He won't turn it off.

His hand retreated from the lamp and fell back to his side.

After taking one brief glance around the room, he slowly walked out and resumed his place at the head of the dining table.

While Jeremy surfed the internet on the laptop at the dining table, and Abby was reading a website on the desktop in the living room, Ray sat for a moment—truly sat. It was a little after 4:00 AM and for the first time in the last couple of days, he felt the soreness in his muscles and the heaviness on his eyelids.

He clumsily reached for his own laptop in front of him with his half closed eyes. *I should look up the FBI*, he thought to himself. He fought back the fatigue while he typed but nodded off a couple of times, and his focus faded in and out. While he waited for the FBI homepage to come up, a thought to say a prayer for Jamie entered his mind, but soon a shroud of dark slumber crept over him.

Chapter 6
Tracy

At 7:02 AM the sunlight snuck through the curtains and draped over Ray's cheek while he slept with his head on top of the dining table. His laptop was in front of him and it remained active with dancing lines on the screen. Abby slept on the couch and Jeremy slept at the dining table opposite Ray. The sunlight slid up to Ray's nose and eyes. He jolted and awoke.

After looking around, he focused on Jeremy in front of him. "Jer!" he called out. "Oh, my goodness! You're going to be late for school." He looked at the time on his laptop and continued calling out to his son, "Come on, Jer. Wake up!"

"Huh?" Jeremy moaned with his eyes still closed.

"School!" Ray walked over to his son. "Go wash up. I'll drive you."

Jeremy, with his eyelids half-open, mumbled, "What? I'm not going."

The talk about Jeremy's school reminded Ray to call Jamie's, in case by some miracle she showed up there. As he dialed, he called out to Jeremy again, "Yes, you are. I know you're tired, but you can't skip class."

While the phone rang, he shook Abby awake.

"Hello," Ray said when the school receptionist answered, "this is Ray Lee. I'm calling to see if my daughter, Jamie Lee, was dropped off at school today."

She placed him on hold while she radioed the schoolyard supervisor, checked the office sign-in sheet, and called Jamie's classroom. She reported back to Ray that Jamie had not been at school. He asked if she was picked up from school yesterday, and the receptionist confirmed, "Yes, Mr. Lee. Tracy picked up Jamie as usual. Is something wrong?" She expressed concern, but Ray could not spare the time to explain. He cordially thanked her and asked her to phone him if Jamie showed up.

He shook Jeremy's shoulder. "Jeremy, I said you're not skipping school."

Abby sat up on the couch and asked, "Any news detecting Tracy's Fastrak?"

"No," Ray said despondently. "Nothing yet. But you should get to work."

"I could come back later," Abby said.

"You really don't need to," Jeremy said, groggily sitting up.

"What he means," Ray clarified, "is that you've helped so much already, and we don't want to take you away from your life."

"Sifu Ray, it's okay," she said, "I want to help."

Jeremy gave a sigh with attitude and stood up to go to the kitchen.

Ray, feeling embarrassed, tried to divert her attention away from Jeremy. "I'm not going into work today, so I'll monitor the radio frequency alerts. You should get to your job. I wouldn't want you to get in trouble."

"It's perfectly fine," she assured. "I work at a bio lab, so it's flexible as long as I get in before 9:00 a. m." She glanced at her watch. "I'll check back later with you when I get off work, Sifu." She picked up her purse and headed for the door.

"Thank you, Abby."

"Good-bye, Jeremy," she called towards the kitchen, seeing Jeremy behind the counter pouring a glass of juice. But he didn't answer.

"Bye, Abby," Ray again intervened to cover for the rudeness of his son. "We'll see you later."

He closed the door behind her and immediately turned to him. "What is the matter with you, Jeremy? She just spent the entire night helping us look for your sister. Why do you treat her like that?"

Jeremy was quite still as he drank his juice in the kitchen.

Ray shook his head. "I'm taking you to school. Go get ready. Hurry up."

"I said I'm not going," Jeremy stated bluntly.

"What do you mean you're not going? I know you cut classes, Jer, but not today. Today, you're going."

"I said I'm not going," Jeremy combated his father's insistence with sternness in his voice and defiance in his eyes.

"I'm not asking. I'm telling. You're not cutting."

"How could I go to school with Jamie missing? I'm staying to look for her."

"I don't need your help. I can monitor the signal. What I need is for you to do what you're supposed to do!"

Jeremy shook his head at Ray and started to walk to his room.

Ray anticipated his intent and moved quickly to stand in the hallway, blocking Jeremy's path to his room.

"Get out of my way," Jeremy said. He clearly didn't like his father physically blocking him from entering his place of retreat.

The two of them stood face-to-face like alley cats on a fence trying to pass in opposite directions. After last night, Jeremy reconsidered forcing his way through.

"The only reason you're going to your room is to change your clothes and get your backpack," Ray declared.

"What the heck? How can you be thinking about school at a time like this? You're ridiculous!"

"It's a school day, Jeremy, and that's where you're *supposed* to be! We're not going to let everything fall apart. Something is going to go the way it's supposed to!"

Jeremy insisted, "I'm not sitting in class and learning geometry while my little sister is in trouble! If school is so important to you, then you go!"

Ray opened his mouth and took a step towards Jeremy to give a final rebuttal when the laptop beeped. Beep-beep-beep. They both looked at the screen, which had a flashing green textbox on the bottom right-hand corner. It continued to beep. They scurried over to the hailing laptop.

"What is it?" Jeremy asked.

"It's Jamie. Tracy just crossed a toll station!" Ray scanned Jeremy's face for a split second as Jeremy looked back at his father with inquisition. "Get in the car," Ray said as he grabbed the laptop, cell phone, and car keys. "They're 20 miles out on the Interstate heading southbound."

They scrambled out of the house. Jeremy locked the front door while Ray unlocked the car. They jumped inside the car and peeled out of the driveway. While Ray was looking in the rearview mirror, he saw the same grey, four-door sedan was back but parked a little farther from their house. He found it incredulous that the stranger returned after last night, but he could not go down this rabbit trail.

They sped down the residential street.

"What are we going to do once we get to the toll station?" Jeremy asked. "They won't be there when we get there."

"I don't know yet," Ray confessed, "but this is the only lead we have. We at least have her car model and license plate. According to this ID info, she's not driving the same car."

Ray took side streets whenever there was a slight congestion or a stop at a red light. He kept his car in constant motion until he reached the freeway, which felt like fifteen minutes when it actually only took him less than three minutes. He wove through the slow moving traffic on the freeway, cutting off other cars and instigating angry honks. Once, he charged into the carpool lane by crossing the double solid, yellow lines, he blazed down the highway at 79 miles per hour.

"We should go faster," Jeremy said.

"We can't risk getting pulled over by a cop," Ray replied. "We'll lose more time that way."

They quickly approached a truck going only 67 miles per hour in the carpool lane. After tailing him for a few seconds, Ray broke through the double solid, yellow lines again into the fast lane to pass the truck and jump back into the carpool lane. He resumed his 79 miles per hour speed but soon slowed to 65 miles per hour when he noticed the perched highway patrol car underneath an overpass up ahead. Cruising by the policeman with the radar gun trained on the passing traffic, Ray waited until he could no longer see the patrol car and then floored the pedal to get back to 79 miles per hour.

Ray glanced at the laptop resting on Jeremy's lap and said, "We're looking for a silver Ford Focus with the license plate GH555TX."

They finally passed through the same toll station that Tracy and Jamie had gone through fifteen minutes earlier.

Ray moved into the middle lane, driving just slightly faster than the flow of traffic. Both of them scanned each car as they drove by them. Although realizing it was futile to do so since the car would no longer be there anymore, they felt motivated and hopeful knowing that Jamie had passed this point just fifteen minutes before.

"They're not going to be here," Jeremy said with frustration. "We need to get up ahead. Drive faster."

"Just make sure you look carefully."

Then the laptop beeped again and another flashing green box appeared on the screen.

"They crossed another toll station?" Jeremy asked. "That's not possible. There isn't another one that close."

"No," Ray looked closely at the screen, turning his head back and forth between the screen and the road. He slowed the car down to 63 miles per hour. "It's something else. It looks like it's coming from a retail store. She must be using a credit card with a RFID microchip in it! They just recently installed those chips in credit cards. The radar picked up the frequency when she used her card to make a purchase. They stopped somewhere!" Ray and Jeremy looked at each other with excitement. "What's the address the frequency is originating from?"

Jeremy read off the address on the screen and punched it into the GPS on his cell phone, which directed them to take an exit off the freeway two miles ahead.

Ray accelerated up to 75 miles per hour, snaking around other cars and having to hit the brakes a couple of times as he came up fast behind a slower vehicle. Jeremy threw out suggestions for lanes to take and cautioned his father about a slower car up ahead, but the backseat driving only made Ray anxious.

Finally, they exited. Jeremy told him to take a left turn but the left turn lane was lined with a dozen cars waiting for a red light to turn green. Ray got into the right turn lane instead, turned right, and then spun around in a U-turn, upsetting an oncoming vehicle. He drove straight, heading in the direction he needed, and passed the line of cars still waiting for the light to change.

Jeremy googled the address on his cell phone. "They're at a Target store! It's only three miles away!"

Ray sped through a couple of yellow lights, avoided hitting a pedestrian, and overtook a motor scooter, which made the driver swerve out of shock.

They saw the red Target sign a block away. Ray gassed it.

He slowed as he approached the driveway of the enormous parking lot filled with cars.

They both surveyed the areas on opposite sides of their car, as they drove moderately up and down the aisles—balancing a slow but rushed pace.

"Remember," Ray said, "silver Ford Focus with license number GH555TX."

"Why are they here?" Jeremy asked. "Man, I can't wait to get my hands on her."

"Think straight, Jer," Ray said as beads of sweat bubbled above his brows.

"Why are there so many people here on a school day?"

"Focus."

The lot was fuller than they expected on a Wednesday morning. Every silver car caught their attention, especially the ones that were pulling out of a parking spot, driving up an aisle, or pulling out of the lot. They checked out the people coming out of the store and every woman with a little girl. When Ray turned left to go up the next aisle, he came to a sudden stop in front of a large Hispanic man pushing a shopping cart. The pedestrian gave Ray a dirty look and deliberately crossed the street slower to agitate Ray. Ray wanted to blow his horn but resisted so as not to alarm Tracy of their presence.

As they completed the turn, Ray noticed a young woman in the distance just disappearing around the side of the Target building.

"There!" Ray pointed. "Over there, at the edge of the building. That's Tracy!"

He drove fast down the road, swerving around an elderly pedestrian, and slowing down for a mother crossing with a stroller. As soon as she passed, he sped up again and then came to a crawl as he neared the edge of the building. His heart raced.

They both peered around the corner as Ray stopped the car. Scanning a smaller section of the parking lot beside the Target store, Ray saw a silver Ford Focus in the middle of an aisle.

"That's it," Ray exclaimed.

The trunk was open. As soon as it closed, they saw Tracy speaking to a man in a beige suit. They shook hands and were parting. He walked to the driver's side of a brown SUV with tinted windows that was parked next to her car.

"Let's go!" Ray stepped on the gas again and told Jeremy, "Get ready!" He didn't know what he exactly meant by that, but at this point he didn't know what to expect. They simply had to be ready for anything and not miss a beat.

As they quickly approached, Jeremy used his camera phone to take several pictures of the other man and his SUV as he got inside. The brown SUV pulled out and began to drive away. Ray pulled in front of the silver Ford Focus as Tracy was opening her driver's side door to get in. She looked up immediately, and her flustered expression gave away her guiltiness.

She got inside her car and fumbled to insert her keys into the ignition until she dropped them. They fell by the gas pedal. She didn't have time to reach down and feel around for them, not while Ray and Jeremy jumped out of their car. Tracy got out of her car and ran.

"Tracy!" Ray yelled as he chased her. He looked inside the silver car as he passed but did not see Jamie inside. "Tracy!"

She kept running towards the tree line that marked the edge of the parking lot.

Jeremy raced past his father and made a beeline for Tracy. He closed in on her as she reached the trees. When he was about eight feet from her, he dove, catching her by the knees and sending her body slapping on the dirt, like a pancake on a skillet.

She kicked and grunted. Jeremy's instinctive Wing Chun techniques deflected the kicks, as he scampered towards her and she tried to slither away on her back. Ray came and grabbed her forearms, then pushed her right elbow across her chest to trap the arm and render her other arm useless. Ray mounted her torso, pinning her to the ground.

Jeremy came around Ray and lunged down to punch her in the face, but Ray blocked it with his free hand.

"No," Ray commanded his son. "We need her." He looked at Tracy. "Where is Jamie?"

Tracy

She squirmed like a wild dog that had been hog-tied. Thrashing her legs, she tried kneeing Ray in the back. He was stunned by Tracy's feral reaction.

"Get her legs, Jer," Ray told Jeremy.

Jeremy went and pinned her legs down by her knees.

"Where's my daughter?" Ray demanded. He pressed her arm across her chest more firmly and raised his other hand with an open palm, threatening to strike her square in the face. "Tell me!"

She stopped struggling, as she could no longer move. She stared at Ray through her panting breaths. Her crazed eyes threatened Ray.

"How did you find me?" she asked angrily. "Get off of me!"

"Not until you tell me where Jamie is! What have you done?"

"I don't know what you're talking about!"

"Stop lying! Tell me now," Ray demanded, pressing her trapped arms into her chest until he knew it hurt her.

"Tell us," Jeremy echoed, "before I beat the crap out of you!"

"I don't have her."

Jeremy punched the side of her knee. She screeched in pain. Ray looked around suspecting her loud screech to draw attention. It did. Several nearby shoppers looked at what was happening by the tree line. Ray saw their eyes examining the event and beginning to form conclusions as they pointed towards him.

"We can't do this here," Ray told Jeremy. "I need to flip her."

Ray came up a few inches off her body and pulled the arm he had pinned across her body towards the side to rotate her upper body while Jeremy flipped her legs around. They got her on her stomach. Ray took a breath as he thought about what he was doing.

"Do it!" Jeremy said.

Ray punched the back of Tracy's head, knocking her unconscious. He exhaled.

"Let's go," he said.

They carried her limp body to their car and strapped her in the backseat.

"You drive her car," Ray told Jeremy, finding the keys on the floor of the driver's side. More people pointed at them, and Ray heard someone calling security. "Let's go."

They got in the cars and drove off with their kidnapped perpetrator.

. . . .

The father and son sat on the dining room chairs placed in the living room while they watched Tracy's motionless body lying on the couch. They arrived home seven minutes prior but didn't wake her. They were catching their breath, calling the police, and thinking over what they were going to do. Ray also phoned the FBI. He would've even called the Coast Guard and Marines if he thought that were possible.

After waiting a few minutes, Ray could wait no longer. "Okay, Jeremy. Go get a wet towel and a glass of water. Let's find out what's going on."

As Jeremy got up to go to the kitchen, the doorbell rang. Both Ray and Jeremy stiffened as they looked at the door and then at each other. Ray moved towards the door and glanced back at Tracy to make sure she wasn't suddenly waking from the doorbell. He peeked through the peephole. It was Abby and Deon.

Ray let out a sigh of relief and motioned to Jeremy that it was okay. He opened the door halfway to conceal his captive. "Hey, what are you guys doing here? It's the middle of the afternoon. Don't you both have school or work?"

"Hey, Sifu," Deon greeted in return. "Today's my short day at the college. I wanted to check on what was going on, 'cause I feel for you looking for your daughter."

"I got the rest of the day off," Abby said, "since we got everything done for the project at the bio-lab. How's the progress?"

"Can we come in?" Deon asked.

"Well, okay, but don't be disturbed by what you're going to see," Ray agreed with some apprehension.

Once they entered, their attention was immediately drawn to the blond woman passed out on the couch.

"Whoa," Deon exclaimed, "who's the chick, Sifu?"

"Oh my," Abby asked, "is this Tracy?"

"Tracy?" Deon repeated as he got closer to examine her. "This is the perp that took your daughter?"

"Where's Jamie?" Abby inquired.

"We don't know yet," Ray replied as he closed the door and locked it. "We were just about to ask her."

"What are you going to do with her?" Deon asked.

Jeremy approached with a wet towel and glass of water. "She's going to talk and tell us where Jamie is," he said with a cold nonchalance.

"Yeah, that's what I'm talking about," Deon concurred.

"We're going to keep this civil," stated Ray. "We're going to ask her, and she's going to tell us. Jeremy, wake her with the towel and water."

Jeremy poured water on her face, then slapped her face with the wet towel. After repeating the action and shaking her a few times, she suddenly awoke. She moaned and rose swiftly but uneasily. She held her head like someone with a hangover. Jeremy stepped back. Her attention finally focused on the people semi-encircling her. Her eyes opened fully, scanning Ray and the others. Ferocity returned to her demeanor.

"What do you think you're doing?" she interrogated fearlessly.

"Tracy, what is going on?" Ray questioned. "Where is Jamie?"

"Let me go," she demanded with an even tone. "You can't keep me. You will regret what you're doing." Her confidence continued to catch them off guard. Perplexity appeared on her face as she asked, "How did you find me?"

"I want my daughter back, Tracy." Losing his patience, Ray's stare narrowed.

She glared back at Ray with squinted eyes. She leaned forward like she was about to rise from the couch, but Jeremy and Deon took a half step forward, tightening the ends of the semi-circle and clearly warning her against taking any offensive action.

"Jamie, Tracy. What have you done with Jamie?" Ray interrogated. "Where is she? I don't care why you did it. I only want her back."

"You're not leaving here until you tell us," Jeremy said with a clenched fist. "Just let me hit her," he said to Ray without taking his eyes off of her.

Tracy looked at Jeremy with a wicked half smile. "You stupid kid. I put up with your crap long enough. Go ahead. Try to hit me."

Jeremy's face reddened.

"No, Jeremy!" Ray shouted.

Jeremy launched at her.

Tracy sprang from the couch and blocked two of Jeremy's straight jabs at her face, grabbing his second punch and flipping him over the couch.

Deon lunged at her with both his massive arms spread wide open. She quickly side kicked him in the ribs, dropping him to his knees.

Ray was immediately upon her as she threw two wide-arcing punches at his head, both of which Ray effortlessly deflected. She tried to kick his groin, to which he closed his knees inward and blocked. She grabbed his shirt to pull him in and knee him, but he blocked it crossing his arms in front of him. He was composed, fluid, and automatic with his movements. The close distance Tracy created gave Ray the opportunity to fire a short jab into her rib cage with his right hand, causing her to wince. With his left, he grappled her right hand that clung on to his shirt and wrenched her wrist, contorting her arm. She screeched, like a cat that got its tail stepped on.

"Smack her down, Sifu," Deon yelled, rising from the floor. "Make her talk!"

Ray held her there, watching her grimace in so much pain that she couldn't make a sound anymore.

"That's it, Sifu," Deon cheered again. "Let me hit her for you. I'll make her talk."

Ray held the woman whom he had trusted for the last two years, welcomed into his home, and allowed to befriend him—the fiend who snatched his daughter. He cranked her wrist further, causing her entire body to writhe.

"Ray!" Abby screamed.

Ray snapped out of it and shoved her back onto the couch. He took deep breaths, an automatic response to slow his own heart rate back down and calm himself. Jeremy rose from behind the couch. Tracy cradled her limp wrist.

"No, you guys step back," Ray said firmly. Looking at Tracy, he warned, "I'm going to tell you one last time, tell me where my daughter is." Tracy tilted her head down and looked off to the side. "Tracy, look at me. What is it you want?" Still Tracy was non-engaging. "Look, I called the police. They're on their way here so you better tell me now, or you're going to tell it to them."

She slowly looked up through a web of wild strands of hair. Her wicked smirk and snake-like squint made Ray's stomach quiver. Abby took a step back, stunned by the sudden and unexpected evil expression.

"You have no idea," Tracy said in a low tone. She giggled with an awfully narrow smile. "Jamie is gone. You're not getting her back. You're a loser, Ray. You're a deadbeat, washed-out bum wallowing over his dead wife. You're not even a man. You're pathetic. You don't deserve Jamie."

Ray felt the heat on his neck and shoulders exude through his skin. It was beyond reason that Tracy turned out to be this kind of person. "Who are you?" Ray asked with incredulity, "Are you psychotic? Is this an alternate personality? I knew you, Tracy. Why are you doing this to me?"

"There you go," she said condescendingly, "you're the victim again. Boohoo. Poor, poor Ray. You're pitiful, and I'm done playing house with you and your dumb teenager. I'm too good for your broken family. No, I'm not crazy. Far from it. I'm intelligent, calculated, and destined for great things. This is just the first step for me."

Ray couldn't help feeling it. As angry and hateful as he felt towards Tracy, her words stung him. Perhaps it was because they were words that came from a person who had been in his home and knew him, and perhaps it was because he felt some accuracy in her insults. But he was also overwhelmed with desperation, and there was one thing in this moment he knew he needed—to get his daughter back.

"Tell me, or I will…" Ray's face was close enough to hers that his breath blew aside the wild strands of hair draping over her face. He considered what threat or violent action he was willing to carry out. How far would he go to make this woman tell him where his daughter was? "Tracy, don't make me hurt you again." He paused. "I will," he said matter-of-factly.

She laughed hysterically. Ray released her shoulder and stepped back from her.

"You don't know what you're up against," Tracy mocked. "No matter what you do to me, Jamie is ours."

"Ours? Who are you talking about?" He grabbed her by the shoulders and shook her vigorously, like he was trying to rattle the answer out of her. "Who has her? Is it that man you were with in the parking lot? Does he have Jamie? Who is he? Tell me!"

The doorbell rang.

Not Easily Broken

Chapter 7
Police

"Police," a deep, male voice announced through the door.

"Thank God," Abby said as she went to open the door.

Ray walked to the entrance.

Two officers stepped in with stone-cold faces. Ray thought these officers were exactly what was needed, because by their expressions they seemed to be all about the facts and getting the job done—no-nonsense cops. Perfect.

One officer was short and stocky with a bald head that appeared as solid as a bowling ball. He had a tattoo of a sickle on the side of his head. The curved blade of the sickle wrapped around his right ear, while the handle extended around the back of his neck. The other officer was tall and older with short brown hair and a bushy mustache. His thick cheekbones, protruding brows, and deep set eyes in large concave sockets sent a terrifying chill. The skin on his face was flaky and had dozens of craters, creating a rough texture, like a surface that needed sanding.

"Officers," Ray greeted them with relief, sounding like a runner who had just gotten his first break after a mile sprint. "I'm glad you're here. She," he said pointing at Tracy with a straight, stiff arm, like a spear, "took my daughter. Please, make her tell you where Jamie is."

"I'm Sergeant Pierce," the cratered-faced policeman introduced. "This is Officer Bohr."

Officer Bohr stood with his feet evenly squared off. His thick, stubby right hand rested on his gun as he robotically scanned the living room.

"My name is Ray Lee," Ray returned the introduction but was not interested in cordiality. "I reported yesterday that my daughter went missing."

"I'm aware of the report," Sergeant Pierce stated.

"She did it," Ray said, looking at Tracy. "I don't know why. I don't really care. I only want my girl back."

Sergeant Pierce said to Ray while watching Tracy, who sat on the couch still cradling her wrist, "Tell me what happened, Mr. Lee. I've read the report you filed about your missing daughter. Give me the specifics from your perspective."

Ray gathered his thoughts of all the crazy events from the last twenty-four hours and did a quick mental arrangement of them into a coherent exposition. "This is Tracy Pendleton. She was the babysitter of my daughter Jamie Lee."

"For how long?" Sergeant Pierce interrupted.

"Two years," Ray answered. Re-gathering his thoughts, he continued, "Tracy told me she was taking Jamie to an art class at the community center yesterday, but they never went. I checked. I called the community center. Their names were not on the guest sign-in sheet. When I came home, Jamie and Tracy were not here. I called her cell, but the number was disconnected. So we went to her apartment but found her place vacated, like she tried to move out in a hurry. Then my son and I tracked her down and found her at a shopping center parking lot. We brought her back here. We've been trying to find out from her where Jamie is. She refuses to say."

Sergeant Pierce never took his eyes off of Tracy while Ray gave his testimony.

"Please make her talk," Ray said.

Sergeant Pierce walked to Tracy with a stern, evaluative look. Tracy met his stare with a strange mixture of confidence and cowardice, like a wounded cat that could still hiss. After standing over Tracy for a moment and sizing her up, he turned sideways so that his left shoulder pointed at her while his right shoulder pointed at Ray. He kept his face on Tracy.

"Ms. Pendleton, where is Jamie?" Sergeant Pierce asked plainly.

"I don't know," she replied with a tremble.

"What do you mean you don't know?" he probed.

"I picked her up from school as usual." Her tone changed completely. Her pitch was higher and softer. Her inflections and expressions were apologetic, an act that would've gained any audience's sympathy. "I took her to the art class but there was no sign-in sheet as Mr. Lee mentioned. I know how much she likes drawing. She had a good time. I took her out for ice cream later. Then she was feeling sick so I brought her home—here. I stayed with her while Mr. Lee taught his Wing Chun class as he normally does on Tuesday nights. He always promptly came home at the same time. So since I had to move out the next day, because my lease ended, I left a little earlier but just five minutes before Mr. Lee got home. Just five minutes, like at 9:05 PM. That was the last time I saw Jamie, Sergeant."

"You lying wench," Jeremy yelled from behind her.

"Hey!" Sergeant Pierce pointed at Jeremy with a hairy, rugged finger. "Back up."

Police

"Jer," Ray said, "let the policemen do their job. Sergeant, she *is* lying."

"Ms. Pendleton," Sergeant Pierce continued, "why didn't you answer Mr. Lee's calls?"

"I'm sorry," she said. Her apologetic tone sickened Ray. "I didn't have enough money to pay my cell phone bills this month so the company temporarily turned off my service. I'm a student. I'm struggling to pay tuition. That's why I babysit. But I don't get paid that much. I'm sorry I didn't have a way to be reached. I'm doing the best I can with what I have," she said with a slight whine.

Sergeant Pierce watched Tracy coddle her wounded wrist, which had swelled.

"Sergeant," she said. "Officers," she said looking at Officer Bohr as well, "I'm sorry. I didn't know that leaving Jamie for just five minutes would cause so much trouble. I shouldn't have done it. I'm a good babysitter. I just made a small mistake. She promised me she was going to be good. She was supposed to watch TV and eat her snack, which I prepared for her. I reminded her not to go outside or open the door for strangers. I locked the door before I left. She's a good kid. I thought she'd be okay." She tilted her head to peer around the sergeant at Ray and said, "I'm sorry, Mr. Lee. I thought it would be okay for me to leave her for just five minutes. I texted you to let you know. Didn't you get my text?"

Ray shook his head. His breathing was audibly heavier. "Tracy! Stop lying. You have Jamie. So cut the act and tell Sergeant Pierce where she is."

"Mr. Lee," Sergeant Pierce corrected, "speak to me. Not to her."

"Sergeant, with all due respect, you can tell she's putting up an act, right? Make her tell you."

Sergeant Pierce turned his head toward Ray, looking insulted. "Make her?" His evaluative stare was now upon Ray. "Is that how you think I should do *my* job?" His voice chaffed like sandpaper.

Ray, surprised by the shift of attention, felt as though he was suddenly under a hot lamp in a dark interrogation room. "What I mean is—"

He interrupted, "I've heard both sides. Let me assess the facts."

Sergeant Pierce's words summoned an attentive stillness to descend upon the room.

"Let me ask you, Mr. Lee," Sergeant Pierce began, "did you find any evidence that Ms. Pendleton has Jamie?"

"You mean, like…" Ray's lips fumbled.

"I mean, like Jamie's clothing items in Ms. Pendleton's possession, a neighbor reporting they saw Ms. Pendleton taking Jamie somewhere, any traces in your home that Jamie was forcefully removed from here... anything?"

"Well, no, nothing like that," Ray said, "but she did confess just before you arrived that she has Jamie! She said it herself!"

"Did she *actually* say she has Jamie?"

"Well, she said that we would never see her again. That's what she said. I mean, that's a confession, right?"

"I," Tracy chimed in with a whimper, "wasn't sure what I was saying, Officer. I blurted all sorts of hysterical phrases because I was scared. Terrified. They brought me here and attacked me." She caressed her swollen wrist gently and dramatically. "Mr. Lee is a sifu, a master, you know, of Wing Chun kung fu, and he used it on me. Look." She lifted her swollen wrist and then lifted her shirt to show a bruise on her rib cage.

After glancing at Tracy, Sergeant Pierce turned his body to face Ray completely with his back towards Tracy. "Mr. Lee, so far I don't hear any evidence that Ms. Pendleton is a reasonable suspect. All we have is hearsay and speculation from you."

"But—" Ray responded, then stalled to form a good rebuttal.

"Sergeant," Abby chimed in, "she *is* lying. She's trying to fool you."

"Are you insulting me, miss?" Sergeant Pierce asked with a crease between his brows. "I've been doing this job for a long time."

"Sir," Abby tried to clarify, "I'm not implying that. I'm saying—"

"Who are you? Who are any of you?" Pierce asked as he looked at Deon judgingly.

Deon returned the glare.

Ray asserted, "She was the last to see Jamie, and she's been avoiding us. She tried escaping. Everything she told you is a deception!"

"You said she tried escaping. Where did you find her, Mr. Lee?"

"At a Target parking lot in –"

"Parked?"

"Yes. She was –"

"Parked at a shopping center hardly appears to be a fast getaway for a kidnapper."

"She was meeting someone. It looked like a hand-off. That was probably her partner in all of this."

"Did you *see* Ms. Pendleton hand Jamie to this other person?"

"Well, no. Not so much, but—"

"More speculation?" the sergeant challenged.

Taken aback, Ray could not believe the gradual turning of the situation.

"The more you talk the more your story sounds imaginative."

"This is unbelievable!" Ray blurted with defiance.

The sergeant stiffened and displayed his loss of patience. "Let me tell you what I've gathered so far."

Again, a renewed silence with a command for attention hovered the room.

"What I hear is," Sergeant Pierce continued, "you illegally went into Ms. Pendleton's home. That was breaking and entering. You followed Ms. Pendleton to a shopping center. That was stalking. Ms. Pendleton was brought to your private residence, and I'm guessing she was brought here against her will. That was kidnapping. What I see is Ms. Pendleton has been forcefully held here. That is unlawful imprisonment. What I also see is Ms. Pendleton is injured from an attack, in which she claimed you were the perpetrator. That is assault and battery."

Ray suddenly noticed he was standing in between the two officers, like he was trapped in a flanking tactic. He noticed Officer Bohr now had his left hand resting on his Billy club while his right hand remained on his sidearm. He couldn't believe what was happening. How did the tables turn? How was he the one on trial? But of course with the way Sergeant Pierce laid out the evidence against him, he looked like the villain.

Sergeant Pierce concluded, "What I can tell you, Mr. Lee, is that I have potentially five different reasons to arrest you right now." He looked around the room. "And I can count everyone in this room as accomplices." He looked over his shoulder at Jeremy. "That includes your boy, who could get up to two months in juvenile hall and six months in bootcamp. Not to mention, Mr. Lee, that the charges against you for assaulting Ms. Pendleton would warrant more severe punishments given that you are a professionally trained and certified martial artist. Your hands are considered weapons. You could be tried for assault and battery with a deadly weapon. That could put you away for a long time, leaving your boy fatherless."

Ray looked at Abby and then at Deon, searching for a hint of what to do. Abby offered a look of disbelief and reflected the same level of astonishment as Ray felt. Deon flashed an expression of anger, like he wasn't surprised by the turn of events. His hate for the officers simmered on his face. Jeremy was out of view, covered by the towering sergeant, but Ray considered carefully the threat against his son.

Tracy remained seated with her back hunched over, like a frightened, stray dog. Her knees were locked side-by-side and her shoulders concaved in, keeping a closed and unchallenging posture. She rested her wounded arm on her lap with her hand hanging limply over the side of her thigh. She peered at Ray through the strands of hair draped over her face. She looked like a young, naïve college girl. With tented brows, drooping eyes, and a quivering bottom lip, she appeared dehumanized, like a slave in a brothel.

"You tell me, Mr. Lee," Sergeant Pierce stated, "what I should do here? Now, Officer Bohr can handcuff you and take you in. But if Ms. Pendleton chooses not to press charges against you and your accomplices, then Officer Bohr and I will write this off as a bad misunderstanding in a domestic issue." He waited for a few seconds for a response.

"Sergeant," Tracy said kindly, "I don't want to press charges. I loved Mr. Lee's family, and they're suffering enough already with their missing daughter. I just..." She started to cry. Tears ran down the side of her cheeks and soaked into the fallen strands of hair on her face. "I just hope dear Jamie is okay. I can't believe she's missing. I don't want anything to happen to her." She looked at Ray with pained eyes and whimpered, "I'm so sorry."

"That's it," Sergeant Pierce said. "This matter is over."

"I want to go home to ice my wrist," Tracy said.

"We can take you to the hospital for medical attention, Ms. Pendleton."

"No, thank you," she said. "I think they brought my car here." She saw her set of keys on the kitchen counter. "I can drive. I just want this day to be over."

"I don't even want to ask how your car got here," Pierce said to Tracy, glancing at Ray and Jeremy.

Ray shook his head with pursed lips.

"Do you have any more objections, Mr. Lee?" Pierce asked Ray.

"No," Ray answered wisely, "no, I don't, Officer."

"Sergeant."

"No, I don't, Sergeant."

"Ms. Pendleton." Sergeant Pierce moved toward Tracy. He took her arm and helped her up. "Officer Bohr and I will drive behind you and escort you until you are at a distance away from these premises."

They slowly moved toward the door. Ray wanted to block them from leaving. He wanted to stop the only lead he had to Jamie from walking out his door. But he could tell that Officer Bohr was ready for action and was a man who acted without feeling. Bohr's left hand was no longer resting on his billy club but was gripping it instead. Ray's only hope for recovering his daughter was going to disappear out his front door and there was nothing he could do to stop it.

Police

"Do you have everything, Ms. Pendleton?" Sergeant Pierce asked.

She felt her back pocket, which showed a bulge in the shape of a cell phone. "Yes, I do." She grabbed her keys off the counter.

Officer Bohr opened the door with his right hand while his left still gripped the billy club.

Sergeant Pierce escorted Tracy toward the door. "Come on, Ms. Pendleton. Nice and easy," Sergeant Pierce said to Tracy while supporting her arm.

"This is bull, man!" Deon shouted as he took two steps towards the door.

Officer Bohr gave Deon a car-stopping stare. He then slowly stepped through the threshold and closed the door shut. The last thing Ray saw was the side of Bohr's head with the large sickle tattoo accented by the white, shiny skin.

Ray moved to the window to watch them help Tracy into her car. He tried processing what just took place and what to do next. He knew the sergeant's assessment was logical, but it wasn't right. That was law enforcement, an institution that deciphers right from wrong through a system of reason, evidences, and due process. It was an institution that defended the victims and brought the perpetrators to justice. But the representatives of this institution deemed him to be the real perpetrator and his lost daughter to be an inconsequential effect of a domestic issue. Where was order?

. . . .

"What just happened?" Abby asked with outfaced palms. "What was that?"

"You can never trust the po-po," Deon exclaimed. "Crooked cops! Did you see the way the bald one looked at me? Like he was going to take me on. I would've slammed his chrome dome on the floor!"

"I can't believe this," Abby said. "We thought the police were going to help us. How could they have helped Tracy? *She* was the criminal."

"Crooked cops," Deon repeated. "I've seen plenty of them."

Ray's blood boiled, but he forced his mind to consider rationally what happened. "The sergeant made a logical case against me," he admitted.

"Come on, Sifu," Deon objected.

"The evidence was stacked against me, and I couldn't risk dragging all of you down." Ray looked at Jeremy protectively. "There was nothing I could do."

Deon was wound up and upset, looking like he was ready for a fight.

"Evidence! What evidence? That was all a joke. They were crooked and you could see it!"

"Sifu Ray," Abby said, "something was very wrong about the whole thing. It was like they were helping her. But I don't get why they would do that. Can't believe how screwed up this is."

"I agree. It did appear like they were helping her. Maybe that's why I've had a hard time getting their cooperation lately," Ray replied. "But they had a case."

"Case or not. The whole thing was jacked," Deon commented.

"Sifu Ray," Abby said, while opening her laptop, "I found this on the first night Jamie went missing, when you were having us do research. I found this." She typed. "Here, look."

Ray leaned over her shoulder and was looking at the website for the FBI.

"Abductions are a federal crime and the FBI is the direct agency that handles it. There's a number here—."

Before she finished speaking, Ray dialed the number on the screen and turned on the speakerphone function. An automated message greeted Ray, giving numerical options. Ray pressed the number for reporting cases of abductions.

"Federal Bureau of Investigation. Jana speaking. How may I help you?"

Ray began to report the case of Jamie's kidnapping.

The operator interrupted, "Let me verify that you are calling from Los Angeles, California."

"Yes, I am."

"You've called the national office in D.C. Let me direct you to our field office there."

"Sure. Thank you," Ray said anxiously.

They waited, listening to jazz music played through the phone.

"Hello. Federal Bureau of Investigation, Los Angeles field office. Derrick speaking. How may I help you?"

Ray repeated his story.

"You're reporting a kidnapping. Let me direct you to our division that handles missing children."

"Okay."

"Hello. This is the division of missing children and child exploitation of the Los Angeles field office. Gary speaking."

"Gary, I'm trying to report the kidnapping of my daughter, Jamie. Her babysitter took her, and I believe she has already transferred her to an accomplice. I need help getting my daughter back. Please—"

Police

Gary interrupted, "Is this Ray Lee of 555 Sunnyvale Dr., Los Angeles, California, 90038?"

Caught off guard, Ray stuttered, "Yes, yes. This is. How do you—"

"Mr. Lee, the local authorities have already made us aware of your *case*. They have reported to us that they evaluated your case and are presently monitoring it. They are couriering your file to us, which we will review. But they have advised us that your case contains legally questionable issues."

"Legally questionable?" Ray started to lose his composure, but focused on remaining calm. "Gary, you have to understand that the police officers who came to my house were not trying to help me. There was something wrong with the way they were handling—"

"Mr. Lee. Your case has been red-flagged in the FBI's system. We will review your case and proceed with caution."

"Please hear me out."

"While it is under review, your case is in the hands of your local authority."

"But that doesn't make sense. It says right here on your website that the FBI is directly responsible for handling child kidnappings."

"That is correct. But until we have definitively determined that your daughter's absence is the result of a kidnapping, it is not yet our exclusive responsibility. As mentioned, the report provided by the police will be reviewed in order to determine the nature of your case. But I must inform you that your case has been classified as a "Dubitable Case with Compounded Factors.""

"What do you mean?"

"I have your number, Mr. Lee," Gary said, almost as a warning. "We will contact you when we have completed our review. Until then, please be patient and stand by. I must take another call." He hung up.

"That was strangely wrong," Abby said.

Ray dialed the number for the national office again. "FBI is a big organization. I'll talk to someone else."

"Hello. Gary speaking."

"Gary?" Ray was surprised.

"Mr. Lee. Your adamant calls will not speed up the process. There are protocols we follow and your case will run its proper course." He hung up again.

"What in the world!" Abby exclaimed.

"They're routing my number. Gary is having my calls routed to him," Ray said. "If that's the case, my phone calls could be monitored as well."

"What are we going to do?" Abby asked.

"What about the Amber Alert?" Ray asked.

"The Amber Alert is tied to the California Highway Patrol. I contacted the captain in charge and gave him all the info, but I haven't seen any Amber Alerts posted for Jamie."

"It's been too long. It should've been done by now."

"Has the whole world gone wrong?" Deon asked.

A silence followed Deon's question, until Ray said, "We're on our own."

. . . .

"What do we do now?" Abby asked. "Should we track Tracy's Fastrak Pass again?"

"No, it doesn't seem Tracy has Jamie anymore. Jamie is being held somewhere." Ray thought for a second. "There was that man we saw meeting with Tracy. Their meeting looked like a transaction." He calculated what he observed. "Tracy was plotting something. It was premeditated. Jeremy and I interrupted her plans, and she did not expect that. Whoever that man was, he's part of the abduction."

"Sifu," Abby said, "this is very serious if you're saying there was someone else involved and making a transaction with her. This isn't the whim of a crazy woman."

"It doesn't look like a crazy act anymore, Abby. Tracy was with us for two years. You heard the things she said to us. We all saw her put on an act for the officers. Her meeting with that man in the suit looked like part of a plan."

"But why? Why Jamie?" Abby asked.

"I don't know." Ray sat down on a dining room chair. He fought back thoughts of regret. Maybe if he were more thorough in evaluating Tracy before hiring her, he could've prevented this. But he knew he was as thorough as he could've been. Perhaps if he didn't lose control and did the criminal deeds in the last twenty-four hours, there couldn't have been a case against him. But he knew if he had done nothing, they wouldn't have uncovered this much information about Jamie's disappearance. He had to stop beating himself up. *Think straight*, he told himself.

"If only we had a lead on that man. I think he's our key. If only I had thought straight in that moment, I would've gone after the man in the suit rather then Tracy. They were probably making a hand-off. Jamie was probably in that man's SUV!"

"I took pics of that guy as we were pulling up," Jeremy said holding up his phone. "I got pics of his car too, including his license plate."

"Sweet, dude," Deon congratulated.

"That's good, Jer. Good job thinking ahead in the spur of the moment. A face and a car, though," Ray remarked, "is hard to go off of, but it's something."

While Jeremy still held up his cell phone in one hand, he produced another cell phone in the other hand. "I also have Tracy's cell phone."

Smiles formed on the others' three faces. They looked at each other with a spark of hope, like hikers who found a trail after wandering aimlessly in a forest.

"How did you—" Ray asked curiously.

"After we brought her in, I slipped her phone from her back pocket while she was still knocked out. Then I grabbed my old phone from my room and stuck it in the same pocket so she wouldn't know. But don't worry I took my SD card out." Jeremy looked around the room at their approving faces. "I did it just in case. Can't always trust cops and all," he said, looking over at Deon with a smirk.

"Dang, boy," Deon cheered, "You're slick!"

"Jer, this is great!" Ray praised also. "Okay, we have to work fast before she finds out that her phone is missing and before she can get access to another phone."

He walked to Jeremy and took Tracy's phone. "It's likely she has a wipe-out app on her phone that allows her to erase all her data remotely. Let's copy all of her info from her phone before she activates that app. That will give us her call log as well. One of her recent calls must be to the man in the suit. If we can isolate down which number it is, I can track his cell phone by radar and we can know his location!"

He went to the dining table and opened his laptop.

"Abby," Ray said, "grab Jer's laptop and download the photos from his phone onto it. Then start a search for that license plate number and see what we find. Name. Address. Driver's license. Parking tickets. Anything. Jer, Tracy's phone is probably password protected." He gave Jeremy a smile with a glimmer. "But somehow, I don't think that'll be a problem for you."

"You're finally getting to know me," Jeremy replied.

"Use my laptop to work on Tracy's phone. Drain everything from it." Ray got up to let Jeremy take his place. "Everyone, the man in the suit is our new target."

Jeremy got to work on cracking Tracy's phone. Ray had to admit that he was proud to see his son's witty thinking and skills at work even if those skills were ethically questionable.

"Sifu," Deon said, "I'm not tech-smart, but what can I do?"

Ray looked gratefully at the large, young man before him—the same bully and confrontational guy that tried to take him down just last week. He was puzzled by the shift in his relationship with him, but during this crisis, he welcomed Deon's help.

"I mean, I hope I'm not intruding, Sifu," Deon said. "I know you didn't ask for my help in your family matters, but I'm game."

"That's kind of you."

"I want to help find your daughter. You got some crazy stuff going on, with a psycho-babysitter, suited men, and shady cops."

"I don't want to worry your grandmother," Ray said.

"Oh, she's fine as along as she knows that I'm okay. She's just extra cautious with me being a young, black man growing up in L.A. I guess you might not know about that," he said with a boyish chuckle.

"No. I can't say that I do," Ray replied with a smile. "But seriously, please don't feel you have to stay. It looks like things are getting complicated. This could cause trouble for you."

"Complicated is for sure," Deon concurred. "But I want to be here, though, if it's all right with you. After Grandma knocked some sense into me, she made me come back to you. You took me back with no questions asked and no strings attached. Sifu, that spoke to me. I'm serious. Because nobody welcomes you back for nothing after you wrong them— not where I come from. Grandma said that was grace and it means something." Deon had all of their attention. "Grandma always wanted me to learn to be more sacrificial, which is a tough lesson to learn in my hood. Know what I'm saying? She said being sacrificial is the mark of a true hero. There are too many villains in my hood. Be the hero, she said. Don't be the villain. So I'm here."

Ray didn't quite know how to respond, except to say, "Thank you again."

He considered the insurmountable plight before him. He spoke to all of them, "After what just happened, I don't know if the law enforcement will be on our side. Whether they are or not, finding Jamie will be on us. I want you all to know that I foresee this task to be beyond difficult and dangerous."

Deon declared, "You're not alone."

"This could put you all at risk," Ray warned, "if this whole situation keeps mushrooming. I hate to involve you all more than I already have."

"Sifu." Deon clarified, "You didn't involve us. We chose this."

Abby nodded.

Ray looked at Abby smiling at him with sincerity. This same young woman who spontaneously brought him drinks, which he dismissed as quirky gestures of her naïve attraction to him, was now a significant person to him in his search for his daughter.

These people, Abby and Deon, had become his best friends in the last twenty-four hours. He looked at Jeremy working away on his laptop and felt an increased protectiveness for his son in light of losing his daughter.

"Thank you." Ray's soft gratitude shifted to a serious consideration. "I don't think we're going to get Jamie back easily. I see a fight ahead."

"Bring it," Deon welcomed.

"We're all in," Jeremy said with determination over the collective camaraderie. "Crazy babysitters, crooked cops, suited men, whatever. Let's get Jamie back."

Ray nodded at them with acceptance.

Ray sat with Abby and Deon sat with Jeremy, as they worked on their laptops.

Then Ray received a call. It was Fred.

"Ray," Fred said, "how's the search for Jamie?"

"Whole thing is out of control. I'll have to tell you about it. Right now, I'm in the middle of something."

"I know you're going through a lot, so I hate to tell you this."

"What is it?"

"Miranda wanted me to personally call you to tell you to come in tomorrow morning. The situation is bad. We found something and there are questions for you."

"Can it wait? I'm looking for my daughter. I really can't pull away."

"I know, I know. But it can't wait. They found something on your computer. If you don't come in Thornton will revoke your access to MiraCom's systems."

Ray couldn't risk losing his resource of MiraCom's radar and satellite, especially for tracking down the suited man. "Tell Miranda I'll be in first thing in the morning."

"I have to warn you though. It's ugly here."

Chapter 8
Scrutiny

At 7:00 AM, Ray pushed himself to leave the house. He told Abby and Jeremy to contact him immediately as soon as they finished siphoning the information off of Tracy's cell phone or found anything from the suited man's license plate number. Fortunately, Tracy had not yet activated her wipe out feature.

He walked into the main lobby of Miracom with its vaulted ceiling and patterned, marble floors. He greeted the usual guards in the security booth, the tall six-foot-one-inch Hispanic man in his forties and the shorter five-foot-three-inch African-American woman in her thirties. He never could remember their first names. He thought it was Jorge or Jose and Shawndra or Sandra. On their badges, it only indicated their last names. "Good morning, Officer Hernandez. Morning, Officer Cole," he greeted.

"Morning, Mr. Lee," Officer Cole replied with a pleasant smile. His formality humored them. They were friendly to him. Ray sized them up and could tell that beneath their dark blue uniforms, they were fit, strong, and capable of beating down the toughest adversaries. Officer Hernandez had a lot of bulk, and Officer Cole was small but lean and muscular, likely able to react quickly and pack a sharp punch. Even as a Wing Chun master, he felt secure having these two formidable professionals guarding the front of their building, especially during the present crisis.

But this morning, the two security guards weren't letting him simply pass through with his badge and fingerprint ID.

"Mr. Lee," Officer Hernandez said while he looked down at Ray from his towering height. Officer Cole sat beside her partner with her usual smile. "Please wait here while I call Ms. Miranda to inform her that you arrived."

Ms. Miranda, that was how she was known in this forty-story building with eight hundred employees. Ray was not sure if anyone knew her last name except for that one person who handled the records in the human resources department.

"What's the issue?" Ray asked, surprised by the out-of-the-ordinary procedure.

"Nothing," Officer Cole replied while her partner was on the phone with the security guard on Ray's floor. "Ms. Miranda wanted to be informed when you arrived and gave us specific instructions to ask you to wait here."

Ray felt a twisting nervousness in the center of his chest. Heat beneath his skin rose from under his collar, up his neck, and along his cheeks. He knew he did a couple of things that were not technically legal or according to proper protocol, but this procedure was extreme.

Two more security guards walked out of the lobby elevator. They approached Ray, and one of them said, "Mr. Lee, please allow us to escort you to Ms. Miranda's office. A meeting is scheduled to take place the minute you arrive."

They gestured to Ray to walk toward the elevators. As he walked away with them, he glanced back at Officer Hernandez and Officer Cole who smiled and gave assuring nods.

The three of them entered the elevator, which felt small with the two guards standing on either side of him. The classy, antique-ish design of the elevator and playing of symphonic music clashed with his feeling of being a convicted prisoner going to see the warden. His heart thumped. He tried to slow it down with discreet, deep breaths.

"Why the formality, boys?" Ray asked before realizing he might have belittled them by calling them "boys," though that's what they looked like to him: two blonde-haired, Caucasian young men in their mid-twenties.

"Nothing, Mr. Lee." The same one that spoke earlier responded. "Ms. Miranda wanted to make sure you went straight to the meeting the moment you arrived. Our company is in a more dire situation than you may know since you've been gone."

The explanation didn't relieve Ray's unnerving feeling over this peculiar, and even insulting, procedure, as if he were an invalid incapable of taking the elevator up to his office floor, or worse, as if he were an untrustworthy suspect who needed to be held in custody. Then again, his use of company equipment to locate his daughter was unauthorized and illegal.

They finally arrived at the 37th floor.

After the elevator dinged, its doors opened. He walked with the security guards through the large room of cubicles, as prying eyes from inside the maze of cubicles watched the formal escort pass by. Ray felt their judging stares. The guards didn't walk fast enough for him, but he didn't want to walk ahead of them for fear of them perceiving his brisk pace as an attempt to get away.

To Ray's surprise, they passed Miranda's office. They were heading to the conference room.

Finally, they arrived. The security guard knocked on the door and upon hearing Miranda's voice opened it. Ray walked past the guard holding the door open and entered the dim, narrow conference room. The guard closed the door behind him.

Miranda sat with an expectant expression at the head of the end of a rectangular, black conference table. Marvin sat on her right with the look of a terrified kitten-look. Comb-over Thornton reclined by her left with scrutinizing eyes. Several others sat along both sides of the table. Fred sat on the corner of the table closest to him. Ray felt like he walked into the principal's office for a parent-teacher meeting.

The window shades were drawn, blocking out any sunlight. The ceiling lights were at half-brightness. The flat screen behind Miranda was the brightest source of light.

"Have a seat," Miranda commanded Ray.

There was only one seat left, the one at the tail end of the table, directly opposite of Miranda. Ray sat down and set his bag on the thinly carpeted floor. His thoughts periodically ran away to wondering about the progress on cracking Tracy's phone.

The Thunder Queen spoke. "We have a serious matter," she said plainly and followed by a discomforting pause. "Ray, I'm aware that you are in a personal crisis of your own with the search for your daughter."

"I'll be honest," Ray said nervously, "I'm having a difficult time concentrating because my mind is on my daughter."

"I understand," Miranda stressed. "But our crisis here has turned into a catastrophe that could impinge on millions, including military and law enforcement establishments. You understand the gravity of the situation? The safety of your daughter is important. I'm not denying that. But the real threat of millions being gravely affected and social structures being compromised has to outweigh the needs of any individual, including yours and mine. Are you here with me? Because I need you to be."

"Yes, Miranda," Ray forced his compliance. "I'm with you."

"We discovered some unauthorized actions we need you to address."

"Ms. Miranda, I only did what I did as a father desperately trying to find his daughter," he said quickly with animated gestures, but his eyes couldn't meet Miranda's so they aimlessly roamed the tabletop.

"I don't know what your fatherly concern has to do with our situation, but I need you to explain the unauthorized firewall we discovered on our main server."

"Oh." Ray was caught off guard and not expecting this to be the topic under examination. He took a second to recover from his near self-incrimination. "I—"

"Mr. Lee," Thornton interjected, "do you realize this is a company operating with the highest levels of protocol because we are dealing with the highest levels of communication and surveillance that affect the stability of society?"

"I was trying to—"

"You do understand that our radars and satellites are used by the military and government institutions?"

"Yes, sir. What I did was—"

"You are not a rookie," Thornton declared and watched Ray, like he was probing his thoughts. "You do understand procedure, don't you? Especially in a period of extreme crisis?"

"Yes, Mr. Thornton, I do understand protocol." Ray snuck a quick peek at Fred from the corner of his eye, reaching out for some kind of back-up from his friend, though he knew even his best friend was helpless to do anything. "I was simply trying to—"

"Then," Mr. Thornton interjected an angrily, "you should've known that the proper procedure would've been to present your firewall program to Marvin, the head of systems security."

Ray opened his mouth in a third attempt to explain, but it was futile. He saw Fred shake his head at him.

"And then!" Mr. Thornton's volume elevated. "The head of systems security would present your firewall program to the systems security team for analysis, evaluation, and editing to approve it according to Miracom's criteria."

Ray sat in his chair with all eyes staring at him, except Fred's.

"Instead, you invented your own private program, abused your Class 9 access, and installed an unauthorized software onto the main server that bars anyone from having access to it! Do you think Miracom is your personal home?" The gleam on his dome-like forehead refracted like an interrogation lamp in the dim room. "Your action is outrageous, particularly as one of our senior employees. How are you any different from those hackers who infected us with the virus?"

"With all due respect," he asserted, "after speaking with Marvin briefly, I saw the signs of a potential total systems corruption, which, as you know, would plunge all the operations of Miracom into chaos. As you clearly stated, if Miracom's systems were compromised, entire social infrastructures could be in jeopardy. I did what I could to assist and preserve the order of our company and the order of everything that

Scrutiny

depends on us." He was proud that he said that with conviction.

However, Thornton continued his relentless battery. "Are you part of the systems security team? Did we hire you to create security programs?"

"No, I was not hired for that." Then Ray's phone vibrated in his pocket. He wanted to pull it out and look at it, but he was under the gun.

"You stepped out of line, Ray Lee." Thornton laid down the verdict that sounded like the definitive statement silencing any debate. "I've read your file thoroughly. Your record showed that you have been a very process-oriented person and never went out of bounds. I've also been brought up to speed on your personal losses. Perhaps, Mr. Lee, the tragedy of your late wife and the recent disappearance of your daughter has clouded your rational judgment! Is that possible?"

Ray smoldered underneath his breath. The disrespect for his wife and daughter made him want to charge across the table and pummel the degrading man. All he could do, though, was to take in the denigration. His phone vibrated again! It kept vibrating.

"We cannot allow—" Thornton continued.

Ray pulled the phone out of his pocket, discreetly kept it at his side, and glanced down to read the message. Jeremy wrote, "We have something!"

"Excuse me! Are we inconveniencing you?" Thornton yelled.

"No, sir." Ray looked up. "I'm listening."

"We cannot allow this kind of rogue behavior," Thornton exclaimed with a higher pitch as he turned his face toward Miranda. "This company has to run on procedures and policies, not on pet projects of entrepreneurial individuals! Mr. Lee," he said sharply, honing his judging eyes onto Ray, "you are to remove this personal firewall from our main server and if the internal investigative department deems you still suitable to be employed at Miracom, you can keep your job."

"Ms. Miranda—" Ray felt a surge of urgency to defend himself not for the sake of his job but for his daughter. He still required Miracom's resources. So far, they didn't seem to know about his unauthorized use of the equipment for personal surveillance. Under the present crisis, that kind of minor infraction went unnoticed.

Miranda put up her palm, a known gesture that squelched further talk and claimed the floor. "Ray acted in an immature manner and in violation of company standards."

Thornton nodded his comb-over head.

She turned to her right to look at Marvin. "Explain our situation as it currently stands."

"Well, okay. Yes," Marvin juggled his words as he received the baton to speak. "Okay. So, the virus as we can tell is no hoax. It's pure genius."

He clicked on a remote control to cue the screen behind Miranda. Everyone, except for Miranda, turned their heads to look at the screen. She remained facing forward as though she already knew verbatim what was being presented.

Marvin pictorially illustrated on the screen the range and depth of the virus's effect. "Here it is. The virus has affected all of our radars in some way, which can cause interference with public transportation, mass media, police communication, and military surveillance, as you know. It is at present in every part of our system, although its effects are in varying degrees."

"Update us on your efforts to date," Miranda instructed.

"My systems security team and I have been working round the clock." Marvin ran his fingers through his unkempt, brown, and curly hair. "We also called for help from two of our partnering companies and contracted with another professional systems security company to help us isolate and destroy this virus. Even though we have learned more about it, we have not made much tangible progress in resolving or slowing it down." He paused for a moment and looked at everyone around the room, except for Mr. Thornton, and said softly, "I'm sorry."

"Tell us where the virus has stopped, Marvin," Miranda instructed

"Well, the virus stopped just short of the main server."

"You're saying it has not spread into the main server."

"No, ma'am."

"And why is that?"

"I believe… well, it seems at least, it's because of the encrypted firewall that Ray installed. It really is a one-of-a-kind firewall, I must say."

Thornton reclined back in his chair with annoyance. "The ends will not justify the means. His method was illegal."

"While that may be, Ray's firewall so far has been the only positive measure that has halted the virus from causing a total system meltdown. Is that correct, Marvin?"

"Yes, Ms. Miranda," he replied. "That is correct, I have to say. If the virus got into the main server, well, we would be looking at the compromise of our satellites and a complete takeover of our system. That would be bad. Very bad."

"For all practical purposes," she announced to everyone, "Ray's firewall stays."

Ray let out a silent sigh of relief, and, secretly, he was enjoying the sound of *Ray's firewall*.

"And," Miranda added as she looked at Thornton, "since Ray is so

Scrutiny

far the only one who can access the encrypted firewall through his own decryption code, Ray's employment will remain in good standing, and he will remain in active duty."

Thornton looked like he was going to pop off the combed over strands on his dome. "Miranda! You cannot condone insubordination in your company. Miracom *must* operate according to the policies established. The integrity of an institution depends upon the enforcement of its policies."

"We can deal with policies when this crisis clears. Right now, Ray is the one thing that stands between our main server and that inexorable virus. Unless you can offer me a practical solution to keep Miracom intact, Ray stays."

"Your disregard for regulations will be recorded and submitted to the board. It will not go over well for you when it comes time for your evaluation."

"Do what you have to, Thornton," Miranda said with impressive authority.

Thornton appeared to be boiling. Ray conjectured that this elitist board member had difficulty with people who did not subject themselves to his opinion.

"Ray," Thornton ordered, "you will submit your decryption code for your encrypted firewall to Marvin and his systems security team immediately."

"Disregard!" Miranda simply stated. "Ray, you will do no such thing."

Thornton's eyes turned wide and beady, like they wanted to shoot out of their sockets at Miranda.

"Marvin, how good is the encryption on Ray's firewall," she asked without looking at him.

"I think it's very good, actually, Ms. Miranda," Marvin answered. "At first I didn't know where the firewall was from, so my team and I tried cracking it, and we couldn't. It's nothing like what I've seen before."

"Can your team do anything," Thornton attacked the young, sweaty man. "I see a pattern with you, Marvin. It seems you and your team are not capable of cracking anything—not the virus, not the firewall. Your competency level is in question!"

Marvin's face fell toward the black surface of the table with his hands folded in front of him.

Ray said, "The decryption code is one gigabyte of content. I have it stored only in one location, and—"

"Stop speaking," Miranda cut him off. "The decryption code will stay with you and you alone. Share it with no one."

"This is outrageous, Miranda!" Thornton yelled. "What you are doing violates major protocols! You realize you are being just as brazen as this man's actions?"

"We may potentially have a mole." Miranda said plainly, gradually turning her face toward Thornton to meet his confrontation. "The only way Ray was able to install his encrypted firewall around our main server was because he had a high enough clearance level to do it. It's likely the only way that the virus got into our system is through someone who also had a high enough clearance to do it. Does anyone know who the mole is? Is anyone here the mole?"

The room was mute. Thornton's whole head glowed bright red.

"Until someone confesses to being the mole," Miranda concluded with everyone, "Ray stays. Ray's firewall stays. Ray's decryption code stays with Ray. Clear?"

Everyone in the room nodded, except for Thornton.

"No one is to ask Ray for the decryption code. No one is to ask him *about* the decryption code. Ray, you are not to tell anyone where that decryption code is stored—not even your best friend sitting next to you. Clear?"

He nodded. Fred nodded.

"This will not go without consequences!" Thornton blurted as he stood up.

"I don't think you understand the meaning of consequences, Mr. Thornton," Miranda fired back.

With a huff, his footsteps thumped on the thin carpet as he walked toward the exit. He bumped hard into Ray's chair and disappeared out the door.

"Let's get back to some real business," Miranda said.

Everyone tuned into her.

Miranda sat up as straight as a pole. "I'm unleashing our Internal Investigation Department to find the mole. We can assume with certainty that this virus was an inside job. I'm authorizing them with every relentless measure to flush out this culprit. Everyone with a Class 7 clearance level or higher will be interrogated, which includes all of you. Laptops will be sifted, desks will be searched, phone logs and voicemails will be examined, and the check in and out records for the past month will be reviewed."

She scanned their faces. "*Every,*" she said, and her emphatic articulation of that word appeared as though she bit into a piece of meat, "detail will be investigated. Finding this culprit is our answer to being rid of this virus. Ray bought us some time, which is exactly what we need for Internal Investigations to uncover our hacker."

"So," she said, "if you have any information, divulge it to I.I. Because, every unauthorized access or activity *will* be exposed."

Ray plummeted from being affirmed to once-again a suspect-in-hiding. It would only be a matter of time before the I.I. discovered his improper use of company technology to fight his personal battle. Instead of worrying about being condemned as an unethical person who could lose his job, he felt compelled to work faster before he was exposed.

Miranda closed the meeting and dismissed everyone, except for Ray. "Ray," she called to him.

As the others vacated the room, Miranda and Ray were left standing on opposite ends of the long, dark table.

"Is there anything else you need to inform me?" she asked. "Anything that you couldn't say in front of the others?"

Ray tried to remain relaxed, knowing that his guise was vital in finding his daughter. He paused for a couple of seconds, appearing like he was giving her question courteous consideration while not pausing for more than a couple of seconds, because that could make him look suspicious. He shook his head once, but he made sure not to shake it too eagerly. "No," he said. "I can't think of anything else."

"If you think of anything, no matter how remote it may seem, tell me. Got it?"

"Yes, Miranda."

"Right now, this company is counting on you to protect that decryption code. Don't—and I mean this—don't give it to anyone, even if Thornton himself comes after you for it."

"Yes, Miranda. I'm sorry for circumventing the system with the firewall. I should've—"

"Ray." Her tone softened. "Stop apologizing. You are saving this company and the city from falling into chaos. We need more initiative around here. You did well."

"Thank you, Miranda."

"I wish you the best in finding your daughter. We're done here."

He nodded with a slight smile at her before he turned and exited the room.

He went into his office and closed the door behind him. Pulling out his phone, he dialed Jeremy's number as he sat down at his desk.

While the phone rang, he touched the photo of him and his late wife sitting on his desk. It was hard to believe that two years had passed since her death, and now he was fighting to not lose another love of his life.

"Hello," Jeremy answered, "where have you been?"

"What do you have?"

"Tracy activated her wipeout feature. Her phone wiped out an hour ago. But before it did, we copied all the info that was on her phone, including the voicemails. We got the number of that man in the suit. There was a voicemail from him."

"What's the number?" Ray booted up his computer.

Jeremy told him the number. Ray typed it into his computer.

"I'm going to put you on speaker so Abby and Deon can hear too."

"I'm going to track his cell phone with one of our satellites," Ray said. "This is a bigger deal than using our radar. Since there's a tight watch here because of the virus issue, I need to take a few extra steps to do this. I'm going to access the satellite through a roundabout way so it can't be traced back to me. I'm sending the tracking signal to our phones, Jer. Open that app on your phone."

"Got it," Jeremy confirmed. "I see it. He's on the move, but he's in the city!"

"I'll be home in fifteen. Keep an eye on him. We're going after him as soon as I return."

"Ray," Abby said, "You should also listen to this voicemail on Tracy's phone. The man in the suit mentioned something strange."

"Okay, I'll listen to it after I get back."

Ray erased the log of his recent activities on the computer before he shut it down.

"I'm leaving the office, right now."

As Ray got up from his desk, Fred walked in.

"What's going on, buddy?" Fred asked with concern. "After all that intensity over your encrypted firewall, you all right? Smooth move back there, by the way."

"Hey," Ray greeted as he walked to the doorway where Fred stood. "I can't really talk right now. I'm chasing after a lead on Jamie. Fred, there's some really weird stuff going on. I'll update you later. But for right now, I got to go."

"Sure, man. I'll catch up with you after work. So, you can't even show your best friend where you keep the coveted decryption code?"

Ray gave him a look as he slung his backpack on.

"Just kidding," Fred said as he backed away with his hands in the air.

"Catch up with me later," Ray said.

After Fred left, he locked his office door. Something came to mind, and he went back inside his office to the file cabinet by his desk. He used a key to open the bottom drawer. As he pulled it open, a pile of gizmos and gadgets rattled inside. He dug through them to pull out a small device with a USB plug-in on one side and a SIM card reader on the other. He also grabbed another cell phone out of the drawer. He stuffed the device and phone into his bag, locked the drawer, and started for the door but stopped again. He looked back at his desk. He grabbed the photo of Melanie and him and the metallic, sci-fi looking device next to the photo. He placed those into his backpack as well.

He locked his office again and whizzed down the side aisle, past the matrix of cubicles.

He arrived at the elevator foyer. He waited. Six elevators and none of them were arriving fast enough. Finally, one elevator opened. But as he was about to rush into it, Marvin was coming out.

"Oh, sorry," Marvin said, as the two of them did the dance-and-shuffle of trying to get past each other. "By the way," he said, "great firewall."

"Hey, yeah," Ray replied while holding the elevator door open with his hand, "I'm sorry I didn't go through you and your systems security team. I know that would've been the proper thing to do, but I acted in the spur of the moment. I didn't mean to go behind your back. I think I was in an overall crisis-response mode so I reacted."

"Oh," Marvin responded in his usual uncouth manner as he rubbed his hands on the sides of his pants and flashed a gauche half-smile, "it's all right, I guess. I'm glad the encrypted firewall is really helping. That's what matters, right?"

"Yeah, I suppose so."

"The firewall is pretty impressive and your decryption code for it must be awesome."

"Thanks."

"You have to show it to me some time."

"Of course," Ray said with friendly optimism. "Glad to."

"I mean when this is all over. But for now," Marvin said with a little chuckle as he raised his hands, like he was stopping a car that was coming at him, "you're under orders from Ms. Miranda to not say anything."

"All right, I won't."

"It's probably locked away in some secret compartment on a flash drive, huh?"

Ray didn't say anything, except to maintain the best poker face he could muster. He hated poker.

"It's like you're some secret agent now. It's kind of cool."

Ray, again, didn't know what to say. He felt bad for Marvin. He knew Marvin was trying his best. Infringing on Marvin's territory and making him look bad didn't cross his mind when he installed the encrypted firewall. He reminded himself from time-to-time of how young Marvin still was. He would rather aide him in his career than undercut him. He wanted to apologize again, but he restrained himself from being repetitive.

"Besides, it's probably better I don't know, you know? That decryption code is pretty valuable. I wouldn't want someone coming after me for it, like Thornton." Marvin chuckled and raised his hands up again.

"Well, I'm sure it wouldn't come down to that, where someone is actually coming after me for the decryption code!"

"Yeah, sorry. I was just kidding. Anyway, thanks for helping me out. I think if it weren't for you, I probably would've lost my job. Like Ms. Miranda said, you bought us some time."

The elevator buzzed.

"Okay," Ray said to end the exchange, "elevator's getting impatient. Keep up the hard work, Marvin. I know you'll beat this."

"Thanks. See you later."

The lonely ride in the elevator down thirty-seven floors was a welcomed space of solitude. Ray felt a bulge on his backpack from nothing other than his odd, metallic device and his thoughts began to wander, wondering if Jamie was hurt. What could they be doing to her? This device he and Melanie created was broken, but she had the healing touch for Jamie's "owies," whether scrapes, tummy aches, or icky feelings. There was something about Mommy's touch, Mommy's voice, and Mommy's hug that made the pain go away.

Ray could not deny the irreplaceable effect of Melanie. But over the last two years, he also relished in Jamie becoming Daddy's girl. She refreshed him and gave him a purposeful drive for living, especially when Jeremy descended into a dark place. In some way, saving her was also saving him. He tried protecting her with all of his heart. He would sacrifice his own body for her this very instant, if he could.

The elevator dinged and the doors opened to the first floor. Ray speed-walked into the lobby and waved to Officer Hernandez and Officer Cole sitting in the security booth. He appreciated now more than ever individuals in uniform like them who preserved order and safety for everyone else.

He got in his car and headed home with a backpack containing the decryption code, a SIM card reader, and his sci-fi looking gadget. He affixed his phone onto a holder on the dashboard. A blinking red dot revealed the suited man's location.

Chapter 9
Intercept

City traffic couldn't be worse than on a day like today. Ray tuned into the traffic station on the radio. There were reports of road constructions on the freeway heading to his home. He attempted to weave around the cars, but there was not enough room between the bumpers to actually do any weaving. He thought about getting into the carpool lane where the traffic flowed better, but he didn't want to risk getting pulled over and losing more time. At this rate, the estimated time of his arrival at home according to his GPS was twenty-five minutes. He couldn't afford twenty-five minutes in addition to the time it would take to get from his home to the suited man's location.

His phone app tracking the suited man, however, indicated he was only twelve minutes from the man's present position. As much as he wanted to regroup with his team and his son, he exited the freeway and headed towards the suited man. He called Jeremy.

"Yeah," Jeremy answered. "Who is this?"

"Jeremy," Ray spoke to him with his earpiece in, "It's me. I'm calling from a back-up cell phone. I'm not coming home. Traffic is too bad. I want the three of you to get in Abby's car and track the suited man. You have it on your app, so we'll convene at his location. Looks like he's on the move still, so we'll need to track him until he stops. But don't get ahead of me and don't try to confront him."

Ray paused for a couple of seconds to listen for a response, but all he heard were rustling sounds. "Jeremy," he said, "you got all that?"

"Yeah," Jeremy replied, "we got in Abby's car, and we're pulling out."

"Good. Let's stay on the phone while we drive."

"I'm putting you on speakerphone."

"Okay. Tell me what you found."

"For starters, the jerk's name is Gordon Morrison. Abby got his driver's license, date of birth, and address off of his license plate number."

"Good. Go on."

"The car he's driving is a black 2010 GMC Terrain."

"That's the same SUV we saw him drive away in yesterday."

"According to the phone logs, Tracy was definitely coordinating with this jerk. There were a ton of phone calls between the two of them in the last month. He's totally in on Jamie's kidnapping."

"Sifu Ray," Abby said, "I think you should listen to this one voicemail we got off Tracy's phone."

"Do you have it where you can play it for me?"

"Yes, we do," she answered, "We played it off Tracy's phone and recorded it onto mine."

"Good thinking."

"Here it is. This voicemail to Tracy was just three days before Tracy took Jamie," Jeremy said.

Ray heard a beep and then a man's voice: "Tests are confirmed. Taggot act is good. You have a green light. Deliver Jamie on time. This is my last message to you."

Ray was silent as he thought hard about every word in the message. Hearing Jamie's kidnapper concocted a mixture of abhorrence in his stomach and a shiver along his spine. Gordon spoke in a methodical manner with short to-the-point statements, like it was merely business as usual. It didn't matter to him that he was stealing a little girl or that this girl belonged to a family.

The questions began to crop up as Ray mentally replayed Gordon's sentences – *Why does he want Jamie? He sounded like he was the one in charge, but who is he? Was he the top of the food chain in this scheme or was there another higher than him?* The more Ray processed the voice message the more the mystery mushroomed.

"Sifu Ray," Abby asked. "Are you still there?"

He reverted back to the present company on the phone. "Yes, Abby. I was just thinking about the message."

"Strange, isn't it?"

"He said something about tests. What tests? You said this voice message was prior to Jamie's kidnapping, correct?"

"Yeah, that's right," Jeremy confirmed.

"So it's not referring to tests they ran on Jamie, thank God. But what kind of tests are they talking about?"

"And," Abby added, "he said something about good taggot act. What does that mean? Everything's cryptic."

"Yo, Sifu," Deon chimed in, "this guy Gordon sounds like a stiff, like a professional. What do you want us to do when we get to him? Say the word, and I'll take this guy down for you."

"No," he immediately replied. "We don't know where Jamie is. By now, there's a good chance that she's not actually with him, but he has her kept somewhere. He's our lead. We need to follow him until we get a clue as to where Jamie is. No hasty actions."

"Why don't we jump him, Sifu," Deon contended, "and beat his stiff butt until he tells us where Jamie is?"

"No. We don't know what we're dealing with anymore. You all understand? We don't know who this guy is and if there could be others involved."

"Got it, Sifu," Deon complied. "It's your call. I'm just saying if you want his butt whipped, just give the word."

"For now, we need more intel. If we're going to get Jamie back safely, we need to be cautious and calculated."

He checked the tracking app on his phone and noticed his approach to the red dot. "All right, I'm about to close in on Gordon in less than two minutes."

"We're about five minutes away," Abby said.

"Remember, hang back at a safe distance to watch and follow him. I'm not sure what we're looking for yet, but let's look for some kind of opportunity to learn Jamie's whereabout."

Ray exited the freeway into the downtown district during a busy Friday lunch hour. Slow moving lines of cars filled the streets while pedestrians flooded the sidewalks and crosswalks. There were professionals in suits with briefcases, tourists in shorts with cameras, and homeless people in dark brown, soiled clothes with shopping carts. A farmer's market in a corporate square by the city hall attracted a plentitude of people.

He was only a few blocks away from Gordon's location, but his speed slowed to fifteen miles per hour. He stopped at a red traffic light. While a herd of pedestrians crossed the street in front of him, he saw on his tracking app that Gordon stopped moving. Gordon was inside some kind of complex. The light turned green.

He drove another three blocks, until the blue dot on his tracking app indicating his own position was next to the blinking red dot indicating Gordon's. He scanned as far down the street as he could for an open parking space, but there were none. So, he pulled into a yellow loading zone, knowing that within seven minutes the parking enforcers would hungrily swoop in to issue $80-citations, especially during the busy lunch hours in downtown. But he couldn't afford to search for parking.

He sent a text message to Jeremy, writing, "I'm at the Fig At 7th complex. Going in. Approach carefully."

Jeremy sent a reply text message: "I'm sending everyone a pic of

Gordon I pulled off of his driver's license. This is our guy."

"Good job, Jer."

Ray grabbed his backpack and stepped out of his car. As he closed his car door, he spotted a parking enforcement vehicle coming in the opposite direction on the other side of the street. He accidentally made eye contact with the officer in the car as she passed by. He instinctually turned his head with a flick, though a little too late, and walked around his car onto the sidewalk. From the corner of his eye, he saw the parking enforcer make a sharp u-turn to his side of the street. As he quickly walked away toward the complex, the parking enforcer drove up to his car.

With his cell phone in hand, he walked briskly to the opening of the complex until his blue dot was directly on top of the red dot. He was on top of Gordon! Standing on the edge of the complex, he looked down into a giant hole in the ground. The complex was an underground spiral of shops and restaurants that sank down four levels. At the bottom was a food court with a large, open patio of tables and chairs.

He got on the escalator and descended. He tried to spot Gordon as he went down, but too many red sun umbrellas covered the patio.

Gordon had not moved from his location for the last several minutes. As Ray descended from one escalator to another, he closed in on his unsuspecting target.

He reached the bottom of the complex and heard a musician playing on a grand piano near the center of the patio. Slowly walking along the outer edge of the large patio, he discreetly scanned the outside area, the shops, and food court. He honestly did not expect to be searching a shopping mall in the middle of downtown with all of these people around. He imagined being at a rundown warehouse in an obscure industrial district that was scarce of people or perhaps at a house embedded in a quiet suburb. But not this. He checked his tracking app again to make sure he wasn't misled. As far as he could tell, the tracking app was working properly.

He inspected the faces of each suited, Caucasian male from a careful distance while remaining in the shadows. He reasoned that since the kidnapping was a coordinated effort with his babysitter who knew his family well, Gordon plausibly knew who he was and what he looked like. Ray couldn't chance being seen by him.

He checked his tracking app again. His blue dot was half overlapping Gordon's red dot. Gordon was somewhere very close, even next to him. A group of businessmen stepped off the escalator. Three ladies in business suits came out of the food court. A family of tourists stood by the grand piano, enjoying the music.

Finally, he saw the back of a man's head partly lit by the sunlight. He was seated at a table in the center of the patio, and he had his cell phone to his ear.

Suspicious that this was the sought-out perpetrator, Ray walked to the right along the outer edge of the patio to get a look at his face. He checked the photo that Jeremy sent to his phone. When he could see the side of the man's face from behind the man's right shoulder, Ray stopped. It was Gordon.

Ray sat down at a table that was about fifty feet away from Gordon but remained behind Gordon's right shoulder.

His phone vibrated in his hand. It was a text message from Jeremy: "We're here. Coming down."

He replied with a text: "He's here in front of me on the patio. Come carefully, but don't approach me. I don't want us crowding together and drawing his attention."

"Got it."

Ray sent a text message of instructions to the three of them: "Spread out. Jer, he might know what you look like so stay out of his sight. Right now he's facing south, away from the escalator. Come down and hang back for now. Deon and Abby, since he doesn't know you two, move around to his left side to get a better view of his face."

"Got it," Jeremy replied. "We're coming down to the patio now."

Ray saw Deon and Abby step off the escalator first. They were talking and smiling while their eyes slyly veered toward the open patio. Jeremy was several steps behind them acting as if he was not with them.

While Deon and Abby walked straight, on the left side of Gordon and remaining fifty feet away, Jeremy stepped off the escalator and turned in the opposite direction. He made eye contact with Ray and stopped. Ray pointed with his eyes toward Gordon's direction. Jeremy looked in that direction and then took a seat at a table that was forty feet behind Gordon's head.

Deon and Abby bought sodas at one of the outdoor vendors and moved closer to Gordon as they continued to chat with each other. They sat at a table ten feet away from him, slightly in front of his left side. They sipped their sodas while chatting, appearing absorbed in their topic of discussion. Ray was impressed with their acting.

Ray opened his laptop and took out the SIM card reader. He plugged the USB end of the device into his laptop and opened a program with a banner that read "Cellular Monitoring GSM Intercept."

Gordon was still occupied with his phone conversation. He nodded once. Then the call ended. He set his phone down on the table beside his food tray. He started eating the salad in front of him, taking small bites at a moderate pace—very gentlemanly. The plate of salad was still plentiful, suggesting he just began his lunch. He only chewed a few times before inserting another batch of greens into his mouth. Ray estimated he'd be done consuming the generous plate of leaves in ten minutes.

Ray wrote a text message to his team.

"Here's what we need to do," he wrote.

He saw them casually look at their phones at different instances, while still continuing what they were doing.

"Abby and Deon, I need a good distraction that will pull his attention away from his phone on the table. Jer, I need you to swipe his phone and get me his SIM card. I only need a minute. You'll return his phone back to the same spot when I'm done. He can't know his phone was ever missing."

All three of them replied with text messages that read, "Got it."

"Abby and Deon, you're on. Come up with something fast before he finishes his salad!"

Abby and Deon chatted for another fifteen seconds, having exchanges that appeared more intentionally responsive to one another than before. Abby nodded at Deon. Then their temperaments gradually morphed, beginning with Abby shaking her head, becoming increasingly upset.

Their elevated interaction already caught Gordon's attention. He must be an observant man. But he merely glanced over with a slight turn of his head, and then he returned to consuming his salad.

Deon pulled out a colorful tourist map and vigorously opened it. He pointed at the map. Abby shook her head with closed eyes. She waved a hand of defiance in front of him. He tossed his head back with agitation. Raising their conversation another decibel, he said, "I didn't get us lost, all right?"

"*You* insisted we were supposed to go this way," Abby combated while pointing at the map, "but *I* said we should've taken a right over here."

"You're always accusing me of getting us lost! I was the one who said we should've gone here first."

"And I was the one who said we should've asked for directions. This is why I can't stand going on vacations with you."

"This is why sometimes I can't stand *you*, woman!"

It was the "woman" part that really grabbed Gordon's attention. He turned his head to watch Deon and Abby argue. Now Ray was seeing only the back of his head. Again, he was impressed by his students' dramatic skills.

Abby teared, and her nose reddened. "We always fight on our vacations when we're supposed to be having fun."

"Well, if you stop making a big deal out of everything, we would be. Fine," Deon said, "you know what? Let's ask someone for directions. You'll see."

Deon looked around and made eye contact with Gordon. "Come here," Deon ordered Abby.

Deon looked at Gordon, who tried to ignore them by returning to his salad, but they approached him with their drinks and map in hand.

"Excuse me, mister," Deon said. "I'm sorry to disturb your lunch, but could you *please* help us out? We're visiting from Texas, and we're lost."

"He got us lost," Abby corrected.

"Dang it, woman. Could you give it a break for one minute?" Deon said to Gordon, "She is always accusing me."

"How can I help you both?" Gordon asked with a tone of annoyance.

"Thank you, mister," Deon said. "Where exactly are we, and how do we get to the Museum of Contemporary Art." He knelt down and opened the map on his knee. "This is embarrassing. We've been here for two days, and we're already lost. All these one-way streets, you know? They get us turned around."

"It's fine. I'll show you," Gordon replied in a business-like and stick-to-the-facts manner. He angled his large frame in his chair so that his knees and shoulders faced Deon who was still on one knee.

Abby moved around to stand on Deon's right side to be closer to the map, which encouraged Gordon to have his face pointing away from his phone. Jeremy got up and moved around toward the right as Gordon shifted into that left angular posture, remaining directly behind Gordon's head at forty feet away.

She said, "I told him that we should've turned on this street, but he insisted that it was a one-way and we should go this way, which led us into some underground tunnel."

"Look," Deon said with his hand motioning at her in a chopping motion, "why don't you just let the nice man explain it to us. You know, is there even anything good to see at the Museum of Contemporary Art? Is it worth the trouble?"

"All he wanted to do was watch some UFC fight at the Staples Center," she retorted.

"That's what I'm talking about, right?" Deon sought Gordon's support. "You're a guy. Isn't that the thing to see here? Not some boring museum."

"You two have to figure out what you want. I can show you how to get to the museum," Gordon said blandly.

Jeremy meandered towards Gordon, staying behind him and out of his sight. He was twenty-five feet away.

"I'm sorry, mister," Deon said to Gordon. "This is what happens to us when we get lost on vacation. We fight. If you could explain this to us, it would help. Thank you."

"Fine," Gordon responded.

Jeremy closed in casually. Other people were crossing the patio, getting up from their seats and searching for tables. One couple with empty food trays in their hands would be walking past Gordon's table. He followed them. He was only twenty feet away, walking toward Gordon at the same pace as the couple.

Abby added, "He always gets us lost, so you will have to explain it to him in detail."

The couple was about to pass Gordon's table.

"Dang it, woman," Deon shouted while flicking his right hand up at her, knocking the cup in her hand. Cola sloshed out of the cup, onto the map and Gordon's left pant leg.

In that same moment, the couple walked past the table, and Jeremy, following closely behind them, swiped the phone so silently and stealthily that Ray wished he had caught it on video. Under the commotion, sudden soda accident, and coverage of the passing couple, the theft was perfectly undetectable.

Jeremy walked to Ray. He had the phone opened and the SIM card removed by the time he passed Ray's table. He handed the SIM card to his father as he continued walking by and return to his table.

Ray inserted the SIM card into the reader device that was plugged into his laptop. Upon hitting the "Enter" key, the Cellular Monitoring GSM Intercept program began downloading. The download bar moved swiftly through a rectangle on the screen, greedily taking up the empty space.

All the while, Abby was drying Gordon's pant leg with wads of napkins. "Oh my gosh, oh my gosh," she repeated. "I'm so sorry."

"Dang it, woman," Deon said again as he dried the map and then patted Gordon's thigh with napkins.

"See what you made me do," she accused.

"Stop it already with the accusations! Dang it!"

Gordon, who had his head down and was focused on wiping the cola and ice off of his leg, was also pushing Abby and Deon's hands away from his upper thigh. "It's fine," he said repeatedly. "You don't have to do this. I got it."

But they stubbornly cleaned his left leg.

The download was complete. As soon as Ray pulled the SIM card out of the reader, Jeremy was already walking by his table and taking it from his hand.

"No, no," Abby insisted, "We have to make this right." She continued to pat him down with a bouquet of napkins, getting awfully close to his groin.

While Jeremy walked back to Gordon's table, he inserted the SIM card back into the phone, closed the cover, grabbed an orange food tray off a table, wiped the phone on his shirt under the food tray to clean off the fingerprints, and returned the phone to the exact same spot on the table without a sound. The food tray in hand canvassed his swift action from unwanted eyes. *Smart thinking, son*, Ray said to Jeremy in his head.

"Look. Stop!" Gordon demanded. "You both clearly have your issues. You don't need to involve me."

"So sorry, mister," Deon repeated.

"You need to ask someone else for directions," Gordon said sharply. "I can't help you." He turned in his seat to face his salad again.

Deon and Abby slowly walked away while still fighting, which continued to draw Gordon's attention.

"That poor man," she said. "Can't believe you made me do that to him."

"Stop blaming me for everything, woman. It's so embarrassing being with you."

"And we're still lost," she said as they both faded into the shadows of the outer edge of the patio.

After Ray watched the conclusion of the drama with wicked amusement, he got up with his laptop and headed for the escalator. As he went up the escalator, he looked down to see Gordon take two more bites of leafy greens and then get up abruptly with his unfinished salad. He threw the rest away in the trash angrily.

When Ray got to the top of the complex, Abby and Deon came out of the elevator. Moments later, Jeremy surfaced at the top of the escalator as well.

"You guys were impressive," Ray congratulated.

"What now?" Jeremy asked.

"Let's get out of sight first. Can't risk Gordon spotting us."

They walked into a restaurant with tinted windows and asked to be seated at a booth in a corner. As soon as they sat down, Ray opened his laptop. He still had the GSM Intercept program up on his screen. He typed a few commands, and then inserted an earphone splitter that allowed two sets of earphones to be plugged into the laptop. He handed a single earphone to each of them.

As he clicked on several options on the laptop's finger pad, he said, "I cloned his phone."

They looked at each other with fascination and amusement.

"I cloned his SIM card. I can access his cell phone and listen to his conversations, see his text messages, access his voicemail, and make outgoing calls from his number."

"Dang, Sifu," Deon complimented.

"With my laptop hooked into our satellite, I've turned my laptop into a cellular monitoring and intercepting device. Every conversation will be recorded on to my laptop. You should all know that what I'm doing is very illegal, in case you don't want any part of this."

"You are cooler than I thought," Jeremy said, "in a freaky way."

They listened to silence for a few minutes before a smiling waitress came by to take their orders. They ordered four sodas and a side of seasoned fries to share.

"You never did this to me, did you?" Jeremy asked.

Ray smiled quietly.

The drinks and food came before they finally heard dialing tones followed by ringing. They perked up.

"He can't hear us, can he?" Abby whispered.

"No," Ray answered, "We are undetectable."

Someone answered the call.

But the conversation they heard was inconsequential to finding Jamie. Gordon spoke to a colleague at the America Bank building in downtown about a certain business matter involving another employee. He instructed the other person in a callous manner and ended the conversation with a cold reprimand.

"Well, we know he works for America Bank," Abby assessed, "and with the way he was giving instructions and making decisions, he must be a supervisor or manager."

"He's not just a dude in a suit," Deon added, "He is a snob."

"He doesn't seem like a child-trafficking person," she said.

They ate their fries, washed it down with soda and waited for the next call. Ray received a call on his own cell phone. It was Fred.

"Yeah, Fred," Ray answered.

"Hey, buddy. How are you holding up?" Fred inquired.

"We're hanging in there. Trying to fight this thing."

"We? Is Jeremy with you?"

"Jeremy, Abby, and Deon."

"That's good you have your own search team working for you. What exactly are you all doing right now?"

"Fred, you really don't want to know."

"Yeah, I do. I want to help however I can with finding Jamie."

"Thanks. I'll catch you up later. Are you calling just to check up on me?"

"I wish I were. I called to let you know that they went through your office."

"Who?"

"Internal Investigations. I mean they went through *everything*. They even broke into your locked drawers and cabinets. It's crazy here. Everyone's a suspect, and they're taking no prisoners."

"Did they search my computer?"

"Not yet, but they're starting on that now."

Ray knew it wouldn't take them long to discover his unauthorized and illegal surveillance with company equipment.

"I wanted to give you a heads up," Fred said.

Another call from Gordon's phone was intercepted as a message flashed on Ray's screen and the ringing started.

"I have to go, Fred," Ray said, "Let me call you back later."

"Okay, buddy. Take care."

The ringing in their earpieces continued.

"It's good this jerk uses his phone a lot," Jeremy commented.

"Let's hope we hear something that tells us where Jamie is," Ray responded. He read his laptop screen. "This one is an incoming call. It's from a man named M. That's how he has this person saved in his contacts—simply as M."

"Smart," Jeremy said, "in case his phone was stolen, you at least couldn't know the name of this person. Must be someone important."

"Hello, Marcus?" Gordon answered.

They were as still as statues while listening intently.

"You have the girl?"

"Yes."

Ray's eyes widened and his heartbeats quickened. Jeremy curled his lips.

"How is she?" Marcus asked.

"She's fine. She's been asking for her dad. Whiny kid."

Ray simultaneously felt anger and sadness upon hearing about the mistreatment of his child. He could hear Jamie's voice in his head asking for him, and he would've normally replied to her by calling her "princess." But to his regret, he pictured her calling for him without receiving an answer. It tormented him.

"She has no idea what's going on," Gordon reported. "She still believes I'm Tracy's brother and she's over for a sleepover while her dad and brother are away on an emergency. But she's getting antsy. I can't keep her at the house for long."

Abby looked up at Ray and said excitedly, "House! I have his address from his license plate!"

"How are you keeping her?" Marcus asked.

"She's locked in a bedroom with a doll, a television, and plenty of food and water. There's no phone in there, and the window shutters are nailed shut. No one can see in, and she can't get out."

Marcus chuckled. "Gordon, the babysitter. Didn't know you knew how. What are you feeding her?"

"I'm not a babysitter," Gordon grunted. "I got her a dirty, used doll at a garage sale. She has a bottle of flavored water, a bag of pretzels to chow on all day, and a box of animal crackers. Tracy said animal crackers were the kid's favorite thing, so I got a bunch to keep her pacified. What else are you supposed to feed a kid?"

Ray restrained himself from slamming his fist into the table.

"Glad you're not my babysitter," Marcus responded. "We'll let the experts take care of her soon. PH is going to be very happy about this."

Who is PH? Ray mouthed silently to the three of them.

"We sure we got the right kid this time?"

"Always the skeptic. The lab coats promise we're on the right track," Marcus assured. "Taggot act came across positive and clear. There's no mistake."

"It's my job to be careful. I like to get the correct targets."

"The lab coats ran multiple tests this time and confirmed she's the one."

"This is it then. Our search is over."

"Yes, it is."

"Poor girl, though. Good for us. Bad for her."

"Don't forget PH's vision. We'll all be better because of it. Bring her in this afternoon as scheduled. Remember, come through the service entrance of the building, the one by the loading dock."

"I know the drill. I'll head back to my house in fifteen minutes to get the brat and deliver her. Be sure to put in a good word with PH for me."

"He'll hear all about this," Marcus started to say. "He's personally keeping detailed tabs on the progress. He's been waiting a long time to get his hands on this girl."

"As long as I'm part of the details."

"Oh, you are. Accomplishing this job may even earn you an audience with him."

"Marcus, I've been wanting that day to come. All it takes is getting a little girl into his hands to make it happen. I'll head back to the house now to get the girl and will see you later."

The call ended.

"But we know enough." Ray closed his laptop and coiled up the earphones. "Jeremy, bring up the directions to Gordon's address."

"Already got it," Jeremy replied while he looked at his phone. "His crib is twenty-three miles east of here, right off the 10."

"We have to go. If we leave now, we'll have fourteen minutes ahead of him," he said looking at the time on his phone.

They exited out of the booth. Ray dropped enough cash on the table to leave the waitress a sizable tip. They opened the front door and exited the restaurant cautiously to be sure Gordon was not somewhere nearby.

"Abby, where are you parked?" Ray asked.

"At an all-day parking lot for $20."

"Good. We'll go together in my car."

He led the way to his vehicle, which was only fifty yards away. He pulled the two parking tickets off of his windshield while the others got inside the car.

"I have his house up on my GPS," Jeremy said. "Take a right at the end of the block, get on the freeway, and go east."

Ray's vehicle pulled out of the loading zone space and roared down the street.

"It sounded like Jamie is at this house alone," he said, "If she is alone, that will be good for us. We don't know what we're walking into. Be ready for anything."

"Let's do this," Deon charged.

The car zoomed up the on-ramp and headed east on the freeway.

Not Easily Broken

Chapter 10
Enigma

Images of Jamie being locked in a room of a strange house and thoughts of what she might've experienced crowded Ray's mind. His cold stare at the highway and stiff arms pressing on the steering wheel conveyed the concerns weighing on him. He blinked several times to snap out of his worries and focus on the rescue mission. *Manage your thoughts*, he told himself. *We can't miss this opportunity.*

"We'll get her back, Sifu Ray," Abby said, looking at him in the rearview mirror from the seat directly behind him.

"It might help us to get more prepared by examining the phone conversation we heard between Gordon and Marcus," Ray said. "It could help us know more about what's going on and what to expect. According to the GPS, we'll get there in twenty minutes."

"Well, they're bringing her into some building for something," Jeremy started. "Marcus told Gordon to enter through the service entrance. And who is PH?"

"Doesn't sound like Marcus is the top dog," Deon suggested.

Ray hypothesized, "I think Marcus is Gordon's handler, like Gordon handled Tracy. Marcus sounded like another middleman relaying instructions and managing the transaction. Sounds like this 'PH' person is the one in charge, the one calling the shots. There's a much larger system at work here."

"Geez," Abby exclaimed.

"Marcus also said something about PH's vision. What vision?" Jeremy asked.

Ray said, "If there's a vision, it means there are motives, objectives, and a plan."

"Also, they mentioned professionals in lab coats doing something to Jamie," Abby said and then swallowed uncomfortably when she listened to her own words.

"Man," Deon responded, "this is freaky. What could they want from a little girl?"

Ray didn't respond. He couldn't. At Abby's mention of "professionals in lab coats" he felt an intense urgency and a deep need for answers. *Was this some twisted experiment? Maybe this is some form of high-end child-trafficking ring?* Again, he forced his mind to not be cluttered with speculative worries. Concentrate, he told himself. What was more necessary than answers was retrieval. They had to get Jamie.

"What about this 'taggot act?' We keep hearing that come up," Abby asked as she leaned forward against the back of Ray's seat.

"Tagit? Sounds like the name of some white dude?" Deon suggested.

"Maybe Taggot act means this guy Taggot did something," Jeremy suggested.

"This Taggot guy could be a key player," Ray said.

"Taggot could be one of the pros in the lab coats," Jeremy postulated, "and there's something he's supposed to do."

"Wait, wait," Abby inserted, "the statement Marcus made was, 'Taggot act came across positive and clear.' That was the context. 'Taggot act' was referred to as a noun; 'came' was the verb."

"Abby, you're getting too grammatical for me," Deon commented. "What are you saying?"

"You're saying Taggot Act refers to an action of this guy Taggot," Ray asked for clarity.

"Maybe," she said with uncertainty in her voice. "It's not something he's going to do, but something he did in the past. Maybe."

"It's a weird way of talking about something that someone did," Jeremy commented. "Who talks like that?"

"This whole thing is weird, man," Deon added.

"What else could 'act' mean besides an action? We need to examine the possibilities," she continued. She pulled out her phone and looked up the word in an online dictionary. "One definition for 'act' is a main division in a play, like Act 1, 2, or 3, or maybe Part 1, 2, or 3."

"So Taggot could be the name for some sort of phase," Ray said as he weaved around a slower car in front of him. "That could make sense, because we discovered all of these guys are operating according to some elaborate plan. Tracy had her part and passed Jamie off to Gordon, and now Gordon has his part in passing Jamie off to Marcus. Taggot Act could be the next phase in their scheme?"

"What scheme? What are they putting Jamie through? We're shooting in the dark," Jeremy said while shaking his head. "We're just guessing."

"We have to keep trying," Ray encouraged. "It's all we have to go on. Let's keep this going."

"Jeremy's right. These are still just guesses that don't exactly fit the context of the sentences well," Abby critiqued. "Marcus said to Gordon that taggot act came across positive. If you remember in Gordon's voice message to Tracy, he said taggot act was good. 'Good' is a value assessment. There's something we're not thinking of yet." She looked at her phone again.

Ray glanced in his rearview mirror and noticed how arduous she was in her attempt to solve this puzzle. Seeing her dedication gave him greater confidence in recovering his daughter.

"Sorry, y'all," Deon chimed, "I'm kinda lost with this. I was never good with crossword puzzles."

"Here's another definition," Abby started again. "An 'act' could mean 'a formal decision' that was made or 'a document stating a transaction.' Does that help us?"

Deon stroked the back of his head vigorously while he looked out the window. Ray and Jeremy were quiet with furrowed brows.

"I guess it could mean that they arrived at a conclusion, which they called 'taggot.' Taggot is maybe an inside term for a formal decision. And," Ray said with a pause as he guessed, "the decision was 'good,' meaning it was positive."

Jeremy added unconfidently, "Taggot act is positive, meaning Tracy had the green light. Like, that's their code to give each other the go-ahead. Right? Gordon told Tracy, 'Taggot act is good.' Marcus told Gordon taggot act is positive. Like, that means go ahead—do your thing."

"That could be it," Abby concurred with that possibility, but Ray could tell from her eyes she was still searching, "but it seems like a very complicated way to just tell each other, 'Go ahead.'"

"This whole thing is complicated," Deon chimed again.

"It fits, though," Jeremy said.

"Yeah, it does," Abby affirmed with doubt, "but it fits just about as well as the other possibilities. None of them stand out. I have a feeling this 'taggot act' is more significant than we realize, and we're missing it," she said.

"What are you thinking, Abby?" Ray asked.

Abby tapped on her phone screen and played the voicemail from Gordon to Tracy again. "Let's listen to Gordon's voicemail again."

Gordon's message played: "Tests are confirmed. Taggot act is good. You have a green light. Deliver Jamie on time. This is my last message."

"No, you see?" Abby figured, "Taggot act can't mean a 'formal decision' to give the go-ahead when Gordon said to her right after that, 'You have a green light.' That would be redundant. Why would he speak in code and then repeat what the code meant? That doesn't make sense.

'Taggot act is good,' must refer to something else. Also, taggot act has to fit the previous statement about tests being confirmed."

"It's probably just their own mumbo-jumbo. Does it even matter?" Deon said with resignation. "We're going to get Jamie back right now anyway. This is going to be over soon."

"It could matter," Abby insisted, "because Jamie was specifically targeted. Isn't that what you're all thinking too? Marcus and Gordon made it clear that this was no random kidnapping. It was deliberate. It was selective."

When she said that definitively, Ray's eyes met hers in the rearview mirror. He knew she was right. This entire act of crime followed an algorithm. *Why Jamie?* was the pinpricking question.

Abby concluded, "This taggot act could be the explanation for why this is happening. Don't you all think?"

Ray slipped into the carpool lane, where the traffic flowed more swiftly. "Abby is right," he acknowledged. "The more we can understand why this happened, the more in control we could be of the situation. We can't be in the dark about this anymore."

"Well, then what else could 'taggot act' mean?" Jeremy asked. "We ran through all the definitions we could think of for those words. Right?" There was silence for a couple of seconds. "Abby," he said, looking back at her from the passenger seat, "are there any more definitions?"

"No," she answered quietly while tapping on her phone and looking out the window. Her "no" sounded a bit defeated, like arriving at a dead end on a hiking trail.

Ray saw her mouthing the words *taggot act* over and over as she scanned the screen on her phone. Then she looked outside at the oncoming traffic on the opposite side of the highway. She was thinking. Only the sounds of the SUV hitting the bumps in the freeway could be heard as the men silently gave her space to think.

"We're missing something. We have to think outside of the box about these two words," she inserted.

"What if they're not words?" Deon asked

Ray responded to his speculative question with one raised eyebrow.

"Deon, dude, if they aren't words," Jeremy said, "then the mumbo-jumbo just became *more* mumbo-jumbo."

Abby beamed. "Wait. Deon could be right. He's thinking outside the box. What if they aren't words?"

"What are you thinking of?" Ray pressed.

Her eyes roamed from side to side like an old typewriter in action. "What if... what if 'act' is not a word, but they're just letters, A-C-T."

Enigma

"There's the ACT test my school talks about," Jeremy suggested.

"Could be an acronym," she validated and continued, "and what if taggot was not a name?" She repeated *taggot* to herself out loud a couple of times. Then her eyes widened and the few small lines on her face smoothed over. "What if taggot is spelled T-A-G-G-A-T? You add the act to it and it's not two words but a string of letters: TAGGATACT."

"I'm thinking outside the box with you," Deon said, "but how in the world does that make anymore sense?"

"You know I work in a biolab. Well, it's a genetic research lab. And, TAGGATACT could be a DNA sequence."

The men looked at each other with befuddlement; even Ray turned his head to look at the passengers in the back. They waited to hear more from her.

She continued, "These could be codons, which are triplets of DNA codes. So this would be a sequence of three codons. TAG, GAT and ACT. Gordon said in his message that, 'Tests are confirmed.' What other tests could there be?" She paused for a brief second then asked Ray, "Sifu Ray, has Jamie been getting blood work done?"

Ray thought for a moment. "She did have her blood drawn and examined last month and three months before that. The first time the nurse said it was a routine annual check up. But the second time seemed odd to me when she drew Jamie's blood again. I chalked it up to the doctor's office just being thorough."

"Did the doctor specifically request for the blood work?" Abby inquired.

"The first time he did," he replied. "But he didn't the second time. Or at least I didn't hear him tell me himself. The nurse just came in and told me the doctor wanted to do another blood test." He noticed Jeremy's condemning look of disappointment. "I didn't think anything of it."

"Jamie's always had the same doctor?" Abby investigated.

"Yes, same doctor since she was two," he replied.

"Same nurse as well?"

"No, this nurse started working at this doctor's office about nine months ago."

"Was it the same nurse who did the blood work both times?"

"Yes, it was. Same nurse."

"Ray, I think this nurse might be in on this. It's very likely the tests she ran on Jamie were DNA tests. Whoever these people are, they must've identified a DNA sequence in Jamie that interests them."

Jeremy said with a scowl, "You think this is why they took my sister? For her DNA?"

"I don't have an explanation for why Jamie's DNA is of particular interest," she said, "but this makes the most sense. It fits the context of the voice messages and correlates with the peculiar, repeated blood tests. I think her DNA sequence is the reason they kidnapped her."

Deon blurted, "This is twisted. Sifu Ray, what are you going to do?"

Ray stepped on the gas pedal, causing all the passengers to slump back in their seats. He tailed the car in front of him until there was a small opening in the fast lane next to him, enough for his vehicle to barely fit into. He popped out of the carpool lane, violating the rule about double solid yellow lines and hitting several bendable pylons that formed the barrier for the carpool lane. He got into the fast lane, cutting off a small car. He accelerated some more to pass the car in the carpool lane, trespassing once again over the double solid yellows to get back in the carpool lane. He sped forward.

"What in the world?" Jeremy cried. "Why do they want my sister for her DNA? What does PH want with her DNA?"

"This PH dude sounds like a cold freak!" Deon exclaimed.

The men gave Abby glances as if somehow she would know the answer.

"I don't know," she confessed. "It's very odd. It could be for a number of reasons but none of which would be simple. It could be part of a stem cell project or something. When I get back to my lab, I can research the significances of the codon TAGGATACT."

"Finding more answers gives us more questions," Deon said. "It's never ending!"

"I agree. Our concentration right now is to get Jamie back," Ray declared. The slight tremor in his voice revealed his worry. "At least, we now have a better gauge of what we could be up against. At first, we thought this might've been a random act of a crazy woman. Then we thought this was about child-trafficking. But it's turning out to be something complex and sick. We can also surmise that the people involved are sophisticated and talented. We're not up against a gang of thugs. It's more."

Ray tapped on the steering wheel with his hand. "We'll get answers later. Right now, knowing what we know already, we have to get her back today. There's no other way."

With that, the non-negotiable objective was emphatically stated and their SUV raced down the freeway, weaving around more cars. According to their GPS, they would arrive at Jamie's place of captivity in three minutes.

Ray rapped on the steering wheel again. "Here's the plan."

The quietness in the vehicle allowed for only the road and air conditioner to be heard. All eyes were fixed onto Ray, as he looked straight ahead at the road with his hands at the two and ten o'clock positions on the steering wheel.

"I'll double park the car on the street so we can pull out quickly without anyone blocking us once we get Jamie," Ray said. Saying those last few words sparked a yearning inside of him. He sounded strict, like he was administering a set of instructions to high schoolers. The rigidity in the way he spoke and the specific enunciations he applied to his words indicated he wanted everyone to follow his plan without deviation.

"This has to be done right. We'll only have one chance at this. I'll park half a block away from the house," he continued, "so we're not seen by anyone who might be inside the house."

"Hold on," Jeremy objected already. "Who's going to be the getaway driver? We should have someone waiting in the car, ready to pick us up once we have Jamie. We need a getaway driver."

"This will be covert," Ray countered. "We'll be in and out, simple. We do this together. I don't want to leave anyone by themselves."

"Look," Jeremy persisted, "you're all engineering smart and stuff, but I think I know crime better than you. We should have a getaway driver. Let me be that."

"Absolutely not. No," Ray responded, trying to hide his parental concern over a fifteen-year-old driving—let alone be a getaway driver! "If all of us go in together, we can be in and out faster and we are better off facing whatever it is we might find in that house together. We expect it to be empty since Gordon is not there, but we don't know for sure. We're better together."

"Fine."

"When we get out of the car," Ray continued, "we'll go in together and flush out each room. I'll go in first. Abby and Jeremy next. Deon will go last to cover our rear, in case someone comes up from behind that we don't expect."

"What? No. That's going to take too long," Jeremy criticized. "Why don't we split up and each search every room as quickly as we can?"

"No," Ray replied firmly. "We don't know what's in that house. We have to do this methodically and together. We have one shot. We'll go through each room quickly. It's a house probably with four bedrooms at the most. There can't be more than several rooms to search, including the living, kitchen, and dining. If we average less than ten seconds per room, we'll be in and out in a minute. It won't take long."

"When we enter a room," he said, "we fan out and check every spot, closet, pantry, everything. Call out her name."

"I'm telling you it's going to be too slow," Jeremy insisted. "We need to spread out and ransack the place."

"Jeremy," Ray said impatiently, "we do this right. One shot. We can't split up. If we encounter trouble in one room, we can overpower it together, quickly. If you're by yourself, you can get into trouble and become another victim we have to rescue. We can't afford that. Stick together!"

"Let me cover the rear. I have more training than Deon. No offense, Deon."

"No worries. I'm good," Deon replied. "Just so you know, I can handle things."

"Deon covers our rear," Ray reiterated.

"You want to put your second strongest guy in the middle?" Jeremy asked. "Next to you, I'm the stronger fighter, right?"

"Hey, Jer. Don't sweat it. I got it. I'm a big boy. I might not have much Wing Chun, but I have 250 pounds of football tackle. Them suckers will get what's coming."

"Put me in back," Jeremy insisted.

"No," Ray said. "I want you in the middle."

"That doesn't make sense," Jeremy argued. "What's the point in training me in Wing Chun for the past ten years if you won't even let me cover the rear?"

"Look, Jeremy," Ray contended, "I want you in the middle, because I can't afford anything happening to you. Does that make sense?"

"Yeah, perfect sense," he replied sarcastically. "You don't want anything happening to me, but you're totally fine with something happening to Deon. Right?"

No one said anything for a few seconds while the awkwardness lingered.

Ray felt the sweat pour through his pores from his palms onto the steering wheel. His heart beat irregularly as he breathed with discomfort. He felt too uncomfortable to look back at Deon, though he was curious about Deon's reaction.

"I don't think Sifu Ray has any intention of Deon getting hurt. We're all going to do everything we can to keep each other safe," Abby said trying to soothe the situation.

The tension was not good. They were less than a couple minutes away from their destination and Ray was having a father-son dispute in the vehicle! "That's not what I meant, Jeremy."

"Sure it is. It doesn't matter that you trained me for a decade to fight – for moments just like this! You always said Wing Chun helps me to protect myself and others. Here's the moment. But you'd rather put a guy you hardly know, who's only had a week of training, in a vulnerable position. He's probably more likely to get hurt than me, but that's okay with you. I know how you're thinking."

"Jeremy," Abby intervened, "I'm sure it's not like that."

Jeremy glanced at her and peeled his eyes away as he turned his head, conveying an obvious contempt for her involvement in this argument.

"I already have one child missing. I can't afford for you to get into danger as well. I want you near me." Ray explained in a softer tone though his explanation felt futile to him.

"I'm not a child," Jeremy retorted.

"Yes, you are," Ray countered, "whether you want to admit it or not."

"You don't have to treat me like a child."

"You're fifteen!" Ray shouted. "Of course you're a child! You're *my* child!"

"You know this is baloney. This is a stupid plan, and it isn't going to work."

"Deon," Ray redirected the conversation, "understand that I don't want you to get hurt either, I just need to make sure my kids are with me."

"Sifu, you don't need to explain," Deon consoled. "This is what I'm here for. I'm here to get your back, literally." He laughed. "Don't sweat it, Jer. I'm good with being last. Besides, I ain't afraid of a little roughing up in case things get heated." He said that with a tough expression.

Ray couldn't help feeling guilty for treating Deon this way. "It makes sense at least," Ray added, trying to further justify his scheme. "Women and children in the middle. That's the chivalrous approach, right?" Still, he felt a knot in his stomach and a bitter taste in his mouth. He felt a little less than an honorable man, but he was a father first. His first priority as a father was his children, his family—above his students, friends, or coworkers. Despite his guilt and heavy conscience, he wouldn't change his mind. It had to be this way.

He took a breath and gathered himself mentally. "We'll be fine. Stay together, stick to the plan, and we'll be fine."

They were less than one minute away from the house.

"This plan isn't going to work," Jeremy repeated.

"Don't mean to change the subject," Deon said, "but we assumed that when Gordon said the 'house' that he meant his own house, like where he lives. Do we know that it's his house?'"

"Oh, my gosh. That's a good question," Abby said. "Why hadn't we thought of that?"

"I mean, the big-time crime bosses I hear of will usually have a separate house to be their place of business," Deon added.

"Jer," Ray said, "take my laptop out. The clone of Gordon's cell phone should be up. Write a text message to Marcus as if you're Gordon. Marcus won't know the difference. Write: 'I just need to make sure you have all the details about my work correct. Do you have the correct address of the house where I kept the girl?'"

Jeremy questioned, "Are you sure Gordon talks like that? If it doesn't sound like him, Marcus will know something's wrong and could blow our whole cover."

"Leave out the word, 'just.' Gordon doesn't talk like that," Abby edited.

"Yeah, me and Abby got a good close-up experience of Gordon," Deon said. "Just ask, 'Do you have the correct address of the house?' Leave out the other part. I would also add, 'I want the details of my work to be accurately recorded in the report.'"

"Got it. Send?" he asked his dad.

"Yes. Send."

Only ten seconds later, a reply text from Marcus was received. It read, "Always the obsessive one. Of course I have the address. 555 Forest Lane."

Jeremy looked up the address on the phone's GPS. "It's not the same house! But it's on the same street—actually, same block."

"Smart," Deon said. "Don't keep all the illegal activity going on in your own house, but keep it close by."

Ray exited the freeway. "We're almost there."

Chapter 11
House

Ray parked the SUV a block away from the address to avoid being spotted by unwanted eyes from inside the house. The area they were in was a surprisingly green suburban neighborhood. The canopies formed by the trees over the streets filtered the afternoon sunrays enough to create a comfortable lighting with the perfect amount of shade. Orange and yellow leaves carpeted the sidewalk. The upper-middle class homes on the block were large and pristine with lush lawns and white picket fences. The air was crisp and clear. Not a person was in sight. All was quiet except for the birds singing and the gentle breeze whistling. The tranquility of this neighborhood was wretchedly disturbing given that there was a factory for child trafficking nestled here.

The prettiness of this place sickened Ray. Atrocious crimes against humanity festered behind these perfect walls. He would have preferred to be entering a dingy warehouse, an industrial park, or some ghetto. But his unconscious stereotypes proved shockingly wrong. He normally would evaluate discrepancies between his prejudicial expectations and the reality, but now was not the time.

The four of them moved along a wall of shrubbery that fenced in the house where Jamie was imprisoned. They couldn't see the actual house yet, because the shrubs were too high and thick. As they came to the end of the wall of shrubbery, Ray motioned for them to halt and to arrange themselves into formation. Around the corner would be the driveway of the house.

"Stick to the plan. Stay in formation, and we flush one room at a time," Ray whispered. "If Gordon's facing the same traffic we did, we should have about twelve minutes to get in and out *with Jamie*—plenty of time to clear the house. Let's go."

They whipped around the corner and darted halfway up the driveway but slowed down at the surprising sight of the house. They ducked under an arched doorway and dropped into squatting positions in front of the main door.

"What is this? This ain't no house!" Deon whispered in a demonstrative manner.

The "house" was a large, tan building that appeared to be four times the size of the other neighboring homes they passed. It was two stories high and had the width of two normal houses. They couldn't determine how far back the house went. A massive oak tree grew out of the middle of the front yard. Its upper limbs were slightly higher than the roof of the house, and they extended out wide, like an umbrella, casting a dreary shadow over the front of the house. The main entrance was a huge, brown door made of antiquated, distempered wood with a curved, iron door handle and two deadbolts. All the windows were barred, including the ones on the second floor. The wide, chest-high bushes against the walls of the house would've made it extremely difficult to break in through the windows even if they weren't barred.

They were well hidden from any possible onlookers from the street being under the archway and behind the tall shrubbery that ran the perimeter of the property. They remained in squatting positions to be out of the viewing range of the peephole of the main door.

Abby stepped out to the edge of the doorway to scan the front of the house, and then moved back into a squatting position with the others. "This is some kind of quadriplex. It's one of those houses that have four houses in one. There's one main door, but I'm guessing behind it there's going to be four separate doors, one for each home. My parents used to own something like this as a rental. It allows for multiple occupants."

"We're running low on time," Ray said. "We have to get started."

Abby pushed the four doorbells on the wall. "No answer. That's a good sign, right? Now, how are we going to get through this medieval door?"

"We have no idea what or who is behind this door, so get ready."

He stood up and grabbed the S-shaped door handle to jiggle the door, but there was no wiggle room at all. The door was shut tightly. The latch for the door handle was locked as well. He assumed a fighting pose with one foot squared behind the other. He thrust his back foot like an arrow launching out of a crossbow at the door, nailing the heel of his foot into a spot next to the door handle. A sharp hammering sound echoed across the front lawn enclosed by the wall of shrubs. There was a dent in the wood where his heel struck, but the door did not open. Again, he kicked the door, driving his heel exactly into the same point. The piercing attack of his foot deepened the indentation of the solid wood. But still the door did not open.

"This is too loud. We can't keep banging on the door like that," Abby said.

"It's thick, and the double deadbolts are making it difficult." Ray grabbed the door handle and jiggled the door again. The door felt looser with a half-inch of back-and-forth wiggle room. "It's locked in at least three places, including the door handle. I think the doorframe these deadbolts are lodged into must be thick too. Any normal door would've broken already."

Jeremy nodded his head with a cynical, "Yeah." Ray knew his son was referring to what he did to his bedroom door the other night.

"Well, I think you loosened up this door enough for me, Sifu," Deon said. "It's time for some tackle power. Step aside and let me at it."

Deon backed outside the doorway, giving him ten paces of charging distance.

"Your kick is deadly," Abby said, looking at the dent in the wood door. "But Deon's weight and surface area might be the key to breaking through all three locks."

Deon hunched into a ramming posture, the exact same one that he used not long ago when he challenged Ray. He charged forward, thumping his muscular legs into the concrete like a rhino. After five steps, he angled his left shoulder toward the door. His shoulder muscle and bicep flexed menacingly. In the last two steps he pushed off with his powerful leg and threw his entire body into the door. His left shoulder, bicep, forearm, hip, and thigh crashed into the massive door. The medieval door broke open in surrender.

Deon fell past the door onto the floor inside. The other three rushed in, Ray closed the door and Abby helped Deon up.

"Are you okay?" she asked him as she inspected his left arm and leg.

"Nothing broken," he answered, slowly straightening up and rubbing his arm.

"You just threw yourself at the door," Abby said to Deon. "You could've really injured yourself."

"Got to get through the door to get the girl," Deon stated, panting.

They stood in a small foyer adorned with a stone floor, a cherry wood end table, and an ornate chandelier. There were two doors on each side and two stairwells in front of them leading up to two more doors. Four doors total. The doors were regular doors with no deadbolts but simply doorknobs with locks.

"Which way?" Jeremy asked.

"This is what I was afraid of," Abby stated. "There are four separate homes in this house—two downstairs and two upstairs."

"We have to split up," Jeremy said. "There are four houses and four of us. It's perfect."

"I'm game," Deon said.

Ray stood in the middle of the foyer, turning his head as he considered each door before them. Then he looked at Jeremy and said strictly, "No. We stick together. Stick to the plan. We do the bottom ones first."

"That will take too long," Jeremy said emphatically. "We don't have time to check these one at a time."

Shaking his head, Ray said, "We're wasting time standing here arguing. Being separated is too risky. I can't save you if you're in a house by yourself."

"I don't need saving!"

"Stick to the plan!" Ray ordered, pointing his finger at the floor.

With that, Ray moved to the door on the right and motioned for them to get into formation. He kicked open the door and entered with hands in front, ready to fight.

They walked into a large living room with wood floors, a plush area rug, and fine, brown leather furniture. Deon closed the door behind them. They moved into the next room, which was a dining room, decorated with an eight-person dining set and a vase of flowers as the centerpiece. The place was clean and perfectly manicured.

"This doesn't look like a prison for children," Deon commented. "Nice crib."

"A quadriplex like this could be perfect for holding children," Abby responded.

"These rich folks are sick," Deon said.

"Jamie," Ray called out in a loud whisper.

They entered the kitchen, which had stone floors, darkwood cabinetry, stainless steel appliances, and country-style white curtains drawn over the windows. The granite counter tops gleamed with cleanliness. Nothing lay atop of them except for a small pile of mail and a set of kitchen knives sheathed in a woodblock next to the sink. Ray motioned for Jeremy to grab the pile of mail on the counter, which he did and stuffed into his back pocket. He also unsheathed the largest kitchen knife out of the block. Then he walked to a set of sliding glass doors, parted the curtain, and peeked outside to see a small porch area with a glass table and white metal chairs.

They proceeded out of the kitchen into a spacious hallway. Abby opened the door to a large, walk-in pantry. Down the hallway were three more doors.

"Jamie," Ray whispered into the hallway.

In the other direction, the hallway led back out to the living room. Ray walked further into the hallway toward the three doors. He opened one door and found it to be the laundry room. Walking halfway down, he pushed open a door on the left to an empty bathroom. To the immediate opposite side of that was another door, which he opened and walked into a small empty bedroom. They went inside and quickly checked the closet. They went a little further down the hall. The air smelled like cologne. Their footsteps creaked as they stepped on the wood floors of the hall. All four of them jumped when the air conditioning suddenly turned on.

Ray led them to the end of the hallway where there were two more doors. They inspected the room directly in front of them, the master bedroom. It took slightly longer to search this room and the walk-in closet, master bathroom, bathroom closet, shower stall. They even looked under the king-size bed. Nothing. They exited.

One room left. It was adjacent to the master bedroom. Ray tried to open the door, but it was locked. He looked back at his team with wonder. None of the other doors were locked. This must be it!

A faint whimper could be heard from behind the door. All of their eyes widened. Ray pursed his lips and shot his right foot out so fast it appeared as a blur. His foot smashed through the door.

They rushed in, remaining in their formation, with hands and fists raised. Jeremy held up his kitchen knife. They turned their heads this way and that. The room was smaller than the master bedroom but very sizable. There was a child's bed, a child's dresser, a television on a TV stand with a DVD player and children's DVDs, and a small table with plenty of snacks and boxed drinks. The window shutters outside were closed, so no natural light came in. Three lamps with cartoonish lampshades lit the room.

They fanned out. Deon stayed by the door. Abby checked one of two closets in the room, finding mostly jackets on hangers and boxes of toys. As Jeremy was about to open the double doors to the second closet, a rustling sound came from behind the doors. They all heard it and directed their attention to Jeremy as he yanked both doors open. He looked down and found a little African-American boy, perhaps six years old, with long curly black hair sitting on the floor. The boy's face trembled.

Jeremy squatted and asked softly, "Hey, who are you? What are you doing here?"

The boy stared at Jeremy without blinking, appearing terrified. His lips quivered. Snot ran down from his nose, and his hands were folded in front of him.

"Hey, there. We're not going to hurt you. We're here to help," Jeremy said as he reached out and touched the boy's arm.

Not Easily Broken

The touch triggered an eruption of wild screams from the boy. Tears flooded his eyes. More snot ran down. He screamed in terror, and Jeremy retracted away from him.

Ray came over and tried to shush him, but he continued to scream until Ray picked him up by his arms and brought him out of the closet. Standing the boy in front of him, he knelt on one knee and put up his hands with fingers fanned out to gesture for the boy to calm down. "It's okay," he said over the screams. "We're not going to hurt you. Stop screaming." Finally, he placed both his hands warmly but firmly on both sides of the boy's head. "Please," he said, locked in eye contact with him, "stop screaming."

The boy's screams tapered down to a whimper and then dissolved into heavy breathing. Ray held the boy's head for a moment with his fingers entwined in his curly hair. He maintained their eye contact and secured the boy's calm attention. "I'm Ray," he said. "What's your name?"

"Russell," the boy sniveled.

"Are your parents here?"

He shook his head without breaking eye contact with Ray.

Ray let go of his head and placed his hands on Russell's small shoulders in a fatherly way. "Where are your parents?" Ray asked.

He shrugged and then said, "They don't want me."

"What do you mean? Who told you that?"

"Uncle Gordon."

Ray shuddered with disgust upon hearing the endearing title, but he tried not to show his disapproval to the fragile child. "And what did *Uncle Gordon* tell you?"

"He said they left me and aren't coming back."

"How long have you been here?"

Russell shrugged. "A long time."

"I want to help you," Ray said, tenderly, as he removed his hands from Russell's shoulders. "I'd like to get you home."

"I am home."

"This is not your home. Your parents are looking for you."

"No, they're not. I don't want to leave. Uncle Gordon is taking me on a vacation next week. He said he's taking me far away to a very fun place."

"You're in danger here. You should come with us. You can trust us."

Russell looked at Jeremy, and his eyes ran down to the big knife he held.

"Oh, this?" Jeremy said. "Here. Don't worry about it." He tossed the knife across the room. "See?"

"I like it here. Uncle Gordon takes care of me."

Ray said, "Uncle Gordon is a bad man, Russell."

"Liar!" Russell shouted. "You're bad people. I heard you break into the house! Uncle Gordon said there are bad people who steal children. Leave me alone!" He darted away from Ray and ran for the doorway, but Deon blocked it and grabbed Russell by his forearms.

"Careful, careful," Abby said.

"It's okay. I got him," Deon said. "Come on, little man. It's okay. We're friends."

Russell grunted and yelled while futilely squirming and pulling away from Deon.

"Poor kid has been brainwashed," Abby said.

"He doesn't want to come. We can't take him," Jeremy stated. "Just leave him, and let's go."

"We can't leave him," Ray objected. "We have to rescue him."

"I know you—you want to rescue him, but look at him. He doesn't want to be rescued. He's going to fight us the whole way out and alert the whole neighborhood," Jeremy argued.

"That's because he's been brainwashed. This is part of their tactics in child-trafficking. We're saving him," Ray stated.

"You can't save everyone!" Jeremy argued. "The plan is to get Jamie. Let's go get her."

"Leaving him is wrong," Ray argued.

"It would be horrible to leave him," Abby confirmed. "But Jeremy also has a point. If this boy fights us the whole way, he's a liability to us."

"Sifu," Deon said, "we should try to save him. We can't leave him here."

Feeling the loss of time and urgency, Ray said, "Bring the boy, Deon. Carry him if you have to."

"No prob," Deon responded. "Come on, little man. You'll be all right."

Deon wrapped his humongous arms around Russell, pressed him against his large chest, restrained both of the boy's arms, and carried him out. They quickly exited the house with the boy kicking Deon and letting out shouts of "No." Back in the foyer, Ray led them to the next door on the first floor.

"We lost too much time back there. We should split up into two teams," Jeremy suggested. "Let me and Deon take the top two homes while you and Abby search this one."

"No," Ray replied, kicking open the door. "Stay together. Stick to the plan."

"At least we know the layout of these homes now," Abby said. "We can move through them faster."

They entered the second home and breezed through the living room, dining room, and kitchen. The layout was the same as the first home but reversed—whatever was on one side was on the other side. The décor and furnishing was different, having a modern theme with black and metallic furnishing. They went straight to the room that mirrored the room in the first home where they found Russell. This room was also locked.

"Jamie?" Ray called.

"Hello?" answered a little girl's voice from the other side of the door.

"Stand back from the door," he said and kicked the door open with a loud thud and crackle.

They went inside, except Deon, who stayed in the hallway with the squirming boy wrapped in his arms. Standing before them was a red-haired, freckled girl about five years old, holding a pink, stuffed bunny by one ear.

"Hello," she said with a nervous quiver. She tilted her head to peer around Ray and look at the struggling black boy restrained by a large black man.

"Hello there," Abby greeted as she knelt in front of her. "My name is Abby."

"I'm Sara."

"Why are you here?"

"I lost my mommy and daddy at the mall, but Uncle Gordon found me and brought me here because he said it's safe. He said he's friends with my mommy, and he told her I'm here. He said she's coming to pick me up, but it's been a long time. I know she is busy though with her job. That's what Uncle Gordon says."

"Can I take you to your mommy?"

Sara nodded. "Do you know where she is? I miss her. I want to go home."

"Don't listen to them!" Russell cried from the hallway.

"Who is he?" Sara asked.

"He's just scared. We're taking him to his mommy and daddy too."

"Sara," Ray asked gently, "we're looking for another little girl like you. She looks Asian with black hair. Have you seen her?"

"Asian?" she repeated. "Does that mean like Chinese?"

"Yes," he replied.

She nodded. "I saw them take her upstairs. Uncle Gordon said she lost her mommy and daddy too."

"*Them?*" Ray asked.

"Uh-huh. Them. Lots of uncles live here."

"How many uncles, Sara?" he asked.

"Um," she thought as she looked at her fingers and toes, "maybe twelve."

Ray looked at his team. "We have to go!"

Sara held Abby's hand and followed her out while she clung to the bunny with her other hand.

They returned to the foyer and charged up the stairwell nearest to them. Again Ray kicked open the door, and they hurried in, but having two additional children slowed them down. Again, the décor was different, but the place had the same layout and cologne scent. They went to the same room as in the other layouts, but the door to this room wasn't locked. Ray and Jeremy searched the room while Deon and Abby waited in the hallway with the children.

"Nothing," Jeremy said, coming out of the closet.

"One last home," Ray said with intense anxiety. "She has to be there."

"It's been at least twelve minutes, Sifu," Abby said. "Gordon will be back any minute."

They scampered back down the hallway and into the living room, when they heard a vehicle pull up the driveway. Jeremy went to the window. Parting the curtain slightly enough to peer outside, he saw five men coming out of a silver SUV. They were talking and laughing. Gordon wasn't among them.

Russell perked up when he heard the voices, looked toward the window where Jeremy stood and let out a crazed scream like a tortured cat. Deon secured the boy against his chest with one arm and muzzled his mouth with his large hand.

"The uncles are home," Sara said.

Jeremy saw the men react to Russell's scream. One of them asked, "What's that kid's issue now?" They closed the car doors and walked towards the front entrance.

"They're coming!" Jeremy said. "Five of them!"

"Go!" Ray ordered.

They raced down the stairs into the foyer and made a U-turn to run up the other stairwell. Abby carried Sara and darted up the flight of stairs. Jeremy hung back to push the end table in the foyer against the main door.

"Jeremy!" Ray called from the top of the stairs after kicking the door to the fourth home open.

Jeremy scrambled up the stairs two steps at a time.

He heard a key inserting into the main door. "The door is busted," one of them hollered. He heard the men shoving against the door and saying, "The door is blocked! Someone's inside!"

"Get this thing open," another yelled.

Ray closed the door to the home as he heard the main door in the foyer push open. He and Jeremy moved the couch and chair up against the door as he heard the many footsteps scramble in every direction.

"Check every home!" One of the men said.

"All the doors are busted," said another.

"Find heavy objects to block the door," Ray told Jeremy.

Deon tried controlling the struggling boy, and Abby stayed with the little girl to keep her calm. Then Russell managed to slip his mouth out from behind Deon's hand and let out a scream before Deon could clamp his hand back over the boy's mouth.

"Over here! This one."

All of the footsteps converged up the steps to the home Ray and his team were holed up in.

. . . .

A man outside tried to open the door but couldn't.

The couch served as the main barricade against the door. Ray and Jeremy placed a love seat in front of the couch to reinforce it. They piled side tables, a small shelf, books and a flatscreen television on top of the couch.

More men shoved and rammed against door. "Who's in there?" one of them yelled. "You're trapped. When we get in there, you're dead! You hear me?"

Another vehicle pulled up the driveway. Ray and Jeremy went to the window to see a familiar black SUV. Two men and a woman stepped out of the SUV. The male driver and the brunette were new faces, but the man from the passenger side was no stranger.

"It's Gordon," Ray said.

The ravaging men incessantly shoved, kicked, and charged the door. The door cracked open, pushing the barricade of furniture back a centimeter at a time with each bang against the door. Deon placed his foot against the love seat that supported the couch and gave it a hard shove, closing those centimeters back up. He braced the barricade with one foot while holding the still screaming and squirming boy.

"Better open this door," a man yelled.

"Who's in there?" one of the men asked. Ray recognized the voice to be Gordon's.

"Don't know," another answered, "but they're trapped. They're not going anywhere."

"Get the guns," Gordon said.

The mention of guns sparked fear and desperation in Ray. He could see from the looks on the faces of Abby, Deon, and Jeremy that they felt the same. He looked at Jeremy and felt anxiety over how he was to keep his son from harm. *What did he lead his boy into? What kind of a father would bring his son into this?* He had to somehow gain an upper hand in this situation. But how? Think. Concentrate.

"We're calling the police," Ray yelled. "We're letting them know you're armed and holding us hostage. They'll bring in S.W.A.T. to take you out!"

"Go ahead!" Gordon challenged. "Call the police."

They continued to ram the door furiously.

"Daddy? Daddy, is that you?" A girl's voice was heard through the commotion coming from the end of the hall.

"Jamie?" Ray responded. "I'm coming. Hold this door," Ray told his team.

"They have guns," Deon said.

"Stay low. Sit down and put your backs against the furniture. Hold the door!" Ray sprinted down the hall while Deon and Jeremy braced the barricade. Abby told Sara to stay calm in a corner, promised her that she was going home to her mommy, and then went to find additional items she could throw on top of the barricade.

"Stand back, honey," Ray said at the bedroom door. He kicked the door open. Wood debris and dust fell to the floor as he stepped into the room, but he was suddenly stopped by a pair of little arms wrapped around his waist. He looked down into Jamie's brown eyes. Her hair was neatly brushed, and she wore one of her favorite dresses.

"Oh, God," Ray said, falling to his knees to hug her as if collapsing in surrender. "Oh, God." He embosomed her and soaked in the embrace of his daughter.

"Daddy, I missed you. Where have you been? Tracy took me away and—"

"I know, dear, I know. I'm so sorry. I'm here now. Daddy's going to take you home. We can talk about everything when we get back, okay?"

"Okay," she agreed, "let's go home."

Ray was jolted from his reunion when he heard Jeremy cry, "Ray!"

"Ray? Is that Ray Lee in there?" Gordon asked. "How did you find this place? I underestimated you."

Ray came down the hallway with Jamie in his arms.

"Daddy," Jamie said, "I'm scared. What's happening? Who is this Uncle Gordon?"

"A bad man," Ray answered with poisonous spite.

"What do you hope to gain by coming here, Ray?" Gordon asked. "You found me. I give you credit for that."

The bashing ceased, but the sudden quietness felt more deathly.

"Let us in, Ray. You can't accomplish anything here."

Ray shouted, "What do you want with my daughter?"

"That's not for you to know, Ray. But she is highly valuable. You have to know I'm not giving her up."

"She's not for you to give up because she's not yours. How dare you take her from me? How dare you!"

Manly chuckles were heard from behind the door.

"I'm taking my daughter out of here!"

"Where do you think you're going? The windows are barred. You're on the second floor. There's only one door out of there, which is between you and me. You're not escaping me."

"And you're not getting in. We can hold out until the police get here."

"Oh, you can call the police if you'd like, but I doubt they'll help you. In fact, I may just call them myself. And I doubt you can hold out for very long in there. We're coming in whether you want us to or not."

Gordon's lack of fear and even welcome of the police both puzzled Ray and deepened his desperation. Ray had to be determined.

"I'm taking my daughter out of here, Gordon! You got that? You can't stop me!"

"You know my name too. How did you find all this out? You know too much about me. That's not good for you. Not good at all."

"Threaten all you want. If you come in here, you'll see what I can do to you."

"Oh, who's making threats now? Let me be frank with you, because I'm an honest businessman." Gordon's speech was cold and slimy. "First, I'm not making any deals with you. Because you know too much, you and whoever else is in there with you can't leave here alive."

The four of them looked at each other with concern on their faces. Ray clearly realized the type of people he was up against—mercenaries, terrorists, not thugs! He never expected to encounter ruthless enemies of this sort. The realization of the kind of danger they were truly in became terrifyingly concrete. They were besieged by armed people who promised them death with alarming indifference.

"Secondly," Gordon continued, "I suspect you have two of my other children in there. I can hear one of them. Is that you, Russell?" He switched to his "uncle" tone. "Don't worry. Uncle Gordon is coming for you. Sara, are you in there too?"

Russell managed to squeal through Deon's fingers.

"I also heard a teenager's voice call out to you," Gordon continued, switching back to his "business" tone. "Did you bring your teenage son with you? His name is Jeremy, isn't it? Ray, I really did underestimate you. I wouldn't have figured you would find me and bring your son to my house. I'm guessing you have some friends in there too, maybe two or three. So there's four or five of you in there with children, including Jamie. Open this door, and I promise you the only ones who get hurt are you and your friends. I'll spare Jeremy. If you turn this into a battle, everyone in there will be hurt."

"So you *are* trying to make a deal with me," Ray responded, trying to sound tough. "Not a very good one. You can do better. What is it you want? Money?"

"Ray, Ray. You don't have any idea of what this is about. This is well beyond monetary gains. We don't want your money."

"Then what? Does this have to do with Taggat Act?"

"Oh, you definitely do know too much. Now how did you find out about Taggat Act? It doesn't matter. Let us in. Time for you to bow out."

"You expect me to lay down and hand over my daughter to you? Not going to happen. We're not going down without a fight."

"This isn't going to be some sparring match. Yes, I know all about you too. You're a martial arts instructor. But this isn't a sport, Ray. You're in real trouble. This is the real deal. Before you make this worse, decide if you want to jeopardize the lives of those little ones in there. Do you want to die with that guilt? Do you want your teenage son to die?"

Ray didn't respond.

"Yes, I said 'die' because that's how this is going to turn out for you. Now, I don't like killing children. That's not my business. But if you resist, this can't go any other way than us coming in firing. You got that? You brought this upon yourself, your son and your friends, by coming here and grabbing all of these children. You know, the interesting thing is you probably could've made it out of here with Jamie if you hadn't grabbed the other kids too. But you had to go and try to save all of them. This is on you, Ray. So now, you just need to make the right choice and not make this worse."

"If you come in firing," Ray challenged, "Mr. PH won't be happy if you kill the children. I don't think you'll come in shooting. You have too much at stake. You're fearful that your hide is on the line if you can't produce for Mr. PH."

"He knows about PH! How does he know about PH?" one of the men said.

"Ray, you really need to stop talking," Gordon said. "The more you talk, the more motivation you're giving me to kill you." But there was an obvious nervousness in his voice. Ray had made him anxious.

"What are you doing?" Jeremy questioned. "You're pissing him off more."

"I'm making him desperate," Ray answered. "Clouding his judgment."

"What do we do?" Abby asked softly with a deathly pale complexion, as she held Sara. "Should I call the police?" She held her cell phone in her hand, ready to dial those three digits.

Ray thought for a second. Abby dialed the first number, 9, then he whispered, "Stop. Something's not right about calling the police."

"Yeah," Deon agreed. "He didn't flinch when he heard, 'cops.' Even seemed to like the idea. Only time a crook likes cops is when the cops are crooked."

Ray recalled their dealing with Sergeant Pierce and Officer Bohr.

"What do we do?" Abby repeated.

Ray looked at his son, bracing the barricade. He then went to hold Jamie.

"I'm going to count to three. Then we're coming in," Gordon said.

"It's eight against four," Jeremy whispered with a tremor.

Gordon started counting.

"Sifu," Deon said, "I can't help much with fighting while I'm holding this kid." Russell continued to struggle to break free.

"They have guns," Jeremy said. "What do we do?"

"We can't give in," Ray reiterated.

"Time's up!" Gordon yelled.

The men bashed, pushed, and charged the door, like a pack of ravenous wolves. The door inched open.

Chapter 12
Trapped

"What do we do?" Jeremy yelled as he braced the barricade of furniture barring the door.

"There has to be another way out. All residences have to have at least two exits according to fire codes," Ray said.

"Guns, Gordon," they heard through the door, in between the pounding. Then they heard the insertion of gun clips, followed by cocking sounds.

They heard Gordon say, "Fasten silencers."

"Dear God," Abby called.

"Abby, take the kids into the kitchen," Ray directed.

Abby took Russell from Deon and led the two girls away. Russell's defiant screams intensified. She had to drag him into the kitchen.

"Hold the door," Ray told Deon and Jeremy. "I'll look for a way out."

"This will not end well," Jeremy said.

"Don't think like that. We'll get out, man," Deon encouraged as he put his back into the barricade.

Three bullets shot through the door. Abby screamed.

"Whoever's holding the door, step away," Gordon warned.

Jeremy and Deon hunkered down behind the furniture barricade.

Three more shots pierced through the door, one hit the couch, another the flatscreen, and the other a vase.

"Sifu!" Abby hollered. "Hurry!"

Two more bullets shot through the door. One hit the shelf just behind Deon's head, causing him to flinch forward and let up the pressure he had on the barricade. In that same moment, a huge crash against the door cracked it open two more inches. Deon dove back into his position to brace the barricade, but the opening could not be undone. The siege upon them seemed inevitably hopeless as the wild assailants incessantly pushed the weakening door. The three-inch opening was all the leverage the men needed.

The men shot through and rammed the door. It opened another half an inch.

"We can't hold it!" Jeremy cried.

Ray emerged from the hallway on his hands and knees while bullets rained into the living room. "I found something. You boys hold on. I'll help Abby and the kids out first. Hold on."

He stayed low and went into the kitchen. He led Abby and the children down the hallway where there was a wooden set of stairs going up through the ceiling. It was a pull-down staircase leading into an attic.

"Where does this go?" Abby asked with fearful reluctance.

"To the roof where there's a fire escape to get to the ground. Hurry!"

She had the two girls go up first, and then she shoved Russell up the stairs.

He screamed, "No! Uncle Gordon, help! We're going—"

She immediately clasped her hand over his mouth. She muffled his words as she pushed him through the ceiling and into the dark space.

"Head right to the opening and climb up onto the roof," Ray instructed her.

The front door opened another half an inch. Now there was a four-inch opening.

A hand with a gun reached through the opening in the doorway and started wildly shooting in all directions.

"Aaahhh!" Jeremy yelled with his eyelids tightly shut.

Ray approached the door from the side from the hallway with his back against the wall while the gun was pointed toward the living room, where Deon and Jeremy were. He grappled the hand and cranked the wrist, forcing the gun to drop. Then he wrenched the wrist, like he rang water from a towel. The wrist snapped and the man yelped as the hand slithered back through the opening.

"I hope that was you, Gordon," Ray taunted.

"No, Ray. You're not so lucky," Gordon replied. "But you did piss off a lot of angry guys."

A flurry of bullets carved the door into swiss cheese, bursting splinters in every direction. Ray turned away from the door. Jeremy let out a long cry. Deon unleashed a host of curses.

When the swarm of bullets stopped, Ray saw that the door was shredded. He heard the men reloading their guns and immediately waved for Deon and Jeremy to come to him. They rushed over to Ray, and the three went down the hall to the staircase.

"If you're still alive in there," Gordon said, "we're coming in."

While the three of them ran up the stairs, Ray heard the door breaking apart as they banged on it with the hilt of their guns.

Ray grabbed Deon when he entered the attic. "Help me break this staircase."

Trapped

"Say, what?" Deon asked for clarification.

Standing at the top on one side of the staircase, Ray stomped on it like he was thrusting a downward kick. Deon followed by stomping on the other side of the staircase. Their stomps became in sync and the stairs began to break. Dust rained down onto the floor. Bolts and fasteners loosened. Wood and drywall cracked.

Ray heard the men push through the barricade as the furniture scraped the floor.

"Now! Break it!" Ray called to Deon.

With a final, simultaneous stomp, the two of them broke the staircase off of the ceiling, slamming the wooden steps onto the floor.

"Come on," Gordon said.

Ray pushed Deon along toward the opened hatch leading up to the roof. There was already a stepping stool under the square opening.

"They're in the attic," a gunman yelled. "They broke the stairs. Get a ladder!"

"How did they break the stairs?" another asked.

"Ray," Gordon called. "Come down. You have nowhere to go up there."

Shots fired through the ceiling, Ray had just climbed through the hatch into the open air. He inhaled, like a prisoner who saw the outside world for the first time in years. He saw Abby, Jeremy, and the kids standing at the edge of the roof.

"It's too far," Abby said while holding Russell and Jamie's wrists. "Can't reach it."

"Yes, we can," Ray replied. He ran to them and looked over the edge. There was a fire escape platform but it was about fifteen feet below them. "I'll hang from the ledge. You'll slide down my body like a pole. Abby and Jeremy, go first so you can receive the children as they're lowered down. Deon, you'll be last. Since you have the longest arms, you'll guide the kids as they slide down my body. Abby and Jeremy, be sure you catch the kids. Everybody got it?"

"You're kidding," Abby said, but Ray was already lowering himself down. He hung along the side of the building by his fingers.

"Let's go," Ray invited.

Jeremy grabbed the ledge, faced the wall, and lowered himself. He wrapped his legs around his father's torso. Once his arms were stretched out, he grabbed his dad's arms one at a time. Ray grunted. Jeremy slid down until his arms were around Ray's knees and his feet dangled in the air. Then he released and dropped himself onto the metallic, grated platform.

Ray said, "Your turn, Abby."

"I can't do this."

"Yes, you can."

"I'll help you," Deon said. "Come on. Let's do this."

Abby let Russell go and went to the edge. Russell was too astounded by what was happening with Ray hanging off the ledge and people sliding down his body to make a sound. She crawled to the ledge, feet first, slid her legs over the ledge, and lowered herself down. Deon supported her by her armpits as she worked her way down Ray's body. When her arms straightened out and she was holding onto Ray's forearms, Deon laid flat on his stomach and held her forearms. She then wrapped her arms around Ray's chest one at a time.

"You're almost there," Jeremy said.

Finally, she slid down Ray's body far enough to where Jeremy guided her legs down onto the platform.

"Okay," Ray said with a grunt, his fingers purple and white and his face red. "Jamie is next."

Deon led Jamie to the ledge. Her knees trembled when she looked down and saw her father hanging off the side of the building. Deon started to guide her to go over the ledge.

"No!" she protested with tears. "I can't. Daddy, I can't." She shook her head and pressed herself against Deon.

"This might be too much for the kids, Sifu," Deon said. "I can lower the kids down by their arms if you can catch them."

"Okay, but you have to make sure you're coming down after you lower them," Ray emphasized.

"Sure. Besides, Sifu, you can't expect me to go sliding down your body!"

Ray looked below and said to Jeremy and Abby, "I'm coming down." They stepped to the sides of the platform. Then he let go of the ledge and dropped eight feet onto the platform with a bang.

"I hope they didn't hear that," Abby said.

Deon took Jamie and held her in his hands. He knelt down on the abrasive roof surface as he held her over the ledge by her armpits. He bent over and lowered her against the side of the building, shifting his hands from her armpits to her small arms. He finally laid on his chest and stomach as he held Jamie's hands and dangled her on his long arms. Her little feet hung ten feet above the platform. Ray, Jeremy, and Abby stood directly underneath her.

"Go ahead and let her go. I'll catch her," Ray said.

"Daddy," Jamie cried with terror in her voice.

"I got you baby-girl," Ray affirmed.

"I'm letting go," Deon announced.

He released her. Jamie dropped straight into Ray's arms with Jeremy and Abby offering extra hands on the sides to spot her.

Deon waved at Sara to come to him. She jogged to him at the ledge. He took Sara's bunny and gingerly dropped it down to Jeremy. He then lowered Sara just like Jamie.

"I can hear them," Deon said. "They're coming up!"

He then waved at Russell to come to him, but Russell shook his head.

"Come on!" Deon commanded the little boy.

"What's going on?" Ray asked.

Deon got up from his knees and ran towards Russell with such swiftness that Russell was too surprised to react in time to get away. Deon wrapped his huge arms around the boy's thrashing body and carried him to the ledge.

"No!" Russell screamed.

"We know you're still up there," Gordon hollered from inside the attic. "There's nowhere to go. You trapped yourselves."

When Deon held Russell over the ledge by his arms so that he was still ten feet from the platform, Ray said, "Drop him! There's no time."

Deon released him and the three on the platform caught him.

"Come on, Deon!" Abby yelled.

Deon backed himself over the ledge with his feet going down first. He grasped the ledge with his monstrous hands. As his hands were at his chest level and his head was all that was left remaining above the ledge, Gordon's arms came up through the hatch. Gordon's head emerged through the hatch in time to see the top of Deon's head duck behind the ledge.

"They found a way to get on the fire escape!" Gordon shouted. "The two of you follow me onto the roof. The rest of you go to the window and to the ground floor. Cut them off!"

Deon hung by his fingertips, arms fully stretched. Because of Deon's long arms and height, his feet hung merely six feet above the platform. He let go and dropped onto the platform with a bang.

They hustled down the metallic steps, clanging loudly as they went. Ray carried Jamie, Abby carried Sara, and Deon carried Russell. They descended swiftly past the second floor window as a henchman opened it to see them go by. The window bars blocked him. He shoved on the immovable bars and shouted, "They're going down!"

"Try not to hit Jamie," Gordon commanded while aiming through the metal grates and steps of the fire escape.

Gordon and two other men rained down bullets from the roof but only hit metal barriers shielding the escapees. The henchman from the window tried to stick his gun through the bars to shoot but the openings were too tight.

"They're going down," Gordon yelled to his gang.

Ray and his group reached the ground. They stayed underneath the fire escape, pressed against the building, to shelter themselves from the bullets. Jeremy noticed a door next to them. He grabbed a rake lying on the ground, broke the wooden handle in half and wedged the rake handle between the door and the ground.

"Good thinking, Jer," Ray complimented.

"Now what?" Abby asked.

They scanned the area and realized they were in the backyard enclosed by a high wooden fence. The fence had a gate that led back out to the front driveway, but they could already hear the men scrambling around the front of the house. They also heard men trying to open the jammed door next to them.

Gordon and another henchman fired a few shots onto the ground from the roof to keep Ray's group pinned underneath the fire escape. The children trembled and cried.

"There's nowhere to go," Gordon yelled with mockery. "If you keep this up, you're going to get someone killed, Ray." He fired off another shot.

"We have to go," Jeremy said.

"We're trapped," Abby said.

Ray noticed a set of wooden double doors in the ground on the other side of the jammed door. He presumed the doors led to an underground basement. The doors were shielded by the fire escape. But there was a padlock on them. "Here," he said, pointing at the doors. He picked up an iron rod that lay next to the rake and handed it to Deon. "Deon, would you please?" he invited, pointing at the lock.

Deon shoved the rod underneath the latch and padlock. With one brutish, upward yank, he broke the latch and lock off of the doors.

"If we go in there, we'll trap ourselves in the basement," Jeremy protested.

"It's our only way out right now," Ray stated.

The men in front of the house started to come through the side gate that led into the backyard.

"Let's go," Ray said and took the rod from Deon. He opened the double doors and motioned for them to enter. They rushed in, descending down a set of stairs that led underground. Men came

Trapped

cautiously through the side gate, and other men fired shots through the jammed side door. Ray looked up at Gordon who was moving his head around to try seeing what they were doing. Ray went underground and shut the doors.

"Damn! They're going into the basement," Ray heard Gordon yell to his men from the roof. "Get them! Don't let them go in there!"

Ray slid the iron rod between the handles of the double doors, locking them inside. He turned and descended the steps into the dark.

. . . .

Abby pulled on a string to turn on a light bulb plugged into a socket in the low ceiling. The girls wailed in terror. Russell screamed, "Let me out!" Ray held his arms out and herded the group further into the dingy basement to get them away from the double doors.

"Great, now we're really trapped," Jeremy complained.

The men violently jerked on the doors, but the iron rod held the doors in place.

"It's a matter of time before they get through those doors," Jeremy added.

They heard additional footsteps rumbling outside, telling them that all the men were gradually gathering outside. They heard them say, "Get the axes!"

"Look around," Ray said. "Gordon was upset about us coming in here. There might be something that he's afraid of us finding. Check everything."

"Great," Jeremy said. "We're just going to give him more reasons to kill us."

They fanned out to inspect the walls, corners, and shelves, while the children stood on one side of the room.

"Ray," Gordon called, "you've gotten a lot farther than I expected. I salute you for that. But let's end this cat-and-mouse chase. I have no more patience for this. If you make me come in there after you, I *will* hurt you. I'll torture you. I will put your son in agony. You hear me, Ray?"

"Keep searching," Ray urged his group, trying to keep them focused.

The basement was a bomb shelter. The walls were unfinished brick and mortar. Metal shelving lined the walls and a locked metal cabinet stood in the corner. Deon wrestled with the cabinet but could not open it. The shelves were cluttered with tools, non-perishable foods, flashlights, and chains.

The men fired a few shots through the center of the double doors, but the rod held.

"Where are those axes?" Gordon yelled.

"What if they find it?" one of the men asked Gordon.

"Shut up!" Gordon chided. "You fool, they can hear you. Call the neighbor."

"The neighbor?" Abby repeated as she looked at Ray. But when she saw Ray focused on searching, she resumed riffling through the items on a shelf. She started to move to the next shelf but stopped. "Wait a minute," she said. "I feel something."

The others turned their attention toward her.

"You feel this." She held her hand up with her fingers fanned, like she was touching something. "There's a draft coming from behind this shelf." She inspected the side of the shelf. "There are hinges! Door hinges on this shelf!"

The others came to her to check out the shelf. Ray saw no hinges on the other side of it, so he pulled on that side and it creaked open.

An ax hacked through the wooden, double doors, then retracted, and another ax hacked through.

"Chop it down, boys," Gordon invited boisterously.

The axes hacked at the wooden doors with thunderous pounding and crackling. It wouldn't be long before they shredded this door as well.

"What is this?" Abby peered into a small tunnel that a normal sized person would need to crouch to get through.

"Are we going in there?" Jeremy asked.

"This is like one of those underground tunnels used for smuggling people from one point to another," Ray hypothesized. "It's perfect for their child-trafficking activities, allowing them to move children around or to escape from unwanted searches."

"Where does it go?" Deon asked, as shattered wood pieces fell down the steps behind them.

"Away from here," Ray said plainly. "Grab those flashlights. I'll go first. Deon, you take the rear."

Sunlight streamed through the doors. Jeremy, Abby, and Deon grabbed flashlights off the shelves. Ray stuffed three screwdrivers into his two back pockets, clipped a large metal measuring tape on his belt, inserted a hammer into the back of his pants, and shoved two handfuls of drywall nails into both front pockets. He grabbed a flashlight with one hand and a thick chain with the other. He went into the tunnel, motioning for the rest to follow.

"Deon, close the shelf behind you," Ray instructed as he went.

There was only enough room for a single-file line. Abby and the children went in after Ray, then Jeremy and finally Deon, who closed the shelf. He looked for a way to lock it, but there were no latches. He turned to catch up to the others.

The tunnel was crudely dug out with rough, jagged surfaces. The ground was the same but more uneven. Tripping on a rock or stumbling into a pothole was likely.

"Deon," Ray said, "you okay back there?"

"Yes, sir."

"It's a tight squeeze."

"I got it." Deon's shoulders barely cleared the rocky walls. Every now and then his shoulders bumped or scraped against a protruding stone. His back was exceptionally hunched over, and his knees were bent more than the others. "It's just like football practice. I'll make it."

They heard the shelf behind them creak open.

"They're inside!" Deon notified. "We have to book it."

They shuffled their feet faster, but with their backs bent, they couldn't take big strides. It was like they were trying to sprint through a tunnel designed by dwarves.

"I see light up ahead," yelled one of the men at the end of the tunnel behind them.

"Go after them!" yelled Gordon.

Ray's group was already so far in the tunnel that they could no longer see the entrance. He could only faintly hear his pursuers' voices. In that faint distance behind, he heard footsteps echoing in the tunnel. "Keep going. Don't stop!" Ray exhorted.

But the children started to slow down, creating a distance between him and the rest of the group. "Come on! Keep moving!" he ordered like a drill sergeant.

"How far does this go?" Jeremy asked through his panting. "We must've gone at least a couple of blocks by now. It's hard to breathe in here."

"You're telling me," Deon added with sweat dripping off of his chin.

"The kids can't take much more of this," Abby said.

"We're almost there," Ray encouraged. "Push it."

"The question is," Jeremy said with a shortness of breath, "where is… there?"

"Just be ready," Ray said.

They scampered a little further until Ray's flashlight shone on something. "We're coming to the end. I can see something ahead."

"Oh, good," Abby remarked, panting.

They arrived at a crude wooden ladder bolted into the ground. It extended straight up into some kind of hatch above. Ray climbed up.

"Another hatch?" Jeremy exclaimed.

"Be careful," Abby said with concern.

Ray pushed the hatch partway open with his flashlight and poked his head through the opening. He scanned around first and then shoved the hatch door all the way open until it slammed on the floor. He climbed out onto a nice stone tile floor. One by one he helped them out of the tunnel. Once Deon emerged, Jeremy closed the hatch shut.

To their surprise, they were standing in a fancy kitchen with beautiful, stainless steel appliances, beige granite countertops, cherry wood cabinetries, and brushed nickel knobs. The hatch door to the hole they crawled out of was masked as part of the stone tile flooring—perfectly camouflaged.

"Help me with this," Ray said as he pulled on the large, double-door, stainless steel refrigerator.

Deon helped Ray roll the fridge over the hatch, just in time to block their assailants. The hatch door repeatedly clunked against the bottom of the refrigerator. A shot fired, but no bullet came through the floor.

"Let's get out of here," Ray said.

"Yeah," Jeremy agreed. "Wherever here is."

"Excuse me. Who are you people and why are you in my kitchen?" asked a Caucasian, grey-haired man about five-feet-ten-inches tall standing in the doorway connected to the dining room. He wore a white, button-up shirt, khaki pants, and brown dress shoes. "What are you doing with my fridge?" he asked with perplexity.

The four of them quickly looked at each other with puzzlement.

"You mean, you don't know what's beneath your floor?" Jeremy asked.

"I'm sorry to bring this upon you, sir," Ray said, trying to calm the man down. "I know how this must look, but we're not burglars."

"Well, I figured that since you have three children with you, and I didn't think you'd be so dumb as to try and steal a fridge out of here. I also figured you're not the maintenance crew," he replied. "So if you're not here to rob me, and you're not here to fix anything, what are you doing in my home? How did you get in here?" With each question, he sounded increasingly astounded. "And what is that sound coming from my floor," he asked while looking at the stone tile beneath the refrigerator.

"What's going on, Dad?" A tall, well-built man in his twenties wearing a blue T-shirt and a pair of jeans appeared behind the grey-haired man's right shoulder. He had broad shoulders and a muscular chest.

A woman in her twenties with dirty-blonde hair who was about five-feet-eleven appeared a second later in an adjacent doorway of the kitchen connecting to the hall. "Should I call the police?"

"Call the police," the grey-haired man said.

The woman took her cell phone out of her back pocket.

"No, wait!" Ray asked with his hands held up. "Please. Don't do that. We're not here to harm you or rob you. We're literally passing through. It's hard to explain, but we're leaving, and whatever you do, don't move your fridge."

The grey-haired man looked at Ray's hands that were held out to him as gestures of friendship. He observed the flashlight in Ray's one hand and a chain in the other, and he gave Ray a disbelieving look. "I can't just find you in my home and simply let you go. I want to know why you're here, and I want to know how you got in here."

"Oh, boy," Jeremy commented.

"I know what this looks like, but believe me, this is a big mix-up," Ray tried to assure. "If you'll let us pass, we'll be out of your home. And then you can call the police, because there's something very bad under your kitchen floor. Whatever you do, don't move the fridge. Let the police do it."

"Why shouldn't I just call the police now?" the grey-haired man asked.

"Dad, I'm calling 911," the young woman said.

"Okay, go ahead, but we're going to leave." Ray held out his hands in front of him and slowly stepped towards the man.

"No. You're going to stay," the grey-haired man shouted. He brandished a large kitchen knife from behind his back and sliced Ray's hand holding the flashlight. The flashlight fell to the floor.

Abby screamed as the grey-haired man lurched at Ray with his knife.

The young man was now visibly in the doorway. His broad frame blocked the entire doorway. He reached for something behind his back.

After the grey-haired man swung his knife, Ray kicked him in the stomach. The man stumbled backwards to the counter. As the young man produced a gun from behind his back, Ray flung the chain in his left hand at him. The chain twirled end-over-end and struck the young man in the face before he could take aim. The young man's head flicked backwards. He threw his hand up to his face in pain.

Deon unleashed a barbaric cry and charged at the young man, tackling him onto the dining room floor.

The woman produced a baseball bat from behind the wall and entered the kitchen with her eyes trained on Ray. Abby nestled the children into the corner. The woman tried to go around the fridge to get to Ray but Abby moved in front of her.

The grey-haired man slashed wildly at Ray. Ray evaded each slice with ease, stepping back and to the side, until the man cleared an unobstructed path to the refrigerator. He plunged himself into the refrigerator, knocking it back a few feet.

The refrigerator no longer covered the hatch, but the grey-haired man lay on it. He scrambled to his feet while still standing on the hatch. He stabbed at Ray's stomach, but Ray grabbed his hand and wrenched his wrist, disarming the knife from his hand. With three straight punches to the face, a chop to the throat, and a kick into the chest, the grey-haired man fell back with his head knocking into the dishwasher.

Jeremy jumped on top of the hatch, but he was apparently not the same weight as the refrigerator. The hatch opened and shut, bouncing Jeremy up and down. The woman chopped down with her bat on top of Jeremy, but he rolled out of the way without a split second to spare. The metal bat slammed on the stone tile hatch with a jarring ring.

Abby kicked the bat out of the woman's hands and punched her cheek. The woman charged at Abby, grabbing her by the collarbone and jerking her backward and downward against the stove. The two women tussled with each other in a fierce wrestling match.

Ray stomped on the hatch as someone tried to open it. "Control the center and strike!" he yelled to Abby.

Abby stopped gripping the woman's arms, brought her hands into the center and thrust three palms strikes into the woman's ribs and abdomen. The woman screeched and cowered in pain.

A shot was fired, and Jeremy reacted by darting into the dining room.

Ray tried to stop Jeremy, but the grey-haired man rose and drew two smaller knives from his ankles. He attacked Ray with a flurry of stabbing motions. Ray withdrew and sidestepped until he was against the kitchen sink. The grey-haired man pressed forward with repeated stabs, but Ray grabbed a saucepan from the dish rack and shielded himself. The knife tips dinked against the pan once, twice, and thrice, until Ray commenced a downward block on the fourth time and whacked the edge of the pan into the grey-haired man's mid-section. Then, he swung upward to twang the pan against the man's chin, sending him backwards onto the floor.

Ray saw from the corner of his eye that the young woman had Abby on her back. The two were caught in a mean mix of hair-pulling and throat grabbing. Ray flung the pan like a Frisbee. It struck the back of the woman's head, like ringing a gong, causing her to tumble off of Abby.

The hatch opened partially and a hand extended out of the hole with a gun. The man in the hole randomly fired twice to clear the area around him. He lifted himself out by the arm with the gun, while his other arm pushed open the hatch.

Ray took the hammer out of the back of his pants and slammed it onto the man's gun hand.

The man's fingers instantly opened and released the gun. The bones of the hand were broken. A delayed, angry yelp came from the man. Now with the hatch fully open, the man in the hole grabbed at Ray's ankle with his good hand.

Ray responded simultaneously with a swing of the hammer onto the man's head, knocking him dizzy. He fell back into the hole.

The grey-haired man, with a bloody nose and lips, rose off his back. Ray threw the hammer at him, clobbering him on the forehead. The grey-haired man held his head and writhed on his side but barely moved.

Ray slammed the hatch door on the head of another henchman climbing up the ladder.

He turned towards Abby who unleashed a series of chops to the collarbone and palm strikes to the face of the young woman. The woman fell and hit her head on the doorknob of the pantry door. Ray went into the dining room while Abby gathered the three children.

He found Deon choking the young man in a headlock and Jeremy holding one of the young man's arms. The gun lay off to the side. The man's face turned increasingly purple. His free arm futilely clawed at Deon. Gritting his teeth, Deon squeezed tighter. His massive bicep crushed the man's face while his club-like forearms dug deep into the man's throat. The young man fell unconscious.

Meanwhile, after Abby entered the dining room with the children, she pushed the dining table in front of the doorway to the kitchen and threw a few chairs on top of it, just as the hatch door began to open again.

"Let's go," Ray said and led them into the living room.

Abby closed the double French doors to the dining room and wedged it shut with a chair.

After going through the living room and into the foyer, they reached the front door but stopped short of opening it. They saw silhouettes of henchmen through the door and side windows moving about on the porch getting into position. The door was locked with two deadbolts, like the other home. They heard footsteps coming from the kitchen, which could belong to no other then the henchmen from the tunnel.

"Jacked up!" Jeremy spouted. "We escaped one house to be trapped in another! This is sick!"

"These fools mean business. These are dangerous cats, man," Deon said. Blood oozed from the cuts on his arms and lip.

They panted. The children cried.

Jeremy asked, "Now what do we do?"

Chapter 13
Escape

Ray and his group saw the silhouettes of their attackers through the thin curtains covering the side windows of the front door. Their leather dress shoes rasped on the wooden planks of the porch. They moved into crouched positions with guns drawn. There were four armed men outside and three in the kitchen.

"We're surrounded," Jeremy whispered.

The dining room table jarred against the wood floor, indicating to them that the three from the tunnel were now in the dining room.

"How will we get out? And even if we do, how will we get to our car?" Jeremy asked. "We don't even know where we are."

"Ray," Gordon called from outside the front door, "I'm tired of this."

"Then give up," Ray shouted back.

Gordon laughed mockingly, "You're a piece of work. I don't think you expected things to go this way."

"And I don't think *you* expected things to go this way," Ray taunted back.

Russell whined while Abby covered his mouth. Deon kept the two girls behind him. Jeremy watched for signs of the three assailants inside the house.

"My guys in there told me you took out one of my men and the three house attendants. True, I underestimated you. I guess you are the real deal. But now you're pissing me off. In a couple of minutes, more of my men will show up. You can't take all of us and keep everyone with you safe."

"What do you think I'm going to do, Gordon? Get on my knees and let you do whatever you want with us?"

"Us? I just want the girl," Gordon replied sympathetically. "Either you hand her over to me, or I'll rip her from you. I guarantee you that the latter option will be ugly. Some of your people are hurt already. Don't drag them through this. Don't put your children through this."

"You'll just let us go if you get Jamie?" Ray asked, keeping Gordon occupied while he quickly surveyed the area to come up with a plan.

"I tell you what. We can talk about it. Just open this door. You've already made a mess, Ray. Don't let things get uglier."

Ray glanced back at Jeremy and then at Deon. He noticed Deon's bleeding arm. There had to be a "Plan B" available, if he could just realize it. He looked at Deon, pointed upstairs, and silently mouthed the words, "Search upstairs." He motioned for Jeremy to search the den next to them.

"We armed ourselves when we came into this house," Ray said and shouted louder for everyone to hear, "You hear that? We're armed!"

"With what? Tools? I heard you took out a guy with a chain and another with a hammer and another with a frying pan. What else do you have? Pliers?" Gordon mocked. "I know more than you think. I get reports. It's my job to know."

"Then maybe you can tell me why you want my daughter."

"Stop prying. It gets you in trouble."

"You're obviously child-traffickers with a house designed to be a child prison... the brainwashing of children... trafficking tunnels. But it doesn't seem like you want Jamie for mere trafficking."

"Stop probing, Ray. Just give us the girl."

"What does TAGGAT ACT have to do with this?"

Ray saw the silhouette of Gordon's head shaking.

"You need to stop saying that phrase," Gordon demanded.

"Is it referring to something biological?"

"Shut up, Ray! You're digging a deeper grave for yourself. The more you say, the more you're damning everyone in there who hears you. Just come out!"

Ray heard the unsteadiness in Gordon's voice, and he had to prod further to push him over the edge. "They're not words, are they? It's some kind of sequence. Is it something about Jamie's genetics?"

"You're dead, Ray!" Gordon raged. "You hear me? No matter how this ends, I will make sure you're dead!"

"By your response, I believe I'm guessing correctly. Thanks for confirming my theories. You're far more cooperative than I hoped. By the way, I found out all this stuff from you. You're the leak, believe it or not."

The silhouette of Gordon's head turned to his right and left sides towards his men. Ray suspected he was embarrassed. *Good*, Ray thought. Gordon has acted as an organized, composed, and professional agent. Until now. "Is there anything else you'd like to tell me?" Ray pushed.

"Enough, Ray! I'm counting to five before I order all of my men to charge in." Gordon silently signaled his men with his hand. They scrambled about frantically, almost chaotically.

Escape

The henchman next to Gordon asked, "Aren't we waiting for the backup?"

"No!" Gordon scolded his underling. "They're just a few unarmed people with kids in there. What are you afraid of? We're taking them out. All of them! Only don't hit the girl. Send the rest to hell!"

Jeremy appeared from the den with a golf club and Deon came back down the stairs shaking his head. The three of them huddled.

"No way out upstairs," Deon said.

"There's a way out through the den," Jeremy whispered.

"Ray, you here me? You have to five!" Gordon shouted.

"We can go out the window into a side walkway and climb over the fence to the neighbor's yard," Jeremy suggested.

"One!"

"Nothing upstairs but rooms," Deon reported.

"Okay," Ray laid out the plan, "Jeremy, you and Abby will go out the window with the kids. Deon and I will create a diversion by leading them upstairs."

"Two!"

"What happened to staying together?" Jeremy protested.

"We can't do that now. The important thing is to get you and Jamie to safety."

Ray looked at Deon and asked for a concurrence, "Deon?"

Deon nodded.

"Three!"

"Go," Ray motioned.

Ray kissed Jamie on the cheek. Jeremy led her away by one hand while her other hand clung to Ray's shirt. Their eyes locked with each other. "Go," Ray mouthed to her. "I'll see you in a bit, baby."

"Four!"

Jeremy swiftly led the two girls into the den where the escape window was already opened. Russell writhed violently, dropping his weight to the floor and thrashing his legs. Abby struggled to move him.

Ray gritted his teeth, wrestling with a decision he hated making. "Leave him!"

Abby looked at Ray for clarification. "Are you sure?"

"Leave him," Ray whispered. "Go! Take care of my kids."

Abby offered Ray a reassuring look, let Russell go, and darted into the den.

"Aaahhh!" Russell screamed. "They're up to something! Help!"

"Go in! Go in!" Gordon shouted.

One of the men kicked the door once, but it did not break open the double-bolted door. Ray moved to the door and positioned himself five feet in front of it. The men in the dining room jerked on the French double doors. Ray watched the silhouette of the man outside of the front door ready to kick again. The man kicked the door again and busted it open. Ray kicked the door as it was flying open, sending it swinging shut with such speed it slammed into the handgun and face of the unsuspecting henchman trying to step through the doorway. The henchman fell and became an obstacle to the entrance.

Deon had gone up the stairs.

Gunshots from inside the house and a crash of wood sounds meant the three attackers in the dining room had broken through the wedged French doors and were entering the living room.

Ray ran up the stairs. At the top, he heard Deon whisper to him on his right side. Deon was hiding inside one of the two bedrooms, and he motioned for Ray to go into the next one. Ray did so and closed the door with a slam to make sure Gordon heard it. As his door closed, one of the three henchmen appeared from the living room. The four from the porch, including Gordon, entered.

One of the henchmen said, "ETA on the back-up is five minutes. We could just surround the house and wait for them to arrive."

"What's the matter with you?" Gordon reproached. "You afraid of a guy with a hammer, a college kid, a teenager, a woman, and some kids?"

"I'm only suggesting this could be a lot cleaner with more men," the henchman reasoned.

"He's gotten on my last nerve. We're taking him down now. The back-up can clean up."

Through his closed door, Ray heard footsteps on the stairs. They weren't rushing, but they were coming up simultaneously. He looked behind him at a door to the bathroom. He crawled over quickly to see that it was a Jack-and-Jill bathroom. That's why Deon wanted him to stake out in this room while Deon was in the other. It allowed the two of them to fan out and flank on both sides while still staying connected to each other. *Good thinking, kid,* he thought to himself.

The footsteps were at the top of the stairs. *We're going to get out of this,* he told himself. He wondered if his children had made the escape, but he forced himself to stay focused. The better a distraction he and Deon could make, the better chances the others had of escaping. He had no idea how the two of them would get out of this. But as long as his children were out, that's what mattered. That was the mission. That had to be accomplished.

He made sure his door was unlocked. He positioned himself on the side of the door where it opened, grabbed a handful of nails from his front pocket and waited. He heard some of the footsteps going away from his door, which meant they headed towards Deon's. He had to initiate the distraction. He dropped one of the nails on the wooden floor. He heard the footsteps shift toward his door in response.

His door swung opened until it hit the wall, but no one entered yet. A gun appeared through the doorway. It pointed to the right and then panned to the left, scanning the room like a submarine periscope.

When the forearm holding the gun entered the room, Ray sprang out from the side and grabbed the man's wrist. The gun fired at the far off window but Ray held the gun hand at bay. Simultaneously, Ray anticipated his assailant's partner and threw the handful of nails at the henchman standing behind the one he grappled. The shower of nails stung the second man's face, throat, and eyes. He stepped back and, with a cry, brought his free hand and gun hand to his face.

Ray blocked the first man's free hand from punching him. At the same time, he bent and twisted the wrist, forcing the hand to release the gun. With a kick to his enemy's abdomen, he sent him stumbling back out into the hallway and falling onto the second man. Ray stepped back from the doorway as the men fired a couple of shots into the room. He swung the door shut again.

While the attackers' attention and guns were trained on Ray's closed door, Deon's door opened suddenly, and, with the cry of a Viking, he lobbed a metal desk chair over his head. It struck an assailant in the head and chest knocking him back down the stairs. While the fallen man thudded and thumped down the steps, Deon slammed his door shut.

Ray and Deon turned the disguised child-trafficking home into a nightmarish fun house. The two of them were like mischievous gophers!

The men shot at both doors.

Ray huddled in the corner on the side of the door, where the hinges were. He picked up the gun dropped by his victim. He felt its weight. The handle was still warm. He considered it, and then made up his mind. He threw the gun across the room out of the broken window.

Deon unleashed another alarming battle cry and opened his door, though he was not in the doorway. All the men fired their guns at the blank doorway. Ray immediately opened his door just enough for him to step out into the hallway and grab the nearest assailant to pull him into the room. He closed the door with his foot as he punched the man in the head and pulled him toward the side to avoid the shots from the men outside.

As the dazed man tried to turn around to face Ray, Ray grabbed the arm with the gun with one hand and pulled out a flathead screwdriver from his back pocket with his other hand. He plunged the screwdriver into the man's gun hand. While the gun fell, he kicked the man's knee and elbowed him in the temple, sending him to the floor.

His door busted open. He instinctively backed up against the wall as a tall man stepped in. He came at the man from the side and blocked the gun from pointing at him as a shorter woman entered behind the assailant. He kept the tall man between him and the woman, while he stabbed a second screwdriver into the man's thigh. The woman could not point her gun around her tall partner. Keeping control of the tall man's long arm that held the gun, he shoved him backward by stepping forward and pressing his knee into the tall man's injured leg and palm striking him in the midsection. The tall man fell backwards into the short woman, pinning her against the wall.

Ray smacked the gun out of the tall man's hand. The woman stuck her arm out from behind her partner's body and fired an aimless shot at Ray. Ray grappled her arm and struck the gun out of her hand. After stepping backwards to avoid the tall man's grab, he sidekicked the man's ribs and caused him to fall on his injured leg.

Now that the woman was clear of her partner, she lurched forward with a knife in her other hand. Ray parried the knife and then hit her several times in the stomach and face with a variety of punches and palm strikes. She fell back against the corner of the wall and floor. Her nose and lips bled, and she clenched her stomach. She looked up at Ray with one eye opened but did not move to get up. He kicked the knife out of her hand before turning back towards his door.

While Ray was fighting those two, Deon charged out of his room, threw a metal trashcan at one assailant, and tackled another who stood at the top of the stairs. Deon buried his head into his victim's chest as the two of them bounced down the stairs. Sounds of bone knocked against the wooden steps.

Gordon reflexively turned and pointed his gun at the two bodies crashing down the stairs, but he could not get a clear shot.

While the henchman who was struck by the trashcan was getting up, Ray appeared briefly in his doorway to throw another swarm of nails, like a spray of shotgun pellets, at the man's face. The man clasped his hands over his eyes and went back down to the floor, lying on his back in pain. Gordon reflexively turned to face Ray only to see him already disappearing back behind the wall.

As Gordon turned back towards the bottom of the stairs, Deon ducked into the den, leaving his henchman lying on the floor unconscious. Ray peered around the wall to see Deon disappear out of sight.

Gordon turned towards Ray's doorway and fired his gun maniacally, destroying the doorframe. His barrage of bullets screamed his rage. Ray had him where he wanted.

"I have plenty of bullets," Gordon announced as he changed clips. "I will shoot up this entire house to get you. How many more nails do you have?" he mocked as he kicked the nails at his feet. "Where are the children? Are they in there with you?"

Ray pushed his door closed and then went through the Jack-and-Jill bathroom into the room Deon was in.

"There's nowhere to go," Gordon said as he chambered his gun. He kicked open the door Ray closed and entered the room shooting but was perplexed to find it empty.

"Where is Jamie?" Gordon demanded to know as his eyes searched the room.

"Come get her, if you want," Ray coaxed.

Gordon turned toward the bathroom where Ray's voice came from. Seeing the Jack-and-Jill bathroom, he decided to double back into the hallway. He walked to the door of the other room, where Deon had hid. Again he kicked open the door and entered firing a few shots. When he again found an empty room, he proceeded toward the bathroom with his gun leading the way.

"Where is Jamie, Ray?" Gordon asked. "I want her back."

As he looked inside the dark bathroom with the dual sinks, he pulled back the hammer on his gun before entering. He approached the bathroom cautiously when suddenly something cold and metallic strapped around his neck and choked him.

Ray had snuck back through the Jack-and-Jill bathroom into his former room and went around into the hallway to attack Gordon from behind by wrapping the extended metal tape measure around his neck. Ray yanked backwards and downwards on his tall enemy. Jerking Gordon's head back and down, he said into Gordon's ear, "My daughter is not for you to take."

Gordon's face reddened with pain as he gagged. He pointlessly fired a couple of shots over his shoulder while his other hand clawed at the tape measure. Ray kept the tape short. He pulled as he dug his elbows into Gordon's back. Gordon's head and spine arched backwards, but Ray kept him from falling.

Gordon finally dropped the gun to desperately claw at the strangling tape measure. He could not get his fingers underneath the thin metallic tape and he could not reach far enough behind him to grasp Ray's hands. With his eyes bulging out of his sockets, his face turning bluish purple, and his veins protruding from his forehead, he stepped back and strained so hard that tears streamed out of the corners of his eyes as he used all of his back and neck strength to bend forward.

Ray, taken aback by Gordon's incredible strength and power, was flipped over Gordon's back. Ray landed on his tailbone. Gordon shoved Ray's hands away from his neck and stumbled backwards before falling onto his butt.

Gordon coughed and gasped for air. His neck bled from forcing it into the tape measure to flip Ray.

Ray rolled over onto his hands and knees to face his opponent.

They both looked at the gun on the floor in between them. Gordon, still red in the face and catching his breath, clumsily lunged for the gun. Ray swept his leg around and kicked the gun out from under Gordon's hand. The gun slid through the Jack-and-Jill bathroom and into the other room.

Gordon got up and swung wild punches at Ray. Ray parried, ducked and dodged to foil each attack. Then his opponent lurched forward with a hard right punch. Ray deflected it with his left hand and pulled out the third screwdriver from his back pocket with his right hand. As Gordon's body dove forward, Ray stabbed the screwdriver into Gordon's chest. But to his dismay, the screwdriver did not penetrate Gordon's body!

Upon Ray's surprise, Gordon struck Ray in the stomach with his other hand. While Ray staggered back, he grabbed Gordon's dress shirt and ripped the top four buttons off, revealing a bulletproof vest underneath.

Gordon grinned wickedly and advanced toward Ray with his fists raised like a boxer. Ray blocked and dodged the first two punches, flanked Gordon and stabbed his side, but the vest wrapped around his waist and ribs. Gordon back-fisted Ray on the cheek, causing him to fumble sideways.

Through a melee of grabs, punches, and kicks between the two men, Ray finally found his opportunity when Gordon overstepped with his left leg while throwing a punch. Ray parried the punch and simultaneously kicked that left knee, causing Gordon's leg to buckle. He cried in pain, struggling to maintain his balance. Ray struck Gordon's bleeding neck with his fingertips, like darts piercing an open wound.

Just then, he saw the female agent appear in the doorway of the Jack-and-Jill bathroom in the other room. She picked up Gordon's gun and raised it to shoot. Ray immediately grabbed the wobbling, coughing

Escape

Gordon by the collar of his vest and spun him around to use him as a shield. The woman fired a shot into Gordon's chest before a metal stool from her side struck down on her arms. It was Deon!

Ray and Gordon both fell over from the gunshot. Gordon moaned as he looked at the flattened bullet on his vest. Ray's legs were underneath Gordon. He tried to squirm out, but Gordon flipped around to subdue Ray with his large, armored body.

Ray struck him in the face a couple of times, but Gordon did not relent. Ray's enemy appeared overcome with rage.

They scrambled to their feet in a clinch. As they tussled back and forth, Ray glimpsed past Gordon to see Deon busy controlling the woman. He instinctively struck Gordon's body, which, of course, had no effect.

With a growl, Gordon grabbed Ray's throat, drove him back against the wall, and hoisted him up by his neck. Pinned against the wall two feet above the floor, Ray was being strangled to death! His face reddened and then turned blue. How the tables had turned!

Ray desperately kicked at Gordon's armored body and struck his club-like arms to no avail. Gordon's longer arms were fully extended, so Ray could not reach his face.

In the last several seconds Ray knew he had left before falling unconscious, he reached into his back pocket and pulled out the pliers. He clamped the pliers down on Gordon's right hand, below the thumb. He squeezed hard, digging the pliers' teeth into Gordon's flesh. Then Ray cranked the pliers, like pulling a lever counterclockwise. As the pliers rotated, Ray twisted Gordon's hand and wrist, wrenching the hand loose from Ray's neck. Ray continued to crank the pliers and applied his other hand as well to twist Gordon's hand and wrist, making Gordon's entire arm contort.

Gordon finally released his other hand as well from Ray's neck. Ray landed on his feet. As Gordon tried to use his free hand to liberate his warped right hand, Ray surprised Gordon by dropping the pliers and firing repeated short, straight punches into Gordon's face. Simultaneously, Ray kicked Gordon's weakened knee and pressed forward with a vicious flurry of punches. Gordon brought his hands up to shield his face, but the punches fired straight and true.

Gordon stumbled backwards on his weakened knee just as Deon came through the Jack-and-Jill bathroom and charged at Gordon from behind. Ray pressed forward with the pummeling punches to the face, forcing Gordon to defensively stumble back on his weak leg. Deon rammed Gordon's lower back from behind, lifting him up, and flipping him over Deon's shoulder, like a flapjack. Gordon crashed on the floor face first with a boom.

The two men stood over Gordon's immobile body. He breathed heavily, but did not get up.

"I thought you left," Ray said, still watching the motionless body on the floor.

"I wouldn't leave you behind. Besides, I peeked out the window and saw the others hiding in the backyard of the neighbor's house," Deon said.

"What?" Ray turned his attention to Deon, "They haven't left yet?"

"They were waiting for you, but I told them to scat, and they finally went."

"Let's go."

The two of them backed out of the room and scrambled down the stairs, past the unconscious or squirming agents lying on the floor in the hallway and at the bottom of the stairs. They didn't see Russell anywhere. They went out the front door and onto the porch. Ray did not notice the fresh air or blue sky when he went to the street. As soon as they got to the sidewalk, a white, unmarked van zoomed by them. A couple seconds later, Ray became oriented to where they were and realized the reckless van headed toward Gordon's quadriplex. It was also in the direction where they had parked the SUV. Ray remembered that Gordon called for backup.

"Come on!" Ray shouted to Deon, who was right beside him.

The two of them ran after the van. They saw the van pull up beside his SUV. The side door slid open and about a dozen men and women in business casual attire swarmed out of the van at the SUV. They were still a couple blocks away.

Ray and Deon broke into a sprint. Deon was a few paces ahead of Ray. Ray could hear Abby scream as he saw her fight a losing battle against three assailants. Jeremy scuffled with four attackers. He was taking a few hits, but was surprisingly defending himself and doing damage to his opponents as well. Seeing his son being attacked enraged Ray, causing him to push his already cramping leg muscles to run faster. They were half a block away—and several seconds from jumping into the fight.

However, three of the agents had their heads and hands inside the vehicle. Jeremy tried to pull Jamie out of the SUV, but his four attackers preoccupied him. Abby was held down on the ground. Jamie and Sara screamed from inside the SUV.

"No!" Ray yelled.

Ray and Deon were 150 feet away.

Escape

Ray pushed his legs harder and started to catch up to Deon.

Jamie was dragged out of the SUV. His daughter kicked her feet and flailed her arms. She fought like her father had taught her. Another woman tried to grab Jamie's feet but was kicked in the chin before succeeding.

"Stop! Leave her alone!" Ray clamored. Though he strained his voice, his shout was not very loud for the lack of air in his lungs. "Fight, Jamie! Fight them off!" he screamed. "Fight!"

Ray and Deon were 60 feet away.

Jamie landed a few more kicks on her abductors before they finally gained control of her arms and legs. They carried her into the van through the side door.

They were 40 feet away.

A few of the assailants jumped into the van after her. "Jamie!" Ray yelled.

25 feet away.

The side door closed. "Stop!" he shouted.

The other half-a-dozen assailants, who did not get into the van, spontaneously scattered in four different directions once the side door banged shut.

"Jamie!" Ray cried out.

15 feet.

The wheels of the white van spun in place, screeching against the black asphalt and churning up white smoke.

10 feet.

Ray and Deon reached their arms out to the van.

5 feet.

The van peeled off, launching from its stationary position into an angry roar down the street, escaping Ray and Deon's outstretched hands.

"No! No! No!" Ray bellowed loud enough for the entire neighborhood to hear. "Get in," he told the others. Abby and Jeremy were still on the ground. and Deon was keeled over, catching his breath.

He hopped into the driver's seat and saw in his rearview mirror that Sara was sitting in the backseat, terrified. The others climbed in, Abby riding shotgun.

Ray pulled out and drove ahead. He could see the white van two blocks ahead. It made a right turn. "You are *not* getting away!" he squalled. He stepped on the gas pedal. But a large Suburban SUV backed out of a driveway, forcing Ray to slam on the brakes to avoid T-boning the vehicle. The Suburban had backed out in a straight line, virtually becoming a roadblock.

Ray swerved around the backside of the Suburban. Half of his SUV jumped onto the sidewalk, further slowing him down. As soon as he cleared the Suburban and the sidewalk, he raced forward.

He turned where he saw the van turn, and then came to a red light at a major street. He stopped as far out as he could without entering the intersection of whizzing cars. He looked down both sides of the perpendicular street, but he could not see the white van.

"No!" Ray pounded the steering wheel. "No!" He punched the center of the steering wheel.

Once the light turned green, he gassed the SUV and arbitrarily picked a direction, turning left. He strained his eyes to find the white van. After dodging a few slower cars and passing up a couple more, he saw a white vehicle! Swerving left and right to pass cars, he caught up to the large white vehicle, but it turned out to be a white truck.

"No!" He struck his palm into the steering wheel.

He made a sudden u-turn, causing two cars to blare their horns and come to screeching stops. He sped down the opposite direction. He went through the intersection he previously had turned from. After driving wantonly for ten blocks from that intersection, he still could not see the white van. He looked down the side streets.

"No!" He hammered his fist into his door.

The others sat silently, watching Ray's erratic behavior.

Abby watched him with sorrowful eyes.

He ran through a red light. Horns blared at him.

"No!" He pounded the top of his dashboard three times with his palm.

Abby gently touched his arm.

"No," he said.

She squeezed his arm softly.

"No," he said softly as the vehicle slowed to a normal speed.

She kept her warm hand on his arm.

"No," he whimpered.

He brought the vehicle to a complete stop. He closed his eyes. "No."

He stared into the road ahead of him as cars whizzed by and honked. He burst into tears and placed his head on the steering wheel.

Chapter 14
Homeless

Ray sat there, gripping the steering wheel. He didn't blink. He breathed so heavily his nostrils inflated and deflated. His rushing adrenaline showed on his red, sweaty skin. The sound of passing cars filled the silence.

"How could this have happened?" Ray asked. "We had her."

"We'll find another way to get her back," Abby assured him.

Ray, perturbed by her optimism, looked at her with question. *Was she flippantly handing out casual positivity?* He couldn't handle clichéd optimism right now. He saw the cut above her brow, bleeding lip, and scraped cheek. From the corner of his eye, he glimpsed Deon and Jeremy. He looked back at them, noticing Deon's bleeding arm and lumps on the crown of his head and Jeremy's black eye and bloody nose. They all sustained damage, but he felt like their injuries were meritless—hurts without results.

"She's gone," Jeremy blurted angrily. "You think we'll get another chance like this?"

Deon slumped his head, looking at his feet—defeated. Ray was surprised by Deon's genuine sadness over their loss.

"We can't give up," Abby reinforced. "For now, we shouldn't stay here. We can talk about what happened and what to do next when we get to a safe place."

"What's there to talk about?" Jeremy said.

Deon shook his hanging head.

Ray heeded her recommendation to leave. He put the car in drive and headed toward the freeway.

"Where are we going?" Jeremy asked.

"Home," Ray replied. "Like Abby said, we need a safe place to just re-gather ourselves and…," he searched for the words, "to think. I just need to think." His voice trailed off, as he drifted into a fog of thought.

. . . .

Traffic was surprisingly light. The rest of the thirty-minute ride remained quiet. The four in the vehicle seemed to be lost in either a reflection on the events of the day or a pool of remorse and anger over the results of the struggle. The drive gave Ray a chance to calm his emotions and swirling thoughts. He tried to make sense of their encounters. The house, the children, the tunnel, the other house, the mercenaries, the deadly family, the vicious backup, and TAGGAT ACT—what was all of this about?

Ray's phone buzzed. It was Fred.

"Yeah," Ray answered.

"How's it going?" Fred inquired.

"We had her. I had her in my arms!"

"What? Where did you find Jamie? Is she safe?"

"She was held in a child trafficking home. But we lost her."

"So sorry. You found her? That's incredible. What happened?"

"This is a lot bigger than we thought."

"Anything I can do to help?"

"There is one thing. If you can keep Internal Investigations off of me and out of my work or account at Miracom, that would help. Distract them or slow them down. I still need Miracom."

"Yeah, sure. You know I'm good at being a distraction. What are you doing now?

"Heading back home first. Need to reassess the situation. Fred, this whole thing is out of control."

"Well, I need to tell you that things at Miracom are out of control too. Can I talk to you about work? I know I have terrible timing."

"No, it's fine. Did the virus break through my encrypted firewall?"

"No, your encrypted firewall is keeping the nasty bugs out. Most of the system is compromised. The satellites and main radars are the only things unaffected." Fred continued in a different tone, "The internal investigation is another mess. Everyone is a suspect. Distrust throughout the company is tearing us apart."

"It's good that the encrypted firewall is holding up."

"Ray's Firewall seems to be just about the only thing that's keeping this company intact. I'd ask you how you put this encrypted firewall together out of curiosity, but Thunder Queen Miranda made it clear she didn't want you talking to anyone about it. We have been seeing some activity in our systems of someone trying to crack the wall, though. You still have that decryption code in safe keeping?"

"Yes, of course, Fred. You don't have to worry about that. It's not leaving me."

"Whoever is behind this really wants full control of our network. Ray,

I think it's just going to be a matter of time before they break through."

"Any leads on who the mole is?"

"No. There are a lot of speculations. The suspicions run all the way up to the executive level. Even Miranda has been under investigation."

"I'm guessing Thunder Queen gave the Internal Investigations guys a hard time."

"Oh, she did."

"Miranda couldn't possibly be in on this."

"I don't know. I.I. found some dirt in her past that no one ever knew about. They're digging deep. They're desperate to solve this. There's pressure from the military since some of our major radars have been affected. But so far all their findings are inconsequential to connecting anyone to this virus."

"What about Thornton?"

"You would think that comb-over man had some dirt, but so far he's squeaky clean. They've found nothing on anyone, which has heightened the suspicion around here. Whoever is doing this, they are very good at covering their tracks."

"We could've guessed that these guys were good at covering up from the way they masked the virus in the frequency noise."

"And so far, the virus isn't doing anything major to our systems?"

"So far, no. But we—meaning, me, Marvin's systems security team, and Miranda—are suspecting that this virus is simply lying dormant until it can take over the main server. No one would go through all this trouble to just cause glitches. We think this is just a siege leading to a system-wide takeover."

"I was suspecting the same thing. Someone wants control of Miracom."

"Miranda needs you to come in. She wants a closed room meeting with the two of us and Marvin. She's paranoid about who she's trusting. Never seen her like this. She knows you're still facing a family crisis, but she wanted me to reiterate to you the global crisis that could occur if this all goes south. You're the only guy that's preventing that from happening with your encrypted firewall."

"I understand. I'll come in as soon as I can." Ray continued speculatively, "But, if we're not sure about Miranda, how can we securely meet with her? She's the one calling the meeting, right? So she reasonably could be the mole."

"I don't know, but you're freaking me out. We just have to play along and hope that I.I. finds something soon."

"Okay. I'll do what I can. For the moment, I need to get home and figure things out about Jamie. I think I only have another short window of time to find her. And the window is getting smaller."

"I wish I could be there to help. By the way, I hate to point this out, but since you are the only one who's blocking this virus out, you are probably a prime target for whoever is behind this."

"So what's new?"

"Just be careful, buddy."

. . . .

Ray parked the SUV in their driveway. He instinctually looked in his rearview mirror to see if the grey, four-door sedan with the mysterious driver in it was parked on the perpendicular street. He did not see it. He sighed for a moment while he turned off the engine. It broke his heart to imagine how terrified Jamie must be, having been nearly rescued and then violently snatched. He could still hear her screams.

Jeremy was already out of the SUV and walking up to the front door. Ray got out and glanced down the perpendicular street again, particularly under the large tree. No strange stalker there. Ray actually felt disappointed. At least if he were there, it would give Ray something to work with. Maybe he knew something. What were the chances that his recent appearances and Jamie's abduction were a coincidence?

"Crap!" Jeremy shouted as he stood on the porch, looking inside their home.

Ray rushed to Jeremy, with the other two following behind. Ray came up to Jeremy and looked inside to see their couch overturned. He stepped in.

Lamps were knocked over. The upholstery of the couch was cut open. The easy chair was on its side. The dining table was flipped over. The television was on its back with a cracked screen. Sections of the carpet were torn up. The drawers and cupboards in the kitchen were opened and emptied, contents scattered across the floor. There were holes the size of dinner plates all over the walls.

They walked to the middle of the living room, speechlessly surveying the chaos.

The refrigerator was open, with all of its contents dumped on the floor. The closets were rummaged through and the shelves broken down. More plate-sized holes covered the hallway walls. Debris from the drywall wreckage littered the floor.

Ray and Jeremy proceeded toward their bedrooms.

The door to Jeremy's bedroom was open. The doorframe was still busted, but that was Ray's doing. Ironically, it matched the brokenness throughout the house. Jeremy entered while Ray stood at the doorway looking in.

Jeremy's bed was cut open. His computer was missing. His desk was overturned and his dresser was emptied out, with all his clothes strewn everywhere. More plate-sized holes were punched into the walls and through the posters and artwork. Jeremy kicked personal belongings at his feet and cursed.

Ray moved down the hall with a mixture of sorrow and vehemence. *No*, he said as he approached Jamie's room. *Please, no.* He looked inside. The entire room was destroyed like the rest of the home. The little pieces of encouragement notes were littered everywhere. Her posters were ripped from the walls. Her toy chest was broken and all her toys spilled out. Her bookshelf was dismantled. The stuffed animals once sitting on the bookshelf were ripped apart. Her bed was slashed open. Her dresser was disseminated and her clothes dispersed across the floor. The walls were punched through with holes. Her desk was flipped over and its contents dumped out.

His eyes welled up with tears while his fists clenched so tightly his knuckles whitened. He stood in the middle of her room, in the center of the disorder. He felt like the mess swirled around him, while his blood boiled and his heart ached.

He left her room to go to his bedroom. His room was in a similar shape as the rest of the home, but worse. All the carpeting in the room was stripped open. His bed was shredded and moved from its original place. Things were spread everywhere. The mirror was shattered. The holes in his room were as large as tires.

He slowly walked inside his room and felt appalled over his destroyed home. He looked about the displaced items on the floor. He noticed every detail of damage. He picked up the picture of Melanie and him. The glass was cracked, and the backing was removed. He took a few more steps and picked up Melanie's butterfly barrette that Jamie found. He took a couple more steps and noticed something amongst the rubble of contents. His pillow lay on the floor, and on top of it was a handwritten note.

He knelt down and picked it up to read it. Then he walked out of his room and down the hallway. As he passed Jeremy's room, he said to him, "Come to the living room." Ray went into the living room with the note held in front of him. Abby came from the kitchen, and Deon came out from the dining room to join him.

Jeremy cursed as he walked into the living room and said angrily,

"Why?"

"Sifu. Jeremy. I'm sorry," Deon said sympathetically. "This is messed up."

"Could the stalker you chased the other night have done this?" Abby guessed.

"How could one person do all this?" Jeremy remarked.

"It took a posse to do this," Deon said.

"Maybe it's the same people who took Jamie?" Abby suggested.

"But why?" Jeremy asked, infuriated.

"It doesn't make sense," she responded as she appeared to examine her own suggestion, "for them to take Jamie and then come back to ransack the home."

"Maybe this was payback for breaking into their house," Deon said.

"Revenge?" Jeremy said, "This was about revenge?"

"No," Ray finally said, "They were looking for something." He raised the note to his chest level. "I found this in my room. It's a note from the home invaders." He read the note out loud, "Give us the decryption code. We'll be back. Put the USB drive in an envelope. Place it outside your front door, and we won't come inside."

They stared at the note.

Abby, wide-eyed, said, "Dear God."

"They're coming back?" Jeremy asked.

"I'm scared," Sara whimpered. The group almost forgot she was still with them.

Abby put her hand on Sara's shoulder and pulled the frightened girl to her hip. She stroked Sara's arm, while asking Ray, "What USB drive and decryption code?"

Ray exhaled, closed his eyes and bit his bottom lip. He looked to the side then back at them and said, "It's this." He unzipped the small pouch in his backpack and pulled out a red USB drive. "It contains a decryption code that unlocks an encrypted firewall I installed on our main server at Miracom Systems. The firewall is preventing a virus from getting into the main server. Only I have the decryption code to—"

"Wait," Jeremy interrupted with dismay, "you mean *this*," pointing around at the house, "was about your job?"

"You know we've been facing a major problem at work," Ray explained. "We've been battling a virus that's taking over the company's systems. If it does, it would mean total control of our telecommunications, affecting military, law enforcement, and public communications."

"This is horrible," Abby commented with deep sympathy. "How

much can one family take?"

"Like we don't have enough going on," Jeremy spat. "This wasn't even about Jamie. This was about your job!"

"You have to understand how serious it would be for our systems to be compromised, Jer," Ray explained. "It would be catastrophic."

"What do you call this?" Jeremy yelled. "We're standing in the middle of a catastrophe! Right here in our home!"

"I never thought it would come back to my home, to my family," Ray said apologetically.

"Yo, let's not forget these guys are coming back," Deon reminded.

"Then let's stay here and see who shows up," Jeremy said with his chin up. "Let's wait for the punks who did this."

"By the looks of this place," Abby said, "these people are probably very dangerous."

"Dangerous people?" Jeremy mocked. "What kind of people do you think we have been fighting with all day?"

"Hey, these folks do seem to mean business," Deon said. "Normally, I'm good for taking down a bunch of no-good fools, but, man, Sifu, you're in some serious stuff. We already got shot at today. Praise Jesus we're still alive, but I don't know if we're using up our blessings if we have a second go at it in one day. You feel me?"

Ray took note of the wet wound on Deon's arm. "We can't stay here."

"Where are we going? To the police again? The homeless shelter?" Jeremy quibbled.

"We need a safe place to stay," Ray answered. There was a heaviness in his voice. "Jer, pack up some essentials. We'll go to the Wing Chun studio."

Jeremy stormed into his room with more curses.

"I'll take my car to bring Sara home," Abby said to Ray. She bent toward the little girl and asked, "Do you remember your address?"

Sara nodded with round eyes.

"I'll meet you at the studio after I take her to her parents," Abby said.

Ray complied with a nod.

"Want me to come with?" Deon asked.

Abby considered it for a second. "Yeah, it might be good to have a second adult to back up the story of what happened."

"Thank you, both," Ray said. "I'll see you at the studio."

Ray walked into his room to get his carry-on luggage, which was already removed from the closet and opened. He packed clothes. He took the honeymoon picture of Melanie and him out of the broken frame.

As he walked down the hall, he stopped at Jamie's room and packed her encouragement notes. He read again the note written to him, "I'm glad you're my daddy. Thank you for loving me and taking care of me." He placed it gingerly into the small, front pouch of his backpack, being careful not to wrinkle it.

When he turned to leave, he noticed a light coming from behind the overturned desk. He gently moved the desk aside. There was an illuminated pink blanket. He removed the blanket and found the lamp with the Winnie-the-Pooh lampshade lying on its side. The lamp must've been dropped onto the floor when her desk was overturned, but it remained plugged into the outlet. His eyes welled with tears. The undying lamp resurged in him a determination to retrieve Jamie!

As he walked out of the room, the Winnie-the-Pooh lamp lighted the floor in front of him.

. . . .

The evening sky spread a blanket of darkness over the city. The drive to the Wing Chun studio was quiet and tense for Ray and Jeremy. Ray couldn't shake the disturbing feeling of having been invaded in the very place where he rested. The reality of his personal space dissolved. Personal security was erased. First, a kidnapping babysitter was in his home. Then, home invaders were in there. His home was no longer a safe place of rest. It belonged to others now. He was relieved that he had kept his backpack containing his laptop, other electronic devices, work-related materials, sci-fi looking device, and red USB drive with him in the SUV.

Ray turned the corner. The Wing Chun studio was only a few blocks away. If there was a second home for him, it was his studio that he opened over fifteen years ago. It was more than a place of training. It was a place of development, personal growth, and retreat. It was a studio as well as a school because it was a place of creativity, where solutions for situations were discovered. A sense of relief came over him at the thought of being able to lie on the couch in his office even for an hour.

As they drove up to the studio, he saw a large wooden board where the front window used to be. He parked the SUV in front of the studio. The two of them got out and as they walked to the front door, Miguel came out with a broom and dustpan.

"Sifu," Miguel said with surprise, "you're here. I just put that board up. I found it in the back by the dumpster. I'm sorry, Sifu. I don't know who did this."

"What happened?" Ray asked as he inspected the broken window.

"Vandalism and robbery," Miguel responded. "They trashed the place and took the computers."

Ray and the others went inside and found the studio devastated, much like Ray's home. Even the weapons hanging on the wall were thrown down. The invaders smashed the mirrors. They overturned the wooden dummies, though they couldn't break them. They took the computer in Ray's office, ransacked his desk, and ripped the couch apart.

Ray went back out to the main room. Speechless.

"I was driving by and saw the busted window, so I stopped to check it out. Why would someone do this?" Miguel asked. "We have no enemies. Who did this? A rival school? We need to give them some payback, Sifu."

"No," Ray simply said. "Don't go seeking trouble. This is beyond you, Miguel."

"We can't just let this be," he replied.

"Now what?" Jeremy asked the obvious.

"I was just about to call the cops," Miguel said.

Ray examined that suggestion for a moment and then answered, "No. Not yet." Ray's unsettledness was evident in his pacing about the studio as he observed one broken or displaced item after another. "Can't trust them."

Glass crackling beneath footsteps drew Ray's attention. Abby and Deon walked through the front door with shock covering their faces.

"No," Abby exclaimed. "Not here too."

"These fools went too far," Deon declared.

"Hold up." Miguel asked, "This happened somewhere else?"

"Our home," Ray replied.

"Like you said," Jeremy said, "we need a safe place to stay. Where is that now? Nowhere is safe for us."

"You're welcome to crash at my place, if you don't mind slumming it in a little studio apartment," Miguel offered.

"My one bedroom apartment is also open to you," Abby immediately followed that offer.

"My crib is a house. It's just me and my grandma living there," Deon also offered. "You met her. She's tough as a knuckle. Besides, I live in the hood and them fools might be too scared to come there. Know what I'm saying? It's kind of like being safe in a dangerous place," he philosophized with a jest.

"Thank you very much. But I don't think it would be good for Jer and I to stay in any of your homes," Ray said.

"Ah, nah. It's nothing. My grandma would actually like the company," Deon pressed.

Ray looked at Deon, touched with gratitude. "Thank you," he said sincerely, "but having Jer and me in your homes would put you all in danger—more danger, I mean. We couldn't bring this on your grandma."

"Correction," Jeremy clarified. "Having *you* in their homes would put them in danger. You're the one they want."

The cold sting of his words left Ray frozen. The matter-of-fact ease with which Jeremy condemned him took him aback. He unzipped the small pouch of his backpack and pulled out a business card.

The card read, "Nathan Clarkson."

Ray said, "I'll call Elder Nathan."

"The church?" Jeremy said. "You want to stay at a church? Is that even possible?"

Ray dialed, but he got Nathan's voicemail. Ray left a voice message for him explaining that he and his son ran into some trouble, leaving them homeless, and asked if they could stay at the church for a couple of nights until he figured something else out.

"What if he says, 'no'?" Jeremy asked. "What other bright ideas do you have?"

"I don't know," Ray responded.

"Well, that's a first," Jeremy said under his breath.

"I'll think of something, all right, Jer?" Ray retaliated with frustration. "Your badgering is not helping. Just give me the space to think!"

"I'll give you all the space you need." Jeremy put up his hands and backed away. He retreated into the office, kicking a few items along the way.

"Hey, Sifu," Deon said, "you want me to go talk with him?"

"No, leave him," Ray replied. "He needs to cool off."

"Do we just wait for a call back?" Abby asked.

"For now."

. . . .

The group sat on the mats and waited for fifteen minutes. Jeremy didn't come out from the office. All the while, they watched the door, not knowing what to expect or even if they should expect something. Their senses were on high alert. They felt they had to keep looking over their shoulders.

"You know what?" Abby said as she got up. "I can't just sit here. I need to do something. I'm going to try and clean up as much of this mess as I can."

"I'm with you, Abby," Miguel validated as he stood up as well. "I'll grab some boxes from the back to put stuff in. I can't stand seeing our studio like this."

"Want some help?" Deon asked.

"No, no," Abby insisted. "You both did the bulk of the fighting already back at that house. You two need to rest."

Ray and Deon welcomed the time to remain still. The mats invited their muscles to rest. The studio, though in shambles, offered a respite from their harrowing day. As a temporary calm covered Ray, he felt a curiosity to know his brother-in-arms, sitting beside him. He looked at Deon, this young man who was once his enemy had become his comrade in the past twenty-four hours.

"You know, Deon," Ray said, "there's only been one other time I kicked a student out, and she never came back. I was surprised to see you again. I'm glad you did. Just surprised."

"I was surprised too," Deon concurred, chuckling. "Thank my grandma for it."

"She does seem like quite the little lady."

"I went home that night, and my grandma could tell that I was upset because I got an honest butt-whooping. She could always tell if I got my butt whooped by somebody. I told her exactly what happened that night, about how I challenged you, got whooped twice by you, got schooled by your one-inch punch, how I stepped up to Miguel, and got kicked out in front of everyone. I told her, 'I'm never going back to that stupid karate, kung-fu, whatever school!' I think that's exactly how I said it. I couldn't show my face in here again.

"But then grandma smacked me on my big head." Deon smiled and chortled.

Ray returned a smile.

"She told me I was hotheaded and prideful. She said, 'Boy, you have a big head!' She gave me a whole lecture about pride and anger. She pulled out the Bible on me and hit me upside the head with Jesus! I'm telling you, Sifu, it hurt."

They laughed.

"She said you were a gentleman for the way you beat me up without beating me up—said you didn't hurt my body, just my pride. She said I got beat up for a good reason. It was to break my pride. 'And thank Jesus for that,' she said. She wasn't going to let me quit just because my pride got hurt. She wanted me to come back to learn something, and she wanted me to come back with the kind of attitude you said—respectful and humble. She said that if I didn't go back to your school to learn, *she* would whoop my butt."

"That's quite a grandma."

"You don't even know, Sifu. She's five feet tall and eighty-four years old, but she is one tough, old lady," he said with a big smile. "My whole hood knows her."

"Wow. I suspected your answer had to be something good. So all it took was for your grandma to change your mind and your attitude."

"My grandma means everything to me. She raised me all by herself. My mom was doped out. My dad was locked up. But my grandma loved me. I was a bad kid growing up around a lot of bad folks. But she loved me. She sacrificed a lot for me. I didn't know it at first. But one day, I recognized it."

Ray smiled warmly at Deon.

"So when she says something—anything—I listen. Even, if I don't like it. But I know she's always right. After you took me back and she explained to me that was grace, I understood."

"I can appreciate your relationship with her," Ray said, nodding.

"I hope you get to know her someday. She's a special little lady, but she has one of the biggest hearts in the world." He said with a wide grin that showed his dimples. "She has fought hard to make sure I turn out to be a good person and have a good future. I love her a lot, Sifu, even though I don't like it when she sets me straight."

Ray saw a deeper side to this young man that he never expected. There was a beauty to Deon's soul that was a sight for sore eyes in light of the disasters they had faced. Everyone needs people with beautiful souls around them when life is broken. "I'm sure I will get to know her," he said, "and I look forward to it."

"I have to tell you, though. If you sit down with her, she'll give you two things: tea and Jesus. Not necessarily in that order."

Ray looked about, and his eyes stopped at the trophies and plaques on the floor. His largest trophy laid facedown, and a couple of others were broken in two. "That's it." He got up. "We shouldn't wait anymore. It's getting late. Let's go over to the church and see if anyone is there. We need an answer."

Deon and Ray got up and grabbed their things off the floor.

Ray started to walk to the office, then stopped. "Deon."

"Yeah, Sifu."

"Could you get Jeremy from the office for me?"

"Sure."

Moments later, they vacated the studio. Ray and Miguel fabricated some sort of makeshift barrier and lock for the broken front door to deter

Homeless

squatters or looters.

Miguel looked at the front of the school and said, "This is jacked."

"Thank you for being here to take care of things," Ray said to him.

"If there's anything else you need, Sifu, just call," Miguel said.

"I will. Thank you."

After Miguel left, the four rode together to the church that was twenty minutes away. Jeremy kept his eyes closed with his face towards the window during the entire ride. Ray called Fred and told him about what happened to his home and studio. Fred, again, offered his sympathy as well as a place for Ray and Jeremy to stay. Ray gave his best friend the same explanation about not wanting to endanger him and his family.

They arrived at the church at 9:00 PM. The parking lot was empty except for two cars. Ray and Jeremy took their carry-on luggage out of the trunk and walked across the lot. Ray felt unsure about knocking on the door with their carry-ons. It seemed presumptuous. His approach to the building triggered feelings of uneasiness. He hadn't really been devoted. He wasn't sincerely involved with the church. Was it hypocritical of him to ask for such a favor?

They walked up five wide steps leading to the front double doors. An elderly homeless man sat on the porch under the awning, picking at a sore on his leg.

Ray knocked. No answer. He knocked harder. Still no answer.

There were two cars in the parking lot, so there was probably someone inside, unless those cars didn't belong to anybody at the church. Illegal parking happened a lot in the City of Angels. People left things in places they shouldn't or camped out where they weren't supposed to.

"They're in there," the homeless man said through his rotten teeth. "Keep knocking."

Ray looked to the left and right, then saw a smaller door to the side. He walked to it. The sign on the door indicated that this was the church office entrance. He knocked and then noticed the small, white doorbell on the doorframe. He pushed it.

"Push it again," the homeless man said as he accidentally drooled, then returned to scraping his sore.

The night grew cold quickly. A chill steadily blew into the covered porch.

Ray pushed the doorbell again.

Still no answer.

"There's nobody here. Who's at church at 9:00 PM anyways?" Jeremy questioned. "How many times are you going to push that doorbell?"

Ray pushed the doorbell a third time.

The homeless man smiled and chuckled with a hack.

"This is pointless," Jeremy said. "We have to sleep in the car."

Then the door unlocked and opened.

Standing on the other side of the doorway was a man with spotted grey hair. He was a Caucasian man, a little taller than Ray, with mild wrinkles at the corners of his eyes. Ray recognized him as the pastor of the church—Pastor James.

"How can I help you?" Pastor James asked.

"Pastor," Ray addressed, "I'm Ray Lee. This is my son, Jeremy. I don't know if you recognize us, but we attend your church. Well, we attend as often as we can."

"What brings you and your son to the church at this hour?" he asked as he looked at Abby and Deon and took note of the carry-on luggage beside Ray and Jeremy.

"I'm sorry to bother you so late. I didn't even know if anyone would be here. Elder Nathan gave me his card," Ray said, holding up the business card as if it was a document to legitimize his unusual request, "and said if my family needed anything, we could call the church. Well, technically, it was to call him."

"Please tell me your name again."

"Ray."

"Well, how can we help you, Ray?"

"Pastor, we're in trouble. We need a safe place to stay. Can you help us?"

Chapter 15
Wounds

Ray felt nervous. He had never asked for this sort of favor before, let alone asking it from a religious authority figure who hardly knew him. He was independent and provided for his own. But not now. The chilly wind nipped at his neck, but he could feel the warm air sneaking out from inside the church.

Pastor James stood on the inside of the doorway. "Let's have you get out of the cold first, then you can explain your situation to me."

Relieved, Ray invited his group to follow him in.

Ray had not been in the church office before. It looked much like a business office except with a couple of crosses and a few religious posters on the walls. There were cubicles, file cabinets, desks with computers, and a large copier. They walked on a plush, beige carpet with soft padding underneath it. There was no one else here.

"You're working late tonight, Pastor," Ray said, making small talk.

Pastor James led them to his personal office. He opened the door for them to enter first. "Yes," he responded, "Most people don't understand all the demands of the ministry." There was a brown leather couch and a couple of large, leather chairs with cushioned armrests. The pastor closed the door.

"Sit," he invited them.

Ray and Jeremy sat on the couch while Deon and Abby sat on the chairs. The leather of the couch was incredibly soft. Pastor James sat on the brown, leather chair behind his antique desk.

"So," Pastor James began with his hands folded on top of his desk, "briefly tell me about yourselves and explain to me your need."

Ray didn't know what to expect but the formal, interview-like manner was not it. "Well, Elder Nathan knows me." He thought it would be good to drop Elder Nathan's name a few more times, believing that having a contact on the inside would give him some leverage. At least, that's how it worked in the business world.

"Yes, you mentioned that. Good, so you know Nathan. He's one of our best elders," Pastor James said with a smile.

"Well," Ray added, feeling pressure to be overly honest since he was in the house of God, "actually, Elder Nathan knew my late wife. He really just knows me as her husband. She was a member here."

"You said your name is Ray?"

"Yes," Ray tried not to appear annoyed, remembering that the direness of their situation did not afford him the luxury of that emotion, "Ray Lee."

"Lee," Pastor James repeated, "Oh, yes, Melanie Lee."

Ray was surprised by his familiarity with Melanie.

"She was very involved in our church. Her passing was definitely felt here and was a great loss. I somewhat recall officiating her funeral." Pastor James paused for a second while he examined Ray. "Ah yes, now I can place your face. I remember you now, and of course this is her son," he said, looking at Jeremy. "It's Jason. No, Jerry."

"Jeremy," Jeremy corrected, appearing annoyed.

"Yes, yes. Jeremy, that's right," the pastor repeated. "With three hundred people in the church, keeping track of every name is tricky."

"Pastor James, you knew Melanie by her involvement in the church? How was she involved?" Ray knew this question was a detour from their pressing issue, but the mystery about Melanie gripped him. He knew she was a regular attendee and a member, but he didn't know she was so involved that it warranted the pastor's recognition. He felt a bit embarrassed for asking about this.

"I couldn't tell you specifically. Nathan worked directly with her. You can ask him when you see him. But she was quite an influence around here."

These new discoveries about his late wife gnawed at him. *She was "quite an influence?" She worked under Elder Nathan's ministry?* How could there be a significant aspect about her that he was unaware of? She was religious, he knew, but to what degree? He didn't recall her spending any more time at the church outside of attending Sunday services. *When did she take time to be so involved with the church? What did she do? Why didn't he know about it?*

"I'm sorry again for your loss," Pastor James said cordially, "but let's get back to the matter of the trouble you're in." He surveyed their appearances. "By the looks of you all, I'd have to say you've been in a fight," he estimated.

Feeling further embarrassment in front of the pastor, Ray confessed, "I'm afraid we have. I know it sounds cliché, but it's a long story."

"I'm not sure how the church is able to help you in your matter," Pastor James said skeptically.

"Pastor James, I know how this looks."

"Actually, I'm not sure how this looks, to be honest. So, why don't you briefly explain it to me."

Ray felt pressured to get to the point, so he came out and said it. "My daughter Jamie was kidnapped three days ago by my babysitter. The babysitter gave her to an accomplice. We found Jamie and tried to take her back, and that's how we ended up like this." He could hardly believe he said all of that, but a complete and concise report seemed in order for the pastor from whom they were requesting aide.

"Goodness. Kidnapped? Did you retrieve your daughter?"

"No," Ray looked at Pastor James with pinkish, tearing eyes. "We failed." He avoided looking at Jeremy.

"Are you working with the police?"

"The police won't help us."

"I don't understand why the police wouldn't help you," said Pastor James with growing skepticism.

"I tried to file a report with them. They came to our house, but…" Ray didn't know how to explain it without it sounding like a fiction fabricated out of borderline delusion. "Again, it's a long story, but they're not currently aiding us."

"Well, your problem sounds like a matter for law enforcement and not for the church."

"Our home was invaded and ransacked. What I'm asking for is—"

"Ransacked? By the kidnappers?" Pastor James' skepticism increased.

"No. It's a separate issue. It has to do with my job. I'm an engineer at a very high-profile telecommunications company, and…" Again, he didn't know how to explain all that was happening. "That's a long story too. There's been trouble at my work that led back to my home. We can't go back to it. It's not safe."

"Well, would your presence here bring danger to this church?"

"No. No one should know we're here. We're not even that connected to the church. We're not members, and we hardly attend. I don't think anyone suspects us to be here." Ray made his case but felt embarrassed about the evidence he raised.

"Again, this sounds like you need law enforcement. The church can't help you much with kidnappings and home invasions. I'm not trying to shoo you away, but I want you to get the proper kind of help you need."

"I know this is a lot to ask for," Ray pled, "but we just need a place to stay for a night or two. A place that's safe until I can figure something else out."

"How about a hotel?"

Ray got the clear sense that the pastor was not going to easily welcome them. "I would prefer my son and I to stay out of public areas for now." As soon as he said that, he sounded even shadier.

The pastor raised his eyebrows. "I'll be frank with you. I'm still unclear about the kind of trouble you're in and what you could be involving the church in by being here. I have to ask, you're not involved in some illegal activity are you? Are you running from the police?"

"No, no. Nothing like that. We're not running from the police."

"Then why can't you go to them?"

"It's very complicated. Honestly, if they would help me, I would go to them."

"And you're not involved with some rival gang activity?" Pastor James said, glancing at Jeremy and Deon.

Jeremy fought back the pastor's judgmental glance with a scowl. Deon simply shook it off.

"No, Pastor. Not at all. No gang activity."

"The church isn't a law enforcement agency that solves crimes, and it's not a shelter for the homeless. I have the sense that you're in the wrong place."

Ray wanted to walk out. He's never begged before. He looked at his tattered son and knew they needed a refuge. "I just thought that maybe the church would be a safe place for us to come."

"Come on," Jeremy said. "We're obviously not welcome here. Let's go."

Pastor James dipped his head and let out a big breath. He rubbed his folded hands against each other.

"Please. It's just for a couple of nights." Ray realized he was begging.

"I tell you what," the pastor said as his final decision, "since Melanie was such a wonderful person to us, you can stay for one night. Besides, it's getting late. I wouldn't want you and your boy wandering around out in the cold. I'll have Nathan come in tomorrow to assess your situation and determine what to do from there. I wouldn't count on a second night, though, just so you know."

"Thank you, Pastor," Ray said with relief. "We do appreciate it."

Jeremy looked away from the pastor.

"And understand that if there's anything that would lead me to think that you being here would bring harm to the church, I will ask you to depart immediately."

"Understood."

"There's a vacant office room with a couch and a fold-out cot in the closet. Now," he said, looking at Deon and Abby, "these two—are they sleeping here too?"

"Oh, no. We're not sleeping here," Abby assured. "We're friends who were helping out."

"Okay," Pastor James said. "You can settle into that room. There's a kitchen down the hall with a first aid kit. Go patch yourselves up."

"Thank you again, Pastor. We won't be—"

"Very good then," Pastor James concluded while standing up. He walked to the door and opened it. "I'm burning the midnight oil to finish my sermon preparation, so I'm going to let you get settled in while I get back to my work."

"Of course," Ray said while quickly getting up and grabbing his luggage.

They all immediately stood and exited.

"It's right over there," Pastor James said as he pointed to a plain, white door. The ordinariness of the door did not match the rest of the eloquent and pristine office.

"Okay, we'll let you get back to your work."

Pastor James closed the door in front of them.

They stared at his door for a moment until Abby remarked quietly, "He seems charming, doesn't he?"

Ray led the group to the ordinary door. He opened it, and they looked inside. It was a room with blank, white walls. There was a worn, rectangular conference table in the middle, and mismatched chairs surrounded it. A stack of boxes piled in a corner. An obsolete, dusty fax machine sat in a stand in another corner. A bunch of random office items cluttered the side of one wall, and a dirty, fabric couch sat on the opposite wall.

Abby opened the storage closet and pulled out an old-fashioned cloth cot.

"Well, I guess this is it," Abby said with a bright tone. "Home sweet home."

"It really ain't that bad," Deon added.

"Like you said, Sifu, it's safe at least," she said. "After all you've been through today, that's what you really need."

"This will do for the night," Ray concurred. "We'll get some peace and rest here." He sounded exhausted, physically and mentally.

"I don't like it here," Jeremy objected.

"I admit," Ray responded patiently, "it's not a five-star resort, but we're secure here."

"We're not secure," Jeremy contested. "Didn't you see the way the pastor treated us? He doesn't want us here. We shouldn't be here."

"He was being careful. That's all. It's understandable."

"I don't buy it. Something's not right with him," Jeremy argued. "This whole set-up doesn't feel right."

"He checked us out because he doesn't know us," Ray said, trying to calm and convince his son. "Look, we're just all very wound up and more sensitive after all that we've been through. Let's just relax."

"What kind of a pastor doesn't know his sheep?" Jeremy wouldn't relent. "And what was that about him knowing Mom? Huh? Is he one of those perverted pastors who have sexual affairs with other people's wives?"

"Jeremy!" Abby called to silence him.

"I'm just saying this place isn't safe," Jeremy said. His bruised eye was swelling. "Nowhere is safe for us!"

"Jer," Ray said in a strained tone, "it's late, and there's nowhere for us to go. We'll stay here for at least one night."

"Let's go to a hotel," Jeremy said.

"I want to stay out of public places. I want to keep out of sight until we know more about what we're dealing with."

"Then let's go to my buddy's place. Louis will take us in."

Hearing Louis' name made Ray's blood boil as he recalled Louis' belligerence toward him on the night he searched for Jeremy. "Not Louis," Ray said. "I don't want to jeopardize anyone we know."

"Well, that's strange, because you were so ready to jeopardize Deon back there."

"Jer, like I had said I wanted to keep you safe."

"None of us are safe right now. Not here. Not with Pastor Inappropriate!"

"Stop, Jeremy. Don't insinuate things like that." Ray's patience fragmented. His hands were sore. His knuckles were raw. His back ached, and his composure crumbled.

"Why? Because you don't want to admit to it? Because you don't want to recognize when something is wrong?"

"Jeremy," Abby intervened, "where is this coming from?"

"You're tired," Ray said to Jeremy with his last ounce of understanding toward his rebellious teenager. "You just need to get some rest. Let's all rest."

"Don't tell me what I need. You don't know."

"I know you need to settle down. I understand you're upset about today, but—"

"Stop saying that! Stop saying you understand. You think you do, but you don't. Don't you get that? You don't understand."

"We're not going to keep arguing. After all the fighting we did today, you and I are not going to fight here." Ray became stern. "We're staying. End of discussion."

"You can stay here and bond with Pastor Jerk-off, if you want. I don't have to. I'll find somewhere else." Jeremy pulled his rolling carry-on toward the door.

Ray intercepted Jeremy and stood between him and the door.

"Get out of my way," Jeremy challenged his father.

"Look, I want you to –"

"You want, you want. It's always what you want. Well, what you want gets everyone hurt, doesn't it? Doesn't it? That's how we ended up here. That's how Mom died. It's because you got what you wanted."

"Jeremy!" Abby interjected to try to silence him again.

"Hey, man, this is going too far. Let's just chill, all right?" Deon suggested.

Ray's bulging eyes screamed a host of phrases, but his mouth and body froze. He stared at his son with infuriated disbelief, as a crushing weight of guilt befell his heart.

"What? Isn't it true?" Jeremy said, looking at Abby and Deon to solicit their agreement. "Look at what happened today. We're all beat up. We lost Jamie. We lost our home."

"Jer, everything that happened today was awful. But it was not Ray's fault," Abby said. "Bad people are doing this to you and your family."

"Come on, man," Deon said, "we were so close to rescuing your sister, but we didn't know they would come at us like that. They possed up with guns."

"No! It was his fault," Jeremy chided and stuck his finger in Ray's face. Then he looked at Ray to say, "It was your plan. You insisted that we stay together and search each house one by one. If you listened to me about splitting up, we could've been in and out of the house with Jamie before those guys got there."

"We didn't know what we were walking into. I was trying to keep us safe. Trying to keep you safe."

"And how did that work out? Tell me. Look at us!" Jeremy held up his wounds and pointed to Deon's bleeding arm. "Now we're here where we are obviously not wanted." His voice choked with pain.

"We're here to keep us safe! What is the matter with you, Jeremy?"

"What is the matter with me? We're here because of your job!" Jeremy screamed. He inched closer toward Ray. "You did something at your job that put us in this sexually inappropriate place that pretends to be a church!"

"Lower your voice. You're embarrassing us."

"You're embarrassed?" Jeremy said with a mocking smile.

"All I am trying to do is protect this family," Ray repeated with emphatic intensity as he shoved his finger toward the floor. "You want to blame me for what's happening? Fine! Blame me. But you can't blame me for taking care of my family. You're my son, Jeremy, and my job is to keep you safe. So you need to listen to me because I'm still your father."

"You being my father is my problem!"

"Jeremy, that's enough!" Abby scolded.

Jeremy leaned forward so that his face was only twelve inches from Ray's and spoke in a cold, even tone. "You can't keep us safe. You come up with plans that don't work. You don't listen."

"Jeremy, back up and settle down," Ray warned.

"Or what? Huh?"

"Don't keep going, Jeremy. You are out of control."

"Why? What will happen if I keep going? Will we all wake up and see that you don't have all the answers? That you can't take care of anything?"

"Stop."

"You failed as a father, and that's why you can't get Jamie back. You failed as a husband, and that's why mom died."

His son's words stabbed his heart. A blanket of guilt ensnared Ray while an eruption of rage foamed within him. The condemnation of his son's words tore him to pieces. His mind blurred, as if a gavel bludgeoned his head. A swarm of memories and emotions feasted on his soul. The pain was overbearing.

"So stop pretending you can take care of me or this family. Mom's dead. Jamie's missing. I hate you. This family is dead."

Without thinking, Ray's left hand shot up from his side, like a quick-draw, and struck Jeremy's face. The force of Ray's palm sent Jeremy spinning to the floor.

Abby screeched.

What happened did not register in Ray's mind until a second later when his vision focused again and he saw his son lying face down on the floor four feet in front of him. Ray's bottom lip was trembling, his right hand was clenched into a fist, his breathing was in a stuttered pant, and his left palm stung.

Abby and Deon rushed to tend to Jeremy. As Deon knelt on one knee beside Jeremy, he held up a surrendering hand towards Ray.

"Are you okay?" Abby asked while helping Jeremy up.

Jeremy rose slowly and shrugged off Abby and Deon's assisting hands. He stood up, revealing a white handprint on his face, opposite of his black eye. The skin around the white handprint was glowing pink.

"Jeremy," Ray said, relaxing his arms and opening his fist. "I didn't—" With Jeremy's back toward Ray and his face slightly turned to the side, Ray could only see his own handprint on his son's cheek.

Jeremy rotated his head slowly to glare over his shoulder at Ray with contempt. Something else was surfacing through the hatred as the corners of his lips quivered, his brows drooped at the ends, and his eyes misted. He pulled his gaze away from his father as if he was unable to sustain his assaulting glare under the weight of hurt that swelled.

He turned and walked around his father toward the door. Ray did not stop him. His luggage remained in the room, while he walked down the hallway to the kitchen.

Abby and Deon watched Ray for a moment.

"I can go check on him, make sure he's okay," Deon offered.

"Maybe after a minute," Abby recommended. "Give him some space to cool off."

"Yeah, yeah. Good idea," Deon agreed.

"Sifu," Abby said softly, "are you okay?"

Ray blinked a few times before he sat on the office chair at the head of the meeting table. He propped his elbows on the table and buried his face into his hands. He didn't say anything. He didn't cry. He just breathed into his hands. "I'll be fine," he finally said. "I just need a minute."

"Deon, why don't you come with me to the kitchen? We'll look for that first aid kit, and I'll patch you up. Jeremy might be in there, so we'll take care of him too," Abby suggested.

"Sounds good," Deon replied.

The two of them walked out and closed the door behind them, leaving Ray sitting at the head of the table by himself in the room full of worn, discordant items. At first, he didn't think about anything, then too many thoughts crowded his mind. He thought about Melanie. He thought about Jamie. He thought about Jeremy. He looked at his left palm. It still stung. He rubbed it a few times. But when the stinging wouldn't dissipate, he slumped into the chair and dropped his hands onto the armrests.

His mind flipped through his memories of Jeremy's childhood, and he never recalled spanking him. Words and time-outs worked for disciplining him. He had never felt the sting of Jeremy's skin against his own until tonight. Then his mind jumped to Jeremy's words, and he flipped through his memories of Melanie. A sudden rush of sorrow and remorse welled up in him. He didn't know what to do with the deluge of emotions.

His hands gripped the armrests. *I don't know how to do this*, he thought silently. He continued to sit quietly by himself. He didn't cry. He didn't move. He just sat.

. . . .

Twenty minutes later, Abby returned with the first aid kit.

"May I sit with you, Sifu?" she asked.

"Please," he replied.

She sat down next to him on an office chair that didn't match his at all. She set the first aid kit on the table. "Deon is with Jeremy right now. I patched them both up. They're going to be okay. All minor wounds. Jeremy is icing his black eye and his face. He should be fine."

"Thanks."

"Can I take care of your wounds?" she asked.

He looked at her and responded with a half smile. "Please."

She opened the kit and took out some bandages, antiseptics, gauze, and tape. "If only we had some of your magic Chinese ointment from the studio, that would take care of most of our hurts," she said blithely.

"Most of them," he concurred with a small smile.

She treated the cuts on his hands first. His knuckles had some scrapes and the back of his hands had a couple of small cuts. "You know, Jeremy is an angry teenager. Teenagers these days have a lot to be angry about." She talked as she treated him but kept her eyes on his wounds. "He's figuring things out—figuring out the world, figuring out himself. He didn't mean those things he said."

"Yes, he did. I never heard him express those things before now. I didn't know he thought all that. I don't understand him."

"He's not that easy to understand. One thing is clear though: he's hurting."

"He's been hurting for a while."

She started to treat the cuts on his forearm. "When you're hurting, you'll say all kinds of things you don't truly mean. You lash out at people who love you. I know you didn't mean to hit him."

"It just happened. I wasn't thinking. I should never have done that."

"I know. He said some very hurtful things to you. It doesn't warrant what you did, but that would've been hard for any father to take."

"I should be better."

She began to treat the wounds on his neck. Bruises in the shape of fingerprints decorated both sides of his neck—compliments of

Gordon. "I know you're a good father, Sifu. I see what you do for Jamie and Jeremy. I didn't know Melanie, but I'm also sure you were a good husband to her. What Jeremy said about you being responsible for the bad that's happened can't be true. It can't be your fault." She looked at him sincerely.

He looked away and said, "He may be right."

"About what? That you're a bad father and husband?"

"About me being responsible for Melanie's death."

Abby took her hands off of Ray's neck, leaned back slightly and looked at his face again for an explanation. His eyes remained fallen toward the side. His countenance fell.

She took a few more items out of the first aid kit and laid them on the table. She unwrapped a couple of bandages and put some antibiotic cream on her finger. She began to treat the wounds on his face.

"I don't know if this is my place to ask. You don't talk about your late wife with us at the studio. I guessed it was very personal." She applied the antibiotic cream to his cheek and brow. "So, please tell me if I'm overstepping my bounds."

Her strokes on his face were soothing. She had a tender touch that eased him. In Wing Chun practices, he had physical contact with her, but he had not known the softness of her fingertips on the soreness of his wounds. He had the urge to ask for her to apply a little more antibiotics, but she did so without him asking. Every so often, her warm palm brushed his cheek.

"May I ask," she continued, "how did Melanie die?"

He wasn't sure how to respond at first. The last time he was asked that question was in a grief and bereavement support group a year and a half ago, which he attended only once.

"I'm not being nosy," she explained. "It's just that I see how it affects you. But if it's not something you can talk about, forget I asked. I don't need to know." She applied a small bandage above his brow with a delicate touch.

He took a deep breath and said, "It's okay. I can tell you how Melanie died."

Not Easily Broken

Chapter 16
Melanie

"Mel and I were married for fifteen years," Ray began. He felt that telling about how they lived together was the natural way to begin the story about how she died. Starting from the beginning seemed to be the way to tell about the ending. Right?

"We married young—24 years old, fresh out of college," he continued with a tender smile. "We met at M.I.T. in engineering calculus. There weren't too many women in the engineering field, you know. One day I noticed her sitting at the other end of my row in this massive lecture hall. Her tannish blonde hair draped over her shoulders. She wore a black printed T-shirt of the Bee Gees and these short shorts." He smiled with mild embarrassment. "Everything about her glowed except for one thing. She was chewing on her pencil eraser. That disgusted me."

Abby smiled caringly, though somewhat uncomfortably.

Ray noticed her awkward smile. But he enjoyed the sweetness of the reminiscence and felt he had to finish what he started. "I *had* to meet her. But there were thirty students between her and I in our row. When the professor adjourned the session, I jumped up from my seat and literally climbed over and crawled under people to get through the crowd. I must've stepped on several toes and elbowed a couple of ribs. I was about to lose her as I saw her go out the door, and I was still sandwiched between a large fellow and a couple of chit-chatty girls."

He chuckled and ran his fingers through his hair. "I finally got out the door and saw her at the bike racks as she was unlocking her bicycle."

Abby nodded. She stayed attuned and maintained a deliberate focus.

"I approached her, but I honestly didn't know what I was going to say," Ray said, becoming a little animated. "I mean, I had never approached a girl before. Did I mention girls were a rarity in our engineering program? I ran all kinds of lines through my mind—ones I heard from friends, from television shows, from jokes. I couldn't come up with anything, but I had to get to her before she jumped on her bike and rode off."

As Ray's face lit up, Abby reflected sympathetic delight upon seeing his joy. His enjoyment in strolling down memory lane became a little infectious.

He continued with growing enthusiasm as he delved into his story, "I said to her, "Excuse me, I want to inform you as a concerned member of the M.I.T. community that eraser consumption inhibits the C-fiber firing in your neural synapses and can cause memory distortion."" Ray chortled like a little kid.

He said, "I don't even know how I came up with that! Her response to me was, 'Really?' She laughed at me like I was a guy in a Pokemon costume."

Abby giggled at his reference. "I have to admit your pick-up line is pretty original."

He continued, "She asked, 'Is that research well-confirmed by experimental data? Because your thesis implies that memory is stored somewhere in the neural system. Many reputable philosophers would contend that memory is stored in an immaterial mind. You're not a pure physicalist, are you?'" Ray had the largest grin while he shook his head; it was like he heard the sweetest words. "Oh, she was something. Just from that response I knew I must've found the one. She had this smile like she was tickled by my quirky approach. I said, 'Yes, it is confirmed by some dissertation from Montana… I think.' Well, that started a whole conversation between us."

"Can't believe that worked," Abby commented.

"Me either! I asked her where she was heading. She said, 'The Student Union.' I said, 'Me too!' I lied, of course. I had a dentist appointment, which I skipped. I got two cavities that year. We walked across the M.I.T. campus to the Student Union. We got fries and talked about the composition of erasers. That was fascinating for us. What exactly are erasers made out of anyways?" He pondered joyfully.

"Oh, I was such a nerd," he teased himself. "Fortunately for me, she was too."

"Sounds special," Abby commented warmly.

"I haven't gotten to special yet. Special came later."

"I see."

"Is this uncomfortable for you?"

"No, no. Please go on. I want to hear this."

Ray was relieved, because he was enjoying retelling his romance story. "At first it was fun, but weird, like a good weird. I was so nervous. I had never gone out with a girl before. I didn't know if a beautiful, intelligent Caucasian girl like her would go for a cheesy, Asian guy like me. I thought it was strange that I found myself attracted to a Caucasian girl. I always imagined myself finding a nice Asian girl with glasses and a ponytail, like my mother expected. She was like…" He searched for the words with a glint in his eyes.

"It was the short shorts, wasn't it?" Abby kidded.

"Thanks. Those *were* some nice shorts," he agreed. "But there was something else. Something about her soul that emanated a kind of humanity I had not seen in others. There was something about her that was missing in me. She was captivating, I tell you. She was like a good book I couldn't put down."

"Whoa. That's deep. What was it?"

"You know, to be honest. I'm still not totally sure. But when I was with her, I benefited from whatever it was that she had inside of her."

"This is why you miss her?" Abby asked with sympathetic care laced with a tad of selfish disappointment.

"I miss a lot of things about her. But yeah, I think you're right," he looked at his gently folded hands on the table. "That has to be one of the major things I miss about her. She made me feel more… whole."

"I'm sorry. That's a hard thing to lose," she said plainly.

"Well, don't let me wallow too much. Going back to the story, we discovered we both had quirky interests that we didn't admit to others. To this day, I still won't admit some of them to other people. That's how it began for us. We hit it off with our nerdiness." Ray sighed through his smile, entranced in his own world.

"Uh-huh," Abby muttered.

"So we dated," he carried on. "Well, we hung out. We met up after calculus class for fries twice a week. We did that for a semester. We didn't have that determine-the-relationship talk yet. Is that what the kids still call it these days?"

"Not sure," Abby said, "but I get it."

"Okay. Well, we had that talk over winter break, and that's when it all began."

"That's good," Abby said, "because sometimes it never happens, and the girl is left wondering, 'What?'" She chuckled awkwardly. "You know, girls think a guy might like her, but she can't tell because the guy never comes out and says it. It becomes a guessing game. It's very confusing."

He went on, "After that talk, it was time to meet the parents."

"Wasted no time, huh?" Abby commented.

"We were both pretty calculated people. She met mine first. I grew up with only my mom, since my dad was a drunk and a cheater who ran out on us when I was ten."

"I'm sorry. I didn't know that," Abby said with a different tone of interest.

Ray replied, "Nothing to be sorry about. It was for the better. My father's drinking went from bad to hellish. He was bitter. He felt stuck with us—stuck in a life he didn't want. He started getting physical with Mom—shoving her, throwing things at her. I was pretty frightened as a boy. I hate to admit it, but I wished he would leave us. Then, one day, he did. So, it was just my mom, my little sister, and me. That's what got me started in Wing Chun."

"Wow, really?" Abby sounded amazed. "I mean it's interesting hearing your history and your motivation for Wing Chun."

"I figured I was the man of the house now. My mother had been terrorized, and I didn't ever want that happening to her again. I had a little sister to look out for. I started learning Wing Chun when I was ten at the local community center for free. When I got a part-time job at the age of fourteen, I was able to join a regular Wing Chun school."

"It's quite amazing you were that dedicated at a young age. Most teenagers would've been saving up their money to go out to the movies or buy a car. What did your mom think of you doing Wing Chun?"

"I was motivated by my brokenness. Brokenness can be a powerful motivator, especially when you want to make sure you don't go back to that place again. My mom was all for me doing Wing Chun. Being a single mother working a job and a half, she didn't have much time for us. The Wing Chun was at least a constructive recreation to occupy my time. It kept an angry kid like me off of the streets and out of trouble. And, it helped to keep the big bullies off of me. Anyway, I didn't mean to sidetrack."

"No, I like hearing this," Abby insisted. "I appreciate learning about your story. It's rich."

"Well, back to the story about Melanie."

"Ah, yes."

"Mel and my mom hit it off. That was a relief. But meeting her parents was a whole different kind of awkwardness. They weren't too keen on me being Asian. On top of that, they were clueless about Chinese people. I went over to their house for dinner. They served fried chicken and asked me if I needed chopsticks and soy sauce!"

Abby snickered. "Sorry. But even I'm not that bad as a white girl."

"For them to get comfortable with me was a long process, and it required a lot of patience from me to not be offended by their many unknowingly semi-racist remarks. However, that experience brought Mel and I even closer together." Ray looked at the blank wall in front of him. Then he came to and looked at Abby to say, "Sorry. I'm probably boring you with all the details."

"Oh, no," Abby replied politely. "Not at all."

"Okay," he said and continued. "We dated for two years while in college and got married the month after graduating from M.I.T. We couldn't wait."

"Mm, I see," Abby reflected.

"We did all kinds of things together, liking making this contraption." Ray reached into his backpack and pulled out the sci-fi looking device that was the size of two VHS tapes stacked on top of each other with the copper wires in a glass cylinder attached to the side of it. "Like this."

"What is it?"

"It's... nothing." He turned the large dial on it and pushed the buttons. "We never got it to work."

"But you carry it around with you?"

"As a token, I suppose. Of what? I don't know. Maybe as a token of something broken."

"It looks... interesting."

"It was fun to work on. This thing here conjures up so many memories of us."

Abby took the sci-fi device from Ray and examined it. "No kidding."

Ray took the device back from her. "It sounds dumb, but I feel like this thing is a part of me."

"Interesting."

"Well, as you could see, she blessed me with two children. One I adore to death, and the other I want to strangle to death, but I love them both dearly. She and I had all kinds of dreams for family vacations, for what we would do after the kids went off to college, and for what our retirement would be like. We had it mapped out. Merely dreaming up the future together was exciting."

Abby's sympathy emerged on her face. "I can't even imagine."

"Two years ago," Ray said, like he was beginning a new act in a play. His tone changed. "Jamie was four years old, and Jeremy was 13. Jamie started preschool and Jeremy was graduating from middle school and starting high school that year. It was a big turning point for our family." His voice became solemn. "One night on April 7, to be exact, I came home in a crappy mood. I don't remember why exactly. I think it was some combination of a stressful day at my job, working an extra two hours, bad traffic, and rude drivers. I was recently promoted to Lead Engineer in Research and Development at Miracom Systems. There were a lot of new pressures. You know? It's no small thing to work at Miracom, the leading company in telecommunications, specializing in high-powered radars and satellites. I was in charge of the department that developed new products and systems and researched ways for improvements. I loved my job, but I felt the weight of the new role. So I came home that night, and…"

Ray paused. His eyes roamed the surface of the table. When they stopped, he said, "We needed eggs."

He paused again, but his eyes didn't move. He blinked a couple of times and continued, "The eggs were for Jamie's Easter egg decoration at preschool. It was some activity that all the kids were doing. We both forgot about it, and Jamie was supposed to have it done and brought to the school the next day. She asked me to go pick up some from the store while she made dinner.

"I had just walked through the front door. It was already getting late, since I worked the extra two hours. It was 6:30 PM. I said to her…" He took a deep breath. "'Let me go get it later.'

"She said from behind the kitchen counter, 'But Jamie needs time to decorate the eggs tonight.'

"I said to her, 'Why didn't you text me about this earlier, then I could've gone to the store on my way home? Now I have to go back out after I just got home?'

"'I'm sorry,' she said, 'but I didn't realize we were out of eggs until I looked in the fridge.'

"I tossed my backpack down on the floor and said, 'I come home. No "hello." No kiss. No hug. No welcome. Just, "We need eggs." I paced up and down the living room a couple of times, before I said, 'Look,'" Ray said with a stiff index finger on a half-extended arm pointing at the wall in front of him, like he was speaking to an imaginary person, "'I'm tired,' I told her. 'If you want the eggs now, why don't you go get them?'

"She was annoyed, I could tell. She was chopping vegetables. She didn't say anything for a minute. Then she said she needed me to run this errand. She said she had been cleaning and taking care of Jamie. She was tired too, and she was making dinner."

"I said, '*I'm* tired. I've been at the office all day trying to learn the new systems and manage my team while Miranda breathes down my back. Just let me unwind, sit on the couch for a minute and watch some T.V.'" Ray re-enacted the same intensity of frustration as when he first said it to Melanie, except there was a crack in his voice. "I said to her, 'While I'm at work, you get the luxury of being at home anyway. You haven't been out all day. You can go out for 15 minutes to get eggs! Dinner can wait an extra 15 minutes for you to get back.'"

Abby raised her eyebrows.

Ray noticed and said, "Like I said, I was in a crappy mood. And I was a jerk. She stopped cutting the vegetables and looked at me silently from the kitchen while I sat on the couch. I saw her from the corner of my eyes. She rinsed her hands and came over to me."

Ray paused again, rubbed the back of his neck, and exhaled.

"Normally, a fight would've occurred. That was what was supposed to happen next—a fight. But something was different."

Ray was visibly agitated. He crinkled his face. "When she came over, I was ready. I was ready for her to tell me how insensitive I was and how being a homemaker didn't mean she sat at home all day eating Bon-Bons. That, being a homemaker was a real job and I needed to show her more respect. I was ready for that fight." He chewed on the next thoughts, or perhaps the next thoughts chewed on him. "But it never came. We didn't fight." He shook his head. "We were off. We didn't do what should've happened next."

"What happened?" Abby asked.

"She came over," he said with a soft voice, "and sat next to me. She said to me…" His voice broke. His nose turned pink and ran. A trembling frown formed at one corner of his mouth as he continued, "She said, 'I'm glad you're home. I know your job has been hard lately. You rest. I'll get the eggs.' She kissed me on the cheek and then just got up, got her keys, and went to the garage."

He wiped the drainage from his nose. His lips trembled, blurring his pronunciations. "I heard her turn on the engine and pull out of the garage. I heard her close the garage door. The thought crossed my mind to run out and stop her. I thought of telling her I was sorry for being a jerk. I'll get the eggs. But instead, I stood my ground and I felt like I had won. It was 6:42 PM." Tears flowed down his cheeks and over his lips.

Abby waited patiently while he cried.

Tears seeped into his mouth, blurring his words. He wiped his upper lip with the back of his thumb. "Fifteen minutes later—6:57 PM.—I received a call from the police. They told me Melanie was in an accident with a drunk driver outside the grocery store. They told me to come right away."

Abby touched his hand lightly, but Ray retracted his hand.

He wiped his tears and continued, "I told Jeremy to watch Jamie. I stormed out of the house and drove out there as fast as I could go. There were police cars, fire trucks, and paramedics. Red lights flashed everywhere. The accident was on the street right outside the grocery store's parking lot. Her car was mangled. Glass was everywhere. She was struck on the driver's side as she pulled out of the driveway. As I got out of my car and ran to her, I saw her in the driver's seat through the cracked windshield."

He choked, speaking through his sobbing. "There was blood on her. Her face was contorted. She was in pain.

"They used the jaws-of-life to take her out of the car. There must've been seven officers and firefighters working to get her out. It took them ten minutes to cut open the car and pull her out."

He wiped his eyes with his fingers. "I should've gone to the store. It should've been me."

Abby reasoned, "You can't think that you should've died instead of her. I know there's the guilt of losing a loved one, but it wasn't your fault. You can't beat yourself by thinking you should've died in her place."

"But I wouldn't have died," Ray argued emphatically. "That's the point. She was struck by a low-riding sports car. It was a Ford GT. She drove a Mini-Cooper. I drive the SUV, a Chevy Traverse. I calculated it. If it were me instead of her, the sports car would've hit my SUV too low to kill me. It would've practically gone under me. I calculated the dimensions of the vehicles, the velocity based on how far apart the two vehicles were after impact, the angle of impact, and the amount of force based on the damage. The math worked out. It wouldn't have killed me. But with her Mini-Cooper, the Ford GT hit her dead on. I should have gone instead of her!"

Abby was quiet.

He resumed, "I held her head for a total of four seconds while she was on the stretcher being wheeled into the ambulance. I couldn't go in the ambulance with the paramedics because they were fighting to keep her alive. I would've been in the way."

"I followed the ambulance to the hospital." He tried to say something but his words were choked by his sobs. So he repeated, "She died on the way to the hospital—while I was driving behind her." He wept.

For a moment, Ray cried as he slumped back in his chair with his head hanging over his chest. The teardrops tapped on his shirt. Abby didn't say a word, but sat there with him, watching his body tremble with each choking sob.

When his weeping subsided, he continued reflectively, "If only she had fought with me that night. Why didn't she? I insulted her. Why didn't she fight with me? She was a strong woman. She didn't take crap from me or anyone else. If she had fought with me, I would've conceded and gone. I always concede eventually. Something was off that night. It wasn't right."

"I'm very sorry," Abby said.

"Instead, she went, because I was too tired and I wanted to watch

T.V. She went because I wanted to watch T.V.," he repeated louder. "During those fifteen minutes, I *watched* T.V.! But I can't remember what I watched. Some stupid show."

Ray laughed through a burst of tears. "I was watching some stupid show that I can't even remember now. It wasn't even a good show! I wish she had fought with me that night," he murmured. He inhaled and his breathing stuttered. "I haven't watched TV ever since."

He wiped his cheeks with his palms. Then, he held his left hand in front of him. "While I held her head in those four seconds, she muttered something to me. It was just two words. I heard her mumble, 'No crates.'"

"No crates," Abby repeated scooting to the edge of her seat. "What did that mean?"

"Nothing!" Ray shouted. "It didn't make sense." He closed his eyes and furrowed his brows when he said, "It was hard to clearly hear her last words through the paramedics shouting, the commotion from the bystanders, the wind blowing, and the blood in her mouth!" His face muscles tensed and his tear-covered lips pursed.

"I asked her to repeat it," he said, "but she couldn't." He shook his head with his eyes closed. "I thought the last words I would ever hear from her were 'I'll go get the eggs.'" He opened his eyes and went on, "But I replayed what she mumbled over and over again in my head and later realized with clarity what she said."

"What?" Abby asked, prodding with anticipation.

"'No craze.'" He said with tragic defeat in his voice. "Her final words to me were not 'No crates.' It was 'No craze.'"

"No craze?" Abby repeated. "That doesn't make sense either, does it?"

"Of course it does!" he snapped. "Don't you get it? Craze is craziness. Craziness is chaos. Chaos is a lack of control. 'No craze' meant no chaos—be in control! She knew she was dying. She knew it was up to me now. I was becoming the solo parent, and I had to be in control. *I had* to keep this family together. *I had* to take care of it. *I had* to make sure everyone would be okay. I was in control."

"Are you sure?" she questioned sensitively but skeptically. "I mean I could see the connection you're making, but could that be a stretch? Maybe she meant something else, or maybe she actually said something else."

"You weren't there, Abby," Ray contended. "I know that's what she said, and it makes sense. She was weak and barely conscious. She wasn't going to form an eloquent paragraph for me. Saying two words was all she could muster. 'No craze' made the most sense—be in control, don't let the family fall apart."

Abby watched him with serious consideration, like she was thinking intensely about his reasoning.

"I know those two words don't seem like the most ideal last words from your dying soul mate," Ray acknowledged, "but I know my wife. I know how her mind worked. She was a nerd like me. It wasn't unlike her to say something that sounded unusual to others but made sense to me. I clung to her last words to me. 'Keep it together, Ray' is what she basically charged me with."

More tears flowed. He looked down again. He mumbled, "I tried."

Ray stopped talking. The two sat looking at the scuffed, dusty table.

Abby shifted in her seat and inquired, "So, what happened to the drunk driver?"

Ray looked away and a dark anger flushed over his countenance. Creases appeared on his face. A few heavy breaths entered him. "We don't know. He fled the scene and wasn't found."

"What? How was that possible?" she asked.

"He ran."

"How could a drunk guy who was probably injured get far?"

"I don't know. Somehow he managed to get away and the police didn't find him. The car he drove likely wasn't his. The vehicle was unregistered, so the license plates didn't give us any information on him. Dozens of open beer bottles were found inside his car along with a half-smoked marijuana joint."

Abby appeared upset. "The police!" she exclaimed. "Can they catch any perpetrator? Unbelievable!"

"I tried to find him myself to bring him to justice. He needs to be held accountable for what he did!" Ray said with spite. "You can't just take someone's wife and not suffer any consequences. Our world can't work that way."

"Did you get any leads on who he was or where he was?"

Ray shook his head once. "I looked for any surveillance cameras that might've caught him. None. There were a few eyewitnesses that provided some sketchy descriptions, but nothing specific enough for a sketch artist to compose a drawing of him. Without something identifiable on him, there was virtually nothing to go on.

"But I snuck into the impound lot where his car was detained. I took pictures of it. I searched the internet and social media sites. I looked for any matches of this car that could link it to the driver. I tried tracking the previous owner. I hacked into the police records to get the fingerprints

Melanie

they lifted from the car. No matches came up. He might not have been a U.S. citizen, had no driver's license, no social security number, no passport, nothing. He was a ghost."

"You wouldn't think that in this day a person can remain completely anonymous," she commented. "Everything is available online about everyone."

"He needs to be found and brought to justice in order to make things right again," Ray declared plainly.

"I'm sure not finding him hinders you from moving forward," she said. "But stuff like this never goes unaccounted for. It sounds cliché, but he'll get caught someday."

"I think about him almost daily. I'm not a hateful person, but I hate this man. I hate him for the destruction he brought on my family. I hate him for taking my wife. I hate him for not taking responsibility. I hate him for the freedom he still enjoys."

"I had no idea you were carrying this," she said in a soft way that contrasted his hardened, cold exterior.

"I don't call Melanie's death an accident. I call it murder. That's what he did. By fleeing the scene, he committed murder in my eyes."

"You're hurting. Anyone would be," Abby said.

"I'm beyond hurt," Ray said plainly. "I'm angry."

He smoldered. She started to reach out to touch Ray's arm when Deon opened the door and stepped in. She brought her hand back. Ray wiped away a few streaks of tears on the bottom of his jaw with the back of his hand.

"Sorry, am I interrupting?" Deon asked, holding two cups. "I can come back later, because this looks intense."

"No, you're fine," Ray answered and sniffed.

"I brought some water. Coach always said to stay hydrated. With all the action today, we probably could use some hydration."

"Good idea," Ray said, glancing over his shoulder.

Deon placed the two cups in front of them and sat down. His wounded arm was bandaged with gauze and tape. "Jer is in the kitchen. He's going to be all right, I think."

"Thank you for looking out for him," Ray said.

"You know, Sifu," Deon said with an upbeat optimism, "I know things didn't turn out the way they was supposed to. But man, we kicked butt today! I mean, there were like fifty of them with guns and knives, and we took them out, dog!" He reached out to Ray for a fist bump.

Ray raised a loosely clenched fist and tapped his knuckles against Deon's with a tiny smile on one side of his mouth. He complimented,

"We made a good team."

"Heck, yeah, we made a good team!" Deon cheered with a huge smile that squished his big, black cheeks out and upward, forming two big dimples. "I have to say that all of us getting out of that mad house was a miracle. I mean, what was that? Four houses in one with a creepy basement and a secret tunnel that went forever into some crazy white folks' home!"

"It was an elaborate establishment for child-trafficking," Abby stated. "Whatever Jamie's kidnapping is about, these people know what they're doing."

"We need to get to the bottom of this," Ray said. "We have to figure out why they wanted Jamie so badly—why this PH person wants her."

"You really upset Gordon when you mentioned TAGGAT ACT and PH," Abby observed. "That has to be the key to solving this."

"I agree," Ray concurred. "We have to find out what TAGGACT ACT is, who PH is and how this involves Jamie."

"What about the mess in your home, Sifu?" Deon asked. "My grandma and I had our home broken into twice, so I feel your pain."

"I have to deal with that separately," Ray said. "Right now, we need more clues to plan our next move."

"How are we going to get more clues?" Deon asked.

The three were silent with blank stares.

"I'm not sure," Ray said, "Now that Gordon knows we're on to him and what all of you look like, he might be too careful for us to track his movements."

"Or maybe," Jeremy walked in, saying, "we could do something with this." He pulled out of his back pocket a slim, silver portable hard drive. He set it on the table by Ray, then walked around to take a seat next to Deon.

They were surprised to see him.

"What is this?" Ray asked.

"When we were moving the furniture to build that barricade, I saw a furnace vent behind the lazy boy chair," Jeremy explained. "I saw something silvery through the grates. So I opened it with my pocketknife and found this inside the vent. There's got to be something important on this hard drive if it was hidden in a vent behind a chair." He took quick glances at Ray, but didn't actually look at him while he spoke.

"This is amazing, Jeremy," Abby praised. "How in the world did you even notice something in the furnace?"

"That is pretty cool, man. You have some sharp eyes," Deon affirmed. "But I'm guessing you picked up these skills from a certain way of life. I know."

"Let's just say," Jeremy said cryptically, "my activities in the last year helped me learn to spot small, shiny things really well."

"So we didn't come out empty-handed, after all," she added.

Ray nodded. "This is really good." He looked for eye contact with Jeremy, who kept staring at the silver hard drive. "Jeremy, are you okay?"

Jeremy didn't answer. He looked away from the hard drive and off to the side.

Ray said, "Listen. Me hitting you, that—"

"I'm fine. You didn't hurt me," Jeremy cut him off. Still he made no eye contact. "I just want to find Jamie. Let's get into that hard drive."

Ray licked his lips and redirected his attention to the silver hard drive. "Okay," he conceded and refocused his mind on the task before them.

"Hey, you all," Deon chimed in. "I want to be here to help, but I gotta bounce. I haven't been home all day. It's 11 o'clock. My grandma is going to blow from worrying."

"You don't have to be here, Deon. Thank you," Ray said. "You've done plenty for my family. Please get on home to your grandma."

"I should head out too," Abby said to Ray. "Pastor James gave the impression that he didn't expect all four of us to stay the night. Looks like he's burning the midnight oil in his office and maybe waiting for the two of us to exit." She said to Deon, "Come on, I'll take you home."

"Thank you both." Ray stood up. "Thanks for the talk," he told Abby.

She simply smiled.

Jeremy glared at the two of them.

"You have to get some sleep as well," she told Ray. "I know how urgent this is, but you can't keep going without much rest. Your body won't function. Your mind can't concentrate. After getting a taste of what we're up against, you need to be at 100 percent."

"Thanks for drilling that into me. We'll rest up," Ray said and peered over at Jeremy. "We'll tackle this early in the morning."

"I'll come back tomorrow to help, Sifu" Abby said.

As Deon turned to leave the room with Abby, he nodded toward the silver box on the table. "Can't wait to see what's on that hard drive. It has be good."

Not Easily Broken

Chapter 17
Silver

Ray half awoke to a knocking on the door. The door cracked open. "Hello?" someone said. Ray tried to open his eyes all the way, but his eyelids were too heavy. Then the door pushed open enough for a head to poke through. Through his half opened eyes, he saw Pastor James peeking in.

"Good morning," Pastor James greeted him with an exaggerated cheerfulness.

"Morning," Ray mumbled groggily. He slowly rose from the couch.

"Oh, don't get up," Pastor James said with just his head poking through the door. "I didn't mean to disturb you." He glanced over at Jeremy, who was sound asleep on the cot. "I just wanted to check on you both and make sure you're okay. I left at midnight last night and noticed you were sleeping."

"We're fine. Thank you, Pastor James," Ray replied.

"Glad you got some rest from what seemed like an eventful and challenging day. I'm heading out to an early morning breakfast Bible study, but the church secretary will be here in two hours. I'll leave a note, letting her know you're here."

"We appreciate it."

"I'll be back to check on you later."

"Okay, sure."

Pastor James retracted his head and closed the door tightly.

"Creep," Jeremy said with his eyes still closed.

Ray looked at his phone to see that it was only 5:30 AM. His body felt sore. He lay back on the couch and closed his eyes. His mind began to stir a host of thoughts, reviewing the events of the previous few days and wondering what was on the mysterious silver hard drive. After fifteen minutes, he arose and pulled out his laptop.

While the laptop booted up, he looked at Jeremy and the light-purple handprint on his face.

"I can tell when you're watching me," Jeremy said without opening his eyes.

Ray thought for a moment about his first words of the day to his son.

Then he asked, "Does your face hurt?"

"What do *you* think?" Jeremy turned toward the wall, away from Ray.

"I can get a warm towel to put on it for you. Heat will help—"

"I know, I know. Will help the blood circulate and heal faster. Don't worry about it. Besides, the bruise on my cheek matches the bruise on my eye."

Ray watched Jeremy for a moment. The hardness of his son left him speechless. He wanted to explain his actions to him, but what valid explanation could he offer. He knew Melanie would've been upset with him for striking their son. He could hear what she would say: "Nothing warrants you hitting our son. You need to go make this right!" Ray wanted to make things right. *How could I have lost control? How will I recover from this with Jer?* If Melanie were here, she would serve as a buffer and ease the tension so that they could all talk it out. Right now, all Ray could get was his son's backside.

His laptop booted up and chimed just as his cell phone received a text message. It was from Abby, saying she would be over at 8:00 AM. *Guess she couldn't sleep much either,* he thought. He looked at the portable, silver hard drive next to his hand. It could give him access to the mind of his enemy. After all, it must contain something substantial, even incriminating, for it to have been hidden in a furnace behind a leather easy chair. Gordon was already intensely displeased about Ray knowing about TAGGAT ACT and PH. What else would he find on this hard drive? How far down the rabbit hole could this little storage of data take him? That question could be answered in a few seconds. Digging into this hard drive could make him more of a prime target for his daughter's abductors. They wouldn't forgive him for possessing the amount of forbidden knowledge.

He placed his fingers around the silver hard drive, just when his phone rang. It was Fred.

"Yeah, Fred," Ray answered

"Hey buddy, how's it going?"

"Could be a lot better. Jeremy and I spent the night at the church. We're still here."

"Hope that was comfortable," Fred said sarcastically.

"Just glad that we had a safe place to stay."

"How's the search for Jamie?"

"After yesterday's dramatic disappointment, I have to give props to Jeremy for finding a mysterious portable hard drive in the home of Jamie's captor."

"No kidding." Fred reflected with high curiosity.

"I'm hoping this will give us a big lead. It might help us get to the bottom of what's going on."

"Good going."

"What's happening on your end? I'm guessing if you're calling, it can't be good."

"Miranda has been asking for you. You're really needed here. She wants us to work with Marvin and one of his other team members to crack down on this virus."

"What about Internal Investigations? Am I one of their prime suspects with my illegal activity and all?"

"There are no accusations yet, and, yes, they did discover your illegal use of company equipment for personal surveillance. They have locked you out of our system. But Thunder Queen doesn't care about that. Her main concern is this virus. You may have broken some company rules, but you're also the one standing between the virus and the company. That's all that matters to her."

"Where are we with a solution to the virus?"

"Not any better," Fred answered grimly. "Dealing with this crisis is sucking up all of our resources and manpower. The virus is complex and persistent. Plus, the harder we fight it, the more evident it becomes that there's someone working from the inside. We found traces of sabotage and efforts to aid the virus."

"Still no leads on who the mole is?"

"Nothing definitive. Only suspicions. The mole covers his tracks well."

"A lot of suspicion with no target to blame means everyone becomes a target. That'll eventually tear the company apart."

"Whoever is behind this, he... or she, is persistent. This person really wants Miracom's main server. It's serious."

"I can tell you how serious this is by the way my house was ransacked in search of the decryption code. The mole isn't working alone. He or she has help."

"I'm sorry about your home. I know all this happening while your daughter is missing is bad timing. Maybe the sooner we solve this the sooner you can get back into your home at least. Can you come in?"

"I can't come in yet, Fred. Not now. I need to see what's on this hard drive and come up with another plan to save Jamie. Getting Jamie back is my priority."

"I understand, buddy. I'll let Miranda know. She might erupt, but what can she do?"

"Besides, since Internal Investigations found out about my illegal use of company equipment, they might be all over me the minute I step in the building."

"Don't worry about that," Fred assured. "Marvin vouched for you. When the head of systems security sticks up for you, it goes a long way."

"Marvin stuck up for me?" Ray asked incredulously. "Not that I didn't think he wouldn't, but he's so timid. I can't imagine him sticking up at all! Good, old Marvin." He was warmed by the thought of Marvin fighting for him.

"He made a case for how loyal you are and how valuable you are in fighting this virus. So for now, I.I. is withholding any disciplinary actions or further interrogations until we are out of this crisis."

"Great," he said sardonically, "That means I'm safe as long as we're in crisis."

"Take what you can, buddy. Do you want me to tell Miranda when she should expect you to come in? You know the Thunder Queen will want an ETA."

"I can't say for sure, but I'll come up with a way to assist in the effort. I still need Miracom on my side to help me get Jamie back. I'll try to do something from this end. What do we know about this virus so far?"

"Only that it has begun to deliberately attack the main server. After a certain level of replication, it made the main server its primary objective."

"Okay. That means it must be targeting specific command files related to the main server." He silently thought for a moment.

"You still there?" Fred asked during the silence.

"Yeah."

"Marvin and I have tried every angle at solving this puzzle. We haven't come up with much, which is embarrassing. We've put up every kind of anti-virus software we could find or create to fight it. No use."

"Maybe," Ray said speculatively, "we don't have to fight it. Maybe, for now, we can give it what it wants."

"Come again. You want to give the main server to it?"

"Sort of." Ray scooted to the edge of his seat. "What if we create a series of bogus files with similar signatures to the command files in our main server, then upload them to our system? The virus will detect their signatures and be drawn to them. They could divert the attention of the virus and buy us time."

"Decoys!"

"Exactly."

"Genius."

"Send me the reports you and Marvin wrote up on the virus' behavior in targeting specific files. I'll create a decoy file. You and Marvin could use that as a template to replicate variations of it. If we can generate about fifty of these, that'll buy us a substantial amount of time until we can purge this virus for good."

"It's a solid plan. Marvin will be pleased he stuck up for you!"

"How's Marvin doing? This must be a lot of pressure on him."

"He's holding up, but he looks like he's been pulling all-nighters for the last few days. He's a mess."

"Poor kid. He's good at what he does, and he's a hard worker. This problem is beyond anyone to handle on his own."

"That's why we need you, man."

"By the end of today, I should know better when or if I can come into the office."

"I'll let Miranda know. And one more thing. Mr. Thornton will personally come to oversee our crisis. His words were, 'An executive presence is necessary for a speedy resolution.'"

"Miranda must be thrilled about that."

"Since Thornton's announcement, she's been barking at everyone. Just to warn you."

"Got it. Please tell Marvin 'Thank you' for me."

"You bet. I'm sending those reports to you right now."

For the next couple of hours, Ray entered into a focused mode of troubleshooting. He quickly reviewed the reports and worked on developing a file that had the same signatures as the satellite command files. He did not need to design an actual file, but merely the shell of one that looked like the real thing. As usual, his intense laboring emanated a must that made the room stuffy.

Jeremy finally awoke just as Ray finished and hit "send" to Fred with an encrypted file attachment of the decoy file. Then Ray sent a text message with the decryption code for the encrypted file to Fred.

Jeremy rolled over and sat up. "You're at it again."

"What?" Ray asked.

"You're working on something that requires a lot of intense brain energy. I can tell because the room smells like nerd. What was it? Were you cracking into the hard drive?"

"No," Ray said, expecting a backlash from his son. "I was architecting a file for the virus problem at Miracom."

Jeremy sighed with attitude and turned his head to the side. "Whatever. Let me know when you have time to work on saving your daughter."

"Jeremy," Ray said with defensive agitation, "after all that you've seen that I've done and been through in the last couple of days, don't talk to me like that. You've seen how I used my company's resources to track down Jamie. We still need Miracom."

"I'm getting a cola," Jeremy said as he got up to walk out of the room.

Ray looked at his phone as Jeremy walked by him. He saw that it was 8:25 AM. He wanted to begin digging into the silver hard drive. He picked it up to insert it into his laptop, but was interrupted by someone opening the door behind him.

"Good morning," Abby greeted them. "Hope you're rested."

Ray turned around. "Good morning. You're here early."

"That homeless man is still on the porch," she said. "He greeted me, opened the door for me, and wanted to welcome me with a 'good morning' kiss. That was weird."

"He must be friends with Pastor Pervert. I thought he was going to wake us up with a 'good morning kiss' too," Jeremy said, walking into the room.

"So what did you do?" Ray asked Abby.

"I smiled and scooted by him quickly before he could plant one on me!" she said with disgust. "I think he sleeps there all the time."

"I'm surprised Pastor Perv is okay with that," Jeremy remarked.

"Deon said he has a class this morning," she said, "but will drive himself over with his cousin's car after he's done. Should be around 11:00 AM, he said."

"That kid," Ray shook his head with a smile. "Can't believe his dedication. Just a couple of weeks ago, he tried to take me down. He doesn't have to do all this." He then looked tenderly at Abby and said, "And neither do you."

"Please, Sifu," she exclaimed, "Are you kidding? The police aren't helping and you can't do this on your own. If my daughter were missing, I would want all the help I could get."

"Get used to it," Jeremy said to Abby. "He always thinks he can handle everything by himself."

"Well," Abby said while looking at the hard drive on the table next to Ray's laptop, "is it time to uncover what's inside that?"

Ray turned his attention to the silver box. He sat in front of his laptop, while Abby sat adjacent to him and opposite of Jeremy. Ray held the silver box in his hand and looked at Abby and Jeremy as a cue for them to be ready. He plugged the hard drive into the USB port of his computer. After the laptop purred for a second, a message popped up on the screen: "Error: ID recognition invalid."

"What does that mean?" Abby asked with disappointment.

"It means the hard drive has a security function that allows it to recognize and play only on a specific computer," Ray answered.

"Great!" Jeremy said. "Our one lead to Jamie, and it's useless to us."

"Hold on, Jer," Ray said as he ejected the hard drive and disconnected it from his computer. "Don't give up just yet. I'm guessing because this belonged to Gordon, it only recognizes his computer. Remember that whole operation with cloning Gordon's phone? I bet he syncs his phone with his computer." Ray pulled up a menu on his screen.

"So you're thinking that everything needed to ID his laptop is also on his phone," Jeremy concluded.

"That's my bet," said Ray. He dragged and clicked a few times. "I'm importing all of Gordon's data from his phone into the system of my computer. I'm basically cloning Gordon's digital ID from his phone onto my laptop. Let's see if we can trick this hard drive into believing that I'm Gordon."

He plugged the hard drive back into his laptop. A new message popped up: "ID recognition verified." Then a series of folders appeared in the finder menu on his screen. The first folder that caught his attention was the one labeled, "Jamie."

With wide eyes and a clammy hand on the mouse, he automatically clicked on Jamie's name. A list of files came up. Ray clicked on each of them rapidly and briefly scanned them as the windows appeared. The files were reports on Jamie's biography, immediate family history, extended family tree, personal development, and daily schedules. The other files were Jamie's medical records, medical histories of her parents, her blood test results, and detailed summaries of her genetic design. There were even reports from the babysitter, Tracy, of Jamie's weekly activities and routines. As Ray clicked on the files, he began opening photos of Jamie—pictures taken of her outside of her school, at the playground, in her home, and in her bedroom.

"Oh, my goodness," Abby exclaimed with her hand over her mouth.

Ray's eyes widened further until the white around his pupils showed. Thin, red veins spidered all around the white of his eyes. His lips pursed as he fumed inside. He felt the sides of his face heat up. As his eyes scrolled down the list of files, he noticed the file entitled, "Conclusive Action." He clicked on it, opening a report that summarized a special TAGGATACT codon of Jamie's genetic design. He unconsciously read a bold-faced sentence out loud, "Jamie's TAGGATACT codon is confirmed. She is necessary and sufficient for genetic advancement."

What did this mean?

"What the—? They've been studying Jamie!" Jeremy cried.

Ray continued to methodically unearth the content on the silver hard drive with focus. He closed the "Jamie" folder and opened the next one labeled, "Gordon." They were files containing instructions and correspondences between Gordon and Marcus and between Gordon and Tracy. One of the correspondences indicated that Marcus was the "Tactical Field Handler." Some files contained direct orders from PH. PH's actual name was never mentioned in the files or reports—only referred to by those initials.

Ray began to grasp the complexity of his enemy; his opponent was structured, acted methodically, and had plenty of resources. His scanning eyes anchored on to a sentence in a set of instructions from Marcus to Gordon. He unconsciously read it aloud, "Genetic fit is confirmed. Proceed to extraction and delivery."

"The files repeatedly referred to Jamie's genetic make-up and the TAGGATACT," Abby pointed out.

"What is going on?" Jeremy asked. "Why are they so obsessed with her genes? This is freaking me out!"

"Me too, Sifu," Abby added. "This is no normal human trafficking."

"You were right before, Abby," Ray replied, "While we were in the car, you theorized that 'taggat act' referred to a genetic sequence." Ray closed his left hand into a tight fist while his right hand continued to surf the files. "I don't know what's going on, but we're going to figure this out."

He clicked on the folder labeled, "Affiliates." A list of file names appeared. He clicked on them and opened files containing the names of individuals and companies, contact information for them and pertinent access codes for security gates, locks, and logins. Their eyes ran through the myriad of names.

"What is this?" Abby asked.

"These are people and businesses connected with the organization that has Jamie," Ray said. "There are medical institutes, CEOs, VPs, restaurant chains, Tracy's information, and hundreds of other individual names."

"Wait, look." Jeremy pointed at the screen. "Officer Bohr. And look." He pointed further down the list. "There's Sergeant Pierce." Aren't those the same two cops that came to our house and let Tracy walk?"

"Now we know why they weren't helpful to us and were practically siding with Tracy," Abby commented.

"This section of the list are all police officers in Los Angeles," Ray stated. "It doesn't look like the entire police force is on here, but it's a substantial number of them. Even the Police Chief is listed."

"Crap. I knew it!" Jeremy blurted. "Never trust the po-po."

"Oh, no. I know that person," Abby said pointing at a name. "That's one of the board members of the biolab I work for. What are we up against? This is much bigger than we could've guessed."

"And for some reason, they want my daughter," Ray said coldly. "The more we uncover, the more we'll get to the bottom of this and devise a plan to retrieve Jamie. I'll tell you now. They can't have my daughter. Not unless I'm dead."

Ray's cold tone drew silent gazes from Abby and Jeremy.

"Let's keep digging," he stated.

As they had been flipping through the plethora of files, scanning some and carefully reading others, more than a couple of hours already passed.

He clicked on another folder that was labeled, "Locations." This folder contained maps—maps of Los Angeles, world maps indicating bases or structures of some sort in other countries, and schematics of buildings, including restaurants, grocery stores, nightclubs, warehouses, and both domestic and foreign military bases.

"All these maps," Abby noted. "Looks like they want to know where everything is at all times."

Ray commented, "Or they're planning something big."

Ray opened a particular file consisting of several pages of detailed, extensive layouts of the AmeriBank building in downtown Los Angeles. "Why is this building of special interest?"

One more folder left. It was labeled: "ApexGen." He clicked on it, but a window popped up, asking, "Enter password."

"Password protected!" Jeremy said.

"What could it be?" Abby asked.

"Let's see if it might be on Gordon's phone."

"Doubt it would be that easy," Jeremy opined pessimistically. "This looks like an important file too, just by the name of it."

Ray sifted quickly through the content on Gordon's phone. He entered various phone numbers, birthdates, address names and key words from text messages found on the phone. But they were all incorrect. "We have to get this file open," Ray snapped and banged the mouse on the table. "But how? There has to be a way. I know it's the key to telling us where Jamie is and how to get her back!"

"Why is it always the things that people don't want you to get into are the things you have to get into?" Abby asked.

"Now what?" Jeremy questioned.

"Let's just think for a moment," Ray responded. He looked down at the carpet and contemplated, then went back to surfing the contents on Gordon's phone.

"Wait," Jeremy said. "What was that?" He pointed to a message from Marcus that mentioned the access code for an online forum. "Try that."

Ray typed it in. A message appeared: "Password incorrect."

"Dang it!" Jeremy shouted.

They watched the screen, concentrating and thinking through the possibilities they could come up with.

"Dead end again," Jeremy said.

"Just concentrate. I know the answer will come to us," Ray urged.

There was a knock on the door.

They jolted out of their focus and turned to see a woman in her forties extend her head through the door.

"Excuse me," she said in a soft, delightful voice. "Sorry to bother you all. Pastor James told me you were here."

"Yes, hi," Ray greeted, rising from his seat. The others took the cue to rise as well. "You must be the office admin."

"I'm Cherish," she said with a big smile and opened the door all the way to step inside. "Please, you don't have to stand. I didn't want to bother you. Pastor James said you have a lot to figure out for yourselves. You're more than welcome to stay here."

"Thank you," Ray responded.

"Well, I'm only disturbing you to tell you that Mr. Mills is asking for you."

"Mr. Mills? I don't know a Mills."

"Yes, yes, you do. You met him. Everybody who comes to the church during the week meets Mr. Mills. He's the resident on our porch."

"Oh, the homeless man. I mean," Ray tried to excuse himself, "I didn't know that was his name."

"Yes, that's Mr. Mills. Anyways, he's asking for you and said he has something to share with you."

"Oh gosh," Abby responded.

"He's harmless," Cherish assured. "I know he's not too sightly, but he's a dear old man."

"Um, apparently, you haven't received his special good morning greeting," Abby retorted.

"We don't have time for this," Jeremy commented.

"It's up to you, Mr. Lee," Cherish said. "I'm just passing along a message. I can tell him you're too busy to come to the door if you don't want to be bothered by him."

Ray thought for a moment and conceded. "No, that's okay. I'll come out to see Mr. Mills."

"You're kidding, right?," Jeremy opposed. "You're wasting time on a kissing, homeless whack-job?"

"I wouldn't want him bothering Cherish," Ray replied. "It'll be quick. I'll just say, 'Hi.'"

He followed Cherish to the front door of the office. Cherish opened the door and called out cheerfully, "Mr. Mills."

The homeless man turned around.

"You asked for our friend, Mr. Lee. He's right here."

"Oh, goodie!" Mr. Mills cheered with a grin that bared his blackened gums.

"What can I do for you, Mr. Mills?" Ray asked. "Do you need food or money?"

"Nothing," Mills said, spraying as he pronounced the "th" sound.

"Nothing?" Ray repeated with befuddlement.

"Nothing you could do for me. I have everything I need."

"Then why did you ask to see me?"

"To tell you that you're friend has been looking for you."

"My friend? Oh, you mean Deon? The large, black fellow."

"No, no. Not him. A different man. The one in the grey car. Across the street."

Ray felt a chill on the back of his neck as he leaned a couple of inches to the left to look over Mills' shoulder with one eye. He saw the same grey sedan that stalked his family at his house! It was parallel parked across the street, directly in front of the church, with the driver sitting inside. He saw the firelight from the driver's cigarette.

Mills explained, "I figured he was your friend since he came here when you came here. He has been patiently waiting for you. I thought I should tell you, so you don't keep him waiting!"

Ray said, "Thank you, Mr. Mills. It was very thoughtful of you to alert me about my friend." As he strategized in his mind about what to do, he felt his forearm muscles contract and harden. His bottom lip curled inward. He thought about three different responses and the possible ramifications of each of them, but his impulse told him to do one thing. He rapidly evaluated that impulse. He had to decide soon.

Mills cackled, "He sure is patient! He just waits and watches, like he's waiting for a bus that will never come. I know what that's like. Ooh, them buses..."

Ray clenched his hands.

"Mr. Lee," Cherish said, "are you okay? Would you like to invite your friend in?"

Ray didn't blink. He was coming to a conclusion.

"By the way, is that purdy lady in there with ya?" Mills asked with a child-like chuckle.

"Yes, Cherish, I would like to invite him in." Ray sprang from his spot and darted out the door, shoving Mills to the side. He leapt down the flight of five steps. The engine of the grey sedan started. The driver backed up the car.

"Not this time," Ray muttered. He sprinted across the street, yelling, "Stop!" and slammed the driver's window with his palm, cracking it. He grabbed the door handle and yanked, but the door was locked.

The grey sedan lurched forward to pull out of the parking spot and burst down the street, but it only went a few feet and jerked to a halt when two enormous fists hammered on the hood of the car with such force and weight that it rocked the car. The driver and Ray followed the two fists up two large, rippling, black arms that met at a ferocious face.

"When the man tells you to stop, you stop!" Deon shouted.

Ray grinned from one corner of his mouth. He turned back to the driver, glaring at him through the window. "Open this door. Now!"

The driver took his hands off the steering wheel and raised his palms up in surrender. The firelight on his cigarette lit up brightly and two channels of smoke puffed from his nostrils, like upside-down smokestacks. "All, all right. Take it easy," the driver mumbled in a raspy voice with the cigarette between his lips. He slowly unlocked the door. But before he could reach for the doorhandle, Ray jerked the door open, grabbed the man, and seized him from his car. Ray slammed the man's back against the side of the car with his fists gripping the man's shirt and burying into the man's chest. "Who are you?" Ray shouted into the man's face.

The man turned his face to the side and winced. His cigarette fell out of his mouth. "Agh," the man rasped, "don't hurt me!"

"Talk," Ray demanded. "Who are you?"

"I know who you are. I know you can hurt me, but please don't." His raspy voice was like sandpaper with phlegm. He was an older man, perhaps in his late 50s. He had a thin layer of ash grey hair and a balding frontal scalp. The five folds across his forehead, caused by his brows pushing upward, were like a curtain fully scrunched up. He wore a pin-striped dress shirt under an 80's overcoat.

"Why have you been spying on my family? Are you working with Gordon? Did you ransack my house? Do you have something to do with the virus? Tell me!" Ray ordered. "Or I swear. I *will* beat it out of you.

Right now, I have no sympathy for you and whoever else is involved in making my life a living hell." He raised his right hand into an open palm, aimed directly at the stranger's face while shoving his left fist that still held his shirt deeper into the man's brittle chest.

"No, no, don't. Please. Listen. Agh!" He grimaced in pain. "Just, just listen. I can help you."

"What do you mean? Who are you?"

"I don't work with Gordon, but do you have his silver hard drive?"

"How do you know about that? You're one of them!" He pulled his hand back to strike.

"No! I'm not!" he shouted in his raspy voice. "But I used to be."

Ray halted his hand and looked at him in bewilderment.

"Like I said," the strange man said in a normal tone, "I can help."

Not Easily Broken

Chapter 18
Stranger

Ray dragged the strange man behind him by the collar through the church office's front door. Deon followed closely, scanning left and right for prying eyes.

"What is going on?" Cherish, the church administrator, asked in a high-pitched tone. "Is everything okay?" She shuffled sideways to follow Ray and the man he dragged into the church office.

"Everything's fine, Cherish," Ray minimized.

"Should I call the police?" she asked as she went for the phone on the desk.

"No!" the four of them said in unison.

"No police, please," Ray requested as he made his way to the conference room he stayed in. "You don't need to attract all that attention to the church, right? No crime has happened."

"I see, but this doesn't look right to me," she said, trying to keep up with Ray. "Should I call Pastor James?"

"No, don't do that!" Jeremy blurted as Ray scurried into the old conference room, still dragging the stranger.

"He means," Ray clarified from inside the room, "why disturb him? He's probably in an important meeting."

"Well, he is," she conceded, "but—"

"No need to trouble him over our private matters," Ray insisted. "I'll tell you if we need anything." He abruptly closed the door on Cherish as she was about to speak.

Ray shoved the stranger down onto a chair and stood in front of him, Jeremy stood at his side, Deon hovered over him from behind, and Abby stood by the door. The stranger looked up at his captors enclosing him, reading one face at a time.

"Who is he?" Jeremy asked Ray.

"I'm Stanley," the stranger responded.

"This is the stalker who's been outside of our house for the last couple of weeks."

"This is the creep you chased away the other night?" Abby asked.

"Now, now, creep is not quite the appropriate term for me," Stanley corrected her.

"What do you want with us?" Jeremy pointed his finger at Stanley's nose. "Talk! Don't think I won't beat your sorry face."

"Oh," Stanley said, "this is your son, Jeremy. My, this *is* an angry family."

Ray grimaced when he heard Stanley identify his son. The stalker's knowledge about his family upset him more. "How do you know my son?"

"I see, I see you already have been getting a little beating yourself," Stanley pointed out on Jeremy's face. "Yep, I know about Jeremy," he continued, "and about Jamie too. I also—"

"You said you used to work for the people who took Jamie," Ray interrupted.

"Yes, yes." Stanley looked off to the side with narrowed eyes. "I used to until they fired me," he said with a scowl.

"Were you spying on us to help Tracy and Gordon abduct Jamie?"

"No, no," Stanley said with a frown. "They already fired me before that. They never should've fired me!" He returned his gaze to Ray and widened his eyes. "But I knew you were the key. Your daughter, I mean. So I watched you because I knew they would come for her, and I wanted to get back at them by warning you."

"So why didn't you, you liar?" Jeremy raised his voice.

"I, I," Stanley fidgeted with his words, "I couldn't find the right time. They were always watching. Especially that Tracy. She's a crazy one!" He waved his fingers in the air. "I'm not some hero. Not like you guys. I'm just a disgruntled nerd in a lab coat."

"You want to get back at your company for firing you?" Abby asked.

"Yes, of course," Stanley answered sharply. "I was good at what I did, but I made one small mistake, and they discounted a decade's worth of ground-breaking work." He sat up in his chair and performed erratic hand motions. "Let me tell you! All of their accomplishments—*all* of them—are part of *my* research, *my* theories, *my* genius, and *my* hard work as well! They couldn't have achieved half of what they have now without me. Those other eight brainiacs were subordinates to me. If they think they can just cut me out and claim all of my work as if I had no part in it, well, they have something coming!"

Ray pulled up a chair and sat in front of Stanley so that their knees almost touched. Through his glare, he said, "How do we know you are who you say you are?"

Stanley replaced his frown with a stoic business-like countenance. "That silver hard drive there," he said, pointing to it with his eyes. "That hard drive contains reports on Jamie, medical records, correspondences, maps, and most importantly a file labeled 'ApexGen' which you can't get into because you don't have the password."

That piqued their interest.

"We all get one of those little, silver hard drives. I am who I say I am," Stanley reiterated.

"And who exactly are you?" Abby interrogated.

"I, I am Dr. Stanley Q. Morrison, Harvard graduate in molecular biology. I was one of nine scientists spearheading the integration project. We were the brains," he spoke with an aura of pride. "Well, we were the brains, but not the mastermind."

"What integration project? Who is the mastermind? Is it PH? Gordon's handler, Marcus?" Ray unleashed his questions again.

"Marcus? Gordon?" he mocked. "They are the hands and feet! Not nearly the mind. They are the mercenaries on the low end of the totem pole. They are the muscle, but far from being the brain or the mastermind of the company!"

"What company? Who is 'they' that you keep referring to? Who is behind this?" Ray pelted him.

"I, I know. You have many questions. By the way, you all have done very well on your own, I must say. The last two families didn't handle things quite the way you did. Boy, you are making them angry over there. You should be very proud of yourselves. You put up a real fight!" He praised with sinister delight.

"Answer my questions!" Ray barked.

"Fine, fine. We know who's in charge here," he muttered. "You can pat yourselves on the backs later. I, I just wanted to compliment you. That's all." He sat back in his chair and shifted to one side so he could lean on the armrest. "You all should sit down. This will be a lot to download into your brains." He chuckled.

Jeremy, Abby, and Deon pulled up chairs and sat around him with Deon remaining directly behind him.

"Oh, oh, I see," Stanley commented, "I'm the monkey in the middle."

"It's because we don't trust you, perp," Jeremy stated. "And we don't want you bolting for the door."

"I'm not going anywhere. Like I said, I'm here to help," he promised.

"Tell us everything," Ray ordered.

"You know, actually... Let's all sit around your laptop." Stanley chuckled again. "I'm good in a lab with petri dishes, but I'm not a very good explainer. So I think it would be better if I unlock the ApexGen folder, and let you see for yourselves."

The four of them perked up at the idea of unlocking the protected folder.

"Let's get to it then," Ray urged and moved his chair to sit in front of his laptop.

"My silver hard drive was confiscated upon my termination. Those arrogant pricks leave you with nothing! So, it was a good thing you all managed to get Gordon's," he said with a chuckle. "I'm sure that really stuck it to him, that brute."

They got up and moved to sit around the head of the table with the laptop in front of them. Ray clicked on the folder and again a window asking for a password popped up.

"Here. Allow me." Stanley reached over to the keyboard.

"No," Ray said sternly. "Tell it to me."

"Very, very well," Stanley said. "Type in 'apexhumanity001*Now'."

Several files appeared on the screen.

"Click on the video file there with the name, 'Vision,'" Stanley instructed.

Ray clicked on it.

A window opened. Then a video played. The video showed hundreds of people dressed in suits and gowns seated at round tables in a red-carpeted banquet room. Light glittered off the crystals adorning the tables. Ahead was a stage with a podium and a large projection screen behind it. Mild clapping of hands welcomed a speaker to the podium. He was a young man, probably in his late twenties, with neatly combed hair. He had a boyish gait to his walk as he traveled across the stage and took the microphone.

"Him?" Abby asked. "He's PH? He looks like a college freshman."

"No, no!" Stanley snapped. "Quiet and watch."

The young man at the podium gave a welcome to all the attendants of the event. He then said, "ApexGen members from around the world. I give you the man who leads us into the new age—the man who needs no introduction." He clapped his hands above his head and turned to the side. The room erupted into a roar of applause as every person rose to their feet.

"Here comes PH," Stanley announced with a prideful tone, "the mastermind."

An elderly gentleman with wavy gray hair and distinguished wrinkles walked onto the stage from the side. Though he bore the face of a man in his 70's, his stature was like that of one in his 30's. His walk had energy. He stood upright and carried himself with a veneer of strength.

Ray cocked his head forward for a closer look at the elderly man at the podium. "Wait a minute. I know him," Ray said with astonishment.

"What?" Abby responded.

"Yes, yes," Stanley concurred. "You should."

"Yeah, I know him," Ray repeated.

Stanley smiled. The elderly man in the video stood at the podium with a proud grin as he scanned the room and soaked in the deluge of applause.

"That's Vladimir Haagen," Ray said. "He was my and Melanie's old Intro to Bioengineering professor at M.I.T. I used to visit him for office hours all the time to pick his brain. I remember his answer to any question had to do with nanoprobes. That was his weird fascination. He was very well known and respected, but he quit and disappeared during our third year."

"Ah, yes," Stanley said, "your good old M.I.T. days."

"He's PH? He's the mastermind? That can't be—" Ray asked.

Stanley pointed at the screen and whispered, "Quiet and listen!"

Haagen patiently waited for the cheers to expire before he began to speak. The camera zoomed in on him. He said,

> For centuries, ApexGen has searched tirelessly to unlock the power within our humanity, a power that could only be realized by certain enlightened individuals with more highly evolved inherent traits. To my fellow enlightened ones, a toast to you!

The room resounded with the movement of arms raising their champagne glasses and echoes of, "Here! Here!" and "Salut!"

After sips of champagne, Haagen continued,

> If there is one thing that unites us in this world, it's suffering. Who does not know suffering? But while the problem unites us, it is the solution that divides us. For, the solution is not available or achievable by all, as is the nature of things. We can and will solve the problem of suffering. We can and will eliminate pain. We will bring order to chaos. My fellow enlightened ones, you are recipients of the solution. You stand on the right side of the dividing line. The reason the solution divides us is because the solution to pain lies in power. Not all have the right to power—not all deserve it—because it

is not in their nature. Suffering victimizes the weak, who lack the power to control what happens to them. Power means freedom from pain and disorder. Power liberates us from pain. You, enlightened ones, are the powerful ones.

Another wave of applause rolled through the room.

Your parents, as well as my parents, and multiple generations of our ancestors believed in a dream of a better humanity—not just a better world, but a better humanity defined by a class of people who reign at the apex of the human hierarchy. With the persisting work of each generation, we became more intelligent, more advanced, more evolved, and more enlightened, climbing towards the apex of power. At this two-hundred and seventy-second annual ApexGen banquet, I have an important announcement to make that radically affects our almost three centuries of searching for that solution that unlocks the power of our higher humanity and rightly divides us from the weak.

Such a silence fell upon the room that one could hear the rubbing of Armani fabric against the satin, cushioned chair when someone shifted in his seat. Haagen had a dead, poker gaze as he appeared to be looking at each person. He opened his mouth, but no sound came out. Until three seconds later, he spoke.

"I must announce… that the rumors you've heard are true. We found the solution!"

Glee and jubilation electrified the room. The camera panned to capture the expressions of the audience. People mouthed, "What?" with astonishment. There were smiles of triumph, drunk with domination.

We have reached the end of our search, and it is my honor to declare that we are the genesis of a better humanity! We uncovered the key to our technological-biological synthesis that will unlock the ultimate evolution. We have the technological tool and the genetic key in hand.

A mural-size image of Jamie flashed on the screen behind Haagen. Ray's heart sank, and his breathing stopped.

With tributes to our forbearers who did not lose the dream and who persevered in advancing us forward, it is my privilege to stand with you as the generation that begins a new humanity! We are on the horizon of actualizing our rightful place on the human hierarchy!

The crowd stood and pounded their palms together, bouncing a thunderous applause across the room. One man sitting in the front raised his glass and shouted, "Haagen!" Others followed and echoed, "Haagen!" Haagen raised his glass to the audience. He then leaned forward and said into the microphone in a cool tone, "We are retrieving the key as we speak. We have much work to do. But the hour is at hand, and it won't be long until I'll see *you* at the top."

They drank, and Haagen walked across the stage with his glass raised towards the crowd. Applause and chatter broke out amongst the attendees. He exited. The video faded to black.

"What was that?" Jeremy yelled. "What *was* that? Key?"

"Explain, Stanley," Ray ordered. "Who are these people? Why is my old M.I.T. professor involved in this?"

"Questions. Questions. This is ApexGen," Stanley began in a formal tone. His sudden shift into a semi-professional manner seemed unnatural, "whom you have been battling against. Its leader is Vladimir Haagen, your old professor. 'PH.'"

"How? What?" Ray exclaimed while he wrapped his mind around this disclosure.

"Now, now, just hold on. I know. Questions. Questions," Stanley said, fluttering his fingers in the air in front of his face. "I will try to answer all of them. ApexGen is a secret organization that has been in existence since the dawn of the Modern Age. Its belief is that the human race can and will recognize its fullest potential. Then, when it does, sickness, suffering, and pain, even death, will be eradicated—totally, completely. But not everyone will achieve this, sadly. Only the genetically, intellectually, and physically elite of the human race will achieve this perfect state. ApexGen is the long lineage of collected people who are at the apex of the human hierarchy."

"Hold up," Deon chimed. "You mean these bozos think they were born better than everybody else."

"Well, well, yes," Stanley immediately answered. "That's what ApexGen believes, and frankly, it's true. I was one of their top scientists. I did the research myself. There are those who are born with genetic advantages that allow them to either be stronger or smarter than others. It follows the theory of evolution and natural selection. It makes complete sense."

"Bull!" Deon rebuked. "I've heard this kind of junk before. Fools who think they're superior make up some mumbo-jumbo about genes to validate their oppression of others. It's nothing more than racism."

"I, I can understand why you would be upset. If I had an inferior genetic make-up, I would be too. Fortunately, I don't."

"Did you just imply that I'm inferior to you?" Deon challenged.

"You, you cannot deny the differences in people's genetic make-up. Some are shorter, taller, broader, have thicker bone structures, or have better skin because of hereditary traits that have survived and been passed down for generations. You're born with this. You have no control over it. There are even prevalent genetic traits common in specific races that give those races certain intellectual advantages. These genetic qualities affect neurological capacities—that means thinking power. So intelligence is also a genetic factor. I'm sorry to say," Stanley responded with a sympathetic look at Deon, "but the black race *does* possess inferior intelligence due to DNA coding. That was a belief held throughout much of the Modern Age, and that was the grounds for slavery."

Deon snapped to his feet, flipping the chair with his legs so that it bounced off the wall. "Evil, greed, and selfishness were the grounds for slavery!" The other three rose to hold Deon back from crushing the scientist, although he displayed a surprising level of self-restraint. "Are you listening to this racist punk? My grandma has been through too much racism in her lifetime for me to sit here in this redneck's presence and let him degrade me, my family, and my people!"

"Relax. Please," Ray urged with an extended hand toward him.

"It's men like him that create slavery, oppression, and hell for others," Deon yelled.

"Boy, boy. This whole group has a lot of anger," Stanley remarked.

"Stanley, shut up. Stop speaking," Ray ordered. He looked at Deon, who fixed a red glare at Stanley. "I know how upsetting this is. Hurting him is not going to help us. He's giving us information we need. I need you to be the better man and bear this."

"Yes, like I said, I can help," Stanley commented. "But I can't concur that he'll be the better man. It's not genetically possible."

"I said stop talking!" Ray shot at Stanley. "Deon," he spoke again to his student, "can you keep it together? Look at me." He grabbed Deon's attention. "We don't agree with him, but can you keep it together? I'm going to ask Stanley to keep talking, so can you listen without pummeling him?"

Deon took several deep breaths. His shoulders relaxed.

"Deon?" Ray called to his student again.

Deon removed his hand from his persecutor. "I'm getting coffee. You keep going without me. I'll be back in a few." He walked out and closed the door behind him.

They sat back down.

"I understand why he's upset," Stanley said. "No, no one likes being at the bottom of the totem pole."

"What is wrong with you? Do you have no sensitivity?" Abby reprimanded.

"On the contrary, I'm very sensitive to others," Stanley rebutted. "That's how I know why he's upset."

"Is your entire organization like this?" she questioned.

"Well, well, it's not my organization anymore since they fired me! Haven't you been listening?" Stanley spewed. "But if by the pronoun, 'this,' you mean whether the organization believes in a hierarchy of human classes defined by privileged genetic traits, then, yes, ApexGen is like this. Division is the natural conclusion of the evolutionary process and hierarchy is the logical result of natural selection. It is how nature works itself out. In order for a species to be perfected, those with the weaker traits must diminish and die, and those with the stronger traits must rise and survive."

"What does Jamie have to do with all of this?" Ray interrogated.

"Oh, Oh, yes, your daughter," Stanley said with a perverted grin, "she is the key. At least, we think so with a 99.5 percent confidence level. We had been looking for someone like her for a long time. You and Melanie did a good job, by the way." His grin elongated.

"What do you mean?" Ray pressed. "Be specific!"

"She has a particular genetic code that we need to accomplish our next evolutionary leap."

"It has to do with the TAGGATACT?" Abby asked.

"Yes, yes, you know about TAGGATACT," Stanley said gleefully. "You all are good! You know much more than you are supposed to. When the TAGGATACT DNA coding is repeated a certain number of times and interspersed specifically by another codon, it provides the perfect genetic sequence for nanoprobe synthesis!" He ended his last sentence with a higher intonation, revealing his excitement.

"What are you talking about?" Jeremy asked. "Speak English!"

"Nanoprobes, my, my boy," he said and reached to stroke the side of Jeremy's head, but Jeremy jerked away quickly before Stanley could touch him. With a disappointed reaction, he continued, "Nanoprobes are micro-robots that can be injected into the blood stream. They are marvelous little mechanical creatures that can be programmed and directed. By synthesizing our DNA with nanoprobes, we can enhance physicality, increase brain functions, prevent incurable diseases, regenerate damaged tissue, clear blood clots, increase longevity and even undo mortality!"

"This sounds insane. Is this actually possible?" Jeremy asked.

"This is the kind of stuff I read about at the biolab," Abby commentated. "Once in a while, there would be an article on someone researching nanoprobes on this level."

"Ah, yes, you work at a genetics research lab, Abigail," Stanley said, "so you know what I'm talking about."

Abby was taken aback upon hearing him say her name. "This is more science fiction than theory," she said. "We've seen some test cases of nanoprobes acting on human tissue with some positive results, but—"

"Not, not acting on," Stanley asserted. "Synthesis. Integration. Binding. That's what we're talking about. We're talking about the union between technology and biology, which is the next and final stage of human evolution!"

"You're making this up," Abby accused. "How can any of this be real?"

Deon re-entered the room with a pot of coffee and some paper cups.

"Are, are you going to pour that on me?" Stanley asked, leaning away from Deon.

"Don't give me any great ideas, genius," Deon said sarcastically as he walked past him and sat down next to Abby. He looked at Ray. "I'm good."

"You, you missed the good stuff of my explanation," Stanley chided.

"I'll catch up," Deon replied. "I'm smarter than you think."

"Unbelievable," Ray resumed the discussion. "Professor Haagen used to talk about nanoprobes and the possibilities of a binding process, but he always spoke of it like he was musing over a science fiction tale. It just seemed like a real fascination for him, but none of us thought he was being serious."

"Why, why is it science fiction?" Stanley countered. "Our DNA runs on particular programming. Our cells do what they are supposed to do because they are given certain information based on genetic coding. Nanoprobes are no different. They are little robots running on a program at a cellular level. But nanoprobes can do for our bodies what our genetic make-up falls short in. Where our genetic codes lack the information needed to resolve our fleshly frailties, we can program our nanoprobes to do the rest. The nanoprobes will function like cells in our bodies, but will enhance our bodies by doing what our cells cannot. The nanoprobes can make our brains smarter, our bones sturdier, our muscles stronger, and our immune system more impervious to diseases. Where man falls short, machines can advance." Stanley exuded excitement. "Come, come now, you know with the accelerated advancements in biology and technology, the integration of the two was merely a matter of time and a matter of vision. Now is the time and Haagen has the vision! Professor Haagen, your old professor—he's the visionary!"

Ray sat back and rubbed his forehead. "Professor Haagen. Genetics and nanoprobes. My daughter being the key."

"Yes, yes. Jamie has the right TAGGATACT sequence in her DNA. Open her files, please," Stanley requested.

Ray opened the computer files in the folder labeled with her name. Her medical records, medical history, and DNA make-up came up on the screen.

"Huh, that's interesting," Deon remarked.

"What, Deon?" Ray asked.

"Aw, nothing. I was just noticing that me and Jamie are kind of alike."

"Fine, fine. That's all very nice, but don't interrupt me again with your superficial comments," Stanley rebuked.

"Man, I'm really getting tired of you disrespecting me," Deon retorted.

"As I was saying," Stanley continued, "when we discovered your daughter was the key, Professor Haagen said he remembered you, Ray Lee. That's a big compliment. You should feel proud! He spoke highly of you. He was not surprised that the answer would come from you and Melanie. He recalled the two of you being uniquely bright. He said it was too bad that neither of you went the route of bioengineering. He would've mentored you. By the way, it's nice to hear you refer to him as 'Professor Haagen' still. He is a mental giant of our age."

"He's crazy," Ray said. "You know that? I didn't know it before, but I know it now. He's crazy! Stealing other people's children for a twisted biological ideal! You said there were two other families? This is lunacy!"

"You shouldn't say that," Stanley charged with confrontational poise, "especially not when he spoke so well of you. He is the Einstein of our century. You would've been fortunate to be mentored by him, but you were too shortsighted to recognize the opportunity!"

"He kidnapped my daughter!" Ray fired back.

"He's a visionary extraordinaire! He is not bound to sentiments. He's carrying forth a vision that will propel our humanity to the next evolutionary stage of superiority."

"I don't care if he has a cure for cancer, he can't use my daughter for his experiments," Ray declared.

"Well, well, he is using her, I tell you," Stanley said. "And it's not for experiments. It is for extraction!"

"What is he doing to her?" Abby asked.

"First, first, he'll run a few final trials on her blood samples," he answered. "He'll inject the nanoprobes into her blood samples. If the binding is positive, he will then inject the nanoprobes into her. Blood trials are one thing, but you never really know how it will go until you use a live host," he said nonchalantly. "Again, if the binding is positive, then he will take her blood and use her genetic code as a template for gene splicing—taking the TAGGATACT sequence from her DNA and grafting it into the DNA of all ApexGen members, whom he calls the 'enlightened ones.' I like that."

"They're using Jamie as a base for reproducing the DNA codon for the others?" Abby clarified.

"Yes, yes," Stanley confirmed, rubbing his hands together. "But not just a base. A source. That's why she's so important. If the nanoprobes properly integrate with her DNA, she will be apex human prime—the very first human progeny with a fully successful biological-technological synthesis! Then she will become 'The Source' of generating the TAGGATACT template for all the enlightened ones! Every apex human being will bear a piece of her in them. What a privilege for Jamie!"

"This is inhumane!" Abby exclaimed. "Jamie will be used as a crop field for her DNA, simply to be harvested."

"Oh, no, no, think of all those who deserve to be at the apex of humanity becoming finally actualized!" He suddenly frowned and added, "But, but, this is another way they are cheating me! Since they fired me, I am no longer a member of ApexGen and, therefore, cannot be a recipient of the nanoprobe binding. Losing your job is one thing, but having your rightful human destiny stolen is another. They are thieves!"

"What if the injection of the nanoprobes into Jamie doesn't achieve a positive binding? Will they let her go?" Ray asked.

"Oh my, my. Well, well, if the results are not positive, then the nanoprobes will forcibly attempt to bind to her cells by deconstructing her DNA. The nanoprobes would become a cancer. They will digest her from the inside."

Jeremy pounded the table, stood up, and spun around to walk away from the table.

"I'm sorry that is upsetting," Stanley said. "I understand the sentiment. But science can only be fulfilled without sentiments."

"This is not science," Abby said. "Even science is not above ethics."

"Well, well, that argument is debatable. However, I assure you that ApexGen is very careful with live human subjects," Stanley assured.

"Human subjects? You say it like this is a regular thing they do," she pointed out.

"It, it might be good news for you to know that ApexGen has only run this test on two other candidates—those other two families I mentioned—in eight years!" Stanley said. "It was unfortunate that those two did not turn out to be the correct sources, but this shows you how careful ApexGen is. They don't take their test subjects lightly. Many trials are run before we do a live test."

"Great!" Jeremy said sarcastically and rejoined the table. "They *only* crippled and killed two other people! I'm sure we feel much better now. Thanks for telling us that!"

"Sorry, sorry. Not two individuals. I said two families."

"You're sick!" Jeremy spat.

"ApexGen is not what you think." Stanley defended. "They are doing this for the betterment of the human race."

"But you said that ApexGen believes in a human hierarchy," said Ray.

"Yes," Stanley confirmed.

"Then how can what they are doing benefit the human race?"

"Well, well, it will benefit those at the apex of the human hierarchy and that is what is necessary for the human race to flourish. Those who are superior in natural selection must triumph in order for the entire race to accomplish future evolutions."

"You mean betterment for a few arrogant and selfish folks who want to exploit others," Deon corrected. "How much more of this fool's nonsense do we have to hear?"

"I, I would appreciate it if you don't continue labeling me as a fool. I have two Ph.D.s from Harvard. So, so, I know you don't like it, but think about it. If you want a kingdom to thrive, you would need the king, queen, and royalty to thrive. Not the peasants and slaves."

"I would rather be in a kingdom without slaves, fool," Deon contended.

"Now that's science fiction." Stanley laughed. "Slaves or at least the poor working class are important for the development of a civilization."

"You said you want to help us," Ray reminded, trying to get to the practical issue of saving his daughter. "How?"

"And why?" Jeremy added.

"I, I can help you get your daughter back," Stanley said. "I know the facility she is held in. Open the file next to the video labeled 'Master Schematics.'"

When Ray did so, several pages of blueprints for a building opened.

"She's in there? That's not a house," Abby stated. "That's a building with over a hundred floors!"

"It's, it's the AmeriBank building," Stanley spoke matter-of-factly. "I can show you on the diagram where she is held and tell you how to get inside. I can get you access into ApexGen. I can give you tips on how to get past their security and the best routes."

"Why should we trust you?" Jeremy asked.

"My son is right," Ray reinforced. "You clearly believe in what ApexGen is doing. So why help us and hinder them?"

"ApexGen was my life. Yes, yes, I do believe in their cause. And, yes, I believe in their philosophy and goals. And, yes, I want to achieve the next evolutionary leap with the nanoprobes," Stanley shared. "Also, I loved my work there. We were making history. My co-researchers were my friends, and Dr. Haagen was like a father to me."

"Sounds wonderful," Jeremy mocked.

"It was!" Stanley snapped. "But, but they cut me out! I lost my family. They excised, expelled, excommunicated me!" He threw his hand straight up in the air. "I was a crucial part of ApexGen! I was like the eldest son. ApexGen wouldn't be where it is if it were not for my contributions. They have my life's work. I would rather them fail than to succeed without me. I would rather them not evolve than to evolve without me!"

"Sounds like you went through a bad break-up," Abby commented.

"How dare they cut me out!" Stanley blurted. "They don't want me as an employee? Fine. Then they shall have me as an enemy!"

"You have a passionate hate for them, and that could be useful to us," Ray said.

"We need to talk about this," Jeremy said. "Can we step outside?"

Ray looked at his comrades. Their faces expressed the need to consult with each other. "Yeah, sure."

"You stay put," Deon ordered Stanley, as the four of them stepped out.

Cherish looked over at them from her desk. "Everything all right in there?" she asked cheerily. "I heard a little bit of yelling."

"Just fine," Ray replied. "Just some family matters. No biggie."

"All right," she responded. "I'm heading out to lunch with some ladies from our women's Bible study. I'm locking the door. If you go out, just close the door until it sticks, and it will lock."

"Thank you," he said.

Cherish took her purse and went out. They heard her lock the door and greet the homeless man.

"We can't trust this guy," Jeremy said. "He's one of them."

"He defected, and, besides, we don't have other options," Ray responded.

"This dude's nuts and a straight-up bigot," Deon imputed.

"He does seem to be short of a few marbles," Abby concurred, "and his views are obviously twisted, but he knows what he's talking about."

"He has inside info on ApexGen," Ray said. "He's also revealed this much to us already, including giving us access into that locked folder. I think he's proven to be a trustworthy traitor."

"This is a bad idea," Jeremy said. "I can feel it."

"We have the same enemy as he does, and that makes him our ally," Ray summed up. "I know it's not full proof. I'd prefer to run a background check on him first. But as it stands, he's our ticket. He can give us access to Jamie. That's what matters."

"I don't like this cat either, but I see your point. Your call, Sifu," Deon said.

They went back into the room and found Stanley sitting in his chair staring blankly at the surface of the table. The four took their seats around him.

"We'll take you up on your offer to help us," Ray said.

"I, I can only get you inside the building and tell you what to do, but I won't go any further," Stanley specified. "The rest is up to you. I will not put myself at risk."

"Why won't you go further?" Jeremy prodded. "Is it because you're leading us into a trap?"

"Why would I do that, boy?" Stanley accosted loudly. "They don't need any of you. You're inconsequential to their plans. None of your DNA matters. They want Jamie Lee. So why would I lead you into a trap? I won't go any further with you because the AmeriBank building is a fortress, designed to capture unwanted infiltrators like yourselves. I won't risk it. This is your fight. I'm no hero."

"Fine," Ray said. "Get us in, and we'll take care of the rest."

"Aahhh," Stanley sounded, "I, I hear too much confidence in your voice. I can get you in, yes, yes. But heed this, Ray Lee. Once you're in, the challenge is getting to Jamie and getting her out in one piece. You must realize the enlightened ones will not relinquish the key easily. They will fight you with everything they have. You, you will enter the hornet's nest. They are structured, coordinated, and effective. Inside that hive are many assailants, who are superior to you in intelligence and prowess. You, you cannot best this task alone. The four of you going in together increases your odds, most certainly, from a one percent chance of success to perhaps a five percent."

He continued, "I've made my choice to help you with boundaries. The choice you must make is whether you want to risk your life and the lives of whoever goes with you. If, if any of you are caught, you will not be spared. I will only give you the information you need, if you decide to do this. I will not put myself at unnecessary risk by disclosing confidential information, if there's a chance that you will not go through with this. You, you must decide for certain that you will act. There can be no turning back from your decision once I show you to the gates of Hell.

"I feel compelled to state the obvious to you in light of the dangers I'm aware of: your chances are very slim. Of course, you can walk away from this. You can take your son, whom you still have, and walk away."

Ray looked at Jeremy.

"So, so," Stanley said, "decide."

Chapter 19
Revelation

"This is a no-brainer!" Jeremy exclaimed. "Let's go in there, and get Jamie!"

"Let me think for a minute," Ray requested.

"What's there to think about?" Jeremy challenged.

"Stanley, what's the potential of success if three of us went on this rescue operation?" Ray inquired.

"What?" Jeremy questioned.

"Three is better than one," Stanley responded. "In fact, one or two would be impossible. The more the better in case you run into trouble, which you most certainly will. As long as the team is no more than five, because more than five will raise suspicion. Three is fine, but the plan I devised is really meant for four or five."

"You hear that? You need at least four!" Jeremy stated. "You don't have anyone else to help you. The police won't help. You need me!"

Ray thought for a moment and then said, "I'll call Miguel."

"Miguel? He's not as good as I am. I'm far more trained in Wing Chun than he is," Jeremy objected.

"I'll call Miguel first," Ray told Stanley, "and then I'll let you know."

"Fine, fine. Keep in mind though that the opportune time to infiltrate the AmeriBank building is in two days," Stanley explained, "because that's when the annual lab maintenance crew is scheduled to fine tune our instruments. You'll go in as that crew. You don't work for the company for over twenty years and not make a couple of very loyal contacts! ApexGen should've thought about that before letting me go. They'll remember how valuable I am when I stick it to them!"

"You know you really sound like a vindictive ex-girlfriend?" Abby commented.

"We *will* move in two days," Ray declared.

"'We,' meaning the four of us," Jeremy specified.

"I'm calling Miguel," Ray corrected.

"She's my sister!"

"And you're my son!" Ray softened his demeanor. "Whether you like it or not, you're my son." He got up from his chair, picked up his cell, and said to Stanley as he turned toward the door, "Just be ready with that intel." With his back toward them, he said to his comrades, "You guys watch him. I'm calling Miguel."

Ray walked out into the main office area to put some distance between him and the others. He sat at Cherish's desk and called Miguel on his cell phone. Miguel's voicemail answered. After explaining Jamie's situation, he asked, "Miguel, I already appreciate your help with looking for Jamie on that first night she went missing and for taking care of the mess at the studio. But I need another favor." He told him about infiltrating the AmeriBank building and the dangers it would entail. "Would you join me in getting my daughter back? We go in two days. I know it's a lot to ask. I'll wait to hear from you."

Sitting at Cherish's desk, he pondered on what was about to happen, trying to mentally orient himself to the trial he would face. He rose like an old man and proceeded back to the room.

As soon as he walked through the door, Jeremy asked, "So what's the word?"

"I left a voice message," Ray answered. "We'll wait to hear back. "

"A voice message?" Jeremy retorted. "We're trying to decide on Jamie's rescue to save her from biological experimentation and harvesting, and you left a voice message? Miguel didn't pick up. It's decided. The four of us are going in. What's the plan, Stan?"

"Uh, uh, don't call me Stan," Stanley muttered. "It's Stanley or Dr. Morrison for you since you're only a kid."

"It is *not* decided," Ray spoke loudly. "We're waiting to hear from Miguel!"

"You're unbelievable!" Jeremy shot. He kicked the table and slumped back down into his chair.

"By, by the way, who is this Miguel?" Stanley asked. "Just curious."

"One of Sifu Ray's students," Deon replied.

"Students," Stanley repeated. "Oh, oh, you mean from the karate school."

"Kung fu," Deon corrected. "Wing Chun is kung fu."

"Yes, yes, whatever. I'm sorry about what happened to your school."

"You know about that too?" Ray asked.

"Yes, yes, and about your home too. Now you see how far they'll go to get what they want. There's no home they wouldn't destroy or person they wouldn't kill for the greater cause. Right, right now you're standing in their way with that firewall. You're lucky to be staying at this church. I don't think they would suspect you hiding here."

"What do you mean *they*?" Ray stepped towards Stanley. A flush of shock washed over his face. "Are you telling me the people who want the decryption code for Miracom's main server are the same people who took Jamie?"

"Oh my, this is all connected?" Abby asked.

"Well, well, yes. I thought you knew that," Stanley affirmed.

"Can this get anymore complicated?" she wondered.

Ray paced. "What?" He shook his head. "ApexGen is responsible for the virus?" He brought both of his hands up to the sides of his head. "Why? What do they want with Miracom?"

"Okay, okay. You're upset again," Stanley observed. "Look, I handled the biology, so I don't know the details about Miracom, but it all fits with their rise to the top of the human hierarchy."

"I'm really getting tired of this human hierarchy bull!"

"Tell us what you know about their intentions with Miracom," Abby demanded.

"So, so, while genetics is key to dominating the human race, communications is key to dominating society."

"Whoever controls communication controls society," Ray added.

"Yes, yes," Stanley continued, "it's about controlling the eyes, ears, and mouth of the populace. This principle is very sociologically proven."

Ray felt he should've made the connection between the two situations a long time ago. The simultaneous occurrences of his daughter's kidnapping and virus infiltration were too logically coincidental to be random. *Why didn't I see this?*

Stanley hacked a few laughs. "ApexGen didn't expect you to install that firewall on Miracom's main server. That really screwed with their plans. You've become quite the number one enemy for them, Ray Lee." He grinned.

Ray paced some more and glared at Stanley, wiping his smile away. "ApexGen! Who do they think they are?" he exploded. "I'm going into the office tomorrow to bolster the security to our systems and nail this virus. Then I'm going into ApexGen and taking my daughter back! They're not getting anything from me!" His ferocity startled and invigorated his comrades, except for Jeremy.

"You're still going into the office to do work?" Jeremy questioned.

Ray's determination and his words were sharp with fieriness. "It's not about work, Jer. Didn't you hear? This is all connected. They'll have to kill me before I'll give anything to them. Not my daughter. Not my company."

"Uh, uh, they may just do that—kill you, that is," Stanley commented.

"I'm going in tomorrow," Ray reiterated. "We'll go for Jamie the next day as scheduled," he said with a hammering tone that concluded the matter.

"There it is again," Stanley pointed, "that aura of confidence. Be careful. We have someone in Miracom."

"We know we have a mole," Ray said. "Do you know who it is?"

"I, I don't know that. He or she is not listed in our manifest, which means the takeover of Miracom is very much a black op conducted by a secretive and specialized subdivision of ApexGen. Miracom is a prized target. Nobody knows who the mole is, except the executive level administrators and Professor Haagen. But I can tell you this, Ray Lee," he warped back into his bland, serious tone, "you're safer trusting no one. Not close co-workers, bosses, or best friends. Assume everyone is the mole. When it comes to ApexGen, anyone can be. Heck, it could be the custodian!" He chuckled.

Ray dropped into a fixated silence as his eyes ran from side-to-side like a typewriter while his mind roamed over possible names.

"Okay, well, you let me know when Mr. Miguel calls back and when you have made your decision. Then we'll get started," Stanley said. "I, I'm getting some coffee. This church does have coffee, right?"

He got up from his chair, but Ray stepped in front of him to block him. "Deon, show Stanley where the coffee is. Watch him. Watch him pour the coffee and add his creamer. Don't take your eyes off of him."

"Yes, Sifu," Deon replied

"You know, the last time I was in a church was for confession twenty-one years ago! Is the minister here to take confession?" Stanley asked.

"Oh, yes, Pastor James would love to hear your twenty years of sins! You should do it," Jeremy encouraged while Deon escorted Stanley out to the kitchen. "Now what?"

"We wait," Ray repeated.

"You're overprotection is annoying." Jeremy popped up from his chair. "I'm going to the bathroom. Do you need Abigail to escort me too? You know, in case I get stuck on the toilet," he said as he stormed out of the room.

Ray pulled out the chair at the head of the table and dropped into it, sinking into the thin, lumpy cushioning, while Abby watched him sympathetically.

"Sifu, you're bearing a lot on your shoulders," she said. "I understand the caution you're taking with Jeremy. Any parent would."

"I just don't know how to get through to that kid," Ray said. "For some families, tragedy brings them together. For him and me, it drove

Revelation

us apart. I know the way he is has to do with Melanie's death. If I could change that, I would."

"I want to talk with you again about Melanie's accident."

"Melanie's murder," Ray corrected.

"May I show you something?" she requested.

"Sure," Ray replied. "What is it?"

"This may be a little shocking," she warned as she scooted her chair to sit next to him. She pulled out a wad of folded sheets of paper out of her purse.

Ray leaned forward, curious about what could be shocking on the scraps of paper.

"I kept thinking about Melanie's accident last night," she said. "I took the details you gave me regarding her vehicle versus your vehicle, the other driver's vehicle and where she was struck. I'm not an engineer, but I did have one year of engineering calculus and one semester of basic physics. Here…"

She unfolded the wads of paper and laid them out. Hand-written calculations, diagrams, and drawings filled five sheets of paper.

"Check my math and logic because you're more of an expert in this field. But I think I did this right." She pointed to the first sheet. "You said the other driver drove a Ford GT and your wife drove a Mini-Cooper. He hit her dead on the driver's door because both cars were low. You said if he struck you, it wouldn't have killed you because you drive a SUV, Chevy Traverse, and he would've gone under you. Based on the kind of impact you described, I estimated the speed the Ford GT was traveling."

She shifted a second sheet in place. "I checked the dimensions of the Ford GT versus the dimensions of your Chevy Traverse. Here's the big point. Based on the low height and sloped angle of the Ford GT, it would've gone under your SUV, as you said."

She moved a third sheet in place. "But it would've been like a speeding ramp wedging under you. Considering the velocity of the Ford GT and the weight of your SUV, the Ford GT would've wedged under your SUV and sent you flipping sideways three or four times over."

She shuffled her fourth and fifth sheets in place. "That kind of impact would've killed him, of course, and it would've likely killed you too. As a biologist, I could predict the kind of injuries you would've sustained—a snapped neck, severe head trauma, and deep lacerations to the head depending on the debris or shrapnel."

Ray examined the calculations and drawings on the sheets of paper. They appeared sound. He wasn't sure what to say. He hadn't considered how the exact dimensions of the two vehicles and the angular slope of the Ford GT would've affected the outcome. "I hadn't analyzed it this way." He searched for more words. What he really searched for was an answer to what this meant. "This doesn't change anything."

"This changes everything!" she insisted. "You bore her death upon yourself these last two years, saying that if you had gone as she had asked, you both would've lived. But I theorize that if it were you, the accident would've killed you and the driver. In a way, Melanie saved both your lives by going for those eggs—the life of her husband and the drunk driver."

Abby's conclusion drastically reinterpreted that tragic day. Ray hadn't swallowed the new interpretation yet. He re-evaluated the alternative possibility presented to him as he stared at one sheet of paper after another. His eyes ran over the scribbles. He mentally checked her equations and diagrams. He looked for gaps or missing details in her hypothesis. But it all added up.

However, her theory made him feel unsettled. Something in him resisted this conclusion that reinterpreted Melanie's death as a sacrifice to atone for the errors of two people. He didn't want to believe that Melanie had saved him while he was being a jerk. He felt aggravated and confused. Abby's explanation was sound and rational, but it also didn't make sense to him. *The new view changes things.*

He didn't realize he was fiddling with a pen in his hand until he accidentally snapped it in two.

Abby asked, "You okay?"

"Yeah," he said, noticing the two pen halves in his hands. He placed them on the table. "You did all of this," he acknowledged, diverting the attention away from him.

"Well, it really stuck in my mind after you shared all that stuff with me. I kept thinking about it on my drive home. Then I stayed up researching."

"You went through a lot of trouble."

"Oh, no. It's important if it can help uncover the truth of the situation, especially if it helps you to be free from an unnecessary burden. I'm all for taking responsibility for one's mistakes, but I'm also for seeing things as they are. I know this new information probably throws you for a loop. So if you want to talk about it, I'm here."

"Thank you. I may take you up on that at some point," he lied, "but I noticed it's two o'clock, and we haven't eaten all day. Could you order a pizza or something for everyone? Use my credit card."

"Sure, but I could cover this."

"No, use my credit card." He pulled his credit card out and slid it to

Revelation

her. Then he got up. "I'll be back."

"Sure," she said, again looking at him with sympathetic eyes as he turned away toward the door. "Where are you going?"

"Somewhere to clear my head," he said as he walked out the door.

. . . .

Ray walked across the church office area, passing Cherish's desk and several cubicles. He found a door that led into an outside corridor. He didn't know where he was. He had not explored much of the large church property. To the side of the corridor was a green patio with a stone bench next to a fishpond and a fountain. He sat on the bench for a minute, but surprisingly the engineered tranquility annoyed him.

He left the patio, walked to the end of the corridor, and entered another building. He walked down a few dim hallways and found himself in a foyer of a small chapel. The foyer didn't match the rest of the church facility. It had an antiquated appearance. The wood floors were old and worn, but the aged look was good. It felt authentic. In front of him were a pair of small, wooden doors that had an archaic, Renaissance appearance with small stained glass windows and S-shaped door handles. He was not an old-fashioned kind of guy, but the mismatch of the doors from the rest of the church property allured him to go through them. Perhaps the mismatched nature of the doors and whatever lay behind them mirrored the mismatched feelings stirring within him.

He grabbed the black iron door handles and pulled the doors open, not knowing what he'd find on the other side. He stepped into a small chapel with only three short rows of rustic pews. On the back of the pews were hymnals and books of classic prayers. A middle aisle led to the front of the chapel where there was a small stage about a foot high with a modest podium in one corner. At the back of the stage was an elaborate, wooden altar with gold trim. Above the altar hung a large crucifix with a life-sized, articulated carving of Jesus. The head of the Jesus figure slumped over his chest, and a crown of thorns adorned his scalp. Soft, colorful light shining through a set of three stained glass windows on one side of the walls illuminated him.

Ray sat down at the end of the second pew. He didn't feel religious or prayerful. He felt tired. This was the first place of solitude he found. He allowed his sore feet to rest on the worn wooden floors. He let the hard wooden pew support his lower back. His face was warmed by the colored sunlight filtering through the stained glass windows. His mind relaxed in the antediluvian space. He had so much to process, so much to think over, so much to make sense of.

Fifteen minutes later, someone walked in.

Ray heard the antique door crackle open. He turned around to see who entered into his private space.

"Ray Lee," Nathan greeted with a warm smile.

"Elder Nathan," Ray said, cordially rising from the pew.

"Please, don't get up. Sit, sit."

Ray sat back down, and Nathan slipped past his knees to sit beside him.

Nathan said, "I'm sorry I couldn't catch you yesterday. Pastor James told me you were boarding here for a night. He asked me to follow up on you since I knew Melanie and what your family went through."

"He wanted you to check up on us, to make sure we weren't causing any trouble. Didn't he?" Ray surmised.

"Um, yes," Nathan answered with a diffusing laugh. "He's looking out for the church *and* for you. He's the kind of pastor who doesn't deal well with unknowns. Please excuse him." His calm voice had a pacifying effect.

"Is he always business-like and, well, indifferent?"

"He's not so bad. Others have complained about that too. He has his strengths and weaknesses… *and* some weird antics. But that's why he has me and the other elders to complement him. And please, just call me 'Nathan.'" Nathan switched to a tone of concern. "I got here as soon as I was able to. How are you and Jeremy? I didn't see Jamie. Are you homeless?"

"Our family is facing a difficult problem. Problems. It's the reason why Jamie is not with us and we're out of our home. I know you're concerned about us, but I think the less details you know, the safer it would be for you and this church. I'd rather not get others involved unnecessarily."

"I appreciate your discernment about confidentiality. I and the church would at least like to know if we could help with any of your basic needs."

"You're doing plenty. I can't ask for more."

"Then let me ask what your emotional needs are. How are you and your children doing personally?"

"Honestly, it could be a lot better." Ray's shoulders drooped.

Nathan waited for more.

"Look, I know I'm not giving you a whole lot."

"That's all right. Sometimes it's hard to know how to talk about what's going on in your soul. Life has demanded a lot of strength from you as a single father."

"More than you know."

"I'm sure there must be a lot of unanswered questions still since Melanie's passing. Wrestling through those questions is an ordeal, but forgive yourself for not having all the answers, Ray. You can't know everything."

"A question has been on my mind. It seems Melanie was more involved in this church than I realized. Pastor James said that she worked with you. Could you tell me about that?"

"Of course. Melanie was a tremendous blessing to many people. She was involved with the women's Bible studies and other women's gatherings. I oversee the men's and women's ministries at the church, so she and I had a lot of contact."

"What do you mean she was involved in these things? What did she do?"

"She didn't have a specific role. She helped with set-up and refreshments at the women's gatherings. But how she really blessed people was by spending time with them. Sometimes it was over coffee with them or just ten minutes here and there. She provided a listening ear, compassion, and wise counsel. She had no snazzy title or job description. Her ministry was unofficial but significant. She touched a lot of lives simply by doing what she did. Everybody loved her. To this day, I still hear our ladies talk about what they learned from Melanie or how she affected them."

Ray looked confounded, as if being lost in a foreign city, and yet, he had a clear image in his mind of Melanie loving other people. He could picture her doing that.

Nathan estimated, "By your questions and expression, I'm gathering that you didn't know about this."

"No, I didn't." Ray felt a new sadness.

"I'm sorry."

"I thought I knew everything about my wife, but I was unaware of this big chunk of her life. I mean, she would tell me about her church functions or if she was staying at church a little later on Sundays." Ray strained to remember more. "I'm trying to recall if she tried to talk to me specifically about what she was doing, and maybe, I just didn't hear her. I was not as interested in religious things as her. But I regret not knowing about this significant part of her life."

"I'm sorry you missed that part of her. I'm glad to tell you about the good she did. Her legacy lives on in many people."

Ray stared at the hymnal on the back of the pew in front of him.

Then he looked up at one of the stained glass windows. "She didn't deserve what she got."

Nathan leaned back on the pew. "Very few can say they get what they deserve in life—bad or good. I can't imagine how difficult it was—still is—to lose her. I'm a husband and father of three. I could sympathize with you as a fellow man, but I can't imagine the pain you've gone through."

Ray panned his gaze from the stained glass window to the altar at the front of the chapel. His eyes wandered along the ornate carvings on the wooden altar. "Nathan, have you ever faced a decision to save someone you love at the risk of losing someone else you also love? Do you save the person or play it safe and not take the risk of losing more than you already have?"

Nathan leaned his head forward and shifted in his seat. "Wow, there's a question. Without knowing the details, my general answer is to take the risk of losing someone you love in order to save someone you love. But I tend to be a risk-taker and an idealist."

"I'm not," Ray stated. "I don't like unknowns or chances."

"What do you like, Ray?"

Immediately a familiar and secure thought wrapped around his mind. He said, "Control. I like control. Maybe that sounds bad, but it's normal, isn't it? Who wouldn't want to be in control of their circumstances? That's what I like about being an engineer. Equations give only one result. An angle has a specific degree. Two plus two equals four. It can't be sort of four, mostly four, or possibly something else—it's just four."

"Why do you like control?"

"Isn't it obvious? It's to prevent unforeseen mishaps or misfortune and to produce the most beneficial, desired outcomes."

"This is one of the reasons why losing Melanie has been so difficult, isn't it?" Nathan asked. "It was an outcome that didn't fit the equation."

Ray's lips twitched to the side, and his eyes reddened with moisture. He blinked a few times to dissipate the welling tears. "I could've prevented her death. I applied the wrong equation to a situation, and she died for it."

Nathan looked at his folded hands resting on the pew in front of him.

"Since then," Ray admitted, "I haven't been able to produce the right results."

Nathan looked at Ray. "You know why I think you want control?"

Ray waited.

"I don't think it's about minimizing misfortune or achieving desired results."

Ray turned his head to the side to meet Nathan's look with curiosity.

"You want control because you lack peace."

"Come again?"

"You want peace, Ray. You're fighting for peace. Your soul is fragmented and so you try controlling everything because you lack a foundation to ground yourself on. I think Melanie was your foundation. Since you lost her, you haven't been grounded and haven't known peace. That's why significant losses can be so hard and difficult to get over. Losses don't just leave us empty. They expose our brokenness."

Ray faced forward and stared at the surface of the altar. He felt the wrinkled tension on his forehead. His breathing became slow but heavy. He evaluated the validity of Nathan's dissection of him. *I never thought about it like this before. Was Nathan correct?* He wasn't comfortable with being laid open like a book, but he was even more uncomfortable with the plausible accuracy of Nathan's diagnosis of him.

"Anyway, that's what I think. I could be totally off," Nathan said. "I hope I didn't disrespect you."

"No," Ray responded. "I appreciate the honesty." He thought for a moment in silence. Nathan didn't interrupt. "Losing my wife and the mother of my two children at the age of thirty-six wasn't part of the plan." His gaze wandered from the surface of the altar up to the crucifix.

"I don't have any perfect words to console you, but maybe you'll find some comfort in knowing that God has a heart for the hurting."

"You know what never made sense to me?" Ray asked as he examined the sorrowful face on the Christ figure. "This crucifix. This is the central icon of Christianity, right? I never understood why God would choose such a chaotic image to be the icon of Christianity. I hope you're not offended by me saying this, but looking at this crucified Jesus hanging on a barbaric execution device does not represent peace to me. It represents chaos. Is God a God of disorder? Maybe this is why I never connected with that side of Melanie's life. Maybe I was searching for peace and I found none in this religion."

Nathan paused before responding.

"Again, I hope I didn't offend you," Ray repeated.

"Not at all. Likewise, I appreciate the honesty. Here's my opinion. I think you look at the cross and see chaos because you see the path to peace is by what *you* can control. Sometimes, Ray, peace is not achieved by what you do for yourself but by what someone else does for you."

"That doesn't compute for me—peace attained by what someone else does for you? It makes more sense to think that what I do produces the results I seek. I'm not going to wait around for someone else to do something for me that I should do for myself. My actions and choices create the outcomes I want."

"So do the actions of others on your behalf. In your case, you've only learned how to produce and not yet to receive. Learning to receive from another is no weakness, my friend."

"This sounds less and less like two plus two to me."

"It's only understood according to the logic of grace."

"This is getting very deep. I appreciate the discussion, but right now, I don't have the luxury of learning this. I have a big problem to resolve. When all this is done, then maybe we can philosophize together."

"Maybe the solution is not in your control."

"It has to be. This fight is mine. Others may help, but I have to figure this out for the sake of my children. I'm their father and all they have. Thank you for talking with me. If anything, it helped me to gain clarity on what I need to do."

"Ray, I don't know if you're comfortable with this, but could I pray for you?"

"Sorry. I'm not comfortable with that. But thanks for the offer."

"You're welcome to talk to me again if you want."

"Thanks for your time, Nathan. I can see why you're an elder at the church." Ray got up. "If I'm successful, we can continue our discussion." He left the chapel.

. . . .

Ray felt determined in what he had to do. He walked back through the church halls and corridor. He entered the church office to see Cherish back at her desk. Walking through the office, he smiled and waved at her. He opened the door to the old conference room he was lodging in and found Stanley sitting in Ray's usual seat at the head of the table, fiddling with his sci-fi looking device.

"What are you doing? Were you digging in my backpack?" Ray grilled while closing the door. He approached Stanley with scrutinizing eyes.

"Just, just curious. You know me. Scientist. I was assessing your assets for the mission," Stanley replied innocently. "What is this anyway?"

"None of your business, and you have no business going through my belongings," Ray said and snatched the device from Stanley's hand.

"It looks interesting," Stanley defended. "You're not telling me what it is?"

Revelation

"It doesn't matter. It doesn't work," Ray answered impatiently.

"Then why do you carry it with you?"

"Sentimental reasons. Besides, like I said, it's none of your business."

"Fine, fine. The more you have to work with the better you'll be is all. So, what's it going to be?" Stanley asked as Abby, Deon, and Jeremy walked in.

"Sorry, Sifu," Deon apologized. "I left to go use the bathroom for just a minute."

"You're back," Jeremy remarked. "Thought you might've bailed on us to go save Jamie by yourself!"

Ray looked at Stanley and said, "We're going in. Share with us what you know."

"All four of us are going in?" Jeremy wanted to clarify.

"Hold on," Ray said, looking at his phone and noticing he received a voicemail message. He missed a call from Miguel. "There's a message from Miguel," he said. He accessed his voicemail and put the phone to his ear to hear Miguel say:

> Sifu, I'm honored that you would ask me to be a part of the rescue. Seriously. But honestly, I don't think I can. I have a nine-year-old brother I take care of. Ever since our mom left us, I'm all he has. If anything happened to me, he would be all alone. I can't risk that. Hope you understand. I wish I could help. Seriously. I'm sorry.

Ray took the phone off of his ear with a downtrodden countenance. "What?" Jeremy asked, "What did he say? He said, 'No,' huh?"

Ray nodded. "You're still not going. We'll do this with three people."

Jeremy kicked a chair. "Why are you doing this? Why do you keep me out?"

"Why are you bent on going?" Ray shouted. "I know you're angry and looking for danger. I'm not going to satisfy your self-destructive nature. After what happened at Gordon's house, do you think I'm going to subject my son to something worse?"

"Maybe this is not your call to make!" Jeremy protested. "Maybe it's my prerogative to do this!"

"Okay, okay," Stanley inserted, "Your father-son arguments are very, very uncomfortable. Woo! You all like to fight. Good! Save it for ApexGen."

Ray finalized, "My decision is final, Jer. You're staying at the church."

Jeremy stomped to the back of the room and kicked a couple more chairs out of his way. He dropped himself into a clunky chair at the opposite end of the table and glared at his father.

"Stanley," Ray turned to the strange scientist, "tell us your plan. I want to vet it and make sure it's sound."

"I know this place inside and out after working there for as many years as I did. The plan is fully vetted by yours truly," Stanley assured.

He explained, "You'll go in as a crew of bioengineers from one of our ally companies called Mason BioTech. You're there to fine-tune the biolab equipment as part of an annual service. A crew of four is the minimum for the specific tasks. Five is more convincing, but four will suffice. I have uniforms and fabricated badges personally made by my contact at Mason BioTech."

"How trustworthy is your contact," Ray questioned.

"She's very trustworthy."

"But how do you know that?"

"Well, well, let me just say our relationship is more than professional. I'm a special interest of hers, and the other night—"

"Okay!" Abby interrupted, "Say no more. I'm convinced. How about you all?"

"I'm good," Deon concurred.

"Tell us the plan, Stan," Ray said.

Stanley said, "I'll give you the gist of the plan now and save the details until the night before, because you won't remember everything. But, but, first we will see how your day goes at Miracom tomorrow."

Chapter 20
Miracom

Ray awoke to the sound of his alarm. After rolling off the couch, he rummaged through his luggage for the least wrinkled dress shirt and slipped his arms through it. The texture of the shirt bothered him. Everything felt a little grimy to him. As he grabbed his toiletries, Abby, who had slept on the table, awoke and asked, "Do you want some of us to go with you to Miracom?"

Ray paused at the door and responded, "That's not necessary. This is my job."

"I was thinking about Stanley's caution," she explained. "Maybe it would be good for you to have one or two of us accompany you."

"Stanley's mildly paranoid and mostly nuts," he said as he looked at Stanley sleeping in the corner of the room on the floor in a fetal position. "I'll be fine. How tough could this mole be anyway? And I doubt he will be showing his face yet. It's too soon for him to tip his hand when he doesn't have full control of our main server. Why not maintain anonymity? Besides, my work-related stuff is not your fight." He walked out of the room to go to the kitchen sink.

After washing up, he grabbed his backpack, taking his laptop and sci-fi looking device to evade further snooping hands like Stanley's. He left for Miracom.

. . . .

Walking through the front entrance of Miracom felt foreign, like something had changed. He greeted the usual security guards, Officer Hernandez and Officer Cole. He showed his badge, gave his fingerprint I.D., and signed in. "Anything new going on here these days?"

"The usual," Officer Hernandez replied, "a lot of hi-tech problems requiring a lot of smart people's attention."

"That virus has made everyone skittish," said Officer Cole. "And the rumor of a mole has everyone on edge. What's going on with that?"

"That's what I'm here to work on," Ray answered.

"Well, if there's anyone who could nail this sucker, it's you, Mr. Lee,"

Officer Hernandez said.

"Thanks," Ray said as he started walking to the elevators.

"Come back to us with good news today," Officer Cole said loudly.

He waved and entered an elevator.

Ray entered his office, which felt different. It was neat, but it looked like it had been searched. He could tell a few of the items were out of place, like the stapler on the file cabinet was too far to the left. The feeling he got from standing in his office was similar to the feeling of being in his ransacked home—other hands had been here.

He sat at his desk, adjusted his computer screen, which was rotated about ten degrees too far to the right. He pulled open his desk drawers and checked the contents inside. Some of his items were moved and others removed. While he booted up his computer, the hangings on the wall behind him caught the corner of his eye. He perused the many plaques, certificates and diplomas adorning the wall. Below all of it, there was the picture of his family. Seeing the picture of the four of them together, smiling with their arms around each other, recollected a feeling of wholeness that he missed. Even now, he was fighting to salvage a portion of that wholeness.

When his computer chimed, he logged in and saw that Fred was right; his access to the company's system was restored. Marvin had come through for him.

"Ray Lee," Marvin said with his head poking in through the doorway. "So glad you're here! We're in Conference Room 102. Ms. Miranda wants you on our task force."

"Task force? That's what it is now?"

"Come on. Bring your laptop." His head retreated, and his footsteps faded down the hall.

Ray grabbed his backpack and hurried after him. Entering Conference Room 102, he saw Miranda at the head of the table. Fred, Marvin, and four members from the systems security team, Kristy, Rochelle, Jim and Theo, sat around the table. He rarely saw the systems security team and had never worked with them before. They were young except for Jim who was in his forties. The team appeared worn with circles and bags under their eyes, saggy cheeks, and downtrodden faces. The women had their hair up in ponytails, and the men were unshaven. They received Ray with delight.

"Come on in, Ray," Marvin invited. "Glad you're here. We can use the help."

Kristy added, "We could use your expertise, especially since you came up with the encrypted firewall and the decoy files. They bought us a lot of time. Besides, having a fresh pair of eyes would be good; we've been looking at this mess for too long. Everything's running together."

"Glad to be here. Let's nail this thing once and for all," Ray asserted and took a seat between Marvin and Kristy.

"How are things with your daughter?" Marvin asked. "Miranda and Fred told me a little bit of what happened. I'm very sorry you have to come and deal with this while your family is in crisis. Are you closer to finding your daughter?"

"Thanks, Marvin," Ray said. "Things are intense for my family. It's difficult to answer whether I'm close to finding her. I know where she is."

"You do?" Marvin exclaimed with wide eyes. "Well, that's very good news."

"Yes, but getting her back is the big question."

"I don't understand."

"It's a long story, one that I don't need to involve you all in. But I'm here because there's a crisis here that could impact millions. I also have some intel on this virus that could be useful for our battle against it."

"Really?" Fred asked, "You've been gone from work a few days, and you come back with intel on the virus problem?"

"That's a long story too, but it seems the kidnapping of my daughter and this virus issue are connected."

"What?" Fred exclaimed. "How in the world—"

"I don't want to say too much, but the intel came from a credible source."

"Good," Marvin said as he interlaced his long, scrawny, and white fingers and placed them on the table, "we trust what you're telling us. I know you check your facts thoroughly before making a conclusion. What can you tell us?"

Ray felt sorry for Marvin, seeing him carry the weight of this problem. He was motivated to stand with this kid in combating the virus. Without mentioning ApexGen, he told them this virus originated from an organized group aimed at controlling communications globally for militaristic purposes.

"I can't believe this," Marvin said with a frightened look. He appeared as if one last brick was laid on an already crushing load upon his shoulders. "Before we thought maybe it was just a prank from a brilliant college student. Then we thought it was a disgruntled employee who was the mole. But we never guessed it was this serious. I mean, we're actually up against an aggressive organization bent on a takeover?"

Ray asked, "How's the investigation on the mole problem?"

"I.I. is uncovering everything from illegal vacations to parking tickets," Fred replied, "but no real leads on who the mole is."

"There are a lot of speculations," Kristy said. "It's nerve-wracking, honestly."

"Everyone is being interviewed," Marvin said. "I.I. has a few prime suspects, but nothing solid enough to make a conviction. Whoever it is, this person dug themselves in and covered his or her tracks very well."

"It's pretty scary," Kristy said. "I find myself looking at everyone with suspicion. I mean, it could be anyone, right? I can't even go to the bathroom when someone else is in there without feeling paranoid."

"The worst thing we could do is create panic," Fred said. "Let's just stick to the task. Let I.I. do their work, and we'll do ours. With Ray joining us, we might be able to make a dent in this."

"Thanks for vouching for me, Marvin," Ray replied.

Marvin offered a tired smile. "We need you. Plus, they shouldn't seriously be suspecting you when you put up the encrypted firewall!"

Ray requested, "Catch me up to speed. What have you found out about the virus and what have you tried so far?"

Their laptops were open. A router sat in the middle of the table with blue Ethernet cables spidering from it into each laptop, so that all their computers were connected. Also in the center of the table were co-axial video/audio cables with adapters to plug into the laptops, which showed their work on a screen through an LCD overhead projector.

Marvin reported. "So far," he began with his chin drooping and his head shaking, "we ran twenty-two different, top of the line antivirus softwares. But The Mutilator, uh, that is the virus, dismantles each of the antiviruses. It's designed to destroy antiviruses!"

"I'm forwarding the reports to your laptop right now," Theo said.

"The Mutilator?" Ray asked with an odd half smile.

"That's what we call it," Fred said. "We felt it deserved a name. One thing we've been doing is identifying all the malware files associated with this virus one at a time to manually delete them."

"Well," Kristy annotated, "it's a metamorphic virus, which I heard you discovered already from the beginning. So it keeps changing and reproducing itself. Nightmare."

Jim, the older member, added, "We're always a dozen steps behind the Mutilator as it reproduces and rewrites itself."

Theo said, "We know there's a core part of the virus' algorithm that remains the same because the virus' general objective is the same—going after the main server and command files. In fact, your decoy ploy proved that, Ray. Once we uploaded the decoys, all the variations of the virus went for it. But that core part of the algorithm must be so embedded within layers and layers of subroutines that we can't detect it."

"The polymorphic encryption code protecting the virus, which you also discovered earlier," Marvin said, "is making it difficult as well. We can't exactly identify all of the malware files of the virus because the polymorphic code of the virus keeps us from being able to fully recognize them." His tone was sharp with frustration.

"All we do is play catch-up with this thing," Fred commented. "We even created three custom antiviruses specifically to tackle this thing, but no dice."

Ray stared at his laptop screen pensively. His eyes roamed from side to side, like a typewriter. He bit the corner of his bottom lip and looked up at Marvin. "Maybe what we need to do is not chase the Mutilator but make it come to us."

"Um," Marvin rubbed his hands on his lap nervously, "I'm not following."

"We give the Mutilator an emulator," Ray specified.

"An emulator? Like a sandbox?" Fred clarified.

"Exactly," Ray said. "It's the only way to trick it. Instead of writing custom antivirus software to fight it, let's write a custom emulator to give it what it wants."

"That might work, actually," Marvin said with a spark of energy.

"That could take a while," Theo said.

"With all of us working on it," Marvin responded, "we could probably have it done by tomorrow morning."

"It's a long shot still," Fred said, "but what do we have to lose? We tried just about everything else. Thank God for the encrypted firewall."

"By the way, do you still have that decryption code for the firewall? Is it in safe-keeping?" Kristy asked.

"Yes, of course," Ray pulled a small, red USB drive from his backpack. "It's right here." He placed it on the table. "It's on me at all times."

"How's it coming, boys and girls?"

Everyone looked towards the door, but they already recognized the distinct voice.

"Good, Ms. Miranda," Marvin answered. "Ray came up with a good idea."

"I expected nothing less." She walked in and grabbed a chair. Marvin rolled his chair sideways to the corner to surrender the head of the table. "Tell me."

Marvin looked at Ray. "I'll let Ray do the honors."

"Thanks, Marvin." Ray proceeded, "We're going to create an

emulator."

"And what is that?" Miranda asked.

"It's also called a sandbox. It's a virtual world for the virus to play in. It's like the decoy files but a step further. We'll recreate the entire environment of our main server, upload it into our system, and draw the virus into it. It'll think that it's in our main server. Once it thinks it has what it wants, it should demangle itself from its polymorphic encryption."

"A virtual world for a virus," Miranda reiterated rhetorically.

"It's like a holodeck for the virus," Fred clarified. Then he said more quietly, "That is, if you're a Trekker, my analogy would be helpful to you."

"We'll take all that we've learned about the virus so far to create the best environment for it. We'll cater to the virus."

"Then," Fred added, "we can set up an algorithmic quarantine around the virus once it is drawn into the emulator. The virus checks in but doesn't check out."

Ray continued, "As the malware files of the virus are demangled in the quarantine, we'll go in and delete the files one by one until it's totally purged."

"Intriguing," Miranda remarked. "Instead of going *after* the virus, you're baiting and trapping it. What do you think of it, Marvin?"

"It's sound," he said. "It's definitely worth a shot."

"Great. How long will it take to put this into effect?" Miranda asked.

"With all of us working at it into the night, we should probably have it up and running by tomorrow morning," Marvin answered.

"Good. Ray, I'm glad you're back," she said. "I know it must be hard with your daughter's situation."

"Resolving this is actually good for my daughter's situation. Long story."

"And Ray has the decryption code safe and secure on that little red flash drive," Kristy said.

"Is that right?" Miranda asked. "The decryption code is on that red flash drive?"

"Yes, it's right here," Ray affirmed.

"Put that away." Her command was stern. "No one needs to see that."

"I showed it to the task force as part of our discussion on combating this virus."

"I specifically told you not to let anyone know where the decryption code is. Put it away."

Ray swiped it off the table and inserted it in his backpack.

"Sounds intense in here." Comb-over Thornton stood in the doorway with a creepish grin. "Good progress?"

"How long have you been there, Thornton?" Miranda asked without looking back at him to conceal her annoyance.

"Long enough," Thornton answered. "But don't mind me. I'm here in a supervisory role," he spoke directly to Ray. "I just want to see what's going on and check on the progress of resolving our problem. Good to see Mr. Ray Lee back with us and to have a plan in place. This is *the* plan, right?"

"That's the goal, Mr. Thornton," Miranda said. "Let's let the task force work. The sooner we're out of their hair, the sooner they'll have a solution."

"Very well," he agreed, "I look forward to making a good report to the Board."

Miranda walked to the door to scoot Thornton out.

"And Ray," Thornton added, looking over Miranda's shoulder, "I'm glad you still have that decryption code safe and sound. I like the red color too."

"Time to go," Miranda insisted, vanishing with Thornton behind the wall.

"Wow," Fred said.

"Ms. Miranda didn't even trust any of us," Kristy said. "That's disconcerting."

"Don't let that worry you. I'm sure she's just being necessarily cautious," Fred responded.

"Well, let's get to work," Marvin proposed.

"Agreed," Ray said as he walked to the back of the room where dark cherrywood panels hung on the wall, like a large painting. He opened the panels to reveal a large white board. "Let's go old school with this white board and architect our emulator."

For the next two hours, several brilliant minds joined forces to lay out a blueprint for the emulator software. They needed algorithms, subroutines, coding, and command files to not only replicate the main server but to make this the perfect virtual world for it. They wanted to ensure that all of the virus variations were drawn into this emulator. No malware file could be left out. Ray emphasized that the emulator had to be supple enough that the virus would think it found what it was designed for and demangle its polymorphic encryption in the emulator while it was quarantined.

During the next two hours, the men removed their ties and loosened their top buttons. Sweat marks appeared under their armpits. The women's hair appeared frizzier. The whiteboard was covered with six different colors of markings. The table was littered with bags of potato chips and crumbs. The room smelled musty.

Ray sat back in his chair after the two hours and surveyed their blueprint. "What do you think, Marvin? You're systems security head, so you get the final word. Give it the green light or hash it out some more?"

Marvin's eyes scanned one side of the whiteboard to the other and two minutes later, he approved, "I don't see gaps or inconsistencies. I think it should work."

"Then I recommend we divide up the design into modules for each person to work on. Between the seven of us, we'll each create a piece of this," Ray said.

Marvin concurred. He divided up the tasks for each team member, taking advantage of their expertise in certain areas of programming. Once the assignments were delegated, everyone immediately got to work, except for Fred who grumbled about his part. Ray was impressed with how Marvin's team automatically fell into place and worked efficiently once they knew their parts. It attested to Marvin's leadership, which he did not give himself enough credit for. Ray made a mental note to put in a good report to Miranda about Marvin when this was all over.

Ray texted Abby, Jeremy, and Deon a few times to check on them. As he hoped, their morning was uneventful, merely waiting for the invasion of ApexGen the next day.

As each team member created a module of the emulator, he or she uploaded it for cross-checking by one another. Not much talking happened, except for technical points of clarification and advice, until Ray broke the silence by asking nonchalantly, "So anybody have an opinion on who the mole is?"

But the silence was maintained.

Given his recent learning about ApexGen, he had a gnawing urge to find the mole in Miracom, who was connected to the abduction of his daughter.

"We're discouraged from talking about it," Theo said. "Ms. Miranda doesn't want any speculations because that will only heighten the paranoia."

"Of course. Speculations lead to paranoia. Paranoia deconstructs the company." Ray conceded.

"I think," Rochelle chimed in, "it's one of the I.T. guys."

"Come on, you don't know that for sure," Fred challenged.

"I do! There's an I.T. guy who's being heavily investigated," she defended. "It makes sense, right? Those I.T.'s have access to everyone's computers."

"I wouldn't be surprised if it was one of the board members," Jim said. "They have all levels of clearance. They could get in and out of any part of our system easily."

"But those board members are businessmen. They aren't smart enough to invent a virus," Kristy contended.

"I think it would be easy for one of the design engineers to be the mole," Theo said. "No offense, Ray. I know that's your team. But they would be perfect, since all they do is create programs and redesign our systems anyways."

"What about the security guards?" Kristy asked. "I know they're not techies, but they watch everyone. Right? They have eyes on everyone and what everyone does. They're probably watching us right now."

"This is creeping me out," Rochelle confessed. "Ever since this virus and mole issue, I always feel like I'm being watched. I'm leery about who I talk to."

"Well, for sure, it has to be someone with inside access," Fred said. "But this again is just a lot of speculation."

Marvin interjected. "We really should concentrate on our work."

"Our leader has spoken," Ray said disappointedly. It was obvious that no one had any solid ideas about who the mole is. He had hoped to find out, and perhaps even nab the mole to pump him for more inside intel on ApexGen or to cross check the information Stanley has been feeding him. But apparently, this mole had dug him or her self in well.

"I don't know how you're able to do this," Kristy said to Ray. "I would find it hard to concentrate on anything else with your daughter missing and all."

"Concentration has never been his problem," Fred said. "Ray is the most focused man you'll meet."

"Do you have a plan for how you're getting your daughter back?" Kristy asked.

"I do," Ray answered plainly. That made everyone look up from their laptops with curious expressions. "But like Fred said, focus is something I'm good at, and right now, I'm focused on nailing this virus." His daughter was on his mind, but he didn't want to involve them for the sake of their safety.

"Man, after you say it like that, it makes me want to hear your plan," Fred said.

"I just uploaded another module. You all want to proof it?" Ray deflected.

Not Easily Broken

"You're good, Ray," Kristy said with a smile. "Whatever your plan is I hope you get your daughter back."

. . . .

6:00 PM came quickly as Ray worked furiously away with growing perplexity. It was odd. He kept correcting fixes and bugs he found in his and others' modules after they were already proofed. The bugs appeared random. He discreetly looked at everyone without lifting his head. *Could the mole be in this room?*

"This is looking good," Marvin said. "Let's take a look at our final product."

They were all looking at the content on their own laptops through their shared connection.

"I say we run this and see what it does," Fred said.

The door to the room opened abruptly. Miranda entered. "Progress report."

"You're just in time, Ms. Miranda," Marvin said. "We're about to test run the emulator. I should say this is 'Emulator beta.'"

"Let's see it." She stood behind Marvin and leaned over to see his laptop screen.

Marvin ran the emulator program and a separate application showing any malware that entered the emulator. He commentated as the emulator booted, "We tried to make it more attractive than the actual main server. There are certain command files that we suspect the virus is after, and we created more of those and made them more accessible."

Fred said, "This better work."

"Mutilator meet Emulator," Marvin said geekishly as he hit the enter key.

The emulator program stalled. An error message showed.

"I got it," Ray said. He rapped on his keyboard for a few seconds to correct the bug. "Hold on," he said, "found another one." Ray was the only one in the room typing. After a couple dramatic taps on his keyboard, he invited, "Try it again."

Marvin ran it again. They each watched the progress of the emulator on their own laptops with Miranda still hovering over Marvin. The emulator ran. Smiles emerged on a few of their faces. One by one, malware began to attack the files in the emulator. As they did, they were quarantined and their encrypted coding demangled, revealing their algorithm and making them vulnerable for deletion.

Fred tracked each one and manually deleted them. "It's working," he proclaimed. He offered Ray a high-five, to which Ray answered. "There are probably thousands of these malware files, but I deleted ten of them in the last twenty seconds already. It'll take a while. But it's working."

"At least, at this rate," Ray commented, "we can delete them faster than they can replicate. Also, the more we delete, the slower the replication rate will be."

"Finally. We're one step ahead of the virus," Fred said with pride.

"And one step ahead of the mole," Marvin added with a sigh of relief.

"Good work," Miranda praised.

"It was Ray," Kristy said. "He came up with this idea. He has come up with *all* the ideas. He should be part of the systems security team!"

"We couldn't have done this if we didn't work together," Ray responded. "We all created this together." The result of their collaboration was undeniable, but he still couldn't shake his hunch that the mole was in the room!

As Fred continued policing the emulator and viciously eradicating the malware files, the emulator unexpectedly froze. "What happened? We were on a roll."

Marvin and Ray immediately ran diagnostics.

Ray looked into the coding and algorithm of the emulator, and again identified a couple of bugs that hadn't been there before. *How did the bug get there? I proofed this very line.* "Try it now," Ray said.

The emulator ran but for only a minute before it froze again.

"What is going on?" Ray went back to combing over the algorithm.

"It's okay," Marvin said sheepishly, glancing over his shoulder at Miranda without actually turning to look directly at her. "Troubleshooting is normal."

Miranda's lips twisted as she looked at each of them. Everyone raised their eyes to watch her straighten up. "One word," she said plainly and stiffly. "Now." She pierced each of them with her non-blinking stare. She paused, allowing her intensity to emanate from her. "I want the solution *now.*"

"Yes, Ms. Miranda," Marvin murmured. "It'll get done tonight."

"We're not sitting around waiting for the virus to take over Miracom, right?" Miranda questioned as she continued to scan the faces of everyone around the table.

"No, not at all," Marvin replied. "We'll get it up and running."

"I'm going home. I'm going to have a nice dinner. Then I'm going to sleep well tonight. You know why I'm going to sleep well?"

"Why, Ms. Miranda?" Marvin asked.

"Because I'm certain that when I come in tomorrow morning we will have this virus resolved."

"That would mean someone has to remain here during the night to keep deleting the malware," Kristy said with concern.

"Kristy," Miranda said.

"Yes, Ms. Miranda," Kristy responded softly.

"Am I going to sleep well tonight?"

Kristy paused and glanced at her peers in search of help. "Uh, yes. You will."

"Good. Take shifts. Set up a schedule. I don't care." Miranda said. "There's only one word you need to know until tomorrow morning. What is the one word?"

They said in chorus, "Now."

"I'll see you tomorrow." She exited, and it seemed like a hurricane had passed beyond them.

"We have to troubleshoot this thing." Marvin sprang from his seat. "Everybody get on it. Fix any bugs you see, and let's keep running it so that the emulator beta becomes just 'Emulator.' I'll set up a shift schedule on the white board."

Ray crinkled his nose when he came across another bug slowing the emulator. But it was a kind of mistake that was not a typical "typo" or oversight. It looked engineered, an implanted error in the algorithm.

Marvin was drumming up a shift schedule on the white board with times and time slots drawn up. "Okay, I'll have you all voluntarily sign up for a timeslot."

It was no wonder Marvin hasn't been able to resolve this virus problem. Someone on his team has been sabotaging his moves! Ray inconspicuously inspected the faces of the team members around the table. He glanced up at Marvin, who was writing his name for the 2:00 AM to 4:00 AM slot.

"This is probably the timeslot nobody wants. So, I'll take it," Marvin said.

"Marvin," Ray said, "could I speak with you outside?"

"Sure," Marvin responded curiously.

They walked out of the room. Marvin stepped just outside of the closed door to listen to Ray, but Ray motioned for him to walk a little farther away from the room.

"What is it?" Marvin asked with a look of concern.

"Marvin," Ray began, then bit his bottom lip and said, "I think the mole is on your team."

"What?" Marvin responded defensively.

"I know this sounds implausible," Ray said.

"Yes, it does. It's not possible," Marvin vouched.

"I'm finding these bugs in the algorithms that I swear weren't there before, or they're appearing in places I knew I had already proofread. The last couple of bugs I found looked clearly engineered. They were deliberately planted."

"That sounds sloppy. The mole we're dealing with is clean."

"But that's why I think it's someone in the room. The mole doesn't have time to come up with a polished countermeasure to our emulator so he or she is just throwing in bugs on the spot to slow us down. The mole is buying time until he or she can get to a space alone to develop a sufficient countermeasure."

Marvin ran his fingers through his brown, curly hair. "Could it be Fred?"

"No, no. Can't be Fred. I've known Fred for years."

"It can't be any of my team members. I know each of them. We've worked very intensely with each other, especially in fighting this virus."

"I know for sure it's someone in that room. We need to flush out this mole before the shift schedule starts. During the shift schedule, the mole will be the only one working with the emulator for two hours. He or she can undo the entire program."

"Then I guess we would know who it is if that happened during that shift."

"Unless the mole creates a countermeasure that's a sleeper program designed to activate at a later time to corrupt the entire algorithm."

Marvin ruffled his hair and then clenched his curls with both hands, like he was about to yank his hair out on both sides. "How do you propose we flush out the mole?"

Ray thought for a moment. "Push your shift schedule back to start at 7:00 PM. I'll discreetly implement a tracer program to track everyone's activities. I'll monitor for suspicious and patterned activities."

"Can't believe it could be any of the members on my team. If that's true, the mole would've been right under my nose! Ms. Miranda will fire me for sure."

"Marvin, it's not your fault. This mole is good. And he or she is working for a juggernaut syndicate. Marvin, we have to get this person." The thought that the mole could be another lead to retrieving Jamie galvanized Ray to trap him or her.

Marvin shifted and suspired uncomfortably. "Okay," he complied peevishly.

"Trust me. I'll build a solid case with ample evidence. And don't you worry. Once we know who it is, I'll take care of him or her."

They went back into the room and resumed their work, but Marvin was having difficulty. His nervous manners were more apparent, and he avoided eye contact with anyone. He said, "Okay, everyone. We're all going to put in an extra hour today, and we'll start the shifts at 7:00 PM."

"Why is that?" Kristy asked.

"Because," he said shyly, "we have a big task, and it'll go better if we're all working together. Besides, working late should be something we're used to now." He cracked an unconvincing smile.

"What was that all about?" Fred whispered, pointing at the door.

"Nothing," Ray replied. "Just had to clear some stuff up with Marvin."

"Fine," Fred responded. "But I know when you get secretive and spy-like that something is up."

Ray executed his tracer program onto their interlinked laptops with a masked signature so he couldn't be detected. He then texted his crew back at the church to let them know he would be returning late. He asked about how Stanley was doing. They informed him that Stanley didn't do much but ramble about random and nonsensical stuff. Stanley gathered the gear needed for tomorrow's infiltration out of his car. Deon chaperoned Stanley all day, but he had stepped out and hadn't been seen for the last half hour. Ray smiled at the mental image of Deon babysitting the strange doctor, but he wondered where Deon went for thirty minutes. Perhaps he returned home to tend to his grandmother. That put a small smile on Ray's face as well.

With the tracer program, Ray picked up on someone rewriting sound content and inserting bad content into the algorithm of the emulator. He tried to trace the source of the activity but the person attempted to shroud his or her trail by rerouting his or her activity through other laptops to make it look like the source came from others. One trail of activity even appeared to come from his laptop!

He followed each trail and found the majority of the anomalous activity originating from Kristy's laptop. He documented each engineered bug coming from her. A few others appeared to come from the other members on the systems security team, including Marvin and a couple came from Fred. He wasn't able to trace all of it back to Kristy, which was likely a matter of not being able to meticulously scrutinize every trail of activity back to its actual source. However, the volume of anomalous activity originating from Kristy was enough to incriminate her. It was 6:45 PM, and he was ready to draw his conclusion. He thought about conferring with Marvin first, but the evidence was undeniable.

He pushed his laptop aside to look at Kristy. She caught him looking and smiled in response.

"Excuse me," Ray interrupted the clattering of keys. "I have something important to show all of you, and I know this will be shocking." Marvin looked at Ray with wide eyes, and a glisten of sweat appeared on his temples. "I'm going to show this to you on your screens. I've been running a tracer program for the last forty-five minutes to monitor everyone's work because I saw suspicious activity coming from this room."

"Wait," Jim said, "you've been spying on us?"

"Yes," Ray answered bluntly, "because I believe the mole is here."

A dead silence fell on the room. Everyone's face froze.

"I'm sending you my report on what I found," Ray said as he typed and clicked. "A new window appeared on their screens. Our mole has been implanting bugs into the emulator program and rewriting good formulas or inserting corrupt data. She has also been trying to mask the activity by rerouting her work through our laptops. I traced some of the activities back to each of our laptops but the majority came from one source."

"Who?" Marvin asked.

"Kristy," Ray announced.

"What?" Kristy exclaimed.

All eyes gravitated to Kristy.

"Kristy?" Marvin asked.

"Yes," Ray affirmed. "You can see it on your screens. The anomalous activities are undeniable. Kristy," he said looking directly at her with a surge of confidence, "for the last few hours you've been sabotaging our work. You are the mole, aren't you?"

"This is absurd," Kristy protested. "Marvin, you know me. I've been on your team for the last three years. I'm not the mole!"

Marvin scratched the back of his head as he asked, "Kristy, how do you explain this activity in front of us? You have to have an explanation."

"Uh," Kristy stuttered. "Come on! This is inconclusive!" She pointed at her screen. "Everyone's incriminated according to this record, including Ray!"

"That is because I haven't had the time to fully trace every trail of activity," Ray explained, "but you can see the activity that definitively came from your laptop. Based on the current evidence, you can't deny that you did these."

"But—. This is—. Marvin, please!" she pled.

"Kristy," Marvin pled back, "I trust you, but we need an explanation."

All eyes were judging her.

"I'm not going to sit here and be accused by you all," Kristy pouted.

"You're caught, Kristy," Ray accused. "You're with the organization that took my daughter. You're going to give me information about Jamie's captivity."

"I misjudged you, Ray. You're paranoid and insane!" A white flush washed over Kristy's face. "I don't feel safe with any of you." She disconnected her laptop from the Ethernet router, packed her things into her bag and got up. "You can submit your bogus claims to I.I. I'll answer to them. Not to you!"

Marvin surprisingly stood up and walked to the door to block Kristy's exit. "Kristy, we can't just let you walk out."

"What?" she said.

Marvin locked the door and placed a chair in from of it.

"What are you doing, Marvin?" she asked. "This is illegal."

"Whoa," Fred remarked. "This is getting out of hand. We can't hold hostages."

"We found our mole," Ray said.

"We did. Thanks to Ray," Marvin praised, "but there's more going on."

"What?" Ray asked inquisitively, feeling proud to stand by this young man in uncovering this serious matter.

"The game has changed," Marvin stated in an unfamiliar tone. "I have something to tell you. The mole isn't a person."

The other three team members, Jim, Theo, and Rochelle, stood up.

Marvin continued, "It's a team."

"Oh good," Kristy said, "we can finally stop the charade with these guys."

"Hold on," Fred said as he rose to his feet, but Theo, who was next to Fred, elbowed him in the face before he could stand all the way up. Fred fell backwards onto the floor with a thud and remained on his back, holding his face and groaning.

Ray gripped the armrests on his chair to push himself up, but Marvin stopped him by placing his hand on Ray's shoulder. Ray didn't notice Marvin had moved beside him. Kristy stood by the door jammed with a chair.

"Stay seated, Ray," Marvin said in that unfamiliar tone.

The others around the table took steps towards Ray, closing in around him.

Marvin looked down at Ray and said, "We want that little red flash drive."

Chapter 21
Mole

"Marvin?" Ray asked in disbelief. "No. You can't be part of this! You're not an agent of ApexGen."

"Why? Why is that hard to believe?" Marvin contested as he took a step back to look at Ray seated on the chair. "Is it because you saw me as this young, scared, sweaty-palmed, awkward geek?"

"No, it's because you're smart," Ray corrected. "Too smart for this!"

"Oh, quit your condescension. You think you're trying to encourage me with your wiser-than-thou posture. I find it degrading! You miss the fact that I'm a genius! I was about to be the one to take over Miracom."

"Then why was Ray able to stop you, genuis?" Fred mocked from the floor, while he held his hand over his nose.

"We," he said while drawing a circle in the air, pointing at his team members, "created a masterpiece! I liked the name the company gave the virus—Mutilator. But then Ms. Miranda had to involve you. What business was it of yours? You're in research and design. You had nothing to do with security. You had to come up with your fancy encryption wall and your decoy files. Do you know how stupid you made me look? And now, this emulator! Is there no end to you? Will you not cease to make me look stupid before Professor Haagen?" His pale face turned fiery red.

"You're looking stupid all on your own," Fred muttered under his breath.

"Listen, Vladimir Haagen is an insane criminal. You can't follow him," Ray urged. "Look at what he has you doing! You're turning into a criminal."

"No, he's helping me realize the maximal potential of my humanity! And he's *Professor* Haagen to you. He's no criminal. He's the Einstein of our age! His evolutionary stage is well beyond yours and mine." He squeezed his fingertips together in front of Ray. While his face contorted ghoulishly, he said, "You cannot begin to grasp the vastness of his brilliance!" Spittle landed on Ray's arm from Marvin's intense pronunciations. "His brain is masterful and he holds the keys to unlock the potentials of our humanity! You're a lower life. You're a utility for him. Or I should say your daughter is his utility. You're just dead weight."

Ray twisted a corner of his lip as he glared at Marvin with narrowed eyes, but Marvin proudly met Ray's glare.

"Marvin, you're not just being a stupid kid," Fred said. "You're a crook!"

"Name calling, Fred," Marvin addressed his comments. "Very intelligent of you."

Ray took a slow, deep breath to relax himself. He didn't want to give up on Marvin. "Listen to me, Marvin. I've known you for several years. I know you. This isn't you. Think about the inhumanness of all that ApexGen is doing. Kidnapping children? Experimentation on children? What Haagen is doing is unethical. You're not an unethical person! It's not too late for you to stop this."

"Wrong again, Ray!" he shouted. "With all your degrees and diplomas, you still can't grasp the fundamentals. It's because you have a lesser evolved brain. There is no such thing as ethics. Ethics is socially contrived. Order—proper social order—is established by higher powers. Those who possess power is a matter of biology."

"Doesn't that sound like a convenient way to justify wrongful actions?" Ray continued to reason with him. "By making everything relative and claiming there's no such thing as ethics or morality, isn't that just your way of making up an excuse to justify your thirst for power?"

Marvin shook his head and laughed. "There you go again! There's your problem. Lecturing." Marvin shook his head at Ray. "I'm not your kid! Don't talk to me like I'm your teenage son! Respect, Ray. That's what you lack. You belittle people by your condescension. But ApexGen will achieve the proper respect due to the proper people!"

"Are we done yapping with these primitive primates?" Theo questioned. "Let's get this done."

"Quiet!" Marvin ordered. "Don't forget I'm leading! I'll tell you when to act!"

Ray appealed to him relationally. "You know me. I've been you're friend."

"I needed you to think that. I worked on my act a lot to be that stuttering, clammy, unconfident guy. I even defended you against the I.I. because I needed to bring you back into the office so we could get the decryption code." Marvin's words slithered. "Professor Haagen will be proud of us once we dismantle your fancy encryption wall."

"Marvin, I'm going to say this one more time: you're going down the wrong path. Turn around."

Fred slowly sat up to reveal his bloody nose and his blood-soiled shirt. Ray glanced at him to quickly assess his friend's condition. Ray curled the corner of his mouth again.

"Still lecturing. You just can't stop, can you? Now *I'm* going to ask you just once, and then I'm going to take it from you. Give me the little red flash drive."

Ray reclined back in his chair, dipped his chin down toward his chest and looked at them from underneath his brows. "Listen to me carefully. I've tried appealing to your rational side. I'm giving you a chance to discontinue what you're about to do. I've hurt a lot of people this week. Unless you let me walk out of this room with my belongings and my friend, I will hurt you too. Sit back down and let me walk."

"Ray, you really don't know ApexGen. We are the highest rung of humanity—not only in brains but in brawn. But we heard about what you did at Gordon's house. We're intelligent enough to not underestimate you. They don't allow us to bring weapons into this facility." Marvin took out a fat, metallic pen from his pocket. His team members followed suit. "But we're engineers, so we make stuff up." He unscrewed the tip of the pen. Then he pulled out a long letter opener with a sharpened tip and screwed the handle of it onto the pen, creating a dagger. They each had one in their hands. "You're not leaving here with that flash drive."

"You made your choice," Ray said while closing up his laptop and packing it into his backpack.

"We made our choices a long time ago. What's yours?" Marvin gripped his dagger at his side with the tip pointing at Ray.

"I'm walking out of here."

"Oh, crap," Fred exclaimed.

"Ray," Rochelle said, "think about this. Don't make this—"

Ray sprang up, kicked his rolling chair into Marvin's legs, while throwing his backpack on his shoulders, and then attacked Theo. Theo tried to raise his dagger up in front of him, but Ray blocked it with one hand, keeping him from raising it any higher than his belt level, while striking Theo's nose with the palm of his other hand. As Theo fell backwards, Ray barreled into him with a merciless flurry of short, straight punches, knocking him into Jim. Jim lost his balance and collapsed.

Fred saw the space before him cleared, and he crawled toward the table to gather his laptop and briefcase.

Kristy slid across the table with lightning speed with a side kick aimed at Ray's face. He barely brought his guard up in time to deflect her high heel shoe from digging into his eye. Rochelle got behind him and brought the dagger around to his throat. Before she could put the tip of the dagger against his neck, Ray seized her wrist, twisted it, and flipped her over his shoulder onto a chair. She bounced off the chair before hitting the floor, writhing in pain.

Marvin leapt on the table behind Kristy. She stood ready in attack mode. Fred stood up, clutching his briefcase in front of his chest like a shield.

"Bravo," Marvin said, looking down at Ray from the tabletop. "Seems Rochelle is down for the count. Four more to go," he sneered. "Let's see how this goes."

Kristy and Theo simultaneously attacked. In a coordinated effort the two stabbed and sliced with their daggers in what appeared to be a partner-dance with integrated movements. Ray parried and deflected the blows with his hands, elbows, and feet. His ambidextrous movements matched their simultaneous attacks.

Kristy, with a cry of anger, overextended herself as she stabbed. Ray parried her desperate move, clutched her wrist, and pulled her across his body. As she stumbled forward in between Ray and Marvin, Ray pummeled four rapid punches into her mid-section. She doubled over and dropped to her knees.

Marvin attacked over Kristy's head, but Ray caught Marvin's over-reaching arm and yanked hard, causing him to fall over Kristy. As he fell, Ray launched an upward elbow strike at Marvin's chin and catapulted him back onto the conference table.

From her knees, Kristy stabbed at Ray's thigh, but he raised his knee to parry her blow with his leg. With the same raised leg, he thrust his heel into Kristy's eye, sending her backwards onto her back.

Fred cowered in the corner, holding his briefcase in front of him as a shield.

Jim rose and hopscotched over his downed teammate. Marvin popped himself off the table. They both attacked. Ray was surprised by Jim's dexterity for an older man and by Marvin's strength and resilience for a scrawny kid. Everything he knew about Marvin was wrong.

With one hand blocking a low strike from Marvin and his other hand blocking a high strike from Jim, he kicked Jim's groin. Growling, Jim shuffled back a few steps.

Ray took advantage of the opening. After evading a slice from Marvin's dagger, he rolled over the conference table. As he rolled, he randomly grabbed two of the blue Ethernet cables and a co-axial video/audio cable off the table. Standing on the other side of the conference table and watching his two opponents, he bent the cables in half and held them in a wad by the bent ends so that the four Ethernet plugs and two metal co-axial jacks stuck out, forming a kind of barbed flail like the ones used for flogging.

Rochelle, using the table, climbed to her knees. She tried to stand, but her back would not agree.

Fred's eyes widened with disbelief as he watched Rochelle rise halfway. "Is there no end to you people?" He was on the opposite side of the conference table from Ray.

With an outcry, Rochelle boosted herself up onto the tabletop and slid over the table on her elbows and stomach, like a serpent. Her hair was wild and drool strung down from her lips. Jim walked around the conference table and approached Ray on his left side. Marvin walked past Fred and approached Ray on his right side. Ray was near the exit, but he couldn't leave Fred. With Jim on his left, Marvin on the right and Rochelle in front, Ray squared off with his makeshift flail in his right hand.

Ray focused on the men flanking him, but to his bafflement, Rachel grabbed the edge of the conference table and slingshot herself forward with such force that she nosedived at Ray's knees. She wrapped her arms around Ray's legs, burying his knees into her chest. Clamped like a bear in a trap, he couldn't kick or step.

The men attacked.

Standing in place, Ray parried with his open hand and whipped his Ethernet-co-axial flail with his right. He twisted from his waist, rotating right and left. The three men endured cuts and red streak marks on their faces and hands.

Fred clutched his briefcase tighter.

Ray jerked his legs, but Rochelle strangled them like an anaconda.

Fred grit his teeth and with wide eyes and collapsed eyebrows, he rushed Marvin from behind and swung his briefcase up and down, like a sledgehammer, on top of Marvin's head and shoulder. Marvin dropped his dagger and crouched down with his hand covering his injured head.

"You freakish kid!" Fred yelled with his briefcase hanging from his hand at his side. "What is wrong with you?"

Fred looked like he wanted to hit Marvin again, but he was panting and hyperventilating.

Jim stabbed at Ray. Ray gripped Jim's hand and then wrenched it so that Jim's arm and upper body twisted. Ray whipped him in the face, and then he whipped down at the back of Rochelle's head. She screamed but held on to him. Back and forth, he whipped between Jim, whom he held, and Rochelle, who held him. He whipped with ferocious snaps, until they both dropped.

Marvin picked up his dagger and from his squatting position sliced behind him, cutting Fred above the knee. Fred yelped. Marvin was about to thrust his dagger at Fred when Ray grabbed his hand from behind. Ray cranked Marvin's arm behind his back, like an officer arresting a thief. Marvin grunted, arched his back, and dropped his dagger.

Marvin squirmed. Ray was surprised by Marvin's perseverance, because he knew he was hurting Marvin. He cranked Marvin's arm further by pushing his arm upwards behind his back. Any further and he would tear Marvin's shoulder. Still, Marvin withstood the agony and struggled to free himself, twisting and jerking.

"Stop, Marvin!" Ray yelled into his ear. "It's over."

Marvin would not relent. Like a fish in a net, he jostled from side to side, trying to loosen himself from Ray's arrest.

Ray grit his teeth and cranked Marvin's arm another two inches upwards to where Marvin's fingers could touch the back of his own neck! Marvin screeched. Ray knew Marvin's shoulder tore, but to Ray's disbelief Marvin twisted suddenly and loosened himself from Ray's grip.

As Marvin pulled himself away from Ray, Ray grasped Marvin's shirt and ripped it open.

Marvin's bare body showed through his opened shirt, revealing his chiseled six-pack abdomen and well-defined chest muscles. He wasn't bulky in mass, but his distinct musculature looked like rocks gleaming in the dim office light.

Marvin grinned at Ray's surprised look. "Not quite the geeky, scrawny, unassuming kid you thought I was."

"You *are* full of surprises and deceit," Ray stated, "but that's not good enough to stop me from getting out of this room. You're out of henchmen."

"Deception is simply one's brain mastering another by swaying what the other brain thinks," Marvin stated with his right arm hanging lifelessly by his side. "And you're right. My henchmen are down. So I guess you get your pass out of this room."

"You're a real whack job, you know that?" Fred insulted as he inched towards the door.

Ray watched Marvin carefully. He didn't know what to expect from this young man anymore.

"Go ahead," Marvin said and stepped aside. "You earned your pass out of the room," he said before a corner of his mouth slithered into a half-grin.

Ray couldn't read him.

"Let's get out of here," Fred invited eagerly. "You watch freaky boy here while I get the door."

Ray saw Marvin's dagger in front of him on the floor and kicked it away.

Marvin didn't move while Fred removed the chair that was blocking the door. He unlocked the door. Marvin remained in place. He opened the door. "Come on," Fred said as he stepped into the doorway. Still Marvin did not move from his spot. Fred stood in the doorway looking back inside the conference room. Ray walked backwards, not giving his back to Marvin. He approached the threshold of the door, but Marvin remained as he was with the same half-grin.

"That's right, freaky boy!" Fred said to Marvin. "You learned your lesson. You can't take Ray on by yourself, can you?" He squeezed the cut on his leg. "Dang! Freaky boy cut me."

Marvin watched them without blinking, remaining like a statue. The bloody scrapes on his face from Ray's flail brightened to a reddish glow, matching the glaze of sweat on his pale skin.

"What is wrong with that boy?" Fred muttered rhetorically and then said to Marvin, "Wait til Miranda finds out about you!"

"Come on," Ray said. "We need to get out of here."

The two of them walked into a large, rectangular space where there were dozens upon dozens of cubicles. The office doors on either side of the long area of cubicles were closed. The empty chairs, black computer screens, and immaculate desktops in the little cubicles extended for twenty-five yards.

Ray and Fred walked down the side aisle to head toward the elevator.

Only the custodians in short-sleeve, brown uniforms were present, cleaning as usual. Staggered throughout the area of cubicles, they looked like rats in a maze. There were five of them from what Ray could see. A broad-framed Caucasian man and a tall, skinny Indian man with a beard wiped down the desks. A short Asian woman in the aisle they were in dusted the paintings on the wall. A brown-haired, six-foot Caucasian man with hairy hands vacuumed the carpet. And a five-foot-eight Asian man with long bangs in the elevator lobby on the other end mopped the stone tile floor.

Ray looked back toward the conference room to see Marvin standing in the aisle right outside of the conference room. He didn't move. He merely watched them. His half-grin gradually grew into a full grin.

"Move quickly," Ray whispered, feeling something was wrong.

Fred hobbled as fast as he could while clasping the cut on his leg. He stumbled every other step. Ray tried to help by supporting him, but he tripped and fell. Ray looked back and saw Marvin walking towards them.

"Come on," Ray said picking Fred up and dragging him forward.

"Excuse me," he said to the Asian woman dusting a painting.

She smiled and stepped out of their way as they hobbled past her.

In his peripheral vision, Ray saw a small object coming at his face. He dodged barely in time to evade the object. He turned around to see the Asian woman holding her duster upside down, using the wooden handle as a short Billy club. She lashed out. Ray deflected two of the strikes before hitting her in the face with the back of his fist. She took a few steps back, keeping her club held up in front of her.

"Go." Ray walked backwards and nudged Fred to move on.

"Uh, Ray," Fred said.

"This custodian is one of them," Ray said. The woman approached them followed by Marvin. "Keep going. I'll take care of these two."

"Uh, Ray," Fred said louder. "What about them?"

Ray turned around to see the other four custodians closing in on them. The two cleaning custodians dropped their rags and spray bottles. The six-feet vacuuming custodian separated the metal extension of his vacuum cleaner into two metal pipes and held them like fighting sticks. The Asian mopping custodian from the lobby stomped on the end of his mop, making a sharp point and turning his mop into a wooden spear.

"The custodians too? How many more of you freaks are there?" Fred shouted.

"Meet the rest of the team," Marvin introduced.

Interrupting the escalating antagonism with an awkward intrusion, Mr. Thornton came out of his temporary office. "I thought I heard voices out here. Ray! I'm glad to see you," he said obliviously. "Tell me what your progress is."

"Oh no, not Thornton too, right?" Fred asked.

"Not me what?" asked Thornton and noticed Marvin. He frowned. "For goodness sake, Marvin, button up your shirt! You're head of systems security! What is the matter with you?"

"That's what I've been asking him," Fred said.

"Mr. Thornton," Ray replied, "go back into your office and lock your door."

"Excuse me," Thornton responded defensively, "did you just tell me to go back into my office? If you do not have any results, you guessed right that I will not be happy about it. But you do not have the authority to speak to me in that manner. Do you understand? I don't care how highly Miranda thinks of you. Right now, I'm the executive supervisor until this virus nuisance is resolved."

"Mr. Thornton, you don't understand," Ray said as he walked toward the center of a row of cubicles and nudged Fred along. "Listen to

Mole

me. Go back into your room."

"Where are you going? And why do you both look like a mess?" Thornton asked.

The custodians maneuvered through the cubicles to close in on Ray and Fred.

Thornton noticed the odd custodial behavior and reproached, "What's going on here? Get back to your cleaning jobs! Do you know who I am? I telling you—"

As the mop custodian walked past Thornton, he hammered Thornton in the face with the butt of his wooden spear. Thornton fell, like a tree, back into his office.

The custodians and Marvin were merely twenty feet away from Ray and Fred. But they had no direct line of access to them yet, because the two of them embedded themselves in the middle of the cubicle maze.

"Did we just trap ourselves in here?" Fred asked softly.

Ray replied, "We gave ourselves an advantage."

"I don't quite see it." Fred desperately called to his friend, "Ray."

The custodians skulked, like a pack of wolves encircling their prey. They slowly maneuvered left and right, inching closer.

"Yeah, Fred. I know you're scared."

"I don't want to die."

Another custodian, a five-foot-seven Caucasian female, came out of a restroom by Marvin with a plunger in her hand. When she noticed what was happening, she stood on the rubbery bell of the plunger and yanked straight up, pulling the wooden handle off of the bell. She held up the handle like a club and joined the enclosing circle.

"Oh, gee. Their count is up to seven," Fred stated.

Marvin pulled his Miracom ID badge out of his pocket. As he took out his badge, he stretched out a two-foot chain attached to it. The other end was attached to his belt. He unhooked the chain from his belt, removed the badge, and replaced it with a set of keys. There must have been twenty keys in the bundle. He swung the chain with the twenty, spiked keys in a vertical circle, like a medieval morning star.

"Why do engineers have to be so creative?" Fred whimpered, holding his brief case in front of his chest again as a shield. The blood from his cut seeped into his pants.

Marvin and the custodians were only fifteen feet away from them. The circle around the two tightened, but the cubicle walls and desks still separated them.

"Fred, we're engineers too," Ray stated plainly. He took his friend with him into a cubicle. "When I tell you," he whispered, "I want you to duck underneath this desk." The two of them were in the middle cubicle in a row of five cubicles. Neck-high cubicle walls surrounded them. They faced the opening of their cubicle, which was only wide enough for one person to pass through. Behind Ray was a desk with a flat screen monitor and a keyboard. Beneath the desk was a computer tower. A black rolling chair was pushed under the desk. A five-drawer file cabinet was on his left side. A laser printer on a printer stand stood to his right. Hanging on the cubicle wall to his right was a poster-size glass picture frame of serene mountains. Outside the cubicle was a narrow aisle and across that aisle was another row of five cubicles of similar size and layout.

"Why did you trap us in here?" Fred asked.

"Sometimes the best advantage is being trapped," Ray whispered.

"That makes no sense," Fred whined.

Marvin and the custodians were now twelve feet away. The custodians held up their weapons. Ray could see how tightly they gripped their weapons by the tension in their forearms. They were eager to fight. Ray pulled on the two adjusting straps of his backpack to tighten the shoulder straps. The place already smelled like sweat.

. . . .

"Down!" Ray shouted. Fred dropped and scooted under the desk.

The two female custodians holding the duster and plunger clubs charged the opening of the cubicle with Marvin behind them. But they both stalled at the narrow opening. Apparently, they had not coordinated who should enter first! Ray whipped the rolling chair from behind him and shoved it into the opening, hitting the women in the kneecaps and creating a temporary barricade with the chair.

Ray took the keyboard off the desk, ripped its three-foot cord from the computer tower, and wrapped the end of the cord around his right hand. The vacuum custodian with the two metal fighting sticks swung at Ray from behind the cubicle wall. Ray ducked and dodged the custodian's attacks that were limited by the neck-high wall.

Ray swung the keyboard by the cord. His first swing knocked the metal sticks aside. His second swing was wide, hitting the dusting custodian behind him while she was pushing the chair away and then hit the vacuum custodian in the head. The sound of the plastic keyboard cracking on the skulls sounded like popcorn popping.

The broad-framed, Caucasian custodian and tall, skinny Indian custodian, who had no makeshift weapons, were in the neighboring cubicles on opposite sides. They scaled the cubicle walls with alarming speed. Ray whipped the keyboard straight at the broad Caucasian custodian with a snap of his arm. The keyboard darted, striking the custodian in the face, knocking him back into the neighboring cubicle. Without pause, Ray whipped the keyboard in the opposite direction behind him. It sliced in a straight line through the air, and the edge of it struck the tall Indian custodian in the shins as he mounted the top of the cubicle wall. His feet were knocked out from under him, and he fell face forward into Ray's cubicle. His stomach landed on the file cabinet first, and then his face hit the floor. He lay motionless in front of Fred, who was under the desk.

Without hesitation, Ray swung the keyboard up and over toward the cubicle entrance. The keyboard chopped downward on top of the dusting custodian. She brought up her arms above her head, and the keyboard crashed on her forearms, causing her to step backwards, and pushing the plunger custodian and Marvin back.

Ray swung the keyboard again in a wide, horizontal arc. The mopping custodian with the spear in the adjacent cubicle to Ray's left was scaling the wall when he had to leap backwards to evade the bludgeoning keyboard. Ray continued swinging, whizzing it over the cubicle wall at the vacuum custodian with the two metal sticks, who ducked to avoid getting cracked on the head again. The broad Caucasian custodian in the other adjacent cubicle and the three at the opening all backed away to avoid the swift, orbiting keyboard. The Indian custodian slowly rose. While still swinging the keyboard, Ray snapped a quick kick to the Indian custodian's face, dropping him back to the floor.

Swing after swing, the devastating keyboard whizzed through the air in circles and kept everyone at bay. But Ray's swinging keyboard became predictable. So finally, the vacuum custodian timed it right and swung both of his metal sticks down as the keyboard flew at him, smashing the keyboard into pieces. Alphabetical and numerical keys scattered in all directions.

The custodians saw their opportunity and charged. Ray flung the cord at the mopping custodian in the adjacent cubicle. It tangled around the custodian's head, delaying him for a couple of seconds.

Marvin stepped inside the cubicle, swinging his chain and keys, like a morning star, in a figure-eight pattern. As soon as Ray had released the keyboard cord, he grabbed the forty-inch flatscreen monitor behind him. Spinning around to face Marvin, he yanked its cables and power cord out and charged at Marvin. The large flatscreen shielded him against Marvin's vicious chain and key attacks. Ray couldn't see but could hear the screen being torn up by the whipping ball of keys. Ray rammed the screen into Marvin, knocking him back out of the cubicle, pushing the duster and plunger custodians back. Ray chucked the screen out into the aisle at the three of them.

Ray quickly turned right, pulled the glass poster frame off the cubicle wall, and raised it in time to block a punch from the broad Caucasian custodian in the adjacent cubicle who already scaled halfway up the cubicle wall. The broad custodian's fist slammed into the frame, shattering the glass and cutting his knuckles. Ray shoved the frame into him to push him off the wall.

While the broad custodian stumbled back into his cubicle cradling his raw, bleeding hand, Ray flung the frame like a Frisbee over the cubicle wall at the vacuum custodian. The vacuum custodian reflexively brought his metal sticks up to form an "x" in front of his face. When the frame collided with his metal sticks, the remaining shards of glass burst through his x-shaped block, piercing the custodian's face in dozens of places. Screaming painfully, he turned away.

Ray kept them at bay and inflicted serious wounds, sending a message that he would keep them out of his cubicle. However, Ray suddenly switched his tactics and baffled his unsuspecting assailants.

He turned to meet the mop custodian, who crouched on top of the cubicle wall with his wooden spear. The mop custodian seemed to expect Ray to try to knock him back out of the cubicle. So while he perched on the wall, holding on by one hand, he thrust his spear at Ray to keep him away. But Ray grabbed the spear and pulled him into the cubicle. The mopping custodian fell over the file cabinet and on top of the Indian custodian who was trying to rise again.

Then Ray turned toward the cubicle opening where both the duster and plunger custodians were scampering in at the same time again with their clubs. He grabbed the women lodged in the small opening by their wrists and yanked them through concurrently. He immediately pressed their wrists against their chests and shoved them against the cubicle wall on the right, where the broad Caucasian custodian was again climbing over the wall. The broad custodian reached over the women with his non-bloody hand for Ray. Ray allowed the broad custodian to grab his collar, and then stepped backwards hard to pull the broad custodian off balance. The broad custodian fell into the cubicle on top of the two women.

Turning to his left, he blocked Marvin's swinging chain and keys by catching it, but the bundle of keys still hit Ray on the shoulder. Ignoring the stinging pain, he yanked the chain, pulling Marvin into the cubicle as well. As Marvin unexpectedly stumbled inside, Ray punched him in the chest.

The mop custodian stood back up on Ray's left side. He kicked at Ray's head. Ray blocked the kick, but sustained a blow to his ribs when the mop custodian whacked him with the spear. The Indian custodian finally rose. But with the Indian custodian standing, the mop custodian was crowded against the file cabinet.

Ray stepped into the center of the cubicle. Now he had Marvin and the duster custodian in front of him, the plunger and broad custodians on his right, and the Indian and mop custodians on his left. He was almost completely surrounded. The vacuum custodian was behind Ray on the other side of the wall, picking out glass from his face.

Ray scanned them with his hands up in a guard position and taunted, "Come on!"

Infuriated, they attacked all at once. Ray blocked, kicked, and punched back in return, sustaining a couple of insignificant blows to the shoulders and arms but landing a dozen of his own in their faces, chests, and abdomens.

Within seconds, the custodians and Marvin discovered the encumbrance of their tight space. When anyone cocked his or her club back to swing, they accidentally jabbed a neighboring custodian. Marvin's swinging chain hit his fellow comrades or got caught against the cubicle wall. In the frenzy of the crowded confusion, the custodians were hitting each other more than they were hitting Ray!

But Ray chopped and kicked in every direction. They desperately tried to block. But the raising of a forearm to block meant an elbow went into a comrade's face. When the mop custodian raised his spear across his chest, he accidentally stabbed the Indian custodian's side. In a frantic reaction, the duster custodian swung her club wildly only to hit Marvin in the head. The custodians were not expecting to block hits coming from anywhere else but Ray. The friendly fire picked away at the assailants.

The vacuum custodian stood to his feet with one eye open. Seeing his comrades in trouble, he sprang into action and climbed over the cubicle wall.

Marvin yelled, "No! Don't!"

But not understanding his leader, the vacuum custodian jumped into the cubicle, standing on top of the desk behind Ray. Ray was completely surrounded—just what he wanted.

The vacuum custodian swung his two metal sticks wide and hard. Ray ducked and the sticks hit the mop custodian and the Indian custodian on their heads like gongs. With shock, he suddenly realized the trap he entered. He turned to try and exit the cubicle by going back over the wall. Ray quickly grabbed him by the belt and pulled him off the desk and deeper into the cubicle.

There was barely room for any of them to stand, let alone move. When Ray's assailants tried to maneuver or evade, they bumped into a file cabinet, printer, desk, cubicle wall, or each other. In the chaos of the clutter of humans jammed into the little cubicle, the custodians and Marvin were clumsy and apprehensive with their attacks.

But Ray burst into an open season of strikes! He fired punches, palm strikes, kicks, knees, elbows, finger jabs, and chops. Since he was tightly surrounded, he didn't need to aim. Every strike he executed hit something. Plus, Ray effectively exerted full force in very short distances. His enemies suffered punches to the nose and stomach, chops to the jaw and collar, palm strikes to the nose and chest, kicks to the knee and groin, elbows to the head and chin, and finger jabs to the eyes and throat.

Finally, one by one, the custodians went down, but they couldn't even fall properly, because there wasn't enough room for their bodies to lie on the floor. They fell into a corner, on top of the desk, over the printer, against the file cabinet, or onto each other.

Ray stood in the midst of the lattice of brown-uniformed bodies with adrenaline still pumping through his arms. It was done. After surveying the lifeless, entangled forms for a moment, he said, "Fred, come out. Let's go."

Fred emerged from underneath the desk with his briefcase clutched against his chest and cell phone in one hand. His eyes were wide as he stepped over the bodies. "We didn't die. You took them all out. I can't believe you did that. I got it all on video. I mean I knew you were good, but, man, I didn't know you could do that!"

"When you're outnumbered by a gang," Ray said, stepping over Marvin and out of the cubicle, "get into a small, confined space with them."

"You know," Fred said as they left the cubicle, "I will admit that I would've never thought of that."

They hurried to the elevator lobby. Fred hobbled on his wounded leg, grimacing as he went. The building now was eerily still. Ray stopped to peek in Thornton's temporary office. Thornton still lay unconscious on the floor. They continued on. When they reached the lobby, Ray looked back behind him before they turned the corner. Startled, he saw Marvin standing in the distance staring at them. He appeared battered, bruised, and bloodied. He started pursuing them. But he limped and dragged himself in a zombie-like fashion with indifference in his face and hollowness in his eyes.

Mole

"All right, now," Fred commented, "that boy severely creeps me out! What is wrong with him?"

"Let's go," Ray said, feeling that same creepy sensation.

Fred pressed the elevator button repeatedly. Ray went to peek around the wall to evaluate Marvin. He was limping towards them at a slow pace. Ray swallowed hard. He had no question of whether he could beat Marvin at this point in a one-on-one. Marvin looked like he could barely hold himself up. But there was something frightening about this kid, and Ray preferred not to engage him in a third round.

Ray heard a ding sound.

Fred motioned for Ray to come as the elevator doors opened. They rushed inside. Fred pressed the button for the lobby floor repeatedly until the door closed. They both sighed with relief as they looked up at the mirror in the ceiling and surveyed their physical conditions.

After descending thirty-seven floors, they exited the elevator and headed to the main lobby, where the front entrance was.

Officer Hernandez saw them and came out of the security booth, alarmed by their injuries. "What happened to you?" he asked.

"Where were you guys?" Fred asked, as the two of them approached the security officers.

Officer Cole also came out with a shocked expression and stood beside her partner. "You're both hurt. Fred, you're bleeding!"

"No kidding," Fred replied. "Didn't you see what was happening on the security cameras? Why didn't you help us?"

"We didn't see," said Officer Hernandez. "We were told that you were doing highly classified work and you couldn't be observed. We were instructed to turn off the security cams on your floor, but to monitor the front entrance carefully."

"Figures," Fred said. "Who told you that?"

"Thornton. With the mole problem, he didn't want your project leaking out. We need to call an ambulance for you," Officer Hernandez suggested.

"Call an ambulance. Call the police! Call the marines!" Fred added.

Officer Hernandez pulled out his walkie, but suddenly there was a loud crackling sound, his eyes rolled back, his tongue stuck out, and his body convulsed before dropping to the floor, revealing a tazer was held to the back of his neck. The hand holding the stun gun was Officer Cole's.

"No!" Fred exclaimed. "Not you too."

She was ten feet away from them. Ray took two quick steps toward her before she drew her gun.

"Stop!" she commanded. "I'm aware of what you're capable of, Ray

Lee." She took two steps back. "I will shoot you. I don't care if you're dead or alive. Give me the decryption code. Put it on the floor and kick it to me."

"How much of Miracom is infected by ApexGen? Engineers, custodians, and security guards?" Fred asked rhetorically.

"Ray, do as I say," she ordered, "or on three, I will shoot the both of you and take the decryption code from your dead bodies."

The elevator dinged. Out came Marvin.

Chapter 22
Plan

Marvin slogged towards Ray and Fred. The scratching sound from the side of his left foot dragging against the stone floor and the stomping of his right foot as he stepped and pulled himself forward created a chill in Ray and Fred. His right arm draped limply at his side, swinging lifelessly as he stepped and dragged. Stepped and dragged. Stepped and dragged. His left arm was curled in front of his stomach. One corner of his bleeding mouth hung open. His bloody face, battered body, and pale complexion would've been horrific enough, but added to that was his expression of cold indifference. It was like he felt no pain, had no remorse, and had no care for self-preservation. His hollow eyes fixed on Ray and Fred.

Ray looked back and forth between Officer Cole with the barrel of her gun pointed at him and Marvin with his freakish eyes staring at him.

"You're kidding me!" Fred yelled. "Marvin! Why won't you go down? What in the world is wrong with you? That boy must be on drugs!"

"Marvin," Officer Cole shouted, "you okay?"

Only a gurgling sound came from his mouth as he raised his curled, left arm and pointed. Officer Cole's eyes followed the line of Marvin's crooked finger to Ray's backpack. She stiffened her arms and tightened her grip on the gun.

"Take off your backpack and toss it to me," Officer Cole ordered. She turned her aim onto Fred. His eyes widened. Then she lowered her aim. "Or I will start by putting a bullet through your friend's knee cap. You have to the count of three."

Ray rushed a few options through his mind. *What can I do? Cole is ten feet away from him—too far to get to her before she pulls the trigger. Knowing Fred, he wouldn't react in anyway that would evade the bullet. He likely would freeze in place.*

"One," Officer Cole counted.

Marvin was too far back to seize him as a bargaining chip. He thought, *Marvin likely knows he was in no fighting condition, so he would move around to pick up Officer Hernandez's sidearm. Then our situation would worsen doubly. Best bet is to use the backpack as a diversion, since that's what their focus is on.* Ray slung his backpack off and got ready to toss it.

"Two."

Marvin plodded around Fred, avoiding Ray, and went toward Officer Hernandez's body. He slowly squatted and removed the gun from Hernandez's holster. He raised the gun to his stomach level and pointed it at Ray. The side of his mouth that wasn't hanging opened wormed up to a half grin. "Soot im," Marvin mumbled to Cole.

"No, wait," Ray said.

"Don't shoot me," Fred pleaded.

"Three," Cole said.

Suddenly, a hand holding a black canister appeared a few inches in front of Officer Cole's face from behind her head; the hand sprayed pepper spray into Cole's eyes, nose, and mouth.

Cole closed her eyes, shrieked, and fired, but the bullet hit the floor. She pressed her hand and the side of her gun against her burning face as she bent over, revealing Miranda standing behind her!

Marvin, stunned, tried to turn his body to point his gun at Miranda. But as he rotated, a growling cry boomed in the lobby. Deon tackled Marvin from the side, knocking him with such force the gun popped out of his loose hand. Deon completed the tackle by crushing his body into the hard, stone floor.

The Thunder Queen unloaded another dose of pepper spray on Cole, spraying it on the side of her face and into her ear. Cole shrieked all the more. Ray moved swiftly to disarm her. The gun was wet with pepper spray, and he could feel his hand burn from it. Cole fell to the floor, squealing with her face covered.

"Ray. Fred," Miranda said. "Let's go!"

Deon got off of Marvin's warped and immobile body. Miranda looked at him and shook her head. "Of all the people," she said. Then she said to them, "Now!"

The four of them ran out of the lobby to find Miranda's silver Mercedes sports car parked in front.

"Get in." Miranda jangled her keys while running to the car, and the doors unlocked and the engine started during her approach.

Fred and Deon climbed into the backseat. Ray jumped into the front. The car peeled away from the curb before Ray closed his door.

"Miranda," Ray finally exclaimed, "how did you—"

"I found this young man moping around by the gate on the far end of the premises." she replied. "When I saw him trying to get over the gate, I pulled up to him and told him to scat, or I would either call security or pepper spray him myself. He told me he was looking for you."

"Sorry, Sifu," Deon apologized. "I had a feeling you were in trouble."

Plan

"And that you were! Good thing for this young man's intuition," Miranda affirmed. "Deon told me everything! The connection between your daughter's kidnapping, this virus, the mole, and ApexGen. He told me about what you had been through at the child-trafficking house, the tunnel, and the violent encounters."

"I'm sorry, Miranda. Deon shouldn't have involved you," Ray said.

"He didn't have a choice," she said, stepping on the peddle to run a yellow light.

"She told me to get in her car or she would call security on me, Sifu," Deon explained. "Then she locked the doors with all her fancy gadgets in here and wouldn't let me out until I told her what was going on."

"And it was a good thing he did," Miranda stated, "because you would've had a bullet in you if we hadn't shown up!"

"I'm so glad you two showed up," Fred said. "If you didn't, we –"

"What were you thinking, Ray?" Miranda scolded as she made a sharp left turn, slinging the passengers to the right of the car. A deadened pause followed the rhetorical question. "You knew how dangerous these people are, you knew we have a mole issue, you knew there's some elaborate takeover plan, and you still took it upon yourself to come to Miracom alone?"

"I didn't want anyone else getting hurt," Ray replied bluntly. "It's my problem."

"It's arrogance!" she snapped as she slammed on the brakes, skidding to a stop at a red light.

Taken aback, Ray fumbled for the words to say. "What I mean is –"

"Arrogance, Ray," she asserted further. "You hear me?"

"Yes, ma'am," he answered feebly.

"Fred," she summoned.

"Yes, ma'am," Fred answered.

"Did you know about any of this?"

"Uh, well, um. No, not exactly," Fred said.

"Not even your best friend knew," Miranda stated.

"I didn't know who to trust, really," Ray defended.

"That's part of your problem, isn't it?" Miranda assessed mercilessly.

The light changed to green and Miranda launched the car forward with a rev of the engine. "You don't go charging into a place by yourself, knowing you're up against terrorists who infiltrated the company. You've already been shot at, and tonight you had another gun pointed at you. Who do you think you are, Ray? All this I-don't-want-to-get-anyone-else-hurt is a farce for your arrogance in thinking you could take this on by yourself. You should've at least informed me of what you knew about the nature of the mole. This young man had enough sense to come looking for you."

"How did you get here, Deon?" Ray asked.

"Took the bus, Sifu," Deon answered. "Abby and Jer are watching Stanley."

"Deon told me you sought refuge at a church. Where is it? I'm taking you there."

Ray gave her the address.

"Before I take you there," she said, looking in her rearview mirror, "let me lose these bozos first. They've been following me since we left Miracom."

Ray and the others turned around to see a Crown Victoria sedan. It was black, dark blue, or brown—it was difficult to tell in a moonless night. Miranda accelerated with such force the torque threw them back on their seats. The sporty Mercedes pulled away from the tailing sedan with ease. Ray could see their pursuers attempting to catch up.

Miranda turned this way and that, zipping down one street and roaring up another, like a rat zigzagging through a maze. She whipped around corners and raced down straight-aways with a grace that seemed to make the car skim over the asphalt. The car never jerked or swerved. The Thunder Queen flew through street corridors like a breeze in a tunnel. After running through a couple of yellow lights and making a few more turns, Miranda slowed the sporty getaway car to 30 miles per hour. Ray turned around in his seat to look through the back window. The sedan was gone.

Ray turned back around. "That was not the first time you did that, was it?"

"There are many things you don't know about me," she replied.

"I'm starting to think you're called the Thunder Queen for many reasons," Fred jested.

"I didn't know I was called the Thunder Queen," she replied blandly.

A quiet filled the vehicle for several seconds until Fred broke the awkwardness with a question. "So what now?"

"I'm taking you to this church. Then I want to know your plans," she declared.

Ray opened his mouth, but before any sounds came out, Miranda said, "Ray, I don't want to hear about you not wanting to involve me, because we're well beyond that. I need you to suck up your arrogant self-reliance and accept my involvement."

Ray closed his mouth.

"It'll be another twenty minutes before we arrive at the church," she continued, "so why don't we make good use of this time by telling me what happened in my company tonight. First off, tell me what happened to Thornton."

"He got knocked in the face," Ray said, "but he's sound asleep in his office."

"All the better," she said. "Now start from the beginning."

Ray and Fred filled the twenty-minute car ride with updates on the virus situation, identities of the moles they encountered, and details of their battles. Fred injected a few dramatic flairs into the story. The three of them speculated that if there were that many moles uncovered tonight, then more could still be undercover. Miracom was not only infiltrated. It was infested. Yet they agreed that no matter how many moles there were, Miracom was not lost until the main server was commandeered.

. . . .

When they arrived at the church, Miranda pulled into the back parking lot, keeping out of sight. They walked to the front of the church and greeted Mr. Mills the homeless man on the porch. Ray knocked on the church office door.

"Knock again," Mr. Mills invited with a hacking chuckle.

As Ray was about to knock again, the door opened. Abby stood in the doorway, and he felt an unexpected sense of relief at the sight of her.

"You're back!" Abby said with exuberance and warmth. "It got late, and I was wondering. Come in out of the dark."

"Thank you. We almost didn't make it back if it weren't for Deon and Miranda."

"Deon! You went to Miracom?" Abby asked with surprise.

"Yes, I did," Deon replied with a boyish smile.

"And you're Miranda? Ray's boss?" Abby said.

"So you're the Thunder Queen," Jeremy said, walking into the office from the conference room. "Fred and my dad used to tell me about you."

Fred, standing behind Miranda, shook his head adamantly at Jeremy. Ray looked at Jeremy with wide eyes. Jeremy realized what happened and froze in his place, trying not to look at Miranda. Everyone else was silent.

"Well," Miranda spoke up, "now that I know my reputation precedes me, let's get to business."

"Uh, yes," Ray agreed, "come this way. You need to meet a former scientist of ApexGen." He led the way into the conference room.

"Oh, oh, good," Stanley greeted Ray as he walked in. Stanley sat at the head of the table with a pen in hand and several sheets of scratch paper in front of him. The scratch papers were covered with scribbles and drawings written from every orientation; there were no topsides to the sheets. "I was afraid something happened to you."

"Something almost did," Miranda chimed.

"And, and, who is this?" Stanley asked as he scoped out Miranda from head to toe. Then he looked past her at Fred. "And who is that?"

"I'm Miranda. Ray's boss," she introduced. "But apparently, you can call me Thunder Queen."

"What, what kind of a nickname is that?" he mocked.

"So, you're a former scientist of the organization that wants to take over my company?"

"Stanley has inside knowledge," Ray stated, "and he's helping us get in ApexGen."

"You trust this man?" Miranda asked Ray.

"He has given us no reason not to so far. Besides, we don't have much of a choice. He's our best bet," Ray replied.

"Why, why wouldn't you trust me?" Stanley asked defensively. "You have nothing to lose by trusting me."

"And you have nothing to gain if we do," Miranda pointed out.

Stanley looked at Ray and said, "I don't like her. Does she have to be here?"

"I don't care if you like me or not. I care if you're trustworthy," Miranda said. "We've had our fair share of two-faced people. And yes, I have to be here."

"She's here to help, Stanley," Ray explained, "and she wants to know the plan, as do the rest of us. Why don't we get some coffee, and we'll let Stanley elucidate the details of his master plan to us?"

"Fine, fine. Well, grab a seat around the table," the mad scientist invited.

"First," Ray said, "Fred and I are going to get cleaned up. We've been bleeding all over Miranda's nice car."

"Gee," Abby said, taking a closer look at Ray's wounds, "your wounds from the previous fight haven't even healed yet. Let me help you both."

"Sure, Ray could use a nurse," Fred agreed in a mildly slimy way as he nodded at Ray with a grin.

Ray shook his head while he placed his backpack on the table. The three of them went to the kitchen.

. . . .

Plan

They all sat around the conference table. On the center of the table were a few sets of dark blue uniforms with name tags, ID badges, file folders, a thick black binder stuffed with paper, and a dozen equipment items and small toolboxes. The uniforms included caps. The fronts of the uniform shirt and cap had embroidered lettering that read, "Mason BioTech Services."

"Mason BioTech," Abby said, "this is a very reputable company."

"It is a subsidiary of ApexGen. We infiltrated it and annexed it in 1998," Stanley informed. "Now, now, take a file folder and open it."

Ray, who sat adjacent to Stanley's right side, opened the folder in front of him.

"Listen, listen carefully to me," Stanley said, squinting at them. "You cannot miss a detail. This will not be easy. If you are caught, it is over. The first document describes five roles of the service team. The service teams are typically four or five members. Each of you has a designated role from equipment adjustors to equipment assessors to equipment cleaners. All, all of the equipment is extremely sensitive and is expected to be handled with expert care and exactitude. So, so the way you carry yourselves in there is important. If you appear clumsy or careless, you will raise suspicion. Keep, keep in mind that you are a specialized team."

"How are we supposed to know how to carry ourselves?" Deon asked.

"I understand these protocols," Abby said. "I work at a biolab, and while I may not be totally familiar with the brand of equipment ApexGen uses, I have been around these kinds of equipment enough to know how to handle them."

"Good, good," Stanley affirmed, "then you shall be the designated team leader." He handed her a metallic seal to adhere to her ID badge.

"What about the security measures?" Miranda asked.

"I'm, I'm getting there," Stanley said, sounding annoyed. "When you first enter the building, you'll go through x-ray machines. They will x-ray everything. It's worse than TSA! So do not plan to sneak anything in. If you don't want them seeing something, leave it at home. Because they will see it. Any suspicion can blow your entire operation. After you go through the x-ray scanners, approach the security desk and tell them you're servicing in the basement." He dramatically pronounced the word 'basement' while pinching his thumb and index finger together next to his mouth. "You must say 'basement' not downstairs, garage, or cellar."

"All right," Jeremy said, "we got it. Basement."

Stanley continued, "They will ask you to enter your entry code on a wireless keypad. Abby, only the team leader has the entry code, and it must be memorized. You cannot read it off of a sheet or device. You're expected to know it. The code for this visit will be, uh..." He rustled through his scratch papers until he picked one up and said, "Ah, yes. 552738169.4. Be, be sure you get the decimal point too."

"Did you just pull the code from that pile of trash?" Jeremy asked.

"It's, it's the code!" Stanley assured, sounding annoyed again. "I got it from my contact today. What's the entry code, Abby?"

"552738169.4," Abby recited. The faces around the table showed their surprise. "I'm good with numbers," she said with a smile.

"Good, good," Stanley said excitedly. "Then, then each of you will have your thumbprint scanned to verify your identification." Stanley took out his phone, tapped on an app and entered login information. He passed the phone to Ray. "Place your right thumb on my phone. It will scan your print. A digital imprint of your thumbprint will be sent to my contact at Mason BioTech who will finalize your forged identities and send them to ApexGen."

"Hold on," Miranda interrupted. "He's taking copies of your thumbprints?" she said with an appalled tone. "He can save your thumbprint, send it to who knows who, and use it to forge your identity. Ray, how did you meet this man?"

"Um," Ray started, "he was stalking my house."

"Good grief," she responded, "How do you know he's not just playing you all?"

"That's what I've been saying about this racist chump," Deon concurred.

"Maybe it's time to listen to Deon again," Miranda suggested.

Stanley was irritated, "Excuse me, ma'am, but you don't know me—"

"Nobody here knows you," she stated.

"But, but let me finish," he said, "ApexGen fired me. Therefore, I want them to know the impact of abandoning me. Get it?"

"You sound like a bitter ex-girlfriend," Miranda said.

"That's what I said," Abby said.

Stanley huffed.

"What did you get fired for anyways?" Deon asked. "Being a racist?"

"That, that is not relevant," Stanley replied.

"I think it's very relevant," Miranda contended.

"You should tell us," Ray demanded. "It makes a difference. We can't have any secrets from you if we're to go on." He held the phone with the thumbprint scanner app running in his palm, like he held it hostage until Stanley gave him what he wanted.

Plan

"Fine, fine," Stanley surrendered. "It was stupid, in light of all the genius work I did for them. Like I said before, my contact at Mason BioTech is a special person."

"Special, how?" Miranda interrogated.

"I have relations with her," Stanley said blandly.

"OK again, that's good enough for me," Abby said quickly.

"No, no one outside of ApexGen can see our bio-plans, lab results or bio-schematics," Stanley continued, "but she's always asking me about our latest, greatest developments and future plans. It stimulates her. One time, only one time, I took some photos of some of our projects on my phone and sent them to her. You, you know. To impress her, so she can genuinely witness the brilliance of my work."

"I can see where this is going," Abby said.

"I was caught," Stanley said.

"Uh-huh," Abby added.

"They said," he continued, "I breached confidentiality, and ApexGen has a zero tolerance policy on that. What did they even mean that 'I breached confidentiality?' All of those projects were my works! They were my ideas, my plans, my results. Mine! They pretty much belonged to me, so, so I should be able to do with them as I pleased!"

"You were hoping to impress her to get lucky, weren't you?" Fred asked.

Stanley rubbed the back of his neck with his head down.

"Ew," Abby said.

"Wow," Jeremy commented, "I didn't expect this to be the reason. I thought maybe you were working on some risky experiment and blew up a lab or something, but not this."

"That's why I must get back at them!" Stanley shouted. "They can't fire me over something like this. Are we done with the topic of my termination? Can we get back to what really matters?"

"Now that we have our answer," Ray said, "let's get on with it." He placed his thumb on the phone. The screen flashed green once. He passed the phone to Abby who passed it to Deon. Then Jeremy reached for the phone. "No," Ray said. "Not you, Jer. We already had this conversation."

"Miguel already said he can't do it," Jeremy argued. "You need four people."

Ray looked at Jeremy with serious consideration. Then he turned his attention to Stanley. "Stanley, you said it's not ideal, but it could be done with three people, correct?"

"Yes, it's possible," Stanley affirmed, "but it lessens your chances of success."

"I'll do it," Fred volunteered. "I mean, I'll go and be the fourth person."

"What? You?" Jeremy questioned. "You would get beat up by a hobbit!"

"I'm not a fighter, but I'll go," Fred restated.

Ray looked at him with surprise and gratitude. "You would do this? It's dangerous."

"Come on," Fred said. "How long have we been best friends? Your daughter needs rescuing. How could I not help?"

"Bad idea," Jeremy contended.

"No, this is good," Ray countered and placed his hand on Fred's shoulder. "Fred is an engineer. The way he carries himself will grant our team greater credibility. We have our team of four!"

"This is bull!" Jeremy protested. "Why am I here?"

"Very good," Stanley affirmed. "Allow me to proceed then."

Stanley opened a digital map from the ApexGen folder on Ray's laptop. "The actual headquarters of ApexGen is not the actual AmeriBank building. ApexGen is a sixty-floor subterranean fortress."

"Whoa," Abby exclaimed

"Not again," Deon exclaimed. "What's with these people being underground?"

"Take, take the main elevator down," Stanley continued. "Jamie is on the 53rd floor, but the elevator will stop at the 52nd floor and ask you for an access code before the elevator will continue descending. You must get this correct on the first try. If you enter the wrong code, the elevator will freeze and lock you in until a security team arrives. The access code to descend past the 52nd floor is—ummm..." He scratched the top of his head. "Oh, yes, it's 7387#."

"7387#," Ray repeated, "Got it."

"Wait, wait," Stanley said shaking his head, "no, that's not it. It's 7397#."

"Are you *sure*?" Miranda questioned.

"Yeah, you got to be on point, man" Deon stressed.

"Yes, yes. Don't question me. It's correct. 7387," Stanley said. "I mean, 97. 97! 7397."

"Oh gosh, we're going to die, aren't we?" Fred said.

"Okay, listen," Stanley said. "The subterranean fortress descends all the way to the 60th floor. You only want to go to the 53rd floor to find Jamie. But mark my words, you don't not want to go any lower."

"Why? What's below the 53rd floor?" Abby asked.

Plan

"The lowest seven floors are the executive and special agents levels," Stanley explained. "It is the most secretive and highly regarded part of ApexGen, so it is heavily guarded. Not to mention, since that is where the most covert agents, their handlers, and our executives work, you would find yourself in a hornets' nest of the fiercest foes. Gordon was a trafficking mercenary. The executives and special agents make him look like a clumsy Mickey. I guarantee you, you would not come out of there alive."

"Can I say that now I'm a little scared?" Abby said.

"A little scared? I'm peeing in my pants! What did I volunteer for?" Fred said.

"Just stay out of the 54th to the 60th floors, and you should be fine. The 60th floor is the executive level floor and war room. It's where the highest levels of planning happen, where the executives, generals, and head agents meet. Even I have never been there in all the years I was employed as their chief scientist. Plus, we have no schematic of that floor." He showed them the blueprints in the ApexGen folder on the silver hard drive. It did not include the 60th floor. "We have no idea what that floor looks like."

"Got it," Ray reiterated. "Stay out of floors 54 through 60, especially 60. I just want Jamie. I have no reason to go any further "

"There is one more thing I should show you," Stanley said. He showed them a part of the blueprint that indicated a very long stairwell, descending all the way down to the 60th floor. "This is an emergency exit," he pointed out. "This stairwell shaft runs all the way from the top to the bottom. I want to point this out as an alternate means of escape. Don't use it unless you have no other choice. Once you open the door to the stairwell, it sounds an emergency fire alarm throughout the building."

"There is also this," he said, pointing to a part of the blueprint that indicated a ventilation shaft, extending straight down to the 60th floor. "This is an alternate route of the alternate route. The ventilation shaft is plenty wide, and there's a ladder running up and down the entire thing. If for some odd reason you do find yourself in the ventilation shaft, be aware that it is a straight tube that is sixty stories deep. If you slip off the steel ladder, you plummet to your death. There, there is no safety mechanism."

"What dingo built this place?" Deon asked.

Ignoring Deon's question, Stanley continued, "Now, now you see the three ways to descend and ascend the edifice. Of course, the cleanest operation would be to go down the elevator, get Jamie from the 53rd floor, and simply go back up the elevator unnoticed."

Stanley reclined back in his chair and concluded, "That, that's it! You know the layout, you have the security codes, and you know the steps to take." He smiled. "Abby," he asked her quickly, "what's the entry code into ApexGen that you give at the lobby security?"

"552738169.4," she recited without hesitation

"What's the access code for the 53rd floor?"

"7397#. Or is it 7387?"

"Not funny," Fred said.

"Very well," Stanley said. "So, so is this a satisfactory plan?"

Ray examined details of the scheme. "Are there other security checks between the lobby and the 53rd floor? With a highly secured place as this, it must require more than our uniforms, ID badges, thumbprint and a couple of security codes."

"Ah yes. Almost forgot!" Stanley perked up, pointing a finger to the ceiling.

"Great! He almost forgot!" Deon mocked. "He argues that he's some powerful mind, and he 'almost forgot'?"

Stanley gave Deon a dirty look. "To, to enter any room you will need to supply a tiny sample of your blood into a machine. It will check your DNA signature. It's just a prick on your finger. My contact at Mason BioTech will submit your DNA signatures as part of your security clearance. After you provide your blood sample, place your ID badge in front of the scanner by the door, and the door will unlock. If you don't offer your DNA signature, the door will not unlock."

"This keeps getting freakier," Fred commented.

"You mean there are hundreds of employees in the facility getting DNA checked every time they enter a room? There must be a gross amount of blood in the building's system!" Abby noted.

"Your blood opens doors. It's always about the blood."

"Still gross," Abby said.

"So, so." Stanley reached for a small device next to the badges in the center of the table. "Let me draw samples of your blood." The device looked like a large, thick high-tech calculator with a big screen and a nodule on the side where a person could insert an index finger. He pressed a few keys to set up the device. "First, first, enter your name and then follow the directions on the screen. Insert your finger into the hole on the side. It will take a sample of your blood. The data will be sent to my contact."

Ray took the DNA device. "Anything else we should know about?"

"Oh, oh yes! Body heat emissions are also monitored throughout the building. If you linger in an area where you shouldn't be lingering, such as outside a secured door, it will draw suspicion. You have to keep moving. No loitering."

"Are the guards armed?" Ray asked.

"Oh, there's that too!" Stanley lit up again. "The guards are armed with three-million-volt tazer-batons. No, no firearms. Shooting is prohibited in the subterranean section of the building because of the sensitive nature of the equipment, cargo, and subjects inside the facility. But there are ample guards on every floor. They are not of the caliber of the special agents in the lowest seven floors, but they are well-trained and brutal. They manhandled me once over a misunderstanding and ever since then my shoulder pops out of place. Do not underestimate them."

"Crud. Any other bad news you're not remembering to tell us?" Deon asked.

"Oh," he perked again, "cameras of course. Surveillance cameras at every major access point, door, elevator, stairwell, and room, but not in the ventilation shaft."

"ID badges. Access codes. Blood. Body heat monitors. Cameras. Guards who can electrocute you." Deon reviewed. "And we have to act like we know what we are doing as bioengineers or something."

"That's it. You got it... bro."

"Crap," Deon remarked.

"I, I suggest to let Abby take the lead," Stanley recommended. "Let her do most of the talking. Ray and Fred will be the technicians. Deon, since you're not technically skilled in these areas, you will be the tech assistant. Here are your uniforms."

Ray said, "You still haven't told us how we would get out of this subterranean complex with Jamie."

"Oh, oh, yes!" Stanley said.

"You remember something else now?" Miranda mocked.

"That's where my old, personal assistant will be of help to you. His name is Terry," Stanley said.

"Another person?" Ray asked. "Can we trust him?"

"Yes, yes. He was my assistant for eighteen years! He is very loyal to me. He felt I was wronged too, but he is as much a scaredy-cat as I am. The most he will do is make up an excuse for all the lab workers in Jamie's lab to leave the room to assist with a special task. It will last for no more than fifteen minutes. Got that? You have fifteen minutes. Inside the lab, there is a biohazard container the size of a street trashcan. Place Jamie inside. Make, make sure it's empty and clean first." Stanley chuckled. "Seal it. The container is impervious to x-rays. And it is bulletproof! Those biohazard containers are strong enough to contain everything from nitric acid to a grenade blast. They're designed to keep the nastiest things in, so I'm guessing it works in keeping things out too. Interesting, isn't that?"

"Then we just wheel Jamie out the front door," Ray asked.

"Yep, yes, yeah. Wheel her out as normal as you can be," Stanley answered.

"If anyone should ask what's in the container?" Miranda questioned.

"Well, well, then you can tell them, uh… um… hm, let's see…," he stuttered

"We can tell them," Abby intervened, "that it's filled with bio-waste residue containing hydrochloric acid that vaporizes if the container is opened, and once inhaled it would dissolve your lungs."

"Whoa," Fred said. "Did you just come up with that?"

"That's, that's good," Stanley praised while pointing his finger at Abby. "Yes, yes, she'll make a good leader. What are the security codes again?" he asked with a twinkle in his eye.

"552738169.4 and 7397#," Abby recited.

Stanley chuckled. "Great. Well, you're all set to go."

"Would be more set if you had a fifth person on the team," Jeremy said.

"Well, well, like I said before, five is better than four," Stanley said. "It's more believable to have one expert team leader, two technicians, and two assistants to go with the two technicians. I mean, four is fine, but five is a bit more believable. Instilling belief is key to this operation."

"See?" Jeremy pressed.

"No," Ray said plainly. "We're fine with four."

"Sounds like a solid game plan," Miranda assessed. "Is there anything I can do?"

Ray pulled out the red flash drive from his backpack and his sci-fi looking device fell out on to the table.

"Are you still carrying that thing around?" Fred asked.

"What is that?" Miranda asked.

"Nothing of relevance," Ray responded. Then he handed the drive to Miranda. "Would you keep the decryption code on you in case something happens to me?"

Miranda accepted it and placed it somewhere inside her blouse.

"If, if everything is settled," Stanley said, "the team of four should review their profiles in the informational folders and get a good night's rest. You, you will need it. My contact at Mason BioTech will have all of your IDs processed overnight and personally delivered to me in the early morning. Your rescue mission will begin at 9:00 AM tomorrow."

Chapter 23
Trust

The white-walled conference room seemed smaller than normal; the many mismatched chairs and the clutter of boxes seemed to be pressing in on them. There was too much in this room. Even Ray, who was generally comfortable with being in tight, enclosed spaces, felt like the room was shrinking. But no one moved. The group sat in silence for a few minutes, digesting the plan that would take place in less than 12 hours, before they disbanded one by one, starting with Abby.

"I'm going to go out into the office area to review my profile," Abby said. "Not that I don't like you all's company, but it's feeling too crowded for me." She got up. "I need some space to concentrate."

"Yeah, me too," Deon said. "I'll be in the kitchen. I got to study up. The little girl's counting on us. Won't let you down, Sifu." He walked out with his folder.

"I'm going to make a late-night burger and fries run," Fred announced. "All the action, life-threatening scenarios, and rescue scheming made me hungry. Anybody want anything?"

"Um, um, I'll take a cheeseburger," Stanley requested. "But, but, I don't have any cash."

Fred appeared annoyed but said, "Since you're the guy making this rescue operation possible, I'll treat you to a cheeseburger. But don't make this a habit."

"How are you going to get there?" Ray asked. "You don't have your car."

"Oh, that's a good question," Fred said, looking around. "Maybe I just won't—"

"Take mine," Miranda said, "but not a scratch."

"Wow!" Fred was excited. "Not a scratch." He enthusiastically took her keys.

"By, by the way," Stanley said, "I don't want pickles or onions and I want mustard instead of ketchup. Also, tell them to go light on the lettuce. Will they put lettuce on it?"

"Oh, gee!" Fred exclaimed. "Just come with me."

The two of them got up. As they walked out, Miranda said sternly again, "Not a scratch, and you will only go to the burger joint. I know what the current reading on my odometer is."

Only Ray, Miranda, and Jeremy were left in the room.

Ray turned to Miranda in seriousness and said, "Miranda, perhaps there is one more thing you could do for us."

Jeremy got up abruptly and walked to the door.

"Where are you going?" Ray asked.

"I'm not needed here," Jeremy said blandly, "so I'm going somewhere else."

"Don't leave the church," Ray shouted as he watched Jeremy walk through the office and into the church corridor.

"What can I do for you?" Miranda asked.

Ray pulled his laptop to him. Using his restored clearance at Miracom, he accessed one of the satellites. "You can help monitor us while we are in ApexGen," he said. "We'll be deep inside the subterranean fortress. It would be a good idea to have eyes on us while we are in there."

"That's good thinking, Ray," Miranda stated.

"I've set the tracer program to track my cell phone," he said as he showed her the blinking dot on the screen that indicated his current position on the map. "Because we'll be well beneath the earth's surface, I'm boosting the frequency my cell phone emits. I'm also uploading the blueprint of ApexGen to the tracer program so the satellite will tell you exactly where I am on the blueprint."

"You're a good strategist," Miranda complimented in a way that seemed irrevocable. "That's why you were our chief R and D person, and that's why you will get your daughter back."

"Thank you, Miranda," he said, closing his laptop. He left the tracer program running. "I hope I can pull this off, but I might need a miracle."

"Listen to me," she ordered. "You stay focused, stay sharp, and fight hard. You will retrieve her. But Ray, I have to say that I don't entirely trust Stanley. He could be two-faced. I don't know what it is, but there is something about him I don't like. I've been a chief executive for a long time and my skills in judging people have made me successful at what I do. I know you don't have another option, but don't trust him completely. Watch your back with him. Take extra precautions. You understand?"

"Understood. I'll be cautious," Ray said. "You know me. Lining up all my ducks is in my nature."

"Your entire operation right now depends on him. A disgruntled ex-employee with a vendetta? There's too many holes in his story to me. I mean it, Ray. Take some provisionary measures for yourself. Don't rely entirely on him."

"You being our eyes from space will be an added measure."

. . . .

Fred and Stanley came back into the room with their take out food.

"Very well," Miranda said. "I'm going home and getting that good night's sleep. I'll be back tomorrow morning before you leave."

"Thank you, Miranda," he said. "What you did tonight and what you will do for us tomorrow is more than I could thank you for."

"Thank me when this is all done and we come out on the other side of this with our heads intact. Then you can buy me a drink. For right now, stay focused and alert, and don't get sentimental. You will have time for that later."

"Yes, ma'am," Ray complied. "I'll see you tomorrow."

"Bright and early," she said, taking her keys from Fred and heading out the door.

Fred and Stanley sat on either side of Ray. Fred brought burgers and fries out of a white paper bag.

"Here," Fred said, handing Ray a burger. "I've been with you all day, and I know you haven't eaten. Knowing you, you get so focused that you actually forget to eat."

Ray accepted it and replied, "Thanks."

"I got you a double bacon, avocado cheeseburger," Fred said. "I figured with all the workout you've done, you could afford to enjoy a fatty burger. Here's all the ketchup you need." He put a pile of ketchup packets on the table.

Ray smiled as he unwrapped his burger.

Stanley asked while he chewed on a bite of his cheeseburger, "Is, is she always that chipper?"

"Thunder Queen?" Fred said, "Yeah, she is. Not a whole lot of warm fuzzies."

"She's just in control," Ray defended. "It's a strong quality of hers that gets misunderstood, but should be admired."

"How, how long has she been at Miracom?" Stanley interrogated.

"Longer than either of us," Ray answered. "Probably for about thirty years. She is part of Miracom's history. Why? What are you getting at?"

"Just, just a suspicion," Stanley stated. "ApexGen has had at least one mole in Miracom for the last few decades. The earlier moles set the foundation for the future work of supplanting the company. That's, that's how we did it. That's how we get into the law enforcement institutions, governments, military, and major companies, like banks and financial corporations. ApexGen patiently laid the groundwork over many years before making its move. The, the earlier moles who paved the way are what we called 'establishers.' That's how Professor Haagen strategizes, and that's how his predecessor strategized. It's a cancerous approach."

"Miranda is no mole," Ray declared. "That's absurd. I'm more likely to trust her than you."

"I don't know, Ray," Fred said skeptically. "The Thunder Queen could make a good mole. She hides a lot about herself from us. I'm not saying she is, but it is an interesting thought."

"The, the way she took your decryption code from you—I, I don't know. It's a high-valued item that ApexGen would kill for. She, she was a bit too ready to accept that burden, like, like she was ready and waiting for you to offer it to her," Stanley continued. "Did it seem too coincidental that she showed up to rescue you at Miracom?"

"But if she was a mole, why would she take out one of her own agents?" Ray questioned. "If it weren't for her, we could've been dead."

"Could've, could've been," Stanley emphasized. "She may have calculated that you would've likely taken out the one security guard and the mangled Marvin, seeing as you had already taken out almost a dozen others. Her, her taking out the security guard and the crippled Marvin was an easy way to infiltrate into this hiding place—this inner circle of yours. Sounds exactly like an ApexGen move."

"But that wouldn't make sense. She had Deon with her," Ray countered.

"What, what better way to get on the inside than to befriend one of your allies?"

"They worked together in rescuing us."

"Did, did she give Deon a choice?" Stanley asked.

"No."

"I, I rest my case."

"You know, we never would've guessed Marvin to be a mole," Fred added. "I'm just thinking out loud, you know?"

"'All, all war is deception'—Sun Tzu in *The Art of War*," Stanley quoted.

"He does make some good points," Fred said.

"Don't worry," Ray assured. "Even if she is crooked, I have Plan B in play."

"What's, what's Plan B?" Stanley asked with his head cocked.

"Oh, Ray and his Plan Bs," Fred said.

Shifting in his seat, Stanley asked again, "What is this? What's Plan

B?"

"Fred knows me," Ray said. "Let's just say I always have a safety plan to my safety plan. Stanley, you just focus on getting us into ApexGen. Besides, I still doubt Miranda could be crooked. I can't explain why, but I trust her."

"Like you trusted Marvin," Fred said, "and he turned out to be one creepy boy."

"I misjudged," Ray confessed. "Won't happen again."

"Fine, fine. You can judge however you like. Only remember that ApexGen has agents everywhere, with many sleeper agents in key positions around the world. Mistrust can be a costly weakness." He said and stuffed several french fries into his mouth.

"Well, before it gets too late, it's time for me to vacate this room to review my file too." Ray held up his file folder. He took his last bite and got up from his chair.

"You're not leaving me here, are you?" Fred asked. "Besides, we still have fries."

Ray held the file folder above his head as he swallowed and walked out of the room. He walked through the church office and out into that same corridor that eventually led him to the vintage chapel. But this time he took a left turn through a set of double doors that opened up into a wide hallway. He walked on a plush carpet with elaborate patterns. The light fixtures along the walls were elegant. If he didn't know he was in a church, he would've thought he was in the conference area of a high-class hotel.

He wanted a place to sit in solitude to digest the contents in his folder, but all the rooms were locked. He continued down the hallway until he arrived at the main lobby. One of the six doors to the main sanctuary was opened. The sanctuary was a large, modern auditorium that could seat five hundred people. He decided that would be a good place to hide for a while.

He entered and sat at the end of the last row of cushioned seats. The sanctuary smelled like it had just been vacuumed. There was not much in the sanctuary except for a large, stainless steel cross hanging in the front. A set of large speakers hung above the stage and a few silky banners adorned the white walls.

He opened his folder, but the presence of someone caught the corner of his eye. He looked to the opposite side of the sanctuary where someone was sitting two rows up from him on the last seat. It was Jeremy.

Jeremy just happened to glance over his shoulder as Ray watched him. He got up abruptly and proceeded towards the open door. Ray looked down at his file folder, thinking that he would return to his business-at-hand. But his conscience nagged him to call out to his son. "Jeremy!"

Jeremy stopped, turned his head slowly with his eyes closed, and then opened them. "What?"

"Come here," Ray summoned. He felt it was time to lay everything out with his son. He didn't know what the outcomes of tomorrow might be. There was a likelihood that this could be the last time he would get to talk to Jeremy. He felt like it was his one last ditch-effort to break through to his son. "We need to talk."

"What's there to talk about?" Jeremy challenged. "I'm not going on this rescue mission for Jamie. You don't need me."

"Not about that," Ray said.

"Then what?"

"We need to talk about what's going on with you—inside of you."

"Nothing's going on with me. I'll leave you alone to what you are doing. Big day tomorrow."

Jeremy took three more steps to the door and entered the doorway when Ray said, "I get that you want to be destructive."

Jeremy stopped in the doorway. He turned his head slowly and looked back over his shoulder at Ray. "What?" He asked again, "What are you talking about?" He turned to face Ray while remaining in the doorway.

"I'm talking about you wanting to be violent."

"That's what you think? That's why you're keeping me out of this mission?"

"Isn't it? Isn't that what this is for you? A chance to let out your anger?" Ray persisted. "You insist on being on this dangerous mission because you're on some kind of destructive path. You want to let out your hate for life. Maybe you're hoping you'll get hurt yourself. But I'm not going to support you in going down this road."

Jeremy shook his head. "You don't get it," he muttered.

"You're angry. I do get it."

"Stop saying that. You don't get me. You don't have a clue about me."

"Oh, come on! You were the same way at Gordon's house. You wanted to cover the rear. You wanted to split up to go search the houses on your own because you wanted some action. Isn't that right?"

"No," Jeremy replied.

"I've seen the posters and drawings in your room—the images of violence and destruction. I see what's brewing in you and it's not healthy.

You think destroying things, or yourself, will make you feel better?"

"No. That's not it. I don't know," Jeremy mumbled.

"I saw you at that party, drinking, and partying like you didn't care about anything anymore. You don't care about yourself, so you just want to throw yourself in harm's way."

"Stop telling me what I'm feeling."

"You think I don't know, but I'm still your father, and I know you better than you think. If you just let me in… just talk to me instead of festering inside."

"No." Jeremy left the doorway and stomped rapidly toward Ray. "No! No! No!" Jeremy shouted as he approached. "You're not right. You don't get it."

"I can see your anger," Ray said. "You can't tell me you're not angry."

"Yes, I'm angry. I'm mad as hell, all right?" Jeremy shouted.

"Well, you need to stop," Ray said matter-of-factly. "I miss your mom too, but this anger of yours is eating you alive. It will kill you."

"Don't you think I know that?" Jeremy shouted so loudly his voice boomed off the walls. His bottom limp trembled. The pause between them gave them both a chance to catch their breaths. "I know what my anger is doing to me better than anybody else. I can feel it. I'm less of a person everyday." His voice cracked.

"Then why do you keep this up?" Ray asked softly.

"Don't you think I would stop how I'm feeling if I could? Do you think I like being this way? Do you think I want to be that angry teenager?" Jeremy paused. His bottom lip trembled. "Do you think I wouldn't rather be thinking about junior prom, getting A's in school, what college to go to, or asking a girl out on a date? Don't you think I hate being this way?" His eyes welled up and he tried not to look at his father. He didn't blink to not push the tears out.

"Then, Jer," Ray said gently, "what can I do to make this better for you? It kills me to see you like this? You saw the school counselor, we went to a couple sessions of family counseling, and we went to a grief group a couple of times. None of them worked for you. What will work? What will fix this?"

"I don't know if you can… fix it," Jeremy said plainly. Though his nose and cheeks were red, he managed to restrain any tears from dropping. "Maybe there are some things you can't fix because you can't go back into the past and change things. Maybe some things are just supposed to stay broken because the loss is too great."

"I can't believe that. Everything can be fixed. We just have to find a way."

"Really? Do you really think so?"

"Yes."

"Can you bring Mom back?"

Ray couldn't respond immediately. The question surprised him and stabbed his heart. "You know I would give anything if I could."

"But you can't. You can't change that. There are some things you lose that you can't get back, and nothing else in this world can replace it."

"I know." His son's words seeped into his own soul like poison. He began to ache, but he tried to stay focused on his son. For the first time in over two years, Jeremy was actually opening up to him. He told himself, *My son needs me.* "Please tell me how I can help you."

"Can you help yourself?" Jeremy asked.

Again, Ray was taken off guard. "What do you mean?"

"Have you gotten over Mom?"

"You know that I miss her dearly."

"Have you healed or recovered from her death?"

Ray hesitated. Then he found the right words. "I'm working on it everyday."

"Bull!" Jeremy retorted. "I see how you retreat to your bedroom late at night. What do you do in there? Cry? I see how you keep yourself so busy with work and Wing Chun. For what? To cover up how messed up you still are? You pose like you have it altogether and like you're in some position to fix others. But you can't fix things because you're just as messed up. Aren't you?"

"I'm not messed up, Jeremy. I have my tough moments, but I get through them, because…"

"Because what? Because you have to take care of your family? That's the ruse you keep hiding behind! You hide how messed up you are behind your children."

Ray felt exasperated. "What do you want from me?" He didn't know these kinds of thoughts festered in his son. After not having a deep conversation with his son for two years, he was caught off guard. His son's questions enveloped him like a trap. He took two breaths before saying, "Am I not supposed to care for you and Jamie? Am I not supposed to protect you as my son? Am I not supposed to be your father?"

"I don't know," Jeremy muttered, throwing up his hands.

"You don't know? So you're badgering me, but you don't know?"

"No, I don't know, okay?"

"Well, then what? What am I supposed to do? Tell me."

"Maybe do nothing!"

"Nothing? You'd rather me do nothing, and that will make things better?"

"Yes!"

"Yes?"

"No. I don't mean nothing. I don't know!"

"Then what do you mean? What is it you want from me?"

"Maybe you're just supposed to be honest with me!"

Again, a pause descended upon them. Suddenly, the space between them felt smaller. For a moment, they just breathed as Ray allowed that last statement his son said to permeate his mind.

"How can I trust you if you can't be honest? How was I supposed to talk with you?" Jeremy's lower lip trembled again.

"I was just trying to take care of you, trying to keep our home under control."

"I know. I see it." Jeremy closed his eyes tightly and shook his head. He looked at his father and said, "But every time you do, every time you try to fix things, I didn't know you. When you pretend you aren't messed up, I feel farther away from you." Jeremy bit his trembling lower lip. "Maybe the people at the party were destructive as you call it. They drink. They smoke. They do drugs. They party. They look for fights. But I know them. The girl you saw curled up to me on the couch—her parents just divorced. The guy you put through the coffee table—his older brother got locked up. The other guy you knocked over the couch—his dad beats him every other day. I could sit with them because they were honest with me." Jeremy's eyes reddened.

Ray listened quietly and never took his eyes off of his son.

"There were many times I wished I could sit with you." His nose reddened and the glassy bubble of water formed over his eyes. He didn't blink, keeping the water in. "But I couldn't stand being around your fronting, trying to fix me, like you had it altogether, when I could see that you were just as jacked up as I was."

"I had to be strong for you, Jer," Ray explained.

"But I needed you to be weak with me."

Ray didn't say anything. Suddenly, he felt the curtains were drawn back. He wanted to reach out to his son to touch his shoulder or stroke the side of his head. He wanted to say something. But he remained quietly attentive. He simply stayed present, allowing the words of his son to seep into his heart.

Jeremy's eyes watered all the more. He broke eye contact with his dad and quickly looked away, but it was too late. A tear fell from his eye onto his reddened cheek. The tear slowly rolled down to the corner of his mouth. He blinked and a couple more tears fell. Ray found his nose starting to run and his eyes welling up. He didn't know this was how his son felt. He didn't know this was what he thought. He didn't know how he had been. Jeremy sighed lightly.

Ray turned one of the chairs around for Jeremy. Jeremy sat on it. Ray sat down as well.

"I don't want to be this way," Jeremy confessed softly. "I don't want to be angry anymore, but I don't know how to stop." He held his hands in front of him with his palms facing up.

Ray wanted to ask what kept him from stopping. He wanted to ask what he could do to help him not be angry anymore. He thought of suggesting going back to counseling as a family. He thought of mentioning a tip he read online. He searched for the right thing to say, and came up with two good responses. But instead, he said, "I'm angry too." Ray looked down at the floor between them. "I'm angry at the jerk who took Melanie's life. I'm angry at Jamie's teacher for making her do an Easter project that required eggs. I'm angry at the paramedics for not helping Melanie hold on for just ten more minutes so I could say goodbye to her at the hospital. I'm angry at myself for not going to get the eggs and being in that accident instead of her."

Jeremy now looked at his father's face, like he looked at the first page of a new chapter in a half-read book he had cast off for a long time. Ray could not see his son's sympathetic eyes, because he kept his face toward the floor.

"I can't tell you how many times I replayed that day in my head," Ray said. "All the things I thought I could've done—should've done—that would've made everything turn out differently. I've come up with thirty-one alternative actions I could've done that would've significantly changed the outcome, where your mom would not have died. The more I think up more alternative actions, the more I don't forgive myself."

"I heard you and Mom fighting that day," Jeremy said.

"I regret that fight everyday."

"I felt mad at you."

"I could understand you being mad at me."

"But I was also mad at God and the whole world. I knew in my head that I couldn't blame you. I mean, it wasn't like that was the first time I heard you two fight. All couples fight, right? I told myself that your argument didn't kill her. That drunk driver did."

"You don't have to be gracious to me," Ray said with his eyes still drawn to the floor space between them.

"But I know it's true even if I didn't feel it was true. You didn't kill

Mom. The drunk driver did."

Ray didn't lift his head up, but shook it once. "I tried searching for that drunk driver. I can't tell you how much it angers me that he got away."

Jeremy nodded. "Me too. It's wrong. It's not fair. Mom was the nicest woman. How could that happen to her?" Jeremy's face fell toward the same floor space between them that Ray's face was anchored to. "Do you remember when she stayed up all night to make that Halloween costume for me because the store ran out of Green Lantern outfits, but she knew how much I wanted to be Green Lantern that year? Or when we were at the grocery store and that old lady in front of us didn't have enough food stamps for all her groceries and Mom covered the difference for her?"

"Yes, I remember," Ray looked up at Jeremy, smiling. "And there was the time when she drove three hours to your youth camp to bring you clean underwear, because you forgot to pack them! I told her, 'Leave him. Let him go commando. He's out in the woods anyways!' But she insisted you have your underwear. Oh, she was incredible."

"Yeah." Jeremy laughed, and more tears fell out of his eyes. He sniffled. "She didn't deserve to die."

"No, she didn't. And yes, she *was* the nicest woman. She was a far nicer person than I am. It isn't fair," Ray echoed.

Jeremy asked, "What kind of a world is this? Why do good people suffer and bad people get away? Is this how life is? Why would God allow this?"

Jeremy asked all the right questions but Ray had no sufficient answers. "I don't know." He tried to come up with something wiser to say; perhaps he could recall an old adage. But those three words were the most sincere words he had.

"I don't know how to feel better. I feel guilty for wanting to feel better, like I'm betraying her if I felt better about losing her."

"You can't do that to yourself. You can't put that guilt on yourself." As Ray said that, he felt the weight of his own words echoing back at him. "She loved you and would never want you to punish yourself."

Jeremy's shoulders suddenly trembled. Streams ran from his eyes and nose. "Dad." He looked up at his father with eyes screaming in pain. "I did something she told me not to do. She told me not to date that freshman girl because I was only in seventh grade. She told me I was too young and that girl was no good for me. I told Mom, 'Okay,' but I went behind her back and dated that girl anyway for nine months. I would lie to her about where I was. I was feeling horrible. I finally broke it off in eighth grade. I was going to tell Mom the truth that night, but she never came home for me to tell her." He wept and wept some more. "I'm sorry. I want to tell her I'm sorry."

"Jeremy." Ray reached out, placed his hand behind his son's neck, and pulled him in, embracing Jeremy with both arms and allowing him to weep on his shoulder.

"I hate myself," Jeremy cried.

"No, no, no, my son. No." Ray whispered, "She forgives you. I know she does."

The world felt like it spun slower. The sanctuary felt smaller. Tomorrow felt farther away.

"I'm here for you," Ray said solemnly. "I'm hurting, but I'm here."

For five minutes they held each other—five solid minutes in the fleetingness of time.

When they pulled apart, Ray said, "You lost your mother. I lost my wife. We both lost a great deal."

They sat there for a moment like they were still listening to each other, although neither spoke. It seemed words were not needed.

"And now we're faced with losing Jamie," Ray reflected.

"Your daughter. My sister," Jeremy said, wiping his tears. "You and I are both threatened with losing someone again. You're trying to rescue your daughter. I want the chance to rescue my sister. How could I sit on the sidelines while my father risks his life for my sister? I'm part of this family."

Finally, Ray understood.

"I know what you might say," Jeremy intercepted Ray's thought process. "I know saving Jamie won't bring Mom back. But I'm not trying to bring Mom back. I'm trying to bring my sister back. It's something I feel I should be—need to be—a part of."

"You might not like hearing this, but you're a lot like me," Ray said.

"I know. Scary. Like looking at yourself in a mirror."

"Well, I hope you're good at pretending to be a biotech assistant."

Jeremy smiled.

"If we're still a family, and I believe we are, then you should have a part in fighting for our family," Ray said. "And I could use your help."

"I probably should've asked this question two years ago, so I'm a little late on this, but how do we heal from this, Dad?"

"You're not late. I think I've come to understand that there is no standard time for grieving. You and I both needed two years to do it—two years to hurt, be angry, and say good-bye." Ray said, "I think trying to save Jamie together will be our first step toward feeling whole again."

Jeremy nodded.

"Come on," Ray invited and sniffed, "let's talk to Stanley. We still have to make sure he can get your ID set up." Even as he said this and they walked out together, he felt uncertain about involving his teenage son in this dangerous venture. It went against his common sense for the safety of his child. But he knew this was something he had to do with him. The danger of losing his son in this was great, but if he didn't do this with Jeremy, he knew he would've already lost his son.

They walked back through the hallway. Ray jested, "Hope you can handle this. Your punches and palm strikes looked rusty to me."

"Don't worry. Like you always said, it's like playing the piano. Once you learn it well, it never leaves you. You taught me well."

Ray placed his hand on his son's shoulder. It seemed like a while since he made a gesture like that to his son. Ray smiled.

They entered the old conference room and found Stanley and Fred laughing together. Ray and Jeremy looked at each other.

"What's going on?" Ray asked.

"Oh, hey," Fred greeted. "Nothing. Stanley was going over my profile with me, and then I don't remember how, but we got on this topic of speculating whether the Klingon and Orc languages have a common linguistic origin because they bear some phonetic similarities, particularly with the consonants."

"And then, and then," Stanley chimed in, "we started wondering if Klingons and Orcs procreated, what the babies would look like!"

"We drew some sketches!" Fred exclaimed.

Fred and Stanley broke out in laughter again.

"Wow," Jeremy said.

As laughter tapered down, Fred took notice of the father and son pair. "Is it me, or do you two appear a tad chummy?"

"Stanley," Ray said, "Jeremy is coming with us to rescue Jamie. Can you doctor up an ID and profile for him as well?"

"You, you know," Stanley replied, "it's 11:00 PM." He had a serious expression. "But fortunately for you, my contact and I are night owls. I'm sure she can make it happen. Besides as I said, five is better."

"Speaking of 11:00 PM," Fred said. "I should get some rest. Big, dangerous day and all. I should call my wife. I have a lot of explaining to do." He patted Stanley on the shoulder. "You're all right."

When Fred walked by Ray, Ray whispered, "I would've never guessed."

Fred chuckled and shook his head before he went out the door.

"Well, well, sit down," Stanley invited Jeremy. "Let's get your thumbprint and DNA. So, you'll be going on this rescue mission after all?"

"Yep," Jeremy replied.

Deon and Abby returned to the conference room.

"Look at this," Deon said. "Somebody is promoted to undercover agent status."

"Anything else we should do to prepare for tomorrow besides reviewing our profiles?" Ray asked.

Stanley wrapped up the samples collected from Jeremy. "Just, just get a good night's rest. You, you will need it. Tomorrow is a day you won't get to do over."

Chapter 24
Entry

It's time! Ray's eyelids flipped open, and his heart thumped. He sprang up to a sitting position on the couch. For some reason, he felt foggy. Jeremy was still asleep on the cot. Abby, Deon, Stanley, and Fred were spread out on the floor with blankets and cushions. All sound asleep. He checked the time on his phone. Only 6:00 AM. He rubbed his eyes. His vision was hazy. He went to the kitchen with his toiletries.

After washing up, he did extensive stretches and punching drills to ready himself. He shook his arms and rolled his shoulders to loosen up. He had to be at a 100 percent. But his mind still seemed cloudy.

There was a knock on the church office door.

He went to open the door. It was Mr. Mills. "Good morning, Mr. Mills," Ray greeted. "What can I do for you this early in the morning?"

He cackled. "Your friend is looking for you."

"Friend?"

"Yep! Right over there across the street in that black car." He pointed behind his shoulder with his thumb.

Ray felt tense. No one should know that he is here. The last time Mr. Mills announced a "friend" was here to see him, it turned out to be Stanley. *Who could this be?*

He stepped outside and saw Stanley's grey sedan parked in the same spot, but there was someone sitting inside of it. He looked back inside the church. *But Stanley is sleeping inside the conference room. Who is that? Maybe Stanley slipped past him while he was washing up and decided to sit in his car. I should go check, just in case.*

As he approached the car, he could tell it was not Stanley. The shape of the face, the hairdo, and the height were different. The person looked familiar, but he couldn't make out who it was through the tinted glass and the glare of the sun on it. He went up to the car and tapped on the window with his knuckle.

The door unlatched, then slowly opened with a creek. Out stepped a short, familiar Chinese man. Ray gasped and stared at the man with widened eyes, as if he were seeing a ghost.

"Sifu Chu?" Ray asked, rubbing his eyes again.

"Hello Ray Lee," Sifu Chu greeted.

"But, how?" Ray was dumbfounded. "How are you? How are you here? You're supposed to be in Hong Kong. You were in the hospital."

"I was, fighting lung cancer," Sifu Chu said. He appeared poised and strong.

"But you're here, and you seem fine," Ray felt joyful yet confused.

"You have been going through many trials," Sifu Chu stated.

"Too many, Sifu."

"How are you handling things?"

"As best as I can. I've been shortsighted in many ways, but I'm still learning, as you always taught me to do. I'm not giving up. I'm fighting hard."

"Not hard enough."

Those were the familiar words he recalled hearing from his master. If anyone said, "I'm trying hard," he would say, "Not hard enough." If someone were to say, "It's too hard," he'd say, "Not hard enough." Ray was taken aback a bit though this time. He hadn't heard these words in a while, and hearing them now made him feel guilty.

"I know things are a mess, but I'll get Jamie back," Ray said.

"What did I teach you when confronting a problem or an enemy?" Chu tested.

"Take control of the situation."

"Yes, take control of the situation, and do you have control of the situation?"

"Somewhat. Not entirely. Well, we have a plan."

"A plan is only as good as the execution of it. You have yet to execute your plan, so it is to be determined if your plan is good."

"It will work." Ray breathed heavier. "I know your teachings, Sifu. You don't need to put this pressure on me."

"Pressure? You remember I took you in after your father left you. I trained you. I taught you. When your life was out of control, I helped you find order."

"Yes, you did. How can I forget?"

"And now, you have lost order. Your life is in fragments again."

"I know. But I'm fighting hard to get everything back to the way it should be."

"Not hard enough."

The words weighed on Ray again. He knew these lessons, but he felt frustrated and antagonized. "What would you have me do?" he blurted.

"Do better."

The figure of a tall man walking up the street behind Sifu Chu caught Ray's attention. He couldn't tell who it was yet, because his vision was still hazy. But as the person drew closer, he made out the image of— *It can't be!*— Vladimir Haagen!

"You!" Ray said and stepped around Sifu Chu to confront Haagen.

"Ray Lee," Haagen said. He stopped ten feet from Ray.

"How did you find me?" Ray demanded to know.

"You know me. There's very little I do not know." He had the same accent as Ray remembered from college. "You're residing at a church. How quaint. What did I tell you about religion? It's misleading."

"Why are you here? What do you want?" Ray observed how distinguished Haagen appeared, even more so than he did during Ray's college days. He doesn't seem to have aged at all. In fact, he looked stronger, exuding an intimidating confidence.

"I know what you're up to. I'm here to tell you that you won't succeed. You're on a fool's errand, and I know you're better than that."

"I'm coming for Jamie. How dare you take her? Where is she? With all your intelligence, where's your ethics? You should know better."

"I do know better. I know perfectly. I was your favorite professor, and you were one of my favorite students. I knew you and Melanie had great potential to change the world. Now you two have produced a child that *will* change the world. I'm very proud of you. You have good genes." He said with a slithery smile.

"You're sick. I want my daughter back. I'm coming for her."

"You should come. All those office hours we spent together. You were always interested in my ideas of nanotech and genetic syncretism to unlock the next human evolutionary stage." Haagen held out his hand. "I invite you to come. Join me as you once did. We had a good relationship. I was more than a professor to you. I was your mentor. Return to me and join me."

"I want my daughter," Ray stated. "How foolish of you for coming here. What makes you think I won't take you down and use you as a bargaining chip for my daughter?"

"By all means, try," Haagen welcomed. A van screeched to a halt behind Haagen—the same van that took Jamie at Gordon's house. The side door of the van slid open with a bang. Gordon and ten agents leapt out of the vehicle and formed a semi-circle around Haagen. "You know I wouldn't come unprepared."

"Sifu Chu," Ray called over his shoulder, "this is the man who has my daughter. You and I can take out all of these bastards." He looked behind him, but Sifu Chu was no longer there. Ray looked around, in the grey sedan and down the street, but he was nowhere in sight. He had disappeared!

"You're alone, Ray," Haagen said. "You've always been alone, but you won't be anymore if you step over to my side. Come with me in the van."

Ray stepped sideways toward the church. His hazy vision still had not lifted.

"You have friends in there, don't you, including your son Jeremy?"

Ray quickened his steps into a sideways trot, not wanting to turn his eyes away from Haagen. He needed to get inside.

"It's okay, Ray. Bring Jeremy with you. Bring him to me too. I wouldn't want to split the family apart." He grinned from ear to ear. "This will be a family reunion!"

Ray darted up the steps. Mr. Mills held the office door open for him while he cackled. Ray rushed inside and locked the door behind him. Panting and his heart pounding, he held his hand on the door and leaned against it. Taking a breath, he hollered, "Abby, Fred, Deon, Jeremy!"

"Ray?"

The voice from behind him was delightfully and yet hauntingly familiar. It was a voice he had not heard in two years. *It couldn't be.*

Ray slowly turned around. The outer ends of his eyes, brows, and mouth drooped. His chest inflated with emotion. His knees weakened. His racing heart melted. Tears rained down his cheeks. It took a moment before he could finally say, "Melanie?"

"Ray," she said with sweetest tenderness. She sat at Cherish's desk. She held a pen in her right hand and dozens of notecards scattered over the desk.

He shook his head. "I'm dreaming. How could this be?"

She rose from the chair, placed the pen down on the desk, and walked toward Ray. His heart thumped all the louder with each step of her approach. He breathed deeply.

"You're not real. I should wake up," he told her.

She stepped to Ray and touched his cheek. He leaned his face into her warm hand. Her skin was as soft as he remembered.

"Where is Jamie?"

"I'm sorry," he apologized. "She was taken, but I'm going to get her back."

"Ray, you lost our daughter?"

"No, no, Jeremy and I are going to get her back. We have a good plan."

"You and your plans. You're taking Jeremy with you?"

"Yes. It's a long story, but I think it's the right thing to do for him."

"You're going to lose him too, aren't you?"

"No! I'll protect him."

"Like you protected me on the day of my accident?"

"Mel," he whimpered. His heart broke, like a thousand pieces of glass shattering even further against a cold, hard ground.

"Like you protected me?" she repeated.

"Mel," he said through the tears dripping over his lips. "I've died every day since you left. You can't imagine how much I regret that day. If I could take your place, I would. With all of my heart, I would."

"But you can't, dear," she said tenderly. "But there is one thing you can do."

"What?"

"Take care of this family. I don't want to worry about our children."

"I'm trying," he said with a searing ache in his chest.

"What did I tell you, Ray?" she quizzed. "'No craze,' isn't that what I said? Don't let things get crazy. Now everything is a mess. Jeremy has been drinking and being self-destructive. Jamie was abducted to be harvested for her DNA. What is going on? You let things get out of control."

"I'm sorry, sweetheart," Ray apologized.

"Let me rest in peace."

"Oh God, Mel," he fell to his knees and wept at her feet. "I'm so sorry. Oh, baby, I'm sorry."

"Dad? Mom?"

Ray looked up and through his tear-filled eyes he saw Jeremy standing over him.

"Jeremy," Ray said. "Son."

"There's someone at the door," Jeremy said. He walked around Ray and unlocked the door.

Ray stood up and yelled, "No! Don't open that."

But it was too late. Jeremy had already opened the door, and Haagen stood on the other side holding out his hand as he did before on the street.

"Stay away from my son," Ray shouted.

Jeremy took Haagen's hand. "I'm going with Professor Haagen. Don't worry. He can care for me. He has the answers."

"What? No!"

Ray reached for Jeremy, but his son stepped outside and closed the door.

"Jeremy!" Ray screamed through the door.

"You lost him, Ray," Melanie said. "You lost all of us." She gradually sank through the ground.

"Melanie!"

He awoke into a sitting position and gasped. Sweat soaked his hair and back. Tears covered his face.

"Dad?" Jeremy called to him. "You okay?"

Ray looked around to see the many faces staring at him in wonder. Jeremy sat on his cot. Abby, Deon, Fred, and Stanley sat on the floor around the room with their blankets draped over them. It was apparent that they had just woken up.

"I—uh—had a dream," Ray answered.

"More like a nightmare," Fred corrected.

"You screamed Mom's name," Jeremy told Ray.

Ray's eyes ran from side to side, like he was still searching around to regain his sense of reality. "Um, yeah, I did." He caught a glimpse of Abby watching him.

"Must've been some dream," Abby said.

"It was," Ray concurred.

"Well, well," Stanley said, "shake it off. Whatever the dream was, it won't be as intense as what you're about to face in a couple of hours."

"Good idea," Ray agreed. "I'm going to freshen up." He got up, took his toiletries, and went to the kitchen.

After rinsing his face, he saw Abby approaching him. She wore light blue sweat pants and a grey printed T-shirt. Simple. She always struck him as a simple girl with a sophisticated mind and a sweet spirit. The brush of her bare feet against the carpet created a warm sound. Her unbrushed, dirty blonde hair draped over one side of her face. Her natural beauty without make-up surprisingly offered a sense of closeness and honesty. She approached him.

"Are you okay?" she asked.

"Yeah, just a rough night," Ray replied, wiping his face with a cloth. "The dream was so real. So intense."

"By the looks of you when you woke up, it seemed painful too."

"Yes."

"Still carrying the weight of everyone's life on your shoulder?" she asked with piercing candor and gentle ease.

Ray wanted to answer in the negative, but he felt her words were true. The dream not only expressed what he felt, but he feared that it would be prophetic.

"Hey, kids," Fred addressed from the hallway. "Miranda arrived."

Ray packed up his toiletries and walked with Abby back to the conference room. Upon entering, he found everyone standing around the table. Miranda was dressed in her professional business attire as usual. The edges of her dark grey suit were sharp. Not a wrinkle or piece of lint was on her. She stood in a commanding poise before everyone. Looking at Ray when he and Abby walked in, she said without a smile, "Good morning."

"Good morning, Miranda," Ray returned.

"Stanley just filled me in on the finalized team being five of you."

"Yes. My son will be part of the team as an intern."

"It actually makes it more credible to have a team of five with two interns," Stanley said.

"It's a good team," Miranda approved, making eye contact with each of the five members. "Are you ready?"

"We're getting ready now," Ray said.

"Well, let's get to it," Miranda ordered.

At her command, they scrambled to wash up and get dressed in their uniforms.

Stanley said, "When, when you get dressed, I'll come and check, check your attire to make sure everything is in place. You will get to carry three tool bags in with you. No weapons. I, I will help you determine what equipment will be appropriate—basic tools are acceptable, plus a few uniquely specialized tools. Ray, Ray, I will do a few extra modifications to your appearance because you may be recognizable to a few people in the company, such as Gordon or the mercenaries you engaged at his house, should they happen to be there. I, I will make you less recognizable."

Ray was the first to get dressed while the others washed up in the bathrooms and kitchen. He was dressed in a dark blue uniform. His top was a button-up, short-sleeve, collared shirt. His pants were dress slacks. He wore black leather dress shoes. Clipped to the pocket of his dress shirt was an ID badge for Mason BioTech with his alias, "Richard Long," and the title, "Bioengineer Specialist." Another ID badge for ApexGen was clipped to his belt, but it did not read "ApexGen" on it. Instead, it merely read "AG Authorized." On the badge was a matrix barcode.

Abby and the others walked in dressed in their uniforms.

"Good, good," Stanley approved while he inspected Ray, straightening his collar and adjusting the positioning of the AG ID badge. "From, from time to time, a regular security guard—not an agent—will check your ID. It's, it's routine. He or she will simply scan this matrix barcode on your badge. This matrix barcode contains your name, photo, position at Mason BioTech, supervisor's name at Mason BioTech, DNA signature, and thumbprint. Do, do not be afraid to let them scan you."

He opened a small, plastic container and pulled out a fake mustache. "Ray, you will put this on. It's adhesive. Top of the line mustache. Not the cheap stuff. Also, wear these glasses and this Mason BioTech cap. And, and apply some of this foundation to darken your complexion. That should keep you from being readily recognizable."

Ray noticed that the photo on his Mason BioTech ID badge appeared like he would with all of these disguise elements. He took the cosmetic case, but didn't seem to know how to apply it on himself.

"I, I planned for you to look like this and had these disguises digitally edited onto a photo of you," Stanley explained. He went to check on Abby. Her alias on her ID badge was "Stephanie Satchel" and her title was "Biotech Specialist Lead."

"I don't know if I look like a Stephanie," Abby said.

"Yes, yes, it will do," he said while he straightened her badges. He told her, "Put, put your hair up into a bun or ponytail." While she tied her hair up into a ponytail, he quizzed her, "What, what's the entry code for ApexGen?"

"552738169.4, and I enter that at the lobby security," she said without hesitation.

Stanley looked at her skeptically and turned to check his scrap paper on the table to verify the number. While he shuffled through his pile of papers, Abby went to Ray. "Here," she said, taking the cosmetic case from him, "let me help you."

Stanley nodded his head with a half smile. "And, and what's the access code for the 53rd floor?

"7397#," she replied with the same confidence and readiness, as she applied the foundation on Ray's face.

Again, he verified her answer. "Good, good," he confirmed. "Remember, you're the team leader. So, so, feel free to give the others instructions on what to do or where to go." He turned to Fred, "Fred, Fred, you and Ray are the engineering specialists. Work directly with Abby, but act like you can work independently, like you know what you are doing." He said to Jeremy and Deon, "Remember, you two are interns. Interns don't really say much. It's, it's better you don't talk. You are there to assist. Jeremy, you will be assigned to Ray. Deon, you will be assigned to Fred." He said to Ray and Fred, "You, you two should be comfortable giving instructions to Jeremy and Deon."

Abby affixed the mustache on to Ray. He put on the glasses and cap. The group offered surprised looks at Ray's transformation with a few simple products.

Entry

"Man, we are a good-looking team," Deon said with a grin. He flipped his badge up to look at it. His alias was "Terence Fillmore" with the title "Bioengineering Intern."

Stanley reminded them, "Jamie is on the 53rd floor. That, that is your target destination. Do, do not go any deeper than the 53rd floor."

"Believe me," Ray assured, "we don't intend to. We just want to get to Jamie and get her out. We're not taking a tour of ApexGen."

"And, and if you happen to run into trouble," he said, mostly looking at Abby, "say you are there to complete a full biogen systems recalibration due to detectable traces of anomalies under the executive directive of Mr. Henry Turkins – approval 00HT."

"Whoa, you just lost all of us," Jeremy said.

"Got it: we're there to complete a full biogen systems recalibration due to detectable traces of anomalies under the executive directive of Mr. Henry Turkins—approval 00HT," Abby parroted.

"Wow, you are one strange woman," Jeremy said to Abby, giving her an enigmatic look.

"Good, good," Stanley praised. "That kind of lingo is only used by those under specific orders from the executive level. Henry Turkins is one of the executive board members who specifically directs the biotech division, but he is currently in Italy visiting with our cell in Rome."

"Hold on, what?" Ray said. "What cell in Rome? ApexGen has a cell in Rome?"

"Did, did I not tell you?" Stanley replied. "ApexGen has cells internationally." He read their perplexed expressions and said, "Oh, I see. I suppose I did not. ApexGen is not a localized organization. It is global with secret cells everywhere."

"Just an important piece of information about the enemy that you happened to forget to mention," Miranda accused sharply.

"It, it was irrelevant to the task at hand. There, therefore I did not think to mention it," Stanley said, twirling his finger crazily in the air. "You don't have to worry about the globalization of ApexGen. You only have to worry about your mission of rescuing Jamie. That's all."

Ray swallowed and felt a pressure of anxiety in his chest. "So the ApexGen at the Ameribank building is a cell?"

"No, no, of course not," Stanley corrected. "It is the headquarters. ApexGen is based in Los Angeles because Los Angeles is a perfect international intersection."

"Oh, gee," Fred remarked. "We're going into the head of the dragon?"

"Anything else you conveniently forgot to mention, Mr. Scientist?"

Miranda questioned.

"I, I don't like your tone," he responded to her. "It doesn't change anything. Everything I told you is still the same. Stick to the plan."

The team was in a state of suspension upon realizing they were invading the head of a global beast.

"Well, folks," Deon said, "we didn't get all dressed up for nothing. Let's do this!"

Ray nodded his head. He concurred, "Nothing's changed. We go in, follow the plan, and get Jamie out. And we *all* come out in one piece."

"No man left behind," Deon echoed. "Or woman."

"Okay, okay," Stanley said, checking his phone, "My, my contact from Mason Biotech will arrive here with a Mason Biotech van in ten minutes. She will be your driver. Abby, since you are the team leader, you will ride in front. So, so, let's pack up your tool bags and head out in ten minutes. We, we can't allow that van to park in front of the church for more than a minute. We need to go once she arrives."

"Abby, why don't you also help us organize our tool bags?" Ray said.

For the next several minutes, Stanley and Abby determined which items would go into the tool bags, discerning necessary items to appear convincing, and removing any questionable items. The others familiarized themselves with what items were in the bags, including basic screwdrivers, pliers, wire cutters, wires, soldering irons, pens, and hammers. High-tech instruments and small cleaning tools for servicing sensitive equipment were included. There were three large, black canvas bags. Stanley instructed the interns to carry two of the bags and Ray to carry the third.

Ray took his bag. He placed a few extra hammers of various types and sizes into it. He also took the sci-fi looking device out of his backpack and was placing it into his Mason Biotech bag when Jeremy asked, "You're bringing that with you?"

Ray noticed he was the center of attention as he held the device over the open bag. "Yes," he answered simply.

"Ray," Miranda asked, "what is that? I saw that on your desk. I thought it was a gaudy paper weight."

"Yes, yes," Stanley asked curiously, "I've been wanting to know what it is."

"It's a long story about Melanie and me," Ray said. "Too long to explain now. If our mission is a success, then I can tell you the story over a celebratory BBQ."

"It doesn't even work," Fred said.

"Then why bring it?" Miranda asked.

"Sentimental reasons," Fred answered for Ray. "I know the story behind it. It's about Melanie."

"Ray," Miranda reprimanded, "now's not the time for sentimentality. Stay focused."

"I know. I just," he fumbled, "will bring it with me." He looked at the meter, the large dial, the buttons, the glass tube with the copper coil on the side, and the antennas, the lever on the other side and the thimble-sized cylinders on top. "I don't know if I'll come out of this, and if I don't, I can't leave it."

"Well, well, it looks high-tech enough to pass as a sensitive instrument," Stanley permitted. "I, I don't see any harm."

"If that thing will help you, Ray, then it's a good idea for you to have it," Abby affirmed. "But we are all coming out of there."

"No one left behind," Deon reiterated.

Ray placed the sci-fi looking device into his bag.

"You, you still have that decryption code?" Stanley asked Miranda.

Miranda glared at Stanley. "That's not for you to be concerned with. Your concern is to get this team in there safely and get them out. You understand?"

"Only want to make sure it doesn't fall into the wrong hands," Stanley said. "It's crucial, you know?"

"I'm more aware of that than you would know," she stated. "You keep your head on the task. If anything happens to them, I'm coming after you."

"Bossy, this one is," Stanley said under his breath. The buzzing of his phone interrupted their argument. He checked it and said, "It, it's time. She's here."

"Let's do this!" Deon cheered. "Should we have a huddle and give a shout out?"

"No, no time for shouting," Stanley said. "Uh, uh, go team."

"Wait," Ray said. He surveyed this group, thought about who they were and what they were about to do together and said, "Thank you. Whatever comes of this, know that I know you all are putting yourselves at risk. I also recognize that this rescue could not happen without all of you. I have no words to express my gratitude." He met each of their gazes at him.

"Okay then, since you have no words, you all get out of here and get this done!" Miranda concluded.

"All right, let's do this!" Deon encouraged again.

Stanley led the way. Deon and Jeremy grabbed the bags and went out next, followed by Fred and Abby. Ray started to walk out, but Miranda grabbed his arm.

"Watch your back," Miranda said. "This scientist still doesn't add up to me. He obviously knows ApexGen inside and out, which means he was deeply involved with them. That kind of loyalty is hard to break. Don't leave everything in his hands."

"Watch our backs," Ray said. He opened his laptop. "The global tracking system is on. I have us under the eye of one of our satellites. It's honed on to my phone."

"Don't lose that phone," she ordered.

Shifting gears, he asked, "You do have the decryption code in a safe place?"

She appeared annoyed. "You do not worry about that. Stay focused."

"Where do you have it?"

"You don't need to know that. I don't want your mind on it. You gave it to me. I'm taking care of it."

Ray knew he could not break her resistance.

"Go," she charged. "I'll be watching you."

Ray gave her a single nod before leaving the conference room. During his walk through the church office, he looked at the empty seat at Cherish's desk where he saw Melanie in his dream. He took a deep breath and left the church.

Stanley stood by the van with the side door opened, waiting for Ray to enter. After Ray stepped into the van, Stanley closed the door. The van immediately took off. Fred, Deon, Jeremy, Ray, and Stanley sat around in a rectangle in the back. Abby rode in the front. The driver was surprisingly a young woman in her late twenties. He pictured someone more mature. There must be a twenty-five year age difference between her and Stanley. Ray did not expect this quirky scientist to be a cradle robber. The woman was quiet and appeared nervous. Her hands clenched the steering wheel.

"What's your name?" Abby asked her.

Stanley's partner didn't reply.

"Thank you for doing this. It must be scary for you," she tried again.

She glanced at Abby for a split second without moving her head or replying.

"Don't, don't distract her," Stanley said. "We'll be there in twenty minutes." He turned to Ray and asked, "So, so you had a last minute pep talk with evil Miranda?"

"It was nothing," Ray said. "Just some last minute things to confirm."

"Like, like what?" he pressed. "Did she tell you where the decryption code is?"

"She didn't need to."

"You, you asked, and she wouldn't tell you, would she?"

"That is not the concern right now."

"Beneath her stony exterior, I can tell you there's something else going on. ApexGen agents are experts at hiding their true intentions."

"You just get us into ApexGen. Don't worry about Miranda."

"Oh, oh, I'll get you in. I just hope she doesn't screw you over. I hope you didn't give her any other responsibilities for this mission. You didn't, did you?"

Doubt about Miranda suddenly pricked Ray. The speculation entered his mind: *Yes, I worked for her for the last several years, but I never knew her that well as a person. I only knew as much about her as she revealed to me. She was good at managing others' perceptions of her.* He didn't answer Stanley but redirected his attention to Deon. "How are you feeling?" he asked Deon.

"Good, good idea," Stanley said. "Do a focus level check on everyone before game time."

"I'm good, Sifu," Deon replied. "I'm ready to do my part."

"It's hard to believe I only met you a month ago."

"And yet, you already feel like a long lost uncle to me or something."

Ray smiled and nodded. "Agreed. You've become one of the closest people to me. Thank you. I mean that."

"We'll get Jamie back. I know it's dangerous and all, but we'll get her back."

Ray nodded again. Then it occurred to him to ask, "What will your grandma think? Does she know?"

"Yeah, every night I told her about what was going on. She knows there's a lot of bad in this world, and she feels for your daughter like I do. I left out all them details about nanoprobes and tazer-batons. She don't need to know that. She's proud of me for helping. Worried, but proud. She called this a mission of redemption." He chuckled. "That's my grandma with her fancy terms, but I think I believe it. It's not just a mission of rescue but a mission of redemption. Has a nice ring to it."

"Yes, it does," Ray agreed.

. . . .

When they arrived at the ApexGen facility, Stanley opened the side door but remained out of sight from onlookers. He said, "Remember, you are a specialized Mason BioTech team. Your target is the 53rd floor. Stay in your roles."

One by one, they filed out of the van. Deon, Jeremy, and Ray had their black canvas tool bags. Abby took the lead, and the others walked on either side of her. The large courtyard leading to the building was two platforms with two short sets of steps all made of white stone. The bright, white ground gleamed in the brilliant sunlight. Cars bustled on the streets behind them. Pedestrians fluttered on the sidewalks. Business people went in and out of the building. They walked up the first set of steps, dwarfed by the gigantic Ameribank building. The remarkable glass exterior accentuated the magnificence of this edifice. After walking up the second set of steps and across a large platform, they were about to enter the building. Ray resisted the temptation to look back at Stanley, figuring that doing so could alarm any observing security cameras.

Abby opened one of the eight fifteen-feet-high glass doors. They walked into an enormous circular atrium with a three-story vaulted ceiling. A couple of escalators curled up the sides for the first three floors. A dark marble elevator lobby was straight ahead. Professionals in business suits came and went. Most were arriving as it was the beginning of the workday. Men and women with briefcases, folders, messenger bags, and laptop cases went about their routine business with no awareness of the global danger this building concealed. It was baffling to Ray that the literal foundation of this monumental, extravagant glass and stone edifice was an equally large structure of organized terrorism.

Everyone funneled to the security checkpoint. The security guards wore suits with metallic badges. Abby passed through the x-ray scanner first. The rest of the team followed. They placed the black canvas tool bags on the conveyor belt to go through the x-ray scanners. After they went through the scanners, one security guard stopped Ray from picking up his tool bag.

"We need to open this and check something," he said. He was a tall, dark African-American male. He pulled out Ray's sci-fi looking device. "What is this?"

Ray was about to speak but Abby stepped forward, interjecting, "Please be careful with that. It's a fragile device to measure for microscopic hazardous bio-residue in the lab equipment. One of those costs us a quarter of a million."

The security guard scrutinized Abby with his surveying glare. "Scan it," he told another security guard.

The other security guard, a shorter, skinny Asian female, passed a small scanner over it. The scanner made no noise. "No energy signature."

The taller security guard asked, "Does this even work?"

"Yes," Ray answered. "It just needs to be plugged in is all."

"At least we know there's no dangerous energy emitting from it. It's not a power source, that's for certain," the Asian female security guard said.

"I've just never seen anything like this," the taller security guard said. "And I've seen a lot of things come through here."

"Can we go?" Abby asked, attempting to move the process along. "I'm sorry, I know you're doing your jobs here, but we're on a schedule. We have a lot of equipment to fine-tune in a day. And we will need that."

"Fine," the taller security guard finally said. "Go on ahead."

Ray placed his device back in his bag, and the team walked on to the elevators.

"Can't believe *that* thing almost cost us the mission before we even started!" Fred whispered.

Ray, trying to be discreet, didn't respond.

They approached a semi-circular security desk with seven security guards sitting behind it. Those who showed certain types of ID badges were allowed through immediately. Abby flashed her "AG authorized" badge. A Caucasian male security officer handed her a wireless keypad.

He instructed, "Enter your entry code."

Without hesitation, Abby punched in 552738169.4.

The security officer looked at his screen, then up at Abby and said, "Okay. Place your thumb on the scanner. Then place your AG badge in front of the scanner by the rotating gate with the matrix barcode facing forward. When your ID is verified, the light by the scanner will turn green. Then pass through the gate."

A green light appeared for each of them.

"Take the last elevator on the right."

They walked into the dark marble elevator lobby. There were twelve elevators, six on each side. The elevator doors were made of shiny brass. Everyone went into the other eleven elevators. A security officer stood by the twelfth elevator on the right, watching people as they went into the elevators. He turned away a few business people, telling them this was a service elevator to the basement reserved for maintenance crews.

The team walked toward that last elevator. He checked their AG-authorized badges and pushed the call button for the elevator. The elevator doors opened.

Upon entering, the security guard told them, "Scan your matrix barcode at the bottom of the buttons and select your floor."

The elevator doors closed. Abby placed her AG authorized badge in front of a dark glass scanner. The buttons on the elevator lit up a second later. Abby pressed button 53.

They descended.

Not Easily Broken

Chapter 25
Descend

There was no elevator music.

The digital counter above the door indicated they descended past floor 16, then 17. They descended fast to the 53rd floor. Without looking around, Ray could see from his peripheral vision that there was a camera above him, hidden in a small, silvery reflective dome. The floor of the elevator was a large square surface, spacious enough to roll in heavy equipment. 25 – 26 – 27. Their descent continued, as they plummeted deeper into the crust of the earth.

Everyone faced forward like statues. Their reflections off the dark, silvery doors stared back at them. 31 – 32 – 33. Ray mentally ran over the plan. He psychologically slipped deeper into his role as a Mason Biotech specialist. He thought about Jamie, but refrained from worrying about the condition she could be in. 40 – 41 – 42. Almost there.

He could hear Deon inhale and exhale. Deon's heavy chest rose and fell with each breath. He glanced at him without turning his head and saw drops of sweat running along his left sideburn area. Deon had no sideburns so his sweat drops were more obvious on his bare skin. 50. From what he could tell, Jeremy seemed calm, almost laid back even. Fred started to fidget. He wondered, *what will we find down there?* Then the elevator stopped at 52.

The dark screen under the buttons panel flashed a red light and asked for the access code. Abby started entering it. Ray hoped it would be correct, since Stanley told them two different codes. She entered: 7397#. Nothing happened. A second later, the light on the dark screen turned green, and the elevator continued its descent. 53.

The elevator doors opened. About ten paces in front of them was a small security station with three guards behind it. The hallway was wide, but the security station left only one opening, large enough for one individual to pass through. One guard stood to the right. The other two were on the left, one standing and one sitting. Outfitted in black uniforms with black caps, they looked like military police. They each had baton-tazers strapped to their sides. The batons were two feet long. Since the security guards up in the lobby didn't carry such weaponry, they knew they had entered an unforgiving territory.

Abby led the team out of the elevator. Along the center of the ceiling were more of the silvery, reflective domes like the one in the elevator. More cameras.

"Enter your access code," the seated security guard instructed. "Hold your AG badge with the barcode up to the scanner. Then provide your thumbprint and DNA signature."

Abby entered the access code 7397# again without hesitating to think, looking professional and genuine. She scanned her matrix barcode, placed her thumb on the scanner, and pressed her index finger into a finger impression on a black box.

The security guard read what appeared on his screen. He then looked up at Abby, back to his screen and up at her again. He asked, "What is your name and date of birth?"

She replied immediately, "Stephanie Satchel. November 4, 1981."

"Spell your last name for me," he requested.

"S – A – T – C – H – E – L," she replied without hesitation.

The security guard looked from his screen to her and greeted, "Good morning, Ms. Satchel. We welcome you and your team to the biolabs of the 53rd floor. You may begin your work in Lab 101 and work your way to Lab 112."

"Excuse me, officer," she said, "which is the lab for biotech synthesis?"

He looked at her for a moment before answering, "109."

"Very good, thank you. That will be our biggest job. Knowing which lab it is will help me pace my team to ensure we allow ample time to get it done," she said very professionally.

"You can get started, Ms. Satchel, once we verify the rest of your team."

Ray and Fred went next. They scanned their matrix barcodes, provided their thumbprints on the other scanner, and gave their DNA signatures on the black box with the finger impression. Ray felt a quick prick on his fingertip, like the prick of a tiny splinter. When he removed his finger from the box, he did not see any blood.

The security guard allowed them both to pass without question.

Jeremy went next. While he provided his identification contents, the security guard standing next to the seated one remarked, "Starting them young! Does Mason Biotech recruit teenagers?"

Abby replied, "He's one of our interns. He's twenty years old. He looks young. Good genes. I know twenty is still young, but he completed all the confidentiality documentation and background checks if you need to verify those."

"No, that's not necessary," the seated security guard said as he reviewed Jeremy's profile on his screen. "My partner here is merely jealous at the opportunities these youngsters get, since he didn't get them."

Jeremy passed through the opening of the security station.

Deon approached the counter and offered his identification contents as his previous four teammates did—matrix barcode, thumbprint scan, and DNA signature. When he finished, he waited for the seated security guard to respond. The security guard read the content on his screen, but it was taking longer than the others.

While the seated security guard continued to read, the standing security guard commented, "You're a big fella. Are you an intern too?"

"Yes," Deon answered, staying poised with his back straight and his chin up.

"You could be a football player," the standing security guard said.

"I'd rather apply my intellect than bash it," he said.

Ray and the others withheld their laughter at Deon's answer.

The seated security guard tilted his head slightly to inspect the side of Deon's face. Deon remained composed and facing forward.

"You're sweating," the seated security guard pointed out.

Ray held his breath.

"It was hot in the elevator, sir," Deon replied. "I sweat easily because I'm a big fella."

Ray wanted to crack a smile.

The seated security guard fixed his eyes on his monitor and quizzed, "What's your name?"

"Terence Fillmore," Deon replied.

"Your middle name?"

"Samuel."

"Your home address?"

"431 Stanton Way."

"Your date of birth?"

"August 17, 1990."

"Your birth place?"

"Bend, Oregon. Whitmore Memorial Hospital."

"Your mother's maiden name?"

"Lewis."

"Your blood type?"

"AB negative."

"Your supervisor at Mason Biotech?"

"Carol Matthews, PhD."

"Date you started your internship at Mason Biotech?"

"January 17, 2012. Tuesday."

Then there was a silent moment. Again, Ray and the others struggled to contain their surprise. The seated security officer finally looked up from his screen at Deon.

"Why are you here?" the seated security guard asked.

"As an intern, I assist the bioengineering specialists in the assessment, maintenance, and fine-tuning of the biotechnological instruments."

"Boy, Ralph," the standing security guard said to his seated partner, "you're really grilling this one."

"Have to be sure," Ralph, the seated security guard, said, "and we have to keep these young bucks sharp. Right?"

"That's right, sir," Deon agreed.

"Go on," Ralph told him.

Deon went through and joined his team.

"Great," Abby said, restraining her urge to let out a big sigh. "Let's get started."

Ralph said, "Take a left at the end of the hall. Not right. Lab 101 moved."

"Great. And 109 is…"

"Lab 109 is in the same location on the opposite end of the hall."

"Got it. We should be done by the end of the day."

"We'll be here," Ralph said.

The hallway was bright, similar to hospital lighting. The walls were creamy beige. The ceiling was white. The hardwood floor was an oak color. Bright fluorescent lights shone from the ceiling. The end of the hallway split into a "T."

Once they turned left, another pair of security guards walked past them, heading in the opposite direction toward the other end where Lab 109 was. Ray thought what he suspected the others were likely thinking, *there is a heavy presence of security*.

Abby approached the door to Lab 101. The door was locked. There was a black, glassy scanner by the door. She placed the matrix barcode of her AG badge in front of it. The scanner beeped, and the door unlocked.

They entered into a pristine, white laboratory. All the instruments had their place, and every item was in order. Even the pencils and paperclips were neatly stowed.

"This joint is clean," Deon said.

"Hey," Fred whispered to Deon, "that was pretty impressive back there."

"I studied," Deon whispered back with a half grin.

Ray approached the two of them and flashed a discreetly alarming expression. He motioned with his eyes upward. There was a silvery, reflective dome in the center of the ceiling, like the one in the elevator. They were being watched and perhaps listened to. Ray checked to make sure his cell phone was on. Last night, he boosted the signal on it through some modifications. Miranda should be picking up his signal and seeing his exact location, if all was working properly. Stanley's suspicion about Miranda entered his mind, but he shook it off.

"We're here," Abby said to her team, loud enough for the lab workers to hear. "Let's get to work. Interns, start sanitizing and disinfecting the work areas and instruments. Specialists, run a detection scan on any foreign bio matter on the machineries and then run performance diagnostics on the machines. If there is any bio residue, have your intern do the sterilization. Fine-tune the machines as needed. Watch for electrical feedback. Grab your equipment. Get started."

The team huddled around the three black canvas tool bags. Abby opened them and began handing out tools and measuring instruments to them. They each now had to play out their roles as described in the files provided by Stanley.

Fred mouthed to her, "What?"

She whispered without moving her lips much, "Play along for about forty-five minutes. The people watching us are probably not scientists, but just security. So as long as we look like we're doing the right things and not doing anything inappropriate, we should be fine. After we do two labs, we'll go to 109. My guess is that's where Jamie is." She finished handing out the equipment and then said in a regular volume, "Follow your checklists." She handed those to them, and they broke their huddle.

"I'll check the activities logs for this laboratory, which will inform us where our concentration should be and what specific needs to pay attention to," Abby stated. She typed on a computer on a desk. After reviewing the activities of this lab, her eyes enlarged.

She went to a corner of the lab, where three large refrigerator-like machines with glass doors stood. They were incubators. A blue light illuminated the insides of the refrigerators. "Oh!" she exclaimed.

Ray went to her. "What is it?"

Numerous petri dishes rested behind the glass doors. Some sort of growth was in each dish with various colorations and shapes. Some of the growth protruded out of the Petri dishes. Others actively bubbled with pus.

"The purpose of this lab is experimentations on various bacteria,"

Abby said in a professional tone. She said to the team without turning her eyes away from the incubators, "As a reminder, team, please be sure you are wearing your gloves." Then she resumed her conversation with Ray, reading off the labels next to the petri dishes, "E. Coli, Salmonella, Streptococcus, which is responsible for pneumonia, Campylobacter, Cryptosporida, and there's Yersinia Pestis."

"That's an interesting one," Ray said, playing along.

"Yes, it is, since it was responsible for causing the bubonic plague," she said matter-of-factly. "There's quite a collection here. On this side," she said, stepping slightly to the right, "are genetically altered bacteria. This one is a mutated merger of Streptococcus and Yersinia Pestis. There are two dozen different test groups or versions of the Yersinia pestis alone. Plus, there are many I don't recognize. They are engineering new strands of bacteria. Hm. Fascinating."

Ray detected her shock.

Abby whispered, "What are they doing with all of these destructive organisms?"

. . . .

After 45 minutes of service, Abby came to Ray's side. With their backs toward the silvery reflective dome, she said, "Let me see what the readings look like." Then she muttered quietly, "We'll move on soon. I'm calculating that by the time we do Lab 109 as our third lab, whoever is watching us will be less interested in us."

"Good thinking," Ray whispered back and then said in a regular volume, "What do you make of some of the deposit build-ups in the junctions?"

"Sterilize those areas," she ordered. "Make sure we get all of that residue out. Then run a diagnostic. We need to make sure the build-ups have not affected the instruments' capacities." She whispered, "If they don't arrest us after our second lab job, we'll know that our ruse is working."

Everyone on the team was busy with something. Abby was good at circulating and providing overt direction or whispering hints of what to do to a teammate. Her knowledge was impressive. For the most part, none of them were doing anything actually useful for the lab equipment, but their charade was holding up.

"We're close to being done here, team," Abby announced. "Specialists, complete your final calibrations. Interns, finish the sterilizations. Report when finished."

Five minutes later, Ray reported his finished work, followed by Fred and the interns.

With her back towards the dome on the ceiling, she said, "Very good. Let me see your checklists." She looked them over. "Job well done. Moving on."

Fred said, "Great. This lab looks good."

Ray felt antsy to get to Lab 109, but he knew they had to put on a convincing act for whoever might be watching. He could hardly believe that Jamie was merely down the hall. He felt impatient and worried about her condition.

"We're moving on to Lab 102," Abby announced.

They exited Lab 101 and walked across the hall to Lab 102. Again, Abby scanned her matrix barcode and provided her DNA signature. That was the third time she did that. Ray wondered if her finger was getting sore from the needle pricks.

They entered Lab 102 and immediately heard sounds of animals. Monkeys, dogs, cats, rats, parrots, guinea pigs, rabbits, lizards, and snakes were confined in ventilated, plexiglass cages.

"Okay," Fred said, "quite a collection of experimental goods." He walked to a six-foot savannah monitor. "Check out this exotic beast."

"Careful," Abby warned, "those creatures can bite off your foot."

The savannah monitor approached the front of its cage and slipped its long snake-like tongue at Fred. Fred backed away.

"Same routine, Ms. Satchel?" Deon asked Abby.

"Same routine."

"Um, Ms. Satchel," Jeremy said frightfully, "do we need to sterilize this area?"

Jeremy stood in the doorway of a smaller room in the corner of the lab. Abby and the others entered the lab. To their horror, they found animal parts, organs, limbs, and heads. But something was odd about the animal parts. When they observed them more closely, they noticed the animal parts were connected to other parts that didn't belong, like a monkey's heart and arteries to a cat's head. Some parts showed a kind of bizarre growth, like a monkey's arm severed at the shoulder had a green, translucent, pulsating mass growing out of it. Inside a glass incubator was a sedated parrot with a large, white, and bulbous growth protruding from its abdomen. An unconscious rabbit in a small metal cage had circuitry grafted onto its body. There were many other abominations around the room. Some in transparent boxes and others in glass jars with solution.

Ray thought, *these horrific experimentations violated nature in every way. What audacity must they have to believe they had a right to do such things to living creatures?*

Suddenly, the mouth of the cat's head attached to the monkey heart opened and closed. The parrot made gurgling sounds. The rabbit opened its eyes and looked at them. These creatures were still alive!

Jeremy uncontrollably gasped. He froze in place, and his face paled, like he wanted to vomit.

"Get a grip," Abby said, glancing quickly at the reflective dome in the center of this smaller room. "I know you're an intern, and it's your first time seeing this. This is important work. Don't insult it with your weak stomach." Ray was impressed by her performance. "Since you're new to this," she continued saying to Jeremy, "you won't work in this room." She instructed Fred and Deon, "You two will handle this room."

Jeremy turned and exited. Fred took the clipboard that Abby was handing to him and whispered sarcastically, "Great." Deon went out and brought the black canvas bag into the smaller room, making a disgusted expression as he entered.

"Terence," she said to Deon, "be sure you sterilize that station by the sink well, and don't touch the specimens."

"Yes, ma'am," Deon responded. He joined Fred and whispered to him, "Ain't no way I would touch those things."

"Looks like this lab will take a bit more time," Abby said to the team, "so let's be as efficient as we can. I'll check the activities log for this lab to see if there are any special services we should administer."

Ray knew now that was Abby's code for I'm-going-to-snoop. They were finding out more about ApexGen than they expected. Perhaps too much. Ray and Jeremy worked in the main room, while Abby checked the activities log on the computer. As she reviewed the contents, Ray noticed her squinting. She furrowed her brows and grimaced.

He approached her from behind and whispered, "You look too disturbed."

She composed herself and turned the monitor toward him. He saw grotesque images of experimentations on animals. It appeared ApexGen has been experimenting with various types of integration, synthesis, and grafting as part of their quest for achieving a higher form of life. But in addition, there was a perverse utilitarian impetus—they were reconstructing biological organisms to serve certain purposes. *How far would they go?* Ray thought. *Is there no natural law they wouldn't break? Apparently, biology for them was something to be manipulated without ethical limits.*

"All right," Abby said, closing out of the log, "let's get this done well."

After 40 minutes of work in this lab, Ray came across some documents on the counter next to a set of microscopes Jeremy was sterilizing. The documents were signed, "Vladimir Haagen." His signature was exactly the same as he remembered it at M.I.T., when Professor Haagen signed the reference letters he wrote for Ray. Seeing his actual signature again stirred an evocative emotion. There was a feeling of familiarity, and yet, estrangement. His signature conjured images of his days at M.I.T. and meeting Melanie, intermingled with loathsome feelings toward his old professor for being the mastermind behind a child-trafficking, terrorist group.

"You okay, Mr. Long," Jeremy asked his dad.

"I'm fine." Ray shook himself out of his whirlpool of emotions. "Just double checking my calculations."

After a full hour and a half, Abby announced, "You all should be wrapping up your section by now. If you're having challenges, let me know."

Over the next several minutes, the team members reported to Abby one by one. They looked eager to vacate this lab.

"Let me review your checklists and reports to make sure we didn't miss something," Abby said. She collected their documentations, looked them over and pronounced, "Good job. This lab is serviced and sterilized!" She sounded ready to be done with this lab as well.

Once they exited, Deon whispered to Abby, "Man, couldn't we get out of there any earlier?"

She whispered back, "We had to make it look convincing. Vacating too soon could've tipped them off." She said to the team in her regular volume, "Let's move on to the next lab before we take a break."

Finally, Ray thought. His heart rate increased with anticipation. He mentally shifted from performance to extraction, while reminding himself that he needed to stay in character. He had to restrain himself from walking ahead of Abby, who maintained a professional pace as they walked towards the other end of the hall. But before they could reach their destination, a pair of security officers stopped them.

"AG ID's, please," one of the two security officers said.

Abby handed hers to him first. He took her ID and scanned the matrix barcode with a portable, wireless scanner. He did so with each of the members, while the other security officer stood at attention. He let them pass. The redundant ID checks was effective in reminding employees that the presence of security was heavy and scrutiny was inescapable. Ray thought, *good psychological tactic to keep people in line.*

They continued on their way, passing Lab 107. Ray tried to calm the anxious stirrings in his chest. Lab 109. Abby scanned her AG ID and gave her DNA signature on the black box with the finger impression. The metallic lock above the door handle lit green, and the door unlocked. *So*

Not Easily Broken

far, Stanley has correctly gotten us all the clearance we needed. Good going, Stanley, Ray cheered in his mind. *Halfway there now.*

Abby turned the handle and pushed the door open. A rush of hospital air hit them. She stepped through, followed by Ray. They entered a large room with three sets of beds on either side. Four out of the six beds were occupied by sleeping children.

"Dear God," Abby unexpectedly whispered. She stopped after taking just three steps beyond the door, stunned by the sight before her.

. . . .

"Hello, there," a short, Middle Eastern man with glasses in a white lab coat greeted them. He stood at a counter on the right side, working with test tubes of solutions.

Ray stepped beside her, and the rest of the team crowded in behind them.

"Hello," Abby greeted back, "we're here to service your equipment."

"The guys from Mason Biotech are here," he shouted. "We've been expecting you."

"Great!" a tall, fair-skinned, blond-haired man said as he walked out of a back room. "Some of our machines are a bit shifty."

This lab is occupied! Ray mentally shouted.

"We'll check them out," Abby said. "Would one of you happen to be Terry?" She tried looking at their ID badges.

"Terry?" the short, Middle Eastern labworker responded. "No, he left us a week ago. Not sure what happened to him. Miss that guy. Why? You know him?"

Abby tried not to appear flushed, realizing that Stanley's inside contact was not there. "Oh, no. I mean, yes. Our previous maintenance team had worked with him and mentioned his name to me. That's all." She quickly moved on. "I'll check your activities log and see what particularly requires our attention."

"Right over here on this computer station," the Middle Eastern lab worker said.

She walked to a wireless computer mounted on a rolling stand.

"And don't worry about tippy-toeing. You can make all the noise you want. These subjects are pretty well sedated."

Subjects? Sedated? Ray felt the impulse to clench his hands into fists, but he had to refrain from doing even that. He scanned the room, his eyes roaming from right to left, and then he felt a surge of emotions. *There's Jamie!* He watched the little person lying on the second bed on the left side. His lips curled. He mustered up all of his willpower to keep his emotions from taking over. He reminded himself to breathe and blink.

He walked to the bed with the child next to Jamie, pretending to be systematic. It was an unconscious little boy about Jamie's age. He inspected the machines connected to the child. Multiple tubes and wires were plugged into his arms, legs, chest, and abdomen. The wires were taking readings. Some of the tubes were drawing fluids and others were injecting fluids. *What sort of experiments are they running on these children?* That these children were being used as lab rats infuriated him, but he could not show it.

After a few minutes, which felt like a week, he maneuvered over to Jamie's bedside. She was sedated. To his horror, Jamie was also connected to machines, wires and tubes inserted throughout her body. Her cheeks were pale, and her lips were chapped. Her hair looked unbrushed and unwashed. Her small hands seemed thinner. She looked like she lost weight. *Had she been getting fed? Was she being taken care?* A flurry of thoughts emerged in Ray's mind. Her little body was motionless except for her chest rising and falling from her breathing. He felt the tears pressing against the bottom of his eyes. But he forbade them to surface. His heart wrenched at seeing his daughter like this. He lightly touched a few of the tubes. His fingers trembled. He wanted to stroke her face, but that would have revealed inappropriate compassion. He inspected the machines and tried to decipher what was being done to her.

Jeremy watched discreetly from across the room while sterilizing instruments.

Abby stepped beside Ray and said, "Be careful with these instruments, Richard," she said to him. "These are very sensitive. We can't fine-tune these while they are running on these subjects, but we can diagnose their performance levels."

"Understood, Stephanie," Ray replied, "I'll get on it." He knew she came over to him to bring him out of his trance.

Abby examined the machines connected to Jamie, checking the wires and tubes and the respective machines to which they were associated. She typed on the computer managing these machines to investigate what was being done to Jamie.

"Be careful with those tubes," the blond, skinny lab worker cautioned. "You don't want to accidentally snag one."

"I see a failsafe attachment," Abby said.

"That's right," the blond lab worker confirmed gleefully. "The failsafe is that blue tube inserted into the girl's abdomen."

Ray noticed the blue tube was filled with a liquid that was not moving. The liquid stopped short of going into Jamie's stomach.

"Am I reading this correctly," Abby asked, reading off the computer monitor, "that this failsafe tube is filled with cyanide?"

"That's right," the blond lab worker said. "If any of the other tubes are removed, the cyanide is released into the girl. The tube runs several inches into her abdomen, so it's impossible to pull that out before the cyanide gets into her bloodstream."

Ray and Abby were silent with horror.

"That's why," the Middle Eastern worker concluded for his partner, "you want to be careful not to accidentally snag one of the tubes or wires."

Fred said. "Good to know."

"Only this one has a failsafe?" Abby asked.

"Only that one," the blond lab worker confirmed.

"Now that I have an overall idea of the activities running in this lab," Abby said, "I'd like to survey your bio supplies."

"Be our guest," the blond lab worker welcomed. "All the bio materials are in that storage room." He pointed to an industrial-sized metallic door with a large metal latch.

Abby went to it and disappeared behind the metal door.

Ray stood over Jamie. He tried to appear like he was doing something useful, but he moved slowly, and his attention was drawn to his motionless daughter.

"You okay, over there?" the blond worker asked Ray.

"Yes. Fine," Ray said, trying to bring himself back into the game, but he couldn't shake the emotions that attacked him. "I just haven't seen anything like this before."

"You're one of the bioengineer techs, aren't you?"

"Yes."

"You're probably more used to working with the machines than being around the subjects these machines were meant for, aren't you?"

"You could say that." He constrained his choking emotions and marshaled his next words to continue the discussion. "The…" Ray said with a split second hesitation in saying the next word, "subjects are so young."

The blond lab worker explained, "Professor Haagen prefers to work with children. He says the undeveloped physiology of the children offers more research and experimental potentials."

"May I ask what sort of work is being done on these chil– young subjects?"

"All four of them have a different purpose. The one you're standing over is our prized subject. That's why there's a failsafe attached to her. Professor Haagen would rather destroy the subject than lose her. That's how critical this one is."

"What's so important about this one?"

"That one there is 'Subject Zero,' like ground zero. She is being prepped for nanoprobe synthesis—the newest advancement in biological-technological integration."

"Ay," the Middle Eastern lab worker interrupted, "are you supposed to be talking so much about the subject zero experiment? That's very classified stuff."

"It's fine," the blond lab worker replied. "They already have access to our activity logs. They can see for themselves what's being done." He resumed, "Anyway, my partner is paranoid. The last lab worker leaked information and was dismissed."

"He was given the ax!" the Middle Eastern worker dramatically clarified. "And he was the head laboratory scientist. Imagine what could happen to us if we leaked?"

Ray knew they referred to Stanley.

"We're not leaking," the blond lab worker insisted. "They're from Mason BioTech. They have clearance."

"So," Ray prodded for more information, "this one is just being prepped, but the actual integration process has not begun yet?"

"It's just about to begin once you all are done here. Professor Haagen wants to move the schedule up a day earlier. So far, we are just harvesting her DNA."

Harvesting? Like Jamie is a crop? Ray looked at the clear tube with blood flowing from Jamie's arm into one of the machines.

"Professor Haagen wants an ample supply of her blood. Since we can't give her a blood transfusion because we don't want her blood contaminated, we've had to bleed her slowly, little by little, over the last 36 hours."

Ray fumed! What father could stand by and allow one more second of this cruelty to happen to his daughter? He felt the heat rise to the surface of his skin. His hands tingled with the urge to strike something. Neither of the lab workers was looking at him or any other member of the team. They were busy with their own work.

But he saw Jeremy about ten feet behind the blond lab worker. His son was sterilizing a sharp tool, and he could tell Jeremy wanted to seize the opportunity of attacking that lab worker. Ray glared intensely at Jeremy, grabbing his attention. Ray shook his head a few centimeters in both directions. Jeremy slowly backed away.

Moments later, Abby came out from behind the large, metal door. "Richard," she called, "there are some chemical containers that may have leaked and left some residue. Grab the interns and bring your hazardous waste detectors. Let's check this storage room thoroughly and move anything out that poses a risk, especially to these sensitive experiments. Bring your hazmat gloves and masks."

Ray looked at her like he was asking her what she was doing. He didn't want to leave Jamie's side to go into a closet, but she looked back at him insistently.

"What about me?" Fred asked.

"You keep working here," she replied. "I only need one specialist and the two interns for this task."

"Okay," Fred replied feebly, like a kid who got picked last for a kickball team.

They filed into the storage room with their hazmat gloves and masks. The large, metal door automatically closed behind them. The room was a metal vault with shelves of biomaterial, tools, hospital instruments, drugs, chemical agents, acids, and organic matter in jars.

"So what are we checking for in here, Ms. Satchel?" Ray asked.

"You don't have to act in here," Abby said. "There are five rooms in this lab, and this is the only one without a hidden camera."

"Are you sure?" Jeremy asked.

They all looked up at the ceiling for a silvery, reflective dome.

"Yes," she assured them in her normal volume, "that's why I was gone for a while. I checked this thoroughly. There isn't one in here, probably, because it's the storage space. No experimentations happen in here."

"Shouldn't we be whispering at least," Deon asked. "We still have a couple of goons out there."

"It's soundproof in here," she replied. "While I was in here, I screamed as loud as I could to see if any of you would hear me. No one came to my rescue, so I concluded you cannot hear what's going on in here from outside. This room was built to contain the most hazardous materials from escaping, including fluids or vapors. So sound can't even get out of here."

"I'm guessing this is a dangerous room," Deon observed, glancing at all the chemical contents and biological matter on the shelves.

"Yes, it is. But it's also a room where we can safely talk."

"What's our plan?" Jeremy asked.

"We have at least two problems," Ray assessed. "We have no Terry. Instead, we have two unexpected lab workers out there."

"Three," Jeremy corrected. "When we came in, a woman with a lab coat walked in."

"Three," Ray acknowledged. "Jamie is sedated with cyanide ready to be pumped into her if we try moving her. Stanley didn't warn us about any of this. Options?"

"I found the hazmat drums Stanley told us about," Abby said. "They're five of them in the back. So Stanley was correct about that."

"He better be correct about them shielding out any kind of detection," Deon said.

"Right," Ray agreed. "Our first hurdle is getting those machines off of Jamie without killing her." Tension increased in his voice.

"We can't turn the machines off. Turning off the power will automatically release the cyanide. It's a default failsafe," Abby said. "I studied the machines. As long as the machines keep drawing her blood, the cyanide won't release. The key factor is her blood. If the transfusion tube is disconnected from her, the machine will detect that it is not actively drawing blood and will release the cyanide."

"So now what?" Jeremy asked. "We can't take the machines with her. Can we?"

"I'm not sure what to do yet," Abby confessed. "They made this foolproof. We need a moment to think about this. A wrong move could kill her."

"We need to think fast," Ray said, "I'm guessing those lab workers will get suspicious if we stay in here too long."

They thought hard for alternatives.

Ray pressed, "What's our solution?"

Not Easily Broken

Chapter 26
Unexpected

"How do we save Jamie?" Jeremy asked desperately. "We can't go back out there without a plan."

"But we can't afford to remain in here until we come up with one," Ray said. "Let's go back out there, continue our charade, and at least buy ourselves some time. Then we can come back in here to rethink this."

"Hold up," Deon said, "I don't know much about this techie stuff, but basically that machine is a death machine to Jamie."

"That's correct," Abby said. "It gets what it wants from her, which is her blood, and if it doesn't, then it kills her."

"Sick people," Jeremy exclaimed.

"So," Deon continued with a thoughtful expression, "if it keeps getting blood, then it'll at least *think* it is getting what it wants."

All of their eyes widened with hope, like light bulbs appeared over each of their heads. They all knew where this was going.

"Would that work?" Ray asked. "Could we trick the machine into thinking it has Jamie? With a bag of blood? There must be a blood bank in this lab."

"It's possible," Abby speculated with optimism. "There could not be a break in the flow of blood going into the machine. I did notice the machine could receive multiple subjects. We could hook up an alternate source of blood to the machine and then reroute Jamie's readings to the alternate source! I'll have to take a closer look at the set-up on the computer, but it's possible!"

"Great idea," Jeremy praised Deon.

"That leaves us with the three lab workers still," Ray pointed out. "We can't accomplish this with them being in the lab. How do we get them out?"

"With some kind of bait to lure them out of the lab?" Deon asked.

"Or we can lure them in here," Jeremy said. "Get them in here. Take them out. The cameras won't see it!"

"Dang, kid," Deon said. "You're hard core."

"We would only have minutes from that moment to free Jamie before the security that's watching us suspects something is wrong," Ray said.

"So we need to find the replacement blood first and have that ready before we make our move," Abby said.

"We'll go back out. Do our jobs and inconspicuously search for that bag of blood," Ray said.

They all nodded.

"Abby," Ray said, "you make the call again for us to reconvene in this storage room. You're good at coming up with reasons for us to do certain things."

She smiled, touched his arm, and headed toward the large, metal door. The others followed.

As she emerged out of the room, she said loud enough for the lab workers to hear, "We have to take care of that in there. Richard, use the readings you took to find the right neutralizers for the chemical residues we found."

"Chemical residues?" the blond, skinny lab worker asked.

"That's right," Abby said, "we're finding them on the floor along the edges of the shelf. It's invisible to the naked eye but detectable by our instruments. Did you have any spills or drippage in there?"

"I knew it!" the Middle Eastern lab worker declared. "It's from all of your spills," he accused the blond, skinny lab worker with a sharp tone, and then said to Abby, "I always told him that he was too careless."

"These two are like an old couple," the female lab worker, who walked in later, commented. She was about five-foot-five with short, brown curly hair. "Excuse them."

Ignoring their dispute, Abby added, "Our ultraviolet lights also revealed traces of organic matter on the shelves."

"That too?" the Middle Eastern lab worker exclaimed.

"Yes," Abby affirmed, "so for now the storage vault has to be off limits."

"Oh," the blond worker asked, "can you get that stuff out? Right now?"

"Yes, yes," Abby said.

"That is a top priority, right?" the Middle Eastern lab worker asked.

Ray knew Abby had to make this believable. But now she couldn't have everyone searching for the bag of blood, and she needed to reserve the storage toom for the team's exclusive use.

"Yes, of course. It will be a scrub job," Abby said. "I'll have both of my interns working on it. I'll do progressive scans of the storage room for other contaminants. We want to be sure we sterilize that entire space given the volatile products in there."

"Thank you," the female lab worker said. "You all get the dirty jobs."

"Interns, grab the gear you need, and we'll start the scrubdowns and neutralizations," Abby instructed. "Richard, I want you to use the microcantilever to detect any gaseous traces of acid in the rest of the lab, particularly for hydrofluoric acid."

"Right," Ray pretended to know what she was talking about. "The micro…cantilever… okay."

"You did pack it in Terence's bag, didn't you?" Her subtlety had tact.

"Oh, right, yes. That's where I placed it."

"Let's go!" Abby looked at her team. "We're on the clock, and don't forget to wear your ventilation masks. You don't want to inhale any of the fumes in that storage room."

The team members scattered to perform their assigned duties.

"Gaseous traces?" the female worker asked. "In the rest of the lab?"

"That's right," Abby reinforced. "You have quite a bit of acid stored in there. If I'm finding chemical residue, then it's conceivable that vaporous elements could have gone into the air."

The obviousness of Abby's reasoning left no room for surprise or question. The lab workers exhibited a great deal of concern.

"See? What did I say?" the Middle Eastern lab worker badgered his blond lab partner. He complained to Abby, "He thought he could just wipe it up with paper towels and no one would know. But now we could have been inhaling toxic vapors!"

"Please, you'll be fine," the blond lab worker minimized with an embarrassed smile. "He's always been a hypochondriac!"

"Could any of the vapors have gotten out of the room when we opened the door?" the Middle Eastern lab worker said.

"Possibly." Abby assured, "Let us do our jobs and we'll get it taken care of. Actually, would you be able to vacate the lab for a couple of hours? It's for your safety."

"I wish we could," the Middle Eastern worker said, "but someone always has to monitor these subjects."

"No problem. We'll make do."

"Found the microcantilever," Ray said, pulling out a device from Deon's black canvas bag. He had quickly looked up the microcantilever online with his smart phone to get an idea of what it looked like, while the others were focused on their discussion with Abby.

"Good," she replied, "begin your scan. Start with the storage room. Then circulate to the other rooms in the lab. Let's make sure there are no traces of the toxins outside of the storage room."

Good going, Abby, he thought.

She continued, "I'm going to assess the rest of the equipment out here before I join you. I want to make sure the computers monitoring the subjects are providing accurate readings."

Ray watched Abby go to the machines servicing the other two children on the other side of the room from Jamie, where Fred was working. He took the microcantilever and walked to the large, metal door. As he walked, his gaze remained on Jamie. He tried not to watch her too intensely for fear that he would reveal his concern for this little girl. But he couldn't help watching her and yearning to set her free at that very moment. He wanted to wake her and see life in her again. He wanted to hold her and restore warmth to her body. He shifted his face toward the metal door and realigned his thoughts to the plan. *Concentrate*, he told himself, *Jamie is counting on us.*

He turned the metal lever and pulled the door open. He saw Jeremy and Deon hurry to resume their act of scrubbing the shelves and floors when they heard him open the door. Then they relaxed when they saw it was Ray.

Once the door closed shut behind him, Ray asked, "Have you found anything in here that's useful?"

"We found all sorts of stuff, but no blood supply," Jeremy said.

"Yeah, they have all kinds of chemicals, stimulants, and acids in here," Deon said. "They might not want to keep blood in the same place as all of this stuff."

"One of the other four rooms then," he suggested. "I'll stay in here with you for a few more minutes, and then I'll go back out to look for the blood."

"We'll keep looking around in here to see if there's anything else that could be useful," Deon said.

"Good," he said.

"I can't stand to see her like this," Jeremy stated.

"I know. I don't want her hooked up to those machines one second longer," Ray said with a worried expression.

"We'll get her out of here, Sifu," Deon assured and placed his large hand on Ray's shoulder. "No matter what, we'll save her."

"Thanks," Ray said and patted the hand that was on his shoulder.

They spread out and scoured the storage space, making a record of the items. Ray couldn't tell what most of the contents were, but he suspected they were mostly dangerous substances since they were locked in a metal vault. He checked the five hazmat drums. They were red, shiny, and half the height of a regular street trashcan with a yellow warning symbol on them. They came with a lid that sealed tightly shut and would need to be pried open with a heavy tool. They were empty and just big enough to fit a little child inside, if the child lay curled up on her side. After a few minutes, Ray went out the metal door with his ventilation mask on, which he removed.

Abby continued working on the machines connected to Jamie, while Fred still worked on the machines by the other children on the other side of the room. The lab workers in the main room took note of Ray when he came out.

Abby asked him, "Find anything?"

Ray answered, "I ran the microcantilever and found 0.076 percent levels of hydrofluoric acid in the atmosphere concentrated in one part of the storage room. The interns are working on sterilization of the surface areas. I'll neutralize the atmosphere after they finish in case the residues on the surfaces would be releasing more gaseous vapors."

"Good thinking," Abby approved. "In the meantime, you could come work with me here on this machine." She appeared insistent with her suggestion.

But Ray was focused on finding the needed blood for Jamie, and so he said, "Actually, I thought I could keep measuring the atmosphere in the other rooms."

"Yes, of course," Abby agreed apprehensively.

Ray proceeded to one of the rooms in the lab. The room was an administrative office with desks, file cabinets, and computers. He spent a few minutes in there before moving on to the next room.

The next two rooms were research areas with powerful microscopes, incubators, racks of test tubes, centrifugal machines, x-ray machines, and MRI machines. After spending a few minutes in each of them, he moved on. While he went from one room to the other, he noticed Fred moved around to other stations, but Abby remained at Jamie's.

One room left. This last room was smaller and looked like a patient room at a doctor's office. It was white with ceramic tile flooring. The fluorescent lights above brightened the room. Along the walls were a counter, a sink, and cabinets. In the center was an exam bed for a patient—or subject, as would be the case here. But on the back wall was an enormous blood bank. It was a giant refrigerator with two sets of double glass doors. The inside of the fridge was illuminated with a bluish light. Behind one set of double glass doors were test tubes and vials of blood plus other kinds of fluids. Behind the other set of double glass doors were bags of blood!

Jackpot! Ray thought. *This is it! Now we just need to take out the lab workers, release Jamie from the machines, and deliver her out of this building in one of the hazmat drums.* They were getting closer to rescuing Jamie. Ray had to contain his anxiousness.

The blood was divided into various types, so he grabbed one of each. He placed them into a temperature-controlled cooler that was sitting on the counter and walked out of the room with it.

"What do you have there?" the female worker asked, seeing Ray walk across the lab with the cooler.

Ray hadn't thought of an answer for why he was carrying one of their coolers. He had to think of something fast. "I thought—"

"To run a blood test. You have fresh blood in that container?" Abby intervened.

"Yes, ma'am," Ray affirmed.

"When there's fresh blood used for subjects in labs where we've detected vaporous contaminants, we must test samples of the blood for contamination," Abby explained.

"You mean the acidic vapors did travel out of the storage? The blood could be infected?" the Middle Eastern worker asked. "Those bags are air tight!"

"You never know," Abby responded. "It's just a precaution. Acidic contents have the capacity to permeate through materials."

"If the blood bank could be contaminated, think of what could be in our blood!" the Middle Eastern worker exclaimed.

"Don't get your underwear all up in a bunch," the blond lab worker said. "It's just a precaution."

"I left the testing device in the storage room," Ray said. "I'll run the test in there. By now, the interns probably made some head way in their sterilization work, so I can begin the atmospheric neutralization as well."

"This is our biggest priority," Abby pronounced. "I want our whole team involved in the testing and sanitizing. We'll assess the next steps for the storage room." She motioned for Fred to follow her and Ray in.

"That storage room really is a big deal, isn't it?" the female worker said with a hint of doubt.

"Can't take any chances on a room like this, especially if we already detected airborne evidences of contamination," Abby defended.

"Go," the Middle Eastern worker exhorted, "do what you have to do. Please! I'll feel better about it. By the way, did you find anything in the atmosphere out here?"

Ray didn't respond right away but took a second to answer. In his excitement over finding the blood, he didn't mentally prepare himself for obvious questions. "Um, yes," he said. "Uh, 0.003% detected in the blood bank room."

"Not enough to harm you," Abby said with a smile. "But let's be safe.

Unexpected

Stay out of infected areas."

"This is a nightmare," the Middle Eastern worker said.

Ray, Abby, and Fred slipped the ventilation masks on and entered the storage vault. As soon as the large, metal door closed shut, they removed their masks. Deon and Jeremy came out from behind the shelves and joined the team.

"I found it!" Ray proclaimed. "I got the blood!" He set the cooler down on the floor and opened it.

"Money!" Deon cheered.

Jeremy smiled, baring all his teeth. "Finally," he said.

"Now we need to talk through the next several steps," Ray directed. "We have to cover every detail on how this is going to work."

The metal door suddenly opened.

Caught off guard, the group turned their heads to look towards the door.

The female worker stepped into the doorway with a handkerchief held over her mouth and nose. "I wanted to see how you were working on this." She stepped all the way into the storage room and squeezed her brow together. "Hey, why aren't you wearing your ventilation masks?"

Fred closed the door behind her.

"Oh, um," Abby said.

"You're here just in time," Ray intervened. "We meant to tell you." He escorted her in further by her arm. He tried to think of something fast.

"You actually don't need that," Deon said as he approached her from the side. "Use this instead." He pulled her handkerchief away from her mouth and quickly replaced it with a wad of gauze. He pressed tightly, sealing his large hand over her mouth and nose.

She let out a muffled scream through the gauze, but no one outside could hear. She struggled, but Deon and Ray held her in place. Several seconds later, her eyes rolled back, her eyelids closed, and her legs gave out. She fell unconscious. Deon and Ray gently set her down on the floor.

"Chloroform," Deon said. "I just learned about it in Chem 101 last semester."

Looking at the woman lying on the floor, they all exhaled.

"Good thinking, Deon," Ray said.

"You just happened to have that ready?" Jeremy asked.

"Yeah," Deon replied, "I knew part of the plan was to take these folks out. Found this chloroform and thought it would be a good way of taking them out without knocking them out."

"That's awesome," Jeremy praised with a smile.

"Our timeline just moved up," Ray stated. "It will be minutes before another one of the lab workers comes to check on their partner or may call security, because she hasn't come back out. We can't risk that. We have to act now."

Abby squatted and looked through the several bags of blood.

"We need to lure the other two lab workers in here now and get to substituting this blood for Jamie," he said.

"Is this all you found?" Abby asked.

"Yes, I took one of each type from their blood bank. It was a large refrigerator with an enormous collection of blood," Ray answered.

"So we need to replace Jamie with one of these bags of blood?" Fred asked.

"Yes," Ray spoke rapidly. "In order to free Jamie from the machine, we need to substitute one of these bags of blood for her, otherwise the machine will release the cyanide into her body. One of these bags of blood will act as an alternative source."

"Ray," Abby said from a squatting position, looking up at Ray. She had a bag of blood in each hand.

"The first thing we need to do is figure out how to lure the lab workers in here without making the security watching us suspicious," Ray talked through the steps. "We'll need both of them to come in at the same time. Come up with ways to lure them."

"Ray, the blood—" Abby said again.

"I know," he interrupted. His mind and speech were moving at twice the normal speed. Eagerness percolated through his voice. "Right after we bring them in here, we need to substitute the blood for Jamie quickly because it won't be long before the security watching us sees what we're doing. I suggest Abby and I start working on Jamie while Fred, Deon, and Jeremy finish up securing the lab workers—tie them up to be sure. Abby, this is where we rely on your expertise to make this substitute switch."

"Ray," Abby said again.

"Yes," Ray finally acknowledged her, "what is it?"

"This isn't the right blood," she said.

He looked at the bags of blood in her hands.

"Fine. Look at the other ones," Ray said pointing at the stash in the chest.

"None of them are," she stated.

"What do you mean none of them?" Ray asked with growing concern.

"There's a lot of blood in there," Deon said.

"I took one of each type," Ray reiterated, "Whatever type we need is all there."

Abby sighed, looked into the cooler of blood, and back at the team. "I was afraid of this. I checked the machine hooked up to Jamie over and over. I looked for another alternative means around this."

"What?" Ray asked agitatedly. "Around what? We have what we need here."

"No, we don't," Abby said with sympathy. "The machine recognizes Jamie's blood type. If we insert a blood type that's different from hers and make the switch, the machine will identify the source as a false one. The alternative blood source has to be the same exact type as Jamie's. Anything else will not be an adequate substitute."

"Okay, so which one of those is Jamie's blood type?" Ray asked.

"None," Abby answered sympathetically.

"None of those matches Jamie's?" Jeremy asked in disbelief.

"No," she answered again. "Her blood type is extremely rare. Only 1 percent of the population has that type. It makes sense they wouldn't care to stock her blood type here since they told us earlier that they don't replenish her blood with transfusions."

Ray stared into the cooler of blood he gathered, wanting to believe that the solution had to be in there amongst the dozens of bags of blood. "So what can we do?"

"I don't know." Abby sounded defeated.

"I can't believe this," Fred said. "We got this far."

The cold, silent frozenness of the team was like death. Hope shrank beyond detection. The box of inadequate blood represented the futility of their efforts. Moments passed without a word spoken.

Ray wanted to kick the box of blood. "Why didn't Stanley tell us about this?"

"He forgot, probably, like he was forgetting other stuff until we asked him about it?" Jeremy said.

"But where does that leave us now?" Abby asked.

"Is there another way to free Jamie?" Ray asked.

"None that I've found," Abby answered.

"We need to get the other lab workers in here." Ray was tense and determined, like a lion fixed on a prey. "This time we can't knock them out. We need to question them and force the answer out of them if we have to!"

The metal door unlocked again and slowly cracked open.

"Hello in there," the Middle Eastern lab worker said through the two inch crack. "I just need to ask my colleague something."

Ray grabbed the handle on the inside of the door and kept the door from opening any further. "Just a moment. It's not safe yet." He felt the lab worker tug on the door. He tugged back and closed the crack an inch.

"What's going on in there? Is she okay?" the Middle Eastern worker asked.

"She's fine," Ray answered. "She's helping us. We just need a moment before you can come in." He yanked the door shut. He felt them tugging the door, but he held it in place.

"We can't spook them. We need to lure them in." Ray said to his team, "And we can't pull any punches to get what we need from them. Ready?"

They nodded.

Ray acknowledged their nods. "Okay," he said softly. "I'm opening the door."

He put on a smile and opened the door slowly. Both male lab workers stood in the doorway, looking in with curiosity.

"What's going on in here?" the blond lab worker asked. "This door can't lock. Why couldn't we open it?"

"Our apologies," Ray said, "You're here just in time, though. There's something urgent we need to show you."

Fred and Ray ushered them inside.

"Wait, do we need ventilation masks?" the Middle Eastern worker asked. "Hold on. Why aren't you wearing yours?" He looked perplexed.

"Don't worry," Ray said, insistently leading them inside by their arms.

Fred shut the metal door behind them.

The Middle Eastern worker saw the female worker lying on the floor and yelled, "Crud! Get out!"

He tried to turn toward the exit but Deon rushed him and pinned him against the wall. With Deon's enormous body pressed against him, the lab worker couldn't even squirm. The lab worker's eyes widened with horror. He put up a fight, but he couldn't break free from Deon's constriction.

Simultaneously, Ray put the blond lab worker in a chokehold from behind. "Tell me," he demanded, "how do we turn off those machines hooked up to the subjects?"

Hardly able to move his jaw with Ray's forearm wedged underneath it, he mumbled, "You can't. I don't have the clearance. Only executive level clearances have the password to shut the machines down without harming the subjects."

"Who are they? How do we get them here?"

"I can't tell you. I'll lose my job," he muttered as his face reddened.

Unexpected

"Who are you? You have no idea what you're doing. You're all dead!"

"Tell us who has the clearance!" Jeremy demanded. He kicked the lab worker in the stomach.

The blond lab worker convulsed from the waist down from the kick. He would've dropped to the floor if Ray hadn't been holding him up. He tried to cough from the kick, but Ray's chokehold prevented him. His attempts to cough came out as gurgles.

"Say it," Ray demanded as he tightened his hold around the worker's neck.

"Professor Haagen," the blond worker muttered, "his twelve executive staff members. All lead scientists." His face turned purple.

"How do we get one of them here?"

"You can't.

"Then call them! Call one of them!"

"I can't. I won't."

Abby and Fred watched the interrogation with despondency. As the lab worker refused to comply, hopelessness washed over their faces.

The lab worker vainly clawed and pulled at Ray's arm. But like a guillotine, Ray's arm pressed deeper into the lab worker's neck, cutting off the air in his throat and the blood to his brain. The lab worker struggled, kicking his feet in the air and slapping Ray's arms, but seconds later he fell unconscious.

Ray let him drop to the floor. Hoping that he made a terrifying example of the blond lab worker, he shouted at the Middle Eastern lab worker who was still compressed between the wall and Deon's menacing body, "You! Call an executive staff here!"

"I won't betray ApexGen," the Middle Eastern worker surprisingly uttered with determined resolve. He chanted, "ApexGen! ApexGen!"

"Put him out," Ray instructed.

Deon jammed a wad of gauze soaked in chloroform over the Middle Eastern worker's mouth and nose. The lab worker tried shouting, "ApexGen," but Deon pressed the gauze tighter until the sounds coming from the lab worker were an unintelligible moan and he fell unconscious.

Deon set the lab worker on the floor.

Ray said, "Fred and Jeremy, tie and gag them. We need to figure out what to do. Stanley was one of the nine lead scientists here. He would have had the password for deactivating these machines."

"I can't believe he forgot to tell us," Deon said.

"He was pretty absent-minded," Fred said, as he tied up a lab worker.

"These lab workers also said they moved their schedule up a day earlier, so Stanley might not have expected Jamie to be hooked up to the machine," Abby reasoned.

"What now?" Jeremy asked, while he gagged a lab worker.

"There's a solution to this," Ray asked. "We didn't come all this way to leave without Jamie! We need to go back out there and further investigate the lab for possible solutions. Maybe there is an emergency kill switch for the machines without harming Jamie, or maybe they do have a blood supply for Jamie that they keep in a hidden place because of the high profile nature of her case. The answer is out there somewhere."

Ray opened the metal door, but as soon as he did, he heard a voice.

"What is that?" Fred asked as he finished tying up the last lab worker.

"Hello?" they heard the voice.

Ray gestured to his team with his fingers placed over his lips as he carefully stepped outside.

"Hello, Hello, there," a familiar and quirky voice came from a computer monitor on the desk. "Are, are you there?"

Ray, Deon, and Abby went to a grey, metal desk where the voice came from. It was who they suspected the voice to be from—Stanley. His face was on the computer screen. "Can, can you see and hear me? Are, are you there?" Stanley asked. "I hope you can hear me, because I have an important message for you."

On the computer screen was an option to respond to Stanley's invitation to video chat with him. Fred and Jeremy also came out to join them by the desk.

"What's he doing on the computer?" Fred questioned.

"He probably discovered our dilemma somehow and is calling in to give us the answer," Ray said and casually glanced back at the dome on the ceiling, feeling very nervous about being discovered by the security. But he couldn't ignore Stanley's call. "We have to take this." He leaned over and clicked on the invitation to video chat.

Stanley perked up with delight when he saw them. "Oh, oh, there you are. Good, you're all there."

"Your timing is not very good, but late is better than never," Ray whispered as he reduced the volume on the computer. "How do we get Jamie off of this machine? Give us the password to turn it off."

"Yes, yes, I am contacting you about that," Stanley said. "There, there's some other important things I'm contacting you about too."

"We don't have time. Give me the password first. You can tell me about the other stuff while we deactivate the machine."

"Well, well, first I have to tell you some good news and some bad. First of all, you don't have to keep whispering. You, you see, I was able to make an arrangement."

"What kind of arrangement?" Ray stood up straight and spoke in his normal volume. He felt the silvery, reflective dome watching him from behind.

Stanley scratched his coarse, stubbly face. "It, it started with me being spotted outside ApexGen when we dropped you off. Agents commandeered my vehicle and took my partner and me in."

"What?" Jeremy cried.

"How did you get away, and where are you calling from?" Abby asked.

"Well, well, I'm much closer to you than you think."

"Get to the point, Stanley," Ray demanded. "The security could be here soon."

"No, no, they won't. See? Professor Haagen had a heart-to-heart with me, you see," Stanley said.

"I don't like where this is going," Fred said.

"We reached a very amicable arrangement." Stanley scratched his wrinkled forehead. "He offered me back my old job and welcomed my return to ApexGen." He grinned.

"What are you saying, Stanley?" Ray asked with increasing anger.

"To, to redeem my loyalty to ApexGen, I had to give over two things to them. That, that was reasonable, right? Professor Haagen hopes I learned my lesson, and I have. So, so, I had to give him the decryption code."

"You're not doing this, Stanley," Ray said.

"It, it's done." Stanley scratched the bottom of his flabby chin with both hands. "While, while you were in there working on your rescue mission, I went with a tactical team to the church to seize the little flash drive from Miranda. I, I told them to bring a few extra guys, because I knew she would be a fighter. And, and she was."

"I hate this guy," Fred said.

"She, she hid the little red flash drive on her, as I expected. Unfortunately for her, she hid it in a place where she did not like being searched." Stanley scratched both his sideburns with his thumbs, creating the sound of sandpaper rubbing old wood. "But, but we got it."

"I knew we couldn't trust him!" Deon exclaimed.

"How, however, there is a problem," Stanley continued. "We, we entered the decryption code but it did not disable the encrypted firewall. So, so we are guessing that the code is either incorrect or only partial and you have what we need. I'm thinking that you probably made up a very complex code where you only had to remember part of it. So, so the code you put on the flash drive is incomplete, and you have the rest of it in your head. The, the code on this red flash drive is 488 digits long. Am I correct to hypothesize that the code is actually 500 digits long?"

Ray's expression was like smooth, cold steel, and he spoke with a razor sharp tone. "Tell Haagen that the final twelve digits could be numerical, alphabetical, punctuation, and even wingding characters! And he is *not* getting any of them from me."

Stanley grinned. "Yes, yes, I see." He looked down and scratched the back of his head. White flakes of dandruff floated in the air. "In any case, that was half of my redemption agreement. The, the second thing I have to give over is your rescue mission."

"Oh, no," Fred said, "we're in a lot of trouble."

"As, as of ten minutes ago, ApexGen became aware of you. So, so to state the obvious: you need to give yourselves up. You should be pleased to know that I bargained for a civilized treatment of you. The security will not rush in. Yet." Stanley lifted his chin and scratched his flaky neck with four fingers. "Out of respect to you, Professor Haagen agreed to give you ten minutes to collect yourselves, mentally and physically, and walk out with your heads up. And, and of course with your hands up too. Then, then Professor Haagen would like to meet with you, Ray. That, that really is a privilege. You already know you cannot free Jamie without killing her. It, it is impossible. So, so please, give yourselves up and don't be heroes. You're, you're an engineer who specializes in frequencies, Ray. And who is with you? Another engineer, a biochemist, a football player, and a rebellious teenager. You're not heroes. Give up."

"You sick scum!" Abby insulted.

"You may be a little upset. That is understandable. But, but don't say I didn't warn you about not trusting anyone. So, so really this is your own fault." Stanley scratched the bottom of his nose with his finger. "But, but look on the bright side. I'm home! I'm like the prodigal son."

"Prodigal son, my black butt!" Deon shouted. "You sold yourself to the devil!"

"Don't, don't you dare call Professor Haagen that. He, he will be the father of a new humanity. He will save—"

Ray kicked the monitor with such force it shot across the room and smashed against the wall.

"We're dead," Fred said.

Ray went to one of the black canvas bags. He took out a cell phone. He entered a code and initiated a program on it, and then set it on a chair and placed the chair under the reflective dome.

"No, we're not." Ray's expression of cold, hard steel only became refined. "I modified the cell phone to be a disruptor. It emits a mild electromagnetic pulse, just enough to disrupt all video and audio feeds within a 25-yard range. The security should be getting distorted views of all the labs. They shouldn't be able to see or hear what we're doing. Fred and Jeremy, can you jam the door? Cut the power from the panel. We'll use that emergency manual release lever to open the door when we're ready."

"On it," Fred responded.

"We're still left with two questions," Abby said. "How will we free Jamie without killing her? And how will we get out of here now that we lost the advantage of secrecy?"

"Look around. There has to be an answer here." Ray scanned around the room.

"We won't have much time to come up with a new plan," Jeremy said while working with Fred on disconnecting some wires in an opened panel by the door.

"I don't know what to do yet," Ray said. "I'll figure something out. I have to."

Not Easily Broken

Chapter 27
Redemption

"That's it." Jeremy rejoined the group. "We jammed the door."

"This will buy us some extra time, but I'll bet they have contraptions to pry this door open," Fred said, examining the door. "It's just a matter of time."

"What options do we have?" Jeremy asked.

"I'm thinking," Ray replied.

"I have to admit," Abby confessed, "I'm pretty scared."

"I know," Ray said softly.

"This is hopeless." Fred paced. Ray had never seen him pace. "Maybe we should just give ourselves over to them and not make this situation worse."

"We can't do that," Jeremy objected. "Who knows what they would do to us."

"And that would mean giving up that decryption code and Jamie," Deon stated.

"We also heard Stanley say that Haagen wants to meet with my dad," Jeremy said with concern. "Who knows what that maniac wants with my dad!"

"But if they come charging in here with those tazer-batons," Fred argued, "we're going to get hurt. I don't want to get fried with ten million volts and then get bludgeoned to death! You're not going to fight them all off, Ray. Admit that. Giving up is not what we planned, but the game changed when Stanley turned on us. He was our ticket in here. If we give up, he said we could walk out of here."

" All of us but Jamie," Deon pointed out.

"That's another issue," Fred added. "We can't even free Jamie from that diabolical machinery! We would be fighting them for nothing if we can't even get her unhooked from that system."

"If I had a day or two to plan this out," Ray said, furrowing his brows and rubbing his forehead.

"But we only have twelve minutes at most," Fred pressured. "I was willing to take a risk coming here when we had a chance of success, but that chance is gone. I'm for us pulling the manual release lever, opening that door, and walking out of here with our hands up."

"Can you trust them to keep their word on not hurting us?" Abby questioned.

"What choice do we have?" Fred's hand gestures reinforced his persistence. "Maybe we can't trust them about not hurting us if we surrender, but I'm pretty sure they will hurt us if we resist them. So betting on the odds, I'd say walking out and giving up actually stands a better chance of us not getting hurt. Besides, what would they gain from hurting us if we gave up?"

"Retribution for breaking in here would be a good reason," Ray said. "Shutting us up would be another. Whether we like it or not, by coming here we've seen too much of ApexGen. They won't let us just leave with all that we know now."

"Dang it!" Fred stomped his foot on the floor. Whipping around, he took a few steps away from them, and then faced them again to say, "All right, so we don't have very good options, but I say that *not* fighting them and giving up still offers us a chance to come out of this alive. It's a minuscule chance, I know, but it's still a chance."

Ray understood his best friend's point about giving up. It would seem to be a reasonable course of action given the circumstances. Plus, he could tell Fred was scared. Even though it didn't take much to frighten Fred, this was different. He wasn't merely emotionally scared, but rationally scared. His best friend was thinking with a clear head, making logical arguments for the most sensible choice.

Yet giving up may not be the most sensible choice. He deduced by now that ApexGen was a highly secretive and secured organization with a grandiose sense of entitlement. They wanted to remain covert, and they believed they have the right to suppress others who threatened the organization. Ray and his team infiltrated ApexGen and uncovered much of their activities, understanding their security system, viewing scientific logs, and witnessing their experimental projects. They were now a severe liability to ApexGen. After the violent engagement at Gordon's house and the brutal battle at Miracom, it was clear that members of ApexGen could and would destroy their opponents if necessary to accomplish their agenda. Simply surrendering to them could be an act of handing themselves over to their executioners. He couldn't do that to his team—to Jeremy, to Jamie. Fighting through whatever onslaught awaited them beyond that door could be the best and only course of action, even if the probability of success was close to nil.

But then again, what good was giving themselves over to their enemies or fighting their enemies to escape if neither option granted the rescue of Jamie, which was why they were in here in the first place? What did it matter if they exited as empty-handed as when they entered? Were they presently at a point of simply needing to count their losses and choose the lesser of two evils? Was it hopeless to save Jamie? Was her salvation a completely lost cause?

"We can't give up," Deon urged. "We have to try. This can't be the end."

Ray wanted to hear that, but he still couldn't see a solution.

"It's pointless to fight. Fighting them was never part of the plan," Fred defended. "We were supposed to sneak in and sneak out undetected. Remember? We're not equipped to take on armed squadrons of terrorists!"

"With Jamie," Deon reiterated. "That was the point, to sneak in and out of here *with Jamie*."

"Yes, I get that." Fred's frustration visibly increased. "You don't have to repeat that to me. But it's different now. There were some major unknowns we didn't account for. Don't forget the betrayal factor that totally tips the scale against us! We have no way of freeing Jamie! I'm sorry, Ray. As much as I love her, and you know that I do, we have to admit we are at an impasse with saving her! Think about this. There's no reason for us to fight them if we can't save Jamie. What's the point?"

"Is there no way?" Ray asked Abby. He hoped some bright idea might have occurred to her by now. She had brilliantly been their expert up to this point.

"None that I can see," Abby said regretfully.

"Can we just try one of those bags of blood?" Jeremy asked desperately.

"I'm pretty sure the machine will detect it's the wrong blood," she replied. "Unless we can convince the machine that they have the original subject, the substitute blood won't work. It'll release the cyanide faster than we can pull the tube out of her."

"Hold on. Wait a minute," Deon said, looking at them one at a time. He spoke with a game-changing face. "I have the same blood type as Jamie."

"What?" Abby stood up.

"Say what?" Jeremy echoed.

"Remember when I was saying that Jamie and me are kind of alike and Stanley rudely cut me off? Well, I was noticing that she and I have the same rare blood type—AB negative," Deon stated. "What if we put some of my blood into one of those bags and hooked it up to the machine?"

All of their eyes widened, like light bulbs suddenly appeared above their heads.

Fred said, "Well, why didn't you say this sooner?"

"Sorry, I was so caught up in playing my role, I didn't even think of it," Deon answered.

"Can we do that?" Ray asked.

"That might work," Abby affirmed as she walked over to Jamie's station. She clicked on the computer and scrolled through a few windows. "There must be some empty bags in that room with the blood bank. We'll need a needle and a tube."

They watched her type with anticipation.

"Wait," Abby said. "No." Her hopeful expression suddenly fell into bleakness. Looking back and forth between the wires connected to Jamie and the computer monitor. "How did I overlook this?"

"What now?" Fred questioned.

"All of these wires hooked up to Jamie will need to provide active readings to the machine. The machine will know if it is missing a reading from one of the wires. The tubes also have to be inserted into a subject because they are digitally sensitive to whether they are connected. If any of these wires or tubes are not active, the machine will release the cyanide."

"Come on! We can't get a break!" Jeremy declared angrily.

"They really tried to create a foolproof entrapment for Jamie," Abby said.

"We're back to square one, with no solution," Fred said.

Frustration swept over the group. Though no one moved or said anything, it appeared that everyone was ready to erupt. They were thinking diligently, straining mentally to grasp for an alternative. But the longer they thought, the more their faces dropped toward the floor as if a burden of hopelessness dragged them into a pit. Until an unexpected suggestion sprouted.

"Use *me*," Deon stated, breaking the silence of hopelessness.

"What do you mean?" Jeremy asked.

"I mean use *me* as the alternate source for Jamie," Deon replied.

"You mean hook you up to the machine?" Abby asked for clarification.

"Yes," Deon answered.

Ray dismissed Deon's volunteerism, "That's ludicrous."

"Why?" Deon recaptured their attention to his suggestion. "It makes sense."

"Let's look for a real solution," Fred insisted.

"I *am* a real solution," Deon insisted.

"A solution that does not involve a human sacrifice!" Fred pressed.

"Maybe that's exactly what is needed to accomplish this rescue mission," Deon said. "Maybe this was never going to work without a sacrifice."

Ray objected emphatically, "Deon, that makes absolutely no sense. What we need to do is scour every inch of this lab. There might be something we missed that can give us a way out."

"Sifu, we don't have time for that," Deon said. "We got the perps outside ready to break down this door. You have the solution right in front of you. Take it." His demeanor was inviting and compelling, but Deon's proposal was ridiculous to Ray.

"Giving you up is not a solution! You haven't thought this through, young man," Ray assessed. "You're responding out of impulse."

"Yes, I have thought this out. I know exactly what I'm saying," Deon said. "We have to act, and I'm the only solution." He held his hands out to his side with his palms open, a vulnerable expression of offering.

Ray looked at the large, young black man standing before him with his arms held out. He turned his back to Deon and took two paces towards the jammed door. He looked at the door, like he was looking past it at the probably dozens of security guards on the other side. Then turned to walk back to him with something to say, but he couldn't think of a sufficient response. He opened his mouth and a grunt came out.

Ray looked away from Deon again and then back at him with an intense stare. He said while pointing at him, "Stop this. We need to find a real answer."

"There is no other answer. You know it," Deon declared.

"Deon, do you realize what you are proposing?" Abby asked.

"Of course, I do," Deon assured. "You need an alternative blood source to free Jamie. I'm proposing to be that. I'll provide the substitute blood for Jamie. Without this," he pointed at his chest, "Jamie can't be freed."

"Man," Jeremy said, "did you inhale some of that chloroform? You can't just sacrifice yourself."

"Why not?" Deon replied as if it were an obvious matter. "We all were sacrificing ourselves the moment we stepped into that elevator and came down here."

"Why would you do this?" Ray asked with perplexity.

"The mission is to save Jamie. So let's get it done," Deon answered with an astounding evenness.

Ray did not detect any impulsivity or emotional irrationality in

Deon's thinking. From what he could ascertain, Deon was functioning with clarity. "You have a whole life ahead of you," he said with increasing frustration to the young man.

"Jamie has a whole life ahead of her."

"You don't even know Jamie," Ray reasoned, trying to talk sense into him.

"I don't know her, but I've seen how you love her. Any father who loves a child like that makes that child special. I know that from my grandma's love for me. So I feel like I know her through your love for her."

His reasoning was simple, so simple that it was confounding.

"If you do this," Abby warned, "you won't get out of here. We don't know what will happen to you. You could even die here. You saw the demented practices of these people. You've seen what they do in these labs. Who knows what they'll do to you."

"I know," Deon responded lucidly and without a waver in his voice, "but look at what they're doing to Jamie." He pointed at the pale, little girl lying on the cheap bed with a thin mattress. Wires and tubes protruded from her like a freakish Frankenstein experiment. Again, the simple points he made baffled Ray and wrenched his heart.

Peeling his eyes away from his daughter, Ray looked up at Deon and said in an intense whisper, "Deon, you would be sacrificing your *life*."

"I know," Deon responded with unchanging calmness. "But I would be saving another."

Ray locked eyes with Deon, and the longer he met this young man's gaze, the more his gaze softened. The wrinkles between his brows gradually smoothed out, and the intense curling of his lips relaxed. He looked at Deon with compassion and incredulity.

"I think I can hear them doing something outside the door," Fred announced, standing by the door. "I think our time has run out."

Deon said to Ray, "Let's save your daughter."

Ray asked Abby, "Would this even work?"

"From everything I can tell, a live subject with the same blood type would be the most risk-free solution. It leaves no variables unaccounted for," she said plainly, but her tone melted when she said, "But, Deon…"

"Let's save Jamie," Deon gently repeated. Then he made a powerful gesture that practically and viscerally demonstrated the willingness and seriousness of his proposal: he pulled up a chair, set it by Jamie's bed, and sat down beside Jamie. His massive arms draped over the arm rests. His back was upright against the backrest. His feet were firmly planted on the floor. He sat there waiting.

Redemption

All eyes were on Ray. Ray's eyes were on Jamie, seeing the lifeless body of his daughter. Then his gaze panned to Deon. The contrast of the large, seated man full of strength next to the little, inanimate girl lying on the bed could not be more paradoxical. *What do I do?* Ray asked himself. He could not believe the option before him. *How could I choose this?*

Finally, Deon said softly, "Please accept this."

The outer corners of his eyes drooped, and Ray exhaled. "Okay," he said. "Okay," he said again more quietly, but this time looking at Deon. He nodded at Abby.

"Dad, we can't give up Deon. That's not right," Jeremy objected.

"It's okay, my man," Deon consoled. "I'm giving myself up. It's my choice. Your dad is just accepting what I'm offering. Come on. Let's do this!"

Abby looked to Ray for a cue to confirm his decision. Ray nodded again. Abby sprung into action, operating quickly on the machines connected to Jamie. "I'll prep the machines to receive another source."

"Deon, I can't fathom what you are about to do," Fred said, "but, Ray, even if we free Jamie we still haven't solved the problem of how we would get out of here."

"If we can free Jamie, then surrendering is definitely not an option any longer," Ray asserted. "There's no point in Deon doing this for nothing. We have to get free."

"Word! You all better not surrender," Deon reinforced. "You all have to get yo' skinny butts out of here with your little girl!"

"Yeah, but how?" Jeremy questioned.

"Even at my best," Ray said, "I couldn't keep all of you from getting seriously injured."

"Or killed for that matter!" Fred blurted.

"I have an idea for that," Abby said as she continued prepping the machines.

"You do?" Fred responded skeptically. "I'm sorry for sounding skeptical, but there's an army outside that door. So unless you have a rocket launcher or something like it, I am hard to convince right now."

"What are you thinking, Abby?" Ray asked.

She didn't stop working. "We could use the stuff inside the storage vault. Remember the various acids they have in there that I had you pretending to clean up? Well, get these three chemicals: nitric acid, sulfuric acid, and glycerol. We'll make glycerol trinitrate, or better known as nitroglycerin. In my field, we use nitroglycerin to treat heart issues. It lubricates the arteries and increases blood flow. They probably kept these chemical ingredients in a lab like this for treating their subjects."

"What? You want to cure the agents of clogged arteries?" Fred questioned facetiously.

Ignoring him, she continued, "Nitroglycerin, in its purest form and in high dosages, is also a highly explosive chemical that detonates upon rupture."

"Oh," Fred said.

"Rupture? You mean if we shook it, it would blow up?" Ray asked.

"Shook it. Hit it. Tossed it. Take your pick," she said.

"Are we making bombs?" Jeremy asked.

"Pretty much. Nitroglycerin is basically what is used in dynamite. We can prepare substantial, concentrated mixtures in test tubes. Each test tube could carry the explosive punch of half a grenade or more. It's no rocket launcher, Fred—"

"But it's something like it!" he said with optimistic energy. "You don't stop surprising me. Cute, smart, and freakishly dangerous!"

"Brilliant, Abby," Ray complimented.

"Dang, girl," Deon exclaimed. "What kind of a biochemist are you?"

"The awesome kind!" Jeremy praised.

"Okay, let's get to work," Ray said. "We may only have several minutes. What do we need to do?"

"Bring the ingredients out here, and I'll tell you what proportions to mix them in. Be sure to have a steady hand. And get a chest filled with ice. You have to keep it cold while working with it," she instructed while never breaking her stride in prepping the machine.

"I'll get the ingredients from the storage vault," Fred said.

"I'll get the ice. I think I saw a whole bunch of frozen ice packs in the room with the blood bank," Jeremy said.

Fred and Jeremy scattered to scavenge.

"What should I do?" Ray asked.

"Why don't you just stay with Deon and Jamie," Abby suggested. "Almost there." She glanced up at Deon, checking to see if he had a change of heart. But Deon remained steady and waiting.

Ray went to Jamie's side, opposite from the side where Deon sat. He stroked her face with the back of his hand. The smooth skin on her cheek felt cold still. He brushed strands of her hair back from her face. Deon waited in his chair, resting both of his large arms on the armrests, while he watched Ray.

Clanking sounds were heard from the other side of the jammed, metal door.

Fred and Jeremy returned with the contents. She told Fred the proportions of the nitric acid, sulfuric acid, and glycerol to be carefully mixed together in a single test tube, all done in the ice-filled chest. "Keep all the test tubes of nitroglycerin on ice," she told them. "They have to stay cold to remain inert, otherwise you run the risk of them exploding on you as you move them. Remember: keep them cold!"

"You're sure about doing this?" she asked Deon. "Every wire is digitally sensitive. The machine knows when something is not connected. So again, I need to hook up all of the same wires and tubes that are in Jamie to you, including the cyanide tube, before I can actually switch the source detection from Jamie to you. Once that's done, we can then unplug Jamie. But once we do this, you will literally take her place. There's no turning back once I plug you in." She said this to Deon with emphasis, like she was giving him a last chance to change his mind.

"I know," Deon simply said.

"I want to say, Deon, you don't have to do this." Ray spoke to him with firm sincerity. He emphasized his words in a way to make sure Deon knew Ray was being authentically genuine in what he said.

"I know I don't," Deon said. "But I want to."

Abby looked at him tenderly and lightly caressed the side of his face. He smiled back at her. She took a syringe and filled it with a clear liquid. She inserted the syringe into Deon's side and injected the liquid. She did this a few more times in other parts of his body. "I gave you some local anesthetics so you won't feel the tubes and wires going into your body. The wires will be taking readings from you. The tubes will either be drawing fluid from you or delivering fluid into you."

Ray pulled up a chair and sat down in front of Deon. "I still can't understand what you are doing, Deon. It—this makes no sense to me."

Abby began inserting the tubes and wires into Deon's body.

"We're saving your daughter," Deon responded.

"*You're* saving my daughter," Ray corrected. "What about your poor grandma? What will happen to her?"

"Tell her I love her and what I did," Deon answered.

Abby inserted seven wires and tubes into him. Five more to go.

"What would she say about you doing this? I can't imagine how this will affect her," Ray said. "I feel responsible for you."

"Well, Grandma was the one who always taught me that we have to be ready to make a sacrifice in order to do something good for someone else. 'Good things don't come cheap,' she would say. Have to give something up of yourself to gain something precious for somebody else." Deon had this tenderness and confidence in reiterating the teachings of his grandmother. "Growing up in the hood, it was all about every man for himself, but she tried to teach me to be the opposite—instead of every man for himself, she taught me to be a man for somebody else."

As Abby inserted the empty cyanide tube into Deon's abdomen, Ray held Deon's hand. Cyanide from the machine filled the tube to a point. Ray said solemnly, "I'm trying to find the right words to say to you, but I have none that can express what I think of you or feel about you right now."

"It's okay," Deon said gently while clasping Ray's hand with his. "One day you'll find the right words."

Ray felt the coarseness but warmth of Deon's enormous hand, like a rough but warm towel enveloping his hand on a wintry morning.

"Last one," Abby said.

She tied a tourniquet around Deon's muscular bicep, told him to make a tight fist and tapped on his arm, encouraging the vein to rise. She rubbed alcohol on the spot where she would insert the needle. Ray watched every step of the process. Emotions swirled within his chest. He felt remorse. He felt gratitude. He felt overwhelmed by the mercy of this young man he had known only for a brief time, but felt he knew so deeply. She inserted the needle with a long tube into Deon's vein to draw his blood, and Ray squeezed his hand as the needle pierced into his friend's arm. The needle was long. The tube was large. Rich, red blood flowed from Deon's vein through the tube and into the machine.

Numbers and readings appeared on the machine.

Abby watched the computer screen and read the content that appeared. "It's working," she said. "I'm making the switch." She typed on the computer managing the three machines, moved and clicked the mouse several times, and then hit 'enter.'

Fred joined them. While Abby watched the machine, the others surrounded Deon, with Ray still seated and holding his hand. The assembly was somber, except Deon maintained a peaceful and proud smile. They watched his blood flow from his arm into the diabolical machine. Deon didn't say a word as the machine took from him.

"It's done," Abby said with a sigh and a nod to Ray. "I'm going to unplug Jamie now. It should only take a minute. Here, take this." She took out a vial from her pocket and handed it to Ray. Without releasing Deon's hand, he took the vial from Abby with his free hand. "This is ammonia carbonate I got from the storage." She explained, "It will help Jamie wake up. Put it under her nose once I've removed the last tube. I'll also give her a small shot of adrenaline. She'll still be groggy, but it'll help her wake up."

Abby removed the cyanide tube first from the little girl's frail body followed by the other tubes and wires. Lastly, she slowly pulled out the needle and tube that sucked her blood from her arm. Ray unplugged the vial with his thumb and waved it under Jamie's nose while Abby gave her a shot of adrenaline in her leg. All the while, Ray did not let go of Deon's hand.

Jamie slowly opened her eyes halfway, one at a time. Her pupils moved from side to side until they focused on Ray. "Daddy?" she whispered weakly.

It was the sweetest sound he had heard in a long while. Abby released a big smile and joyous laugh, looking like she wanted to cry.

Jeremy, standing at the foot of Jamie's bed, rubbed her foot. "Hey, kid."

Ray set the vial down on the bed and took hold of Jamie's hand while still holding Deon's. He felt the contrast of the small, soft hand of his daughter from the massive, rough hand of her savior.

Deon gave Ray's hand a firm squeeze and said, "You take your daughter now."

Ray nodded, looking at Deon with intense gratitude. He loosened his grip of Deon's hand and slowly pulled his hand away, feeling the tough skin slip from his fingers. He stood up and picked up Jamie with both hands.

"Daddy?" She said faintly again. "Are you really here? And Jer, too?" She glanced at her brother with a mild smile from one corner of her mouth. Her eyes opened more.

"Yes, princess," Ray affirmed. "We're both here. We came to take you home."

"I'm ready to go home," she said. "I was scared, but I knew you and Jer wouldn't leave me."

"No, baby, we wouldn't leave you," he said looking at Jeremy.

"Could you tell my grandma?" Deon asked.

"Yes," Ray answered. "I'll tell everyone. Everyone will know what you did."

Jamie looked down at the large, black man sitting in the chair beside her bed. "Who is this?" she asked.

"He——," Ray wasn't sure what should follow next. He decided to say honestly what Deon was. "He's your substitute," he said.

Deon introduced himself warmly, "My name is Deon."

"I'm Jamie. Are you a friend?"

"Yes, I'm a friend."

"Thank you."

Deon smiled at her gently for a moment and then urged, "Now quit standing around me like I'm some lost puppy you all just found in a back alley! Git outta here!"

Chapter 28
Harvester

The lab door clunked and clanged.

"Crap! Here they come!" Jeremy shouted.

"Looks like we're out of time!" Fred stated. "Jeremy and I made twelve test tubes of nitroglycerin. Do you think that's enough?"

Jeremy carried the ice chest over to the group standing by Deon. Inside the chest, a dozen large test tubes plugged with black rubber stoppers and filled with clear liquid stood in the ice and cold packs like prongs.

"You two worked fast," Abby remarked with surprise. "Dangerous to work that fast in making nitroglycerin, but you both did it. You must have steady hands."

"This should do it," Ray said.

"What's the plan," Fred asked.

"Simple," Ray replied. "We kill the lights in here. We don't want them seeing Deon hooked up and Jamie freed. Then we blast our way out of here. Save two test tubes. Head to the elevator. Go up as far as we can. When they stop the elevator, we blast our way to the stairwell."

The door cranked, like metal was being bent and crunched.

"Their using some kind of jaws of life to pry that door open!" Fred said.

"Once that door opens, they'll try to storm in here," Ray said. "But we need to push the fight out into the hall, so we don't risk injuring Deon and these other children."

The door creaked. They heard metal scraping metal.

"Jeremy, kill the lights," Ray ordered.

The thick metal door sounded like a car being crushed at a junkyard. Components inside the door were being demolished as their predators forced it open. The door cracked half an inch.

Ray grabbed a large beaker from the counter and put two handfuls of ice into it. He respectfully placed five test tubes into it. He spoke quietly and quickly to them. "Spread out to the flanks. Fred and Abby, take the left side. Jeremy and I will take the right. Jamie, stay with me, princess. I'll throw the first test tube at them once the door opens enough for a person to enter." The door cranked open a few inches. The sound of crushing metal was jarring and horrifying. "After my first bombardment, that will be our signal. After throwing the first test tube, advance forward to push the fight into the hallway. Pace yourselves with the test tubes. Don't throw them too quickly."

The ApexGen security now cracked the door open by several inches. "Almost in there," one security guard called out. "It's dark in there. Light up your sticks!"

Ray and the others heard popping sounds like live wires striking water and saw blue electric lights flickering through the opening of the doorway.

"Don't throw the test tubes!" Abby whispered. "Toss them carefully. You don't want to risk shaking them too much by throwing and having them blow up in your hand."

"Crud! You mean we can blow ourselves up?" Fred shrieked.

"Lob them in an arch and let them hit the floor. They will detonate when they rupture," she further instructed.

"Good to know," Ray confirmed.

The door cranked open ten inches.

"One more thing," she added.

"What else?" Fred asked incredulously.

"Before tossing a test tube, hold it in your hand and warm it up for four seconds. That will make the nitroglycerin active and more likely to blow upon impact."

"Hold and wait before tossing. Just like a grenade," Jeremy stated.

The door cracked open another twelve inches, sounding like hundreds of cans crushing. Flashlight beams peered through the opening.

"This is your last chance to surrender," a security guard shouted, "otherwise we will come in to take down any conscious person. We will hurt you."

"You all got this," Deon encouraged enthusiastically.

"Aim for their lights. Go to your flanks," Ray ordered.

The two teams moved quietly, swiftly, and carefully to move the test tubes at an even level. They squatted down in their positions far back enough from the doorway to stay clear of the explosions. They waited in the darkness. Only small red and blue lights from the machines lit the immediate areas around the machines.

The door cracked open more than two feet but no one entered yet. Smart. They were waiting to open the door wide enough for more than one guard to enter through at once. The security guards shone their flashlights into the lab. The bluish lights from their tazer-batons illuminated their bodies.

Ray lifted a test tube and held it in his hand.

A final crank forced the door wide open and light from the hallway and flashlights flooded straight into the lab, but the two teams being on the flanks were not in the direct pathways of the light. The guards removed the tool they used to pry the door open. At the same moment, Deon shouted, "Hey, fools! What's up?"

The startling shout stalled the guards' for a split second and drew their attention. But before they could focus in on Deon, Ray gracefully flung the first test tube at the flashlights. The tube arched nicely in the air above the flashlight beams. When three of the guards had just stepped into the lab with their tazer-batons fiercely sparkling and crackling, the test tube dropped between two guards.

Ray barely heard the glass break when a sudden explosion complemented with a bright yellow flash blew two of the guards to either side of the room and the third guard back into the hallway. The men did not have a chance to yell when the force of the nitroglycerin hit them. They were simply thrown like silent rag dolls. Grunts came from the guards, who either felt the explosive impact or were clubbed by the body of the third guard flying into the hallway.

Two seconds later, a security guard from the hallway shouted, "What was that? How did they get explosives into the building?"

While he was finishing his sentence, another test tube was already arching in the air, launched by Abby. The second test tube landed into the hallway a couple of feet beyond the doorway. That explosion blew two more security guards back. Screams and yells were heard. While she was lobbing her test tube, Ray advanced forward several feet with the ice chest, and Jeremy was already warming up another test tube in his hand.

"Press forward," Ray said to Fred and Abby as Jeremy tossed a test tube straight up the middle of the hallway, immediately followed by another test tube that Fred pitched like a softball. The two test tubes were only a second apart from each other, but Fred's landed a few feet further than Jeremy's. They exploded like two beats in rhythm. They couldn't tell how many guards they took out, but there were multiple yells.

The hallway was now dark. Lights knocked out. Only the light of the flashlights shone, erratically waving from one side to the other.

"Fall back," a security guard shouted.

Ray's teams maneuvered towards the doorway, staying low and moving their test tubes at an even level. Ray lobbed another test tube far down the hallway. Two seconds later, Abby chucked another. Two more explosions at the far end of the hall.

Peeking around the wall into the hall, Ray saw the inanimate bodies of more than a dozen security guards strewn all the way down. The light of the flashlights and the bluish electrifying lights were reduced to faint flickers on the floor.

"Let's go," Ray said to them.

Fred and Abby moved into the hallway, followed by Jeremy who took the ice chest with him.

Ray looked back at Deon. He saw faintly Deon's face, shoulders, and the arm with the blood tube. The blood from Deon glowed in the faint light. He couldn't make out Deon's facial expression, but he saw him sitting calmly and almost majestically in the chair. He wanted to say something to him. "Good-bye," "thank you," or "take care." But none of the clichéd partings were appropriate. So he said, "I'll never forget this."

He grabbed his black canvas bag, led Jamie by the hand, and rushed into the hall, leaving his friend in the dark room that once imprisoned his daughter.

The team crouched along the wall where the hall made a *T*. Around the corner to their left was the way to the elevator. Bluish, crackling electricity from tazer-batons gave away the position of Ralph and another squad of guards at the security station. From the number of flickering lights and crackling sounds, Ray guessed there was another half a dozen of them around the corner.

A security guard could be heard whispering into an intercom or walkie-talkie. "Back-up needed. Adversaries armed with—." Before he finished his sentence, Ray sidearm flung a test tube around the corner. The tube glided through the air. The radioing guard saw it, tried to catch it, but he fumbled it from one hand to the other. The jostling detonated the test tube, causing a mid-air explosion in front of him.

Another four guards directly in front of Ray's team poured in through the exit door leading to the stairwell at the far end of the hall. The guards around the corner by the elevator radioed to the unit of four to not approach Ray. But it was too late. They were already within Jeremy's tossing range. They attempted to retreat back to the exit door when Jeremy launched a test tube. The tube chased them and landed right behind the unit of four, blowing them into the air. Through the dusty haze, Ray saw the four guards lying motionlessly on their stomachs or backs.

Simultaneously, Abby peeked around the corner at the elevator and tossed another test tube, aiming it at the remaining five guards left trying to take cover behind the security station. The explosion took out four of the five. The fifth, injured but mobile and conscious, stayed hidden behind the security station in front of the elevator. All that remained of the destroyed security station was a scorched frame.

"I need a sitrep, Unit 3," a voice was heard on the walkie-talkie of the last security guard. He answered in a terrified, juvenile way, "We're being blasted!"

"What? Be more specific!" the voice on the walkie demanded.

"I'm the only one left I think," the guard replied.

Ray's team moved forward toward the security station at a steady pace, carefully moving the remaining nitroglycerin with them.

"We had twenty guards down there! All our cameras are knocked out. We're blind. Tell me what is going on?"

"Get me out of here!"

"Calm yourself, officer. We need to assess your situation! Report!"

"They blew us up with test tubes!"

"What? Repeat."

"Test tubes, sergeant. They're blasting us with test tubes! Get me out of here!"

"Must be delirium," the sergeant said to someone else on the other end of the radio. "Tell me where they are now," the sergeant ordered his frightened underling.

"They are—"

Ray snatched the radio from him. The team stood around the cowering officer. The officer clumsily grabbed the tazer-baton on the floor at his side, but Ray kicked him on the side of the head, causing his head to bounce off the wall. He was unconscious.

"Repeat!" the sergeant of the radio ordered. "You broke up, officer. Repeat!"

Fred took the radio from Ray and spoke into it, mimicking the officer's voice, "They're heading up the stairs. Repeat. They're heading up the stairs. Now get me out of here! Get me—" Then he smashed the radio on the floor.

"Good job," Ray complimented. "Now let's go." He took the security guard's cap and tazer-baton.

Abby summoned the elevator. Seconds later, the elevator doors opened. The elevator was empty. Ray stepped in first and held the security guard's cap over the silvery reflective dome. Fred took out duct tape from Ray's black bag and taped the cap to the ceiling while Jeremy entered and pressed the button labeled, 'Lobby.'

The elevator ascended. There still was no music.

"They'll likely discover we're in the elevator, and we won't make it all the way up the 53 floors to the lobby," Ray predicted. The counter above the elevator door indicated they were passing the 50th floor. "Fred, take this." He handed his best friend the tazer-baton.

"Maybe you should give this to the girl," Fred replied, trying to hand the tazer-baton to Abby.

"She has an advantage," Ray stated. "She can fight. You can't."

Fred retracted his offer.

"We have three tubes of nitroglycerin left," Ray spoke as he opened his black canvas bag. "Let's hope it's enough to get us out of the building."

The elevator reached the 47th floor.

As Ray took out two hammers from the black canvas bag, he said, "At whatever point they stop this elevator, Abby, be ready to lob a test tube out the door. We should all be standing on the sides to shield ourselves behind the elevator walls." The elevator reached the 42nd floor.

Fred noticed the sci-fi device inside the canvas bag before Ray zipped it up. "Are you still hanging on to that thing? We're fighting for our lives and you're hauling that big, clunking memoir?" Fred challenged. "Leave it! Leave the bag!"

"It stays with me," Ray said plainly. "Be ready to fight our way through and get to the exit for the stairwell. Save at least one test tube for the journey up the stairs. Let's hope we get close enough to the surface. Our trek up the stairwell will be relatively short from there."

The elevator reached the 37th floor. They watched the counter for a second. The elevator kept ascending. ApexGen security had not stopped the elevator yet.

"When we get out, Abby, take the remaining test tubes in the beaker." Ray took out his cell phone and fingered the touch screen, pulling up apps and entering codes.

"Hope you're calling the Marines," Fred said.

"I'm contacting Miranda. She's supposed to be monitoring my cell by satellite," Ray said.

"She is?" Fred asked in surprise.

"No one knew about it. I was banking on her not being an ApexGen sleeper agent like Stanley supposed. Since he didn't know she was my eyes in space, I'm hoping Stanley and his tact team didn't take her out for good."

The elevator reached the 32nd floor.

"She can provide me with real time schematics of where we are." Ray waited for a response from Miranda on his phone.

Abby watched the elevator counter. The elevator passed the 29th floor. "Why have they not stopped the elevator?"

"Don't jinx it," Fred said.

"They could be funneling us to a floor that is more tactically advantageous for them to take us out," Ray hypothesized.

"I'm scared, Daddy," Jamie said, appearing more awake and alert.

"We'll be okay," he said, rubbing the back of her head. "Stay close to Jer."

"To me?" Jeremy asked.

"Yes. Protect your sister. After Abby lobs the first test tube out the door, I'll lead the charge and carve a path." He twirled his hammers one at a time, loosening himself up. "Back me up, but keep Jamie safe."

"I will," Jeremy said, taking Jamie's hand.

"Has it occurred to anyone that we could actually make it all the way to the top!" Fred insisted. "Stop jinxing it."

The elevator passed the 20th floor.

"I wonder what will be on the floor they are herding us into?" Jeremy asked.

"What is wrong with the Lee family?" Fred asked rhetorically.

Ignoring Fred's comment, Ray said, "If we're lucky, there will only be a handful of security guards on the floor they take us to. I'm guessing their guards are taking the other elevator and rushing up the stairs to the same floor they're trapping us on. So we'll probably get there before they do. That's if we're lucky."

"I'm ready, Dad," Jeremy said.

"I know you are," Ray affirmed. He placed his hand on his son's shoulder.

The elevator passed the 17th floor.

"We're so close," Abby said.

"Get ready," Ray told them.

"Lobby," Fred said with his eyes closed. "Come on. Lobby. Lobby."

Ray's phone buzzed. "It's Miranda! She sent me the live tracking of our location on the building's schematic!"

Then the elevator halted at the 15th floor.

"This is it," Ray stated. "Move to the sides."

Ray, Jeremy, and Jamie stood on one side while Fred and Abby stood on the other.

He told Abby, "Look before you toss."

She nodded with a test tube already warming in her hand. Ray held up two hammers in front of him. Jeremy kept Jamie behind him.

The elevator doors opened.

Electric crackling sounds alerted the team of impending danger. Ray saw five security guards only about twelve feet away! Abby tossed a test tube right to their location. Ray recoiled back against the side of the elevator wall and pushed Jeremy back with his outstretched arm. The blast was so close, so loud, and so strong, that Ray's ears rang. He felt as though the whole elevator swayed, but it was only his head. Before he regained a clear vision, he charged out with both hammers in fighting positions. Still dizzy from the blast, he stumbled for the first few steps into the dusty fog, like he had just walked into an active demolition site. There was no activity.

But suddenly, he saw a menacing blue light charging through the cloud of dust toward his chest. He instinctively parried it to the side with his left hammer, without touching the blue sparks, and with his right hammer he slammed the tazer-baton out of the guard's hand. Immediately, he brought the right hammer up in a backhanded swing to strike the guard on the temple. The guard fell against the wall but not onto the floor. As the guard got up off the wall, Ray hammered him repeatedly throughout the guard's arms, body, and head. The guard fell to the floor.

"Let's go!" Ray yelled.

They raced down a short hallway and through some double doors. Jeremy brought the black canvas bag with him.

They entered a large, grey, and rectangular room well lit by recessed fluorescent lighting in the ceiling. The room was much longer than it was wide. The floor and walls were unfinished concrete. The sides of the room were lined with circuit breaker panels, voltage meters, power switches, and thick power lines. Throughout the center of the room were drainpipes and other kinds of pipes with big valves extending from floor to ceiling. Staggered along the wall, interspersed with the circuit breakers and voltage meters were eight giant, active, and grey generators and four condensers. Each were the size of washing machines. The generators were set in pairs accompanied by one condenser; Ray saw that the condensers were used to cool down the generators by converting the warmer air in the room into cooler air. He calculated these threefold set-ups must mean that the generators were producing a lot of energy.

There were no closets, storage spaces, or other rooms. No cabinets, desks, or shelves. There wasn't even a broom and dustpan in sight. Only thick sheets of black rubber hung on the left wall. These were used to protect maintenance workers from electrical shocks by standing on them. On the other side of the room, about 175 feet away from them, was the exit to the stairwell.

"What is this?" Fred asked.

"There's nothing on this floor," Ray said, looking at the schematic on his phone. "This is their trapping point. There's no place to hide, and there are no resources in here for us to use."

"Can't make anymore nitroglycerin bombs," Jeremy said.

"Not even any tools for us to use as weapons," Abby said while opening one of the double doors they had come through and looking back down the hall. "The other elevator is coming up. It's fourteen floors away."

"Probably filled with a dozen or more security guards," Ray theorized.

"Well, what are we waiting for? Let's get out of here!" Fred started to make a dash for the exit door to the stairwell.

"Wait!" Ray commanded, stopping Fred's hasty move. "There are likely two dozen more guards and agents coming up and down that stairwell to our location. They meant for this floor to be the trapping point. We can't charge into that stairwell."

"Well, what do we do then?" Fred squealed.

Ray examined the room, scrutinizing the eight active generators. The two dozen pipes attached to the floor and ceiling formed a forest-like environment, creating natural obstacles.

Abby was still standing by the double door, watching the elevator. "The other elevator is ten floors away!"

"I hear a lot of rumbling in the stairwell! Footsteps. Lots of them!" Fred yelled.

"We make a stand here in the center of the room and fight them off! Form a circle and keep Jamie in the middle!" Jeremy said courageously.

"We still have two test tubes," Abby said as she closed the door and rejoined the group. "We can blast a few of them as they come in." She reached in the beaker.

"No, wait," Ray said. He smashed the silvery, reflective dome in the center of the ceiling. "Fred, grab those rubber sheets. Everyone come over here." He led them to a spot between two large drainpipes in the center of the left wall. The diameter of each pipe was large enough to easily fit a person. The space between the pipes was about three persons wide. "Wedge ourselves between these two pipes," he ordered. Ray grabbed the black canvas bag and led the way.

"What good will this do?" Fred screeched as he went along with the wedging plan.

They squished between the two drainpipes. In front of them was a forest of two dozen smaller pipes with valves and meters. Fred brought over the rubber sheets. Ray instructed them to stand on the mats and hold up a few in front of them.

"What are we doing?" Fred asked with nervous agitation.

"Take this, princess," Ray said to Jamie, handing her his phone. "A satellite is tracking this phone. In case we get separated, this will help me find you. Okay? I won't lose you again."

She took her dad's phone.

Then Ray reached into the canvas bag and pulled out his sci-fi looking device.

"That?" Fred fretted. "How is your broken desk ornament going to help us?"

Ray reset a few buttons and knobs. "It just needs a little power," Ray said, taking Fred's tazer-baton from him.

"I need that," Fred said.

He unscrewed the bottom of the tazer to reveal two 9-volt batteries. He took one of the batteries out and gave the tazer back to Fred. Fred held his handicapped weapon limply. Ray inserted the battery into the back of his device.

"I thought that thing doesn't work," Jeremy said.

"Right? That's what you told me too!" Fred said worriedly.

"Technically, it doesn't," Ray replied while adjusting the switches and knobs.

"That's not really an answer. Come on, buddy. Don't lose it on us!" Fred pleaded.

"What does that do, Sifu?" Abby asked.

Ray extended the two antennas, flipped the lever on the right hand side, and pushed the "on" button at the bottom. The digital meter came on, showing a reading of '0.' "This was an experimental device Melanie and I worked on. We started it at M.I.T. and continued developing it after we married."

"Yes, we got that already! It's very special to you and Mel. That's why you kept it all of these years. But how's it supposed to save us?" Fred asked.

"Frequency waves have energy," Ray explained. "Frequencies are not just invisible, non-existent things. They actually have energy."

"Say what?" Jeremy responded.

"There are frequency waves everywhere. All around us. Waves are running through us. They come from television, radio, cell phones… everything. And frequencies have energy. In a room like this, these generators and condensers emit an abundance of frequencies, flooding this room with a plethora of energy. That means there's virtually an unlimited source of power."

"Fascinating." Abby was sincerely intrigued despite their

predicament, but her attention was captured by the thuds echoing in the stairwell.

Fred fidgeted uncontrollably. "Great science lesson, but get to the point!"

Ray held the device up in front of him proudly, like a trophy. "Mel and I created a frequency energy harvester. It harvests the energy of the frequencies in our immediate surroundings." He pointed to the two long, extended antennas. "These are receiving antennas. Once the harvester harnesses the energy from the frequency waves in the atmosphere around us, it is supposed to charge up something, like a light bulb or any electronic gadget, by remotely transferring energy to it." He pointed at the two metallic, thimble looking parts in between the antennas. "It could even power an electric car. If it worked, it could power anything without the need for a cord or an outlet. We were going to patent this if it worked."

"If?" Fred squeaked. "Why are you telling us this?"

"The harvester harnesses energy superbly! It gathered energy far better than we could've expected!" Ray spoke with excited pride as he adjusted the knobs and switches on the device. Ray turned the three knobs in the center to maximum. The digital number on the meter read 50 volts and then three seconds later, 325 volts. The voltage indicator climbed rapidly with every second as it harvested energy. "But the problem was the emission of the energy."

The rumbling from the stairwell stopped right outside of the door. They also heard footsteps coming from the elevator outside the double doors. Their pursuers were right outside of both sets of doors!

The humming and motorized sounds of the generators and condensers audibly represented the invisible frequencies spewing into the air. The meter read 520 volts. The rate of increment on the voltage reading sped up. The harvester was like a hungry animal, gorging on the buffet of energy in the air! 1,150 volts!

"It didn't work, per se," he continued as the meter read 2,200 volts, "because the device emitted too much energy and overloaded the target. It literally blew up the light bulbs and fried other electronic devices. And that was with the harvester only emitting a fraction of the energy it collected." Ray tapped on the large dial on the device. "Of course that was a hazard. People could even be electrocuted if they were in the harvester's emission path. We could never patent it."

"Get to the point! The point!" Fred said. "They're outside."

The coil of wires in the transparent cylinder on the left-hand side of the harvester glowed bright yellow. The meter read 3,500 volts. The team heard voices coming from beyond both doors. It sounded like they were coordinating with each other via their walkie-talkies. The meter read 5,945 volts and the cylinder radiated brilliantly.

"Ray!" a deep, abrasive voice reverberated through the double doors. "I'm the commanding officer, Lieutenant Ashford. All your exit points are sealed off. I'm betting you don't have many more explosives, not enough to take out sixty-six security guards. There are thirty-two in the stairwell and thirty-four outside of these double doors. We brought the entire security force on top of you. You hear me? Surrender and we won't harm you. If you blow up any more of my guys, I will beat the snot out of you and your companions, including your son! We will taze you until your tongues hang out of your mouths and you're lying on the ground like invalids."

The meter read 9,200 volts. The glow from the cylinder illuminated Ray's face as he watched the harvester voraciously consume the energy of the frequencies in the atmosphere. The generators and condensers continued to feed the harvester, and the harvester ate without an end to its appetite.

Ray didn't blink. He appeared to be mesmerized by the candescence of the harvester, or perhaps he was lost in how the contraption represented his relationship with Mel. Abby took note of Ray's captivity by the device.

"Say something, Ray," Lieutenant Ashford called, "or we charge in!"

"Ray!" Abby grabbed Ray's attention.

"We're thinking about it," Ray shouted toward the double door, stalling for time.

"You think this is a game, Ray?" The lieutenant sounded agitated. "I don't want anybody else getting hurt. But I will jam this tazer-baton down your mouth if you make this any more difficult! Then I will take both of your children! What's it going to be?"

Ray was silent. He motioned for his team to lift up the rubber sheets to shield themselves. 15,125 volts! "How do I know you won't hurt us if we surrender?"

"You don't know," Ashford said, "but what you do know is I *will* hurt you if you don't surrender."

22,100 volts. "Let me think on it," Ray casually hollered.

"Give me your surrender and lay down your explosives!"

31,300 volts.

"Your time is up. Do I have your word that you are laying down your explosives?"

"Just a second," Ray shouted back. 44,315 volts.

"I'm through playing with you, Ray! We're coming in, and I swear we will beat all you to an inch of your life if you attack us with those explosives!"

"Okay. I promise we will not blast any more of your men. But if you want me, you will have to drag my cold, dead body out of here! If you have the guts, come in!"

58,882 volts! Ray had his hand on the large dial, had his thumb on a button, and aimed it at the generator by the double doors.

Lieutenant Ashford cursed at Ray and gave the signal to rush in! 75,550 volts!

The doors on both sides of the room burst open. Security guards swarmed in like locusts, with their tazer-batons sparkling in front of them. The first dozen guards took a second to visually locate Ray's position. They quickly maneuvered through the pipe forest and closed in on Ray and the others.

Ray waited a couple more seconds for more of the guards to pour in. Then he turned the big dial halfway to maximum and pressed the button at his thumb.

Tentacles of electricity blazed out of the two thimble-like extensions at the top of the harvester. Ray aimed the harvester at the oncoming attackers, electrifying the men and women three to four at a time. He took his thumb off of the button and the electricity stopped. He swung the harvester toward the stairwell door, where a dozen security guards were maneuvering through the forest of pipes. With the dial still turned halfway, he pressed the button again, and tentacles of lightning monstrously reached out and grabbed the guards, zapping them in groups. Ray continued panning the harvester from one side to the other. It still gathered energy while it spewed out electrical shocks. He turned the dial to three-quarters. He shot bolts of electricity left and right, like a son of thunder.

The room went berserk with energy! Gaskets on the pipes burst. Steam and water sprayed out from busted valves. Ray turned the dial to the 90 percent mark. The security guards were caught in a chaotic storm of lightning, cloud, and rain. They convulsed and shook for long seconds before falling to the floor, shuddering in fetal positions. Finally, the generators by the doors sparked, caught fire, and exploded, blowing back any remaining guards around them. Ray powered down the harvester, turning the big dial back to *0* and took his thumb off of the button. Only sparks from the blown-out ceiling lights faintly illuminated the room.

"Give it a second," Ray said, halting his team from impulsively running out onto the wet floor. He placed the harvester back into the canvas bag.

"Man," Fred said, "I'm really glad you had that thing on you."

Dozens of spastic bodies littered the floor. Lieutenant Ashford, as was indicated on his uniform, lay just a few feet from Ray.

"Don't touch the pipes." Ray yelled, "Now!" After picking up the two hammers he set down on the floor, he charged toward the door of the stairwell. He could tell there were just a few guards left in the stairwell that had not entered the room. His team followed him. Jeremy led Jamie by the hand and carried the black canvas bag. They hopped and skipped over the litter of security guards.

Sprinting to the doorway like he was charging into the center of a battlefield, he twirled the hammer in his right hand before he swung and clubbed a security guard on the head. Exiting the room and standing on a small landing in the middle of three security guards, he swung his hammers in every direction, parrying and bludgeoning until tazer-batons were swatted out of his enemies' hands and the guards fell.

"Let's go," he called as he clambered up the steps.

Stomping up the stairs, they arrived at the 14th floor and then the 13th. Fred was already panting, wheezing and sweating profusely. Ray pushed them to pick up their pace. They ascended past the 12th, 11th, and 10th floors. But Fred started to trail behind.

"Dad!" Jeremy yelled as he rounded the corner, carrying Jamie, to enter the 8th floor. "It's Fred."

Fred was behind by two flights of stairs.

The team paused at the 7th floor.

"Come on," Ray shouted. "We're almost there." He could hear his best friend wheezing. "Push it!"

"Keep going!" Fred hollered back, wheezing. He stopped to catch his breath.

"You took out their entire army of security guards back there," Jeremy commented. "Like that lieutenant said, he brought the whole force. So maybe they ran out of security guards to throw at us, and we're home free now!"

"We still have six more floors to go. We're not out of danger yet," Ray said.

He started up the steps, heading to the 6th floor, but as he got to the top of the first flight of stairs and Abby was in the middle of that flight, the door to the 7th floor burst open. A man and a woman dressed in suits grabbed Jamie while she was in Jeremy's arms.

"No!" Jeremy cried out. He fought off the suited assailants with one arm while carrying Jamie with the other.

Another suited man squeezed through the doorway. Abby shouted at them but couldn't jump into the fight while she held the test tubes, nor could she toss a test tube at the guards with them being so close.

"Abby, duck!" Ray hollered.

As soon as Abby squatted down on her step, a hammer sailed through the air and bludgeoned one of the men in the forehead.

Jeremy jerked away from the grasping abductors while striking one in the Adam's apple. He peeled Jamie away from them. Abby reached for Jamie to take her hand. Jeremy deflected the female assailant's effort to subdue him and side-kicked her in the kneecap, causing her to drop to the floor. Ray tried to scurry past Abby and Jamie, but just as he was doing so, the other suited man shocked Jeremy in the shoulder with his tazer-baton. Two more suited men came through the door and engaged Ray. Ray blocked, attacked, and knocked the suited man over, all the while mindful of Jamie's safety, as she was in harm's way.

But it was too late. They dragged his tazed son through the doorway.

"No!" Ray shouted as he smacked the last guard standing in his way on the jaw with his hammer. He chased after Jeremy through the door, but was met by another armed man. He dispatched him swiftly, and caught the glimpse of two men dragging Jeremy into an elevator. "No!" He raced to the elevator as the doors were closing.

Ray was fifteen feet away when one of the men pointed a different kind of tazer at him, a smaller one. He shot tazing prongs at Ray through the closing doors. Ray dodged out of the way with incredible reflexes. But it slowed him down by a second, just enough time for the elevator doors to close further. Ray saw his son's face through the shrinking opening of the elevator doors. Ray tried jamming his hammer between the closing doors as he lunged forward, but they closed shut before he reached them. "Jeremy!" He banged his hammer on the elevator door.

He leaned his head on the closed doors.

"Oh, no," Abby said as she entered the hall from the stairwell, holding Jamie's hand and the beaker containing the last two test tubes.

"No, no, no," Fred echoed as he stumbled in with the black canvas bag and the hammer Ray threw. "This was my fault."

Ray pulled his head off of the elevator door and looked up at the elevator counter. The elevator descended. He turned around and walked toward them. "I'm going after Jeremy."

"We are never getting out of this building, are we? If we go back down there," Fred said, "we'll never survive."

"You're not. I am."

"*You'll* never survive," Abby said emphatically.

"I need you and Fred to finish this rescue. Get Jamie out of here for me. You have two test tubes still. Blow your way through the building lobby if you have to. Just get her out!" Ray squatted to pick up a tazer-baton from the suited man he dispatched in the hall. He handed it to Abby. "Take this. Grab another one in the stairwell."

Abby examined the person lying at her feet. "Who are these people? They're not security guards."

"Agents, I presume," Ray answered as he took the black canvas bag from Fred.

"You mean the specialized killers Stanley warned us about?" Fred asked. "The deadly ones from below the 53rd floor, where he told us to absolutely not go? Those agents?"

"These were more skilled. Faster and stronger than the security guards," Ray said as blood dripped out of his nose.

"You're bleeding," Fred said.

"One of them got me," Ray said.

"You can't go after Jeremy alone!" Fred objected.

"You don't even know where they're taking him," Abby pointed.

Ray looked at the counter for the elevator that Jeremy was in. It kept descending.

"I will turn over this entire structure if I have to in order to find him!"

"Jer has your phone, Daddy," Jamie informed.

"What?"

"While he was fighting the bad people back there, I put the phone into his pocket. You said the phone could keep me from getting lost. I was afraid Jeremy would get lost."

Ray knelt down on one knee in front of his daughter. "You amaze me." Still holding his hammers, he embraced her.

He pulled back to look into her eyes. He kissed her on the cheek. He was pleased to feel warmth and see color return in her. "Get her out of here for me," he said to Fred and Abby.

"We will," Abby agreed, "but how will you track Jeremy?"

"I have another cell phone which I boosted the signal on," he said, tucking a hammer under his arm and pulling out another cell phone from his back pocket with his free hand. "It's my back-up."

"You always have a plan B, even for your cell phone," Fred stated.

"I'll call Miranda. She'll talk me through where Jeremy is being taken." He dialed her number. "You three should start moving. Take the stairs. Don't use the elevator."

Ray squatted in front of the black canvas bag and set the phone down while it called Miranda.

Abby and Fred silently watched in wonder as their leader weaponized himself. He picked up his two hammers and slipped them through his belt behind his back. He took out two more hammers from the bag and slipped them through his belt at his sides. He took out two smaller ones and slipped them in front of him. Finally, he brought out two more hammers. He had eight hammers of different types, shapes, and sizes that could be held by one hand. He pulled out six screwdrivers from the bag and stuck three in each of his back pockets.

He took out his old, red backpack from the black canvas bag. He pulled the harvester out of the canvas bag and placed it in the backpack. "Fred, please, bring this back with you." He handed his red backpack with the harvester to his best friend.

"I won't lose this," Fred said. "Count on it."

Abby, impressed by Ray, watched him with somberness. "Ray." She touched his arm, felt his tricep harden and flex while holding the hammer. She was speechless for a moment while looking in his eyes. "You just be careful and get yourself out of this hell-hole. Don't you dare get stuck down there. You understand? You have to come out."

"I'm coming back with Jeremy." His commanding voice was firm.

"You better." She squeezed his arm. "Jamie needs you. She'll be waiting for you." Her feeling of concern was painted over her face. Ray could tell she restrained herself from tearing. "I'll be waiting for you too," she said. She hugged him.

He hugged her back with both arms while holding his hammers. He felt her warmth, the softness of her body and the sincerity of her embrace. As he held her for those couple of seconds, he felt her gradually melt in his arms. He sensed the tough woman, who could make bombs out of ingredients for treating heart issues, was a tender soul.

"Go," he said, pulling away from her. "Get yourselves and Jamie out. I'll see you on the surface."

"Yes," Miranda answered on the phone.

Ray tucked one hammer under his arm, bent down, and picked up the phone. "Miranda. It's Ray."

"What's happening? It's showing me on the laptop that you are descending."

"It's not me. It's Jeremy. They took him. What floor have they taken him to?"

"They just stopped."

"Where?"

"The 63rd floor."

"I'm taking the elevator down," Ray simply said with a calm, even tone. He pushed the elevator call button and the doors to the other elevator opened right away. The other elevator was already on the 7th floor. The crew of agents must've taken both elevators up. Or maybe, they intended to leave one elevator for Ray to follow them down. A challenge, perhaps.

"You're just going to take the elevator down? They'll be waiting for you!" Fred stated. "And you're going to the 63rd floor! That floor is the pit of hell, where we were absolutely not supposed to go to. It's a dead end trap!"

"I think that's the point. They want me. But I'm getting my son."

"Maybe you should take one of these test tubes," Abby offered.

"No. I want to be sure you all will get out."

"Daddy," Jamie called.

"You'll be okay, princess." He knelt down. "Stay with Miss Abby. Be strong. Have courage."

"I will," she said in her soft voice.

"And be very fast."

"I will!" she replied with a smile.

"I'll see you later?"

"I'll see you later." With that, Ray kissed her on the cheek, got up, and went into the elevator.

As the elevator doors closed, he saw Jamie wave to him. He waved back. He was sealed in the metal box descending to the very bottom. He thought about smashing the silver, reflective dome above his head with his hammer but instead he glared into it. Then he faced forward. He decided to leave the dome be and let them watch him come.

Chapter 29
Haagen

Ray descended. He didn't sweat. He didn't breathe heavily. He didn't fidget. He just rode the elevator down, still as a mannequin.

The lack of music in the elevator allowed him to think. He thought about Melanie. He thought about Jamie. He thought about Deon. He thought about Abby. He thought about how to save his son. He was almost there.

The elevator automatically stopped at the 52nd floor. He recalled the code to enable the elevator to proceed, but he didn't enter it. He didn't move toward the panel that asked for the access code. He merely stared at the panel with the red light. He had a feeling he didn't need to enter the code. He looked up at the reflective dome above him, as if waiting for a response from it. Several seconds later, the elevator reactivated and continued its descent. He faced forward again.

The elevator doors opened slowly. A number on the elevator doorframe read, "63." He stepped into a wide, brightly lit hall and paused to survey the area. The floor was some kind of polished, metal lining. The ceiling had a cold, metallic finish. There were several closed office doors on either side of the hall; the doors were solid wood, painted black. The hall stretched for thirty feet in front of him and opened into a red-carpeted lobby with black leather furniture and brushed nickel coffee and side tables. From what he could tell from his end of the hall, the lobby was an intersection for additional halls, leading to other rooms. The space was well air-conditioned; he guessed the temperature was around 65 degrees Fahrenheit. No one was in sight so far.

"Ray Lee." He heard his name summoned over the intercom speakers. The voice was chillingly familiar. The voice was cool and energetic, laced with confidence and power, like the voice of a nation's leader.

"Professor Vladimir Haagen," Ray said loudly.

"Welcome home, my boy," Haagen said. "I made a mistake in underestimating you, and making mistakes is not characteristic of me. I should've known. You were always one of my brightest students."

"You have my son."

"Yes, that I do. But I would rather you think of this as a reunion. It's been many years. Come in to talk with me."

"I know what you want."

"And I know what *you* want."

"You want the last 12 characters of the decryption code."

"Let's talk."

"You're not getting it."

"If you are not open to discussion, then you also will not get your son."

"You're underestimating me again." Ray walked forward into the hall with his hammers relaxed but ready at his sides.

"Oh, Ray Lee. Very well, let me show you the situation you are in."

The black doors opened and agents stepped out from the rooms. Agents also appeared at the end of the hall in the lobby. Ray paused to survey them. They were poised and disciplined, not like the security guards. There were men and women of various ethnicities, all wearing dark grey suits with no ties. Their suits were perfectly pressed. They appeared to be taller, broader, leaner, and stronger. There was no one shorter or smaller than him. None of them held any weapons in their hands.

Ray faced eighteen agents, seven on either side and four in the lobby. Everyone stood ready but motionless in an old-fashioned Mexican stand off. The atmosphere was calm but thick, like it could be sliced with a knife.

Suddenly, Ray sprang into action and darted forward a few steps. The agents responded instantaneously and charged toward Ray, furnishing batons, tazers, and pepper sprays in their hands. Ray roused the hornets' nest! But the agents' movement toward the center to meet Ray revealed they expected him to go straight up the middle. But instead, after his initial steps forward, Ray cut to the right, blasting through the unsuspecting agent with his hammers. He deflected the attacks of two agents, ducked through a black door, and into a room.

Positioning himself off to the side of the door, Ray hammered one agent in the chest and kicked him in the side of his knee as he tried to enter the room. They tried pouring into the room, but the doorway funneled the agents, allowing Ray to hammer them one or two at a time. He took out four of them before they stopped pressing in. The four piled at the doorway were either unconscious or moaning in pain.

He hid behind the wall again and waited out of sight. No more agents entered, but he heard the crackle of their tazers and their footsteps on the metal floor. By the sounds of their footsteps, they were prowling just outside of the door.

Without warning, Ray appeared in the doorway and threw a hammer, striking an agent on the nose. Before that hammer struck, he was already leaping over the pile of agents in the doorway and flinging another hammer with a backhanded swing at an agent off to the side. The hammer soared sideways, like a Frisbee, and nailed the agent in the corner of the head.

He headed up the middle. As the agents converged on him, he unsheathed two small hammers from in front of him, crouched low, and slung them at two agents further down the hall, smashing them both in the knees. They went down on their faces.

Ray defended against the oncoming attacks, parrying tazers, blocking kicks and twirling out of grabs. In a sudden, unexpected moment, he allowed an agent to grab his neck with one hand only to brandish a screwdriver from his back pocket and stab it under the agent's arm. He produced two more screwdrivers and stabbed them into one agent's thigh and into another's side. With his free hands, he parried an attempt to pepper spray him in the face, redirecting the agent's arm so that another agent was sprayed instead.

But as they persistently pressed in on him, the violent attacks became overwhelming. He felt a kick in his back, which was partly shielded by the hammer sheathed behind him. He felt the graze of a tazer that shocked his left arm, numbing it so that he couldn't effectively use it for a couple of seconds. A baton struck him on the side, but he simultaneously grabbed the wrist attached to the baton, and in doing so absorbed some of its impact. He dragged the wrist past him and stabbed a screwdriver into the agent's abdomen. But as he did so, he felt a baton bludgeon him in his shoulder blade.

Ray spun around in a 360-degree circle and flashed two hammers from his sides. He stood in place and knocked tazers and batons out of the agents' hands with magnificently artistic maneuvers. He danced forward, gliding across the floor. All the while, he swung his hammers with a masterful display of technique. With the claw of the hammer, he hooked the back of an opponent's neck and dragged the opponent to him in order to elbow him in the face. Concurrently, his other hammer parried a tazer attack and then struck the side of an agent's cheek. His simultaneous movements made it appear like he had four arms!

Moving with lightning speed, every movement was executed with the accuracy of an eagle and the gracefulness of a sparrow. But the agents were far more skilled than the guards. He sustained a few blows from batons on his arms, felt the mist of a pepper spray on his hand, and endured a few punches to the face. But he gracefully deflected deadly attacks and concurrently bludgeoned shoulders, heads, and jaws.

He made his way into the lobby. Only four agents were left, each with metal batons, but they remained at a distance from him. Their eyes were fixed on Ray's menacing and yet beautifully moving arms. They apparently were assessing their opponent, learning from what they observed and recalculating their plan of attack. Ray waited patiently for them to come to a conclusion as to how they would try to overpower him.

The four of them shuffled, repositioning themselves. They moved in strategically with the tactics of an ancient Roman army. They came in with their eyes intensely scrutinizing Ray's destructive arms.

Ray blocked the striking batons. Two of them would strike at Ray at the same time, carefully paying close attention to his devastating hands holding the hammers. But to their confusion, he only defended with his hammers. He did not strike. Then suddenly, Ray's legs went into fierce action. Shooting out from the bottom, they did not expect the attacks from below. His feet struck their shins, knees, and ribs. His knees jammed into their stomachs and groins. Three of them went down, handicapped or unable to breathe from broken ribs. The fourth backed away just in time before he also fell with his comrades.

The fourth looked nervous, but furious. He took out a tazer from his pocket. With a baton in one hand and a tazer in the other, he scanned Ray up and down, from head to toe. He screened Ray's legs and arms, feet and hammers. His erratic scanning of Ray indicated he did not know what to make of his opponent! He was a young, brown-haired and blue-eyed man, who was perhaps in his late twenties. The naivete and uncertainty on his freckled face gave the impression of a youthful innocence tainted by corrupt leadership.

Ray shook his head at him, silently calling him to lay down his arms.

The young agent released a barbaric cry and charged!

Ray blocked, blocked, and blocked with his hammers and knees. Finally, he parried and struck with his hammer in one simultaneous move. He did it again. After knocking the tazer out of the agent's hand, he thrust his heel into the agent's stomach. Immediately, he rapidly thumped the agent's chest with his hammers, like a proficient secretary speed-typing on a keyboard. When Ray stopped, the young agent collapsed.

He watched the young man lying at his feet, with a feeling of remorse. He was not much older than Deon.

A shock to his right lower back jolted him out of his trance. He would have fallen to the floor from the electrocution if it were not for a baton striking him across the back, sending him tumbling into a forward roll.

He sprang up with his left leg that still had strength and twirled around to meet the two agents who snuck up on him. They must have emerged from one of the other halls.

They surveyed Ray's condition. He balanced on his left leg while his right leg drooped from his hip. They both showed crooked smiles, like muggers in a dark alley encroaching on a wounded victim.

They rushed forward with the certainty that Ray wouldn't be able to effectively dodge them. As expected, Ray didn't move out of the way. Instead, he whipped both hammers straight out, like arrows launched from crossbows, and they both struck the agents in the faces. By lunging at Ray, they added to the impact of the hammers on their faces. They both fell and crashed onto the brushed nickel tables.

"Ray," Miranda called to him on his cell.

"I'm in the lobby."

"Head to the hall on your right going south."

Ray wanted to retrieve his hammers off the floor, but he felt the urgency to keep moving unless he should get trapped in this intersection. With two hammers strapped to his back and three screwdrivers in his back pockets, he proceeded quickly. After hobbling into the hall for a few seconds, he felt some strength return to his right leg.

"Turn left," she instructed.

It was a narrower hall that was about a hundred feet long and wide enough for two people to walk side-by-side. There were no doors or rooms, nothing but solid walls and contemporary paintings hanging on them. It was strange. At the end of the hall, there was a set of frosted, glass double doors.

"Jeremy is past those doors," Miranda said.

He grabbed a hammer with his left hand and pulled out a screwdriver with his right. He sprinted at the double doors. But when he reached the middle of the hall, the vent panels above him suddenly opened and agents dropped through the ten-feet high ceiling in front and behind him!

They did not wait and were attacking him before they landed on the floor. Ray instinctively swatted a tazer aimed at his face with his hammer and parried with his screwdriver another tazer aimed at his waist. Ten agents dropped through the ceiling and attacked him four at a time, two from the front and two from the back.

He clubbed one with a hammer. After stabbing another in the shoulder, he left the screwdriver in his opponent. He threw the hammer sideways to belt one agent in the ribs.

He produced another hammer, but a baton smacked the hammer out of his hand, causing a dull pain to crawl up his arm.

He felt his situation becoming desperate, feeling pain in his injured parts. He had seven more agents to combat. Batons struck his cheek, arm, and leg. A tazer shocked his left shoulder for a fraction of a second. He defended vigilantly, but the agents did not tire.

The image of Jeremy in the closing elevator flashed before his mind, inspiring him to commence a frenzy of attacks. His knuckles pounded chests, his fingers poked eyes, his palms smashed noses, his elbows broke jaws, and his feet dented stomachs. He whipped out his last two screwdrivers, jabbed them into arms, pulled them out and drove them into shoulders before leaving them there. He elbowed one in the head and contorted the arm of another. Flashing back and forth with chopping hands and kicks to the knees, he struck down the last remaining agents in a final bout.

He stood over his fallen enemies on a triumphant battleground. He bled, blood leaking from his mouth, face, arms, and legs. He felt welts forming on his limbs. He smelled burnt skin and felt numb muscles where he was tazed. He felt burning irritations where he was pepper sprayed. He was wounded and exhausted.

Slowly stepping over the agents, he limped toward the frosted, glass double doors.

"Ray, I heard fighting," Miranda said. "Did you run into trouble?"

"There's no more trouble. Is Jeremy still in there?" He approached the double doors. The frosting was patterned and thick, so no light passed through. The door handles were long, vertical, and chromed metal bars.

"Yes."

"I'm going in." He pushed open the double doors.

Ray entered a circular chamber. The floors were made of marble with mosaic art. The ceiling was vaulted. The room was the size of a large ballroom. Shelves and shelves of books lined the walls. A single, massive dome light, the size of a Smart car, illuminated the entire room. Ray couldn't help but marvel at the engineering of such a large light fixture that emitted a soft luminescent brightness throughout the medieval chamber. The walls were made of stone with ancient Roman carvings. Reliefs of mythological gods decorated the walls above the bookshelves. Busts of old Greek philosophers, like Socrates, Plato, and Aristotle, sat on marble pillars around the chamber as watchful guardians. The antiquated artistry unexpectedly contrasted the rest of the contemporary style of ApexGen.

Haagen

In the middle of the chamber was a massive desk made of stone. The carvings on it were magnificent. Behind the desk sat a familiar person.

"Again. Welcome home, Ray Lee," Professor Vladimir Haagen greeted from behind the desk. His voice echoed in the large, stone chamber, making him sound god-like. His suave composure was intimidating and yet alluring. He exuded confidence and power in his demeanor, but his voice was irresistibly silky.

Around the room were six agents plus another two standing on either side of Haagen's desk. Besides the main entrance behind him, there was only a small side door to his left. To Ray's right, two more agents stood with Jeremy, holding him captive. Standing behind Haagen was Stanley. The sight of him infuriated Ray.

Ray stood twenty feet from the hardened kingpin as blood dripped from his bottom lip. Jeremy cradled his left arm and squinted his right eye, which was swelling shut.

"Ray Lee," Haagen spoke with eloquence. He crossed his legs effeminately and leaned on one side of his ornately carved wooden chair that looked like a throne. "Very impressive. You have earned my respect. But you always impressed me—you and Melanie."

Ray resented hearing him say Mel's name.

"Dad," Jeremy called, coddling his left arm, like a dog holding up an injured paw. He also had a cut lip and a swollen cheek. The two agents standing with him were the same two who took him into the elevator. But one of them had a fresh patch of gauze taped over his left eye. Though hurt, his son still exhibited fieriness. "I fought back."

"That he did," Haagen confirmed. "Like his dad, Jeremy is a fighter."

"It's been a long time," Ray said, deciding to engage Haagen intellectually, knowing that he was in no physical condition to combat the ten agents in this large spacious chamber, which was a disadvantage for his close-range fighting style. After assessing his situation, the prognosis did not look good. "You built quite an empire. I suppose you outgrew teaching graduate students."

"The institute," Haagen said, "was an avenue for identifying bright minds like you and Melanie. Do you still remember the many lessons I gave you in my office hours?" The words oozed out of his mouth. "You wanted the same thing I wanted: an improved humanity, a more advanced society, greater control over the chaos in our world."

"What do you call this, Haagen?" Ray challenged. "You are creating chaos!"

"On the contrary, I am making order!"

"How is this order? You commit terrorism. You kidnapped my

children!"

"Ah, yes. Your children. Special aren't they? Like their mother and father," Haagen said with a smirk. He leaned back on his thick, elaborately carved chair. "As you know, your daughter is of great importance to us." He held up a finger and said, "Allow me to correct myself. She is of great importance to humanity."

"She's already gone, Haagen. You're not getting her," Ray spoke with austerity.

"Yes, I know she's gone," Haagen said matter-of-factly. "Your lady friend threatened to detonate a tube of nitroglycerin in the lobby if our security did not let them out. Of course, we did not want a public scene, so we let them out. She's a feisty one."

Surprised by his nonchalance over losing Jamie, Ray was unsure of what his game was. "Taking Jeremy won't get you Jamie."

"We drew enough blood from Jamie to make many experimental trials and enough to replicate the DNA we need. I would prefer to have a live source on hand, but I'm sure we can always fetch her again if and when we need her. And by the way, we took Jeremy to get you."

"You carry this entitlement, taking what does not belong to you. What gives you the right? There's no difference between you and a common crook! You were a brilliant mind once."

"Is, *is* a brilliant mind," Stanley corrected.

Ignoring the traitor, Ray continued, "You were the most prestigious professor at one of the world's top-notch universities. What happened to you? How did you become a terrorist?" A drool of blood stringed down from Ray's lips as he spoke.

"You know of Charles Darwin, do you not? Of course, you do. Darwin got it half right." He talked in a toxic manner, as if honey spiked with cyanide dripped from his lips. "We are finishing what he started. He was on the right path but he did not arrive, because natural selection was not the end. It was the beginning. The next step of natural selection is, and should be, *intentional selection.*"

Haagen smiled proudly, saying, "ApexGen is taking humanity to the next level for not simply the survival but the advancement of our race. You see, in natural selection, the greater individuals are selected *naturally*, leaving the decision to Mother Nature. But at ApexGen, the greater individuals are selected *intentionally*. Intentional selection is purposefully breeding and artificially harnessing the stronger traits of our race. We concentrate those traits into individuals to engineer a superior class of humans—*us.*"

"You're breeding people, like horses? And engineering people?" Ray retorted.

"Not only breeding the strong, but also encouraging the weak to die off. We also engineer the right DNA to synthesize biology with technology."

"Your nanotech integration theories."

"You asked: what gives us our entitlement? Our superiority does."

"This is a deranged plan, Haagen. You must be able to ascertain that!"

"Look around you, Ray," Haagen waved his hand high above him, as if referencing the atmosphere. "People strive to improve themselves everyday! Since the beginning of history, civilizations were driven to advance—to be better than their predecessors. Our recent, rapid achievements in technology and genetic research have given us the tools to foster a selective and stronger humanity, creating a superlative civilization that would be at the top of the food chain. But this apex is not composed of merely organic matter. It must be organic and technological, because our biology is limited and flawed. Where our organic nature falls short, our technology perfects us!"

He leaned forward with his elbows on his desk. "ApexGen has been around for 20 generations, Ray. The breeding process has been in place for 150 years, since the height of the Modern Age. In the last several decades, we've combined the breeding process with technological creativity, where we can splice desired, genetic traits and fabricate more genetically superior humans. Now we're at the stage of integrating nanoprobes with our DNA to complete our human construction."

Ray asked with a heightened emphasis, "To what extent? At what cost?"

"To any extent! Any cost! There is no greater goal than the triumph of our humanity." With a wicked grin and condescending gaze, Haagen said, "Jamie has what we needed. She has the missing genetic key in her to accomplish our nanotech synthesis. Because of her, we are erasing the horrible aspects of being human!"

"If you know your history of human civilization, then you also know that men like you will be defeated," Ray challenged to buy time. For what? He wasn't sure yet. He needed more time for a solution to emerge. "History has proven that fanatics like you will lose. How long do you believe you can carry on this science fiction?"

"Look at these men around you," Haagen said, unphased by Ray's challenge. "Do they appear to be your average human beings?"

Ray tried to resist falling into Haagen's arrogant invitation, but he couldn't help sizing up the men and taking note of their superior physique.

"We have spent the last century and a half perfecting our humanity," Haagen said with comfort and conceitedness. "We are stronger, faster, and smarter. Our bodies are superlative. Our brains are sharp. We have infiltrated the law enforcement establishments, major corporations, research institutions, military establishments, and government offices. ApexGen has been plotting and positioning itself for 20 generations. Our effect is unavoidable, and our infrastructure is impenetrable. And now we are at the threshold of revealing ourselves to the world, seizing the apex of the evolutionary hierarchy and establishing ourselves as mankind's rulers by right."

A few people entered the chamber from the side door: Tracy, the kidnapping babysitter, Gordon, the child-trafficking mercenary, and Marvin, the mole, who still looked like a mess. They stood behind Haagen and next to Stanley, the traitor. Behind Ray, Sergeant Pierce and Officer Bohr, the crooked cops, entered through the double doors.

"I thought we'd make this a reunion as part of my show-and-tell."

Ray's situation turned from bad to worse. "You can't accomplish your plans without the last 12 characters," Ray said thinking he still had a bargaining chip. "Let Jeremy go, and I'll give you the last 12 characters." He despised himself for striking a deal with the devil, but he had no other cards to play. He was battered. His son was a hostage. They were in a rock-solid chamber 63 floors inside of the earth with a platoon of enemies.

"Ah, yes. The encrypted firewall is an inconvenience," Haagen said. "I did not bring you down here to make an exchange with you, but let me rephrase your proposal in the negative. Give me the final 12 characters, or I will kill your son."

Ray's widened eyes flashed to Jeremy. One of the agents at his side clenched Jeremy's arms while the other agent clamped his hands on Jeremy's head.

"Did you know the average head weighs about 15 pounds?" Haagen shook his head. "The neck is quite fragile to be supporting such a heavy and precious part of us. Another puzzling weakness of our human design."

The agent started to crank Jeremy's head up and to the side.

"Stop!" Ray commanded with his wounded arm outstretched at the agent. Then turning that arm and pointing at Haagen, he said, "You kill him, and you'll get nothing. Then I'll fight through everyone in here to get to you. You hear me? You saw what I can do. I took out your entire security force and the majority of your agents. What more do you have left to throw at me? Nothing will stop me from getting to you!" He tried to make himself seem as big and threatening as possible.

"But look at you now." Haagen's words slithered. "You're empty-handed. No more gadgets. No more tools. You're injured. You're alone. What more can you do?"

Without turning his head, Ray glanced around at the on-looking agents surrounding him and returned his gaze to the formidable man before him. Feeling a creeping heaviness in his chest, the weight of defeat bore down on him. How could he get out of this with his son?

"Aahhh," Jeremy cried.

The agent twisted Jeremy's head further, to where his chin was past his shoulder.

"OK, wait! Stop! Just stop." Ray's once commanding voice petered down to the plea of a father. "Just stop hurting him."

"Twelve characters, Ray, and it stops, or you witness the slow death of your son. His life is in your hands."

Jeremy cried again, but it sounded like a weak gurgle.

"Stop! All right! OK!"

"Twelve-character code, please."

"Six," Ray began with his eyes anchored on Jeremy, whose head was still twisted.

An agent began entering the code onto a laptop on Haagen's desk.

"B," Ray continued, "1, 9, 5, 7, Y, @, j, Q, #."

"Yes? One more digit."

Jeremy grunted painfully.

"M." Ray repeated softly, "M."

The agent entered the last character and then nodded affirmatively at Haagen.

"Very good," Haagen cheered. He looked at Jeremy's tormentors to signal for Jeremy's release.

Jeremy, still grimacing, rubbed his neck. He started to move toward his father, but the two agents restrained him.

"Let my son go!" Ray demanded furiously. "What more do you want from me?"

"We're not done yet, Ray. I still have much to talk to you about."

"You took Jamie's blood. You have Miracom's main server now. There's nothing more I can give you! Let us go."

"There's still one more thing you can give me."

Not Easily Broken

Chapter 30
Bullet

"What more can you demand of me?" Ray questioned tiredly. "There's nothing more I can give you!"

"Oh, don't think of it as a demand. We're past that point. Think of what I want as a request. Plus, you do have one more thing you can give me that I value," Haagen replied.

"Just let my son and me go."

"But I think you will want to hear what I'm asking for. Besides, you should know that simply leaving here is not an option."

"Haagen, just let us go! At least, let my son go. He's just a teenager!"

"Teenager or not, he entered ApexGen on his own accord, and he will bear the consequences of that on his own. However, depending on your response to what I ask for, you can determine the consequences."

"Haagen," Ray said in a mellow tone, attempting to appeal to Haagen's conscience, believing that whatever Haagen would ask of him couldn't be good. "Somewhere in your soul you must realize this is wrong. My son is only fifteen. What you are doing, the things you have done to people, are crimes. It is unethical. It is immoral. It is evil. Somewhere in you, you must realize that. I knew you. For God's sake, Haagen, there must be some good in you."

Haagen sat back and belted out a laugh, mocking Ray's humble petition. "I'm disappointed, Ray. Where's your fight?" He laughed again and then simmered to smiling smugly. "You can't accuse me of being evil, if evil does not exist."

He made Ray's skin squirm, like a thousand ticks burrowed into his arms. "You can't simply erase the notion of right and wrong in order to justify your crimes. Use reason, Haagen!"

"Allow me to show *you* the way of reason! Then you will see the rationale to my request. I will help you understand. You are a church-going, man, are you not? How has that worked for you? In a world of unfair suffering, how could God exist? At least not a good God, which is what religions teach. The chaos and suffering in the world is evidence to the contrary. There is no God in this world. If there is no God, there is no universal morality, is there?" He paused.

Shamefully, Ray recognized Haagen's train of thinking resonated with some of Ray's own doubts since Melanie's death.

"If there is no morality," Haagen continued, "there is no good and evil. Morality is merely a social construct derived by people. The people who invent the standards are those with the greatest power to do so—those with the greatest power to shape society and what society values and thinks. You see? There is no God, and there is no right or wrong; there is only you, me, and the will-to-power. Those who possess power create order." Haagen leaned forward, touching his fingertips together. His fingers were long and skeletal. "As the most evolved human being, I will author morality for our world."

Seeing that this man no longer had a conscience behind his twisted worldview, Ray searched again for another way out. "Your view of the world cannot be correct. You cannot convince me this is the way things are. There are universals in this world, such as love, justice, and truth. I myself may not fully understand what these mean, but I have to believe that these things are real and not made up. To love your child or your spouse are universal principles. Right and wrong also has to be real, which you are ignoring to achieve your own gains. If there are no universals, how could our world hold together? How could anything mean anything?"

Haagen sighed and leaned back again. "Ray, I used to be like you. When my father first told me about ApexGen, I was only seven years old. He wanted me to be aware of this system I was bred into, but as I got older, I rejected it because we were only allowed to court and marry certain individuals from a good breed. I left home to marry my high school love at the age of twenty-two. We were happy and naïve.

"A year later, she developed breast cancer. You know what the probabilities are for a woman to have breast cancer at such a young age? She never smoked. She did not drink. She was a vegan!" He scowled.

Upon listening to Haagen share his personal testimony, Ray thought he was beginning to see his adversary's humanity, but he detected a cold bitterness.

Haagen chortled, shaking his head. "We were determined to fight the disease. We tried every specialist, diets, and herbal medicines. She had both her breasts removed to be safe. We fought it with a vengeance. We were passionate, thinking we could overcome anything together because we had love. Love! The most deceiving four-letter word.

"The cancer returned and spread to her liver, kidney, and lung. Love didn't stop the cancer, Ray! The next two years was nothing but misery. I watched her waste away like a starved animal. If there is a God in this world, he must be a cruel child with a magnifying glass. She died. Then I wasted another year mourning for her."

Ray felt pity for him. "Then you should know, Haagen, that hurting others is wrong no matter what the ends are. You must know that your inhumane acts will not honor the memory of your late wife. She will not rest in peace from what you are doing."

"She is dead," Haagen spat. His expressionless face was stone cold. "She doesn't need peace. It's the living who suffer the dead that need peace." He surprisingly brightened with an enlightened countenance. "You know where I found my peace? I finally came to my senses and realized that her death was not a tragedy. No. No."

Ray's stomach churned with disgust. "How can you say this?"

"You see? She died because she was weak and *needed* to die."

"Haagen, don't degrade your wife." Ray felt offended for his wife as a husband.

"She degraded the human race! Her nature was weak, and her weakness polluted our humanity. Imagine if we procreated! What kind of children would we have produced? Weaklings who would have further polluted the human race, carrying her flaws."

"You are sick," Ray accused.

Haagen sputtered, "She was defective! She had to be removed from the human equation. It was natural selection. Where I failed was to implement intentional selection. My weakness was being blinded by emotional sentiments. I bought into social notions of love. In error, I wasted a year mourning over her death without realizing I should've been celebrating it, because her termination was a cleansing for our humanity. Removing her life from the genetic pool was better for our race!"

Ray's anger boiled as a husband who mourned the loss of his own wife daily. "You trample on your wife's grave. You did not deserve her, and she surely did not deserve you!"

Haagen held both hands in front of him in a bowl shape as if he were offering a fruit. "Initially, it is difficult to comprehend. I know. Embracing ApexGen's philosophy would require surrendering many frivolous social notions that we psychologically cling to, like a security blanket. But these are all merely placebos. Once you do embrace ApexGen's philosophy, you'll see the only rationale that is right for our flawed world.

"Ray, this is a pivotal moment. I am extending to you an invitation, one that you should not take lightly, especially given your present circumstances. In your resistance against us, you have demonstrated your physical prowess and proven your intellectual excellence. We acknowledge your quality and salute you." He tipped his head and opened his hands. "Therefore, we respectfully invite you to join ApexGen. We want to add you to our equation of intentional selection."

Ray saw from the corner of his eye Jeremy looking at him. He squinted his eyes and pressed his brows together as he asked, "You want us to be part of this?"

"Your son as well, of course. We would not ask you to part from your son and seeing what we've seen of him so far, we are optimistic about his suitability."

"This is what you want from me?"

"Yes. As I said, you have one last thing you can give me. It's you," Haagen said with eerie tenderness. "So you see? This is not so much a demand, as you put it, as much as this is an invitation—a proposal, if you will."

Tracy said, "Ray won't accept it. He's too naïve."

"He's a non-believer," Marvin said.

"Give, give him a chance," Stanley said.

Haagen held up his hand to silence them. "This is a once in a lifetime offer. Be part of the apex of the evolutionary hierarchy and have a personal part in forging a superior humanity. If you join us, it means you and your children will live lives of plentitude and security within our system. You will be among the first generation to experience the nanotech synthesis, which means you and your children will be free from sickness, disease, frailty, and mortality. That's power, Ray. That's triumph!"

"And the rest of humanity?"

"We will weed them out gradually. As we evolve, the strongest in the formula will extinguish the weaker. The weak, sick, handicapped, ugly, delayed, homeless, crippled, unproductive, and impoverished will be extinguished. We must do this in order to purify the human equation—in order to perfect your human condition and mine. In so doing, we will create Elysium! We will turn earth into a home for the gods!"

There was a pause while they locked gazes. Haagen waited for a response, and Ray tried to comprehend the offer.

"Ray, you would be part of the solution for a crippled world that has pained you for the last two years with the loss of your wife. You will be part of an answer to ensure that those who live are those who will never suffer, like your precious Melanie did."

Ray looked down, smiled slightly, and shook his head. Somehow facing this man who mirrored his pain gave greater clarity into Ray's own struggle. He said with piercing confidence to Haagen, "I understand you now."

"Before the next words come out of your mouth, consider your answer carefully."

Ray was silent, looking at the space on the floor between them. Then he looked up to say, "With all your professed intelligence, you are actually ignorant, because you have not grasped the foundational principles of life. You understand nothing about life, mercy, justice, or redemption. I feel sympathy for you. You are a hurting man who lost someone significant, as I did. But you don't realize that you're hurting. Your tragedy is that you don't know how to handle your pain, leading to an erroneous view of reality. You are filled not with enlightenment, but bitterness. Your illogic eroded whatever dignified traits may have been in you, and that's truly sad."

Haagen rebutted, "Do not try to be a therapist! Look at you. How have you handled *your* pain? You bear an internal world of chaos and disorder for the past two years, grasping for an answer in a religion designed by men. You lack peace, unable to make sense of your wife's death. You blame yourself. I know you, Ray."

"You don't know about me." In a flash, Ray thought about the lessons impressed upon him in the past couple of weeks—his interactions with Abby, Nathan, Jeremy, and Deon. They had all taught him pieces of a greater truth. "I'm not the man you think I am." He didn't quite know how he had changed, but he knew he was different.

"I've been watching you, Ray. You go to church sporadically on Sundays, straining to find hope and meaning to the senseless loss of your dear Melanie who was taken from you by the kind of degenerates I'm proposing to extinguish!"

"Your own distorted view of the world drove you to madness," Ray countered. His facial expression conveyed that he was thinking hard and carefully looking for the right words. His hand gestures were more intense. "There's more to being human than attaining power to rid suffering. Life is about finding wholeness from being broken. It's about finding redemption out of your mess."

"Find wholeness? From where? From whom if you do not take it for yourself?"

"From God!" Ray shouted, surprised by his own answer.

"Now you're simply grasping for non-existent answers—a delusional outburst of a desperate man," Haagen insulted with disgust. "People appeal to a higher being when they have no answer. Tell me. What has your God done for you? Has he given you peace? Has he given you justice?"

"Haagen, I see your problem. Because you believe everything is relative, you think you have the entitlement to reshape reality in whatever way you deem fit. You impose your subjective expectations upon others."

"Spare me."

Ray insistently continued with greater intensity, hoping to win his enemy over, "You think you're doing what needs to be done in a world full of problems, but you're merely a tyrant. You do not perceive absolutes, so you posit your corrupt subjectivity as the absolute for everyone else. You see no universals, so you do not hold yourself to any accountability. You recognize no higher being and no higher principles, so you pose yourself as a highest authority. But that is nothing more than arrogance." Ray could tell his words—his logic—weighed on the professor. "You know what real power is? It's discovering and embracing the truth no matter how difficult it might be."

Haagen tried to respond, but Ray cut him off: "With all your posing to be a higher life form, you're simply a hurt man who never healed."

The professor had a hardened expression. "And you think you are not hurt?" Haagen scoffed. "If I'm correct, Melanie was crushed by a drunk driver, was she not? The police never found her killer, did they? Your wife never received justice." Haagen tilted his head and inspected Ray. "Your wife is dead, and the drunk driver roams free and is possibly still a drunk. Is this the ordered world you speak of?"

Haagen gave Ray a mocking smile. "This is where we come in. We can bring order to disorder. We have information others lack." He opened his laptop on his desk then looked at Ray. "In fact, we know your wife's killer is still a drunk."

Ray furrowed his brows at Haagen.

Haagen turned the laptop around for Ray and Jeremy to see. The screen showed a mug shot of an unshaven, Caucasian male with a receding hairline and dark circles under his eyes.

Ray looked at the photo skeptically.

"Oh, yes. This is him," Haagen assured. "See, we're better than the police. We tracked this man for the last two years since the accident. His name is Norton Peters."

Beside the mug shot were three images of Melanie's car, Norton's sports car at the point of impact, and a close-up photo of Norton in the driver's seat of the vehicle. This was his wife's murderer! Ray examined the photo with a flurry of questions colliding in his mind and boiling rage in his heart. After all this time, the man who robbed him of his wife was now revealed to him. He didn't know what to make of this knowledge, but upon seeing the photograph of Melanie's mangled car and the identification of the perpetrator, he felt fresh pain, anger, and hate.

"Would you like to meet him?" Haagen asked.

Ray and Jeremy scrutinized Haagen's face with disbelief. Was he serious or just cruelly tormenting them?

Haagen motioned to his right.

One of the agents exited through the side door. A second later, he returned with a bound and hooded man. The agent shoved the victim to his knees before Ray and pulled the hood off.

"Ray, meet Norton, the murderer of your late wife," Haagen introduced. "Norton, meet Ray, a very, very angry husband." Haagen said with a slimy smile.

Ray's eyes were wide as he looked at this man kneeling three feet in front of him.

"What's going on?" Norton asked fearfully. "Why am I here? Who are you people?"

Ray smelled alcohol on his breath, an odor that fueled his painful rage.

"Once Stanley told me you were here, I had Norton picked up so he could meet you," Haagen stated.

"Who are you?" Norton asked Haagen. "Somebody," he pled, "tell me what's going on. Why am I here? I didn't do anything."

"He doesn't even know who you are," Haagen said to Ray. "He doesn't even realize his crime against you."

"You killed my mother!" Jeremy yelled at him.

"What?" Norton sweated. "I don't know you. This is a mistake."

Ray realized his hands beside him were clenched into fists, like hammers waiting to be swung. He felt his breathing quicken and his shoulders tense.

Norton said, "You can't do this. This is kidnapping."

"I can see your pain, Ray," Haagen said. Ray broke his burning stare at Norton to look attentively at Haagen. "Consider this a goodwill gift from me to you to restart our relationship." Haagen reached into his desk drawer and took out a stone chest that was a little smaller than a shoebox. "I am offering you wholeness, Ray." He opened the chest and lifted out a shiny revolver. An agent by Haagen took the revolver and walked it over to Ray.

Ray looked at Haagen with suspicion.

"Take it," Haagen invited.

Ray's shaking hand slowly took the revolver. He examined the gun in his hand, feeling the cold, hard steel. The barrel was remarkably glossy and reflective.

"The gun has one bullet," Haagen said.

Ray looked in the wheel of the revolver and confirmed there was just one bullet.

"That one bullet," Haagen said with an eloquent intonation, "is all you need to achieve justice. My gift to you is justice, Ray Lee. Once you have that, you will have your wholeness. I ask only for your allegiance in return. For you, it's a win-win. You lose nothing. You only gain."

Ray couldn't stop looking at the gun, caught by the weapon's juxtaposing beauty and capacity to destroy.

"Whoa, wait a minute here," Norton said, looking around for someone to help him. He tried to stand up, but the agent behind him shoved him back down to his knees so hard that his kneecaps thudded on the hard stone floor.

Haagen persuaded, "At this very moment, you can right the wrong done to your wife. I have given you the power. You can continue talking to me about universals or you can grasp the meaning of a will-to-power."

Ray gripped the gun tightly and looked at Norton, who stared at Ray like a petrified deer frozen by headlights. The thoughts of Melanie, the remorse of losing her, and the anger of feeling robbed of her swirled in him like a tempest. The cause of his misery knelt before him submissively, affording him the power to assume control, where his life had lacked it for the last two years. He wrestled with what to do. The hate in his heart prompted a reflexive action, and he put the gun to Norton's forehead.

"Yes," Haagen hissed.

"Wait," Norton cried, trembling.

Ray held the gun straight out with his arm taut. His gaze drilled into Norton while sweat rolled down his back.

"Dad," Jeremy called to him, but Ray didn't acknowledge him. "Dad," he said again in a softer tone, and Jeremy's voice echoed in Ray's mind. A fierce debate waged inside of Ray. This was what he always wanted, but was this the way of justice? Was there truly a universal justice that kept the world in order or was there only the kind of justice that a person is capable of executing? Were there universals or was there only this moment?

He blinked several times then looked at Haagen and raised the gun.

"What if I just use this one bullet on you and end this?" Ray challenged, his hand shaking.

"Don't be silly," Haagen said with a smile. "Of course, we accounted for this possible reaction. Yes, you could shoot me, but after that these agents will kill you *and* your son. We have calculated your temperament and assessed that you are not the kind of man who will gamble with those costs. We know you, Ray. Point the weapon at your true enemy—the one

Bullet

who hurt you."

Haagen said while pointing at Norton, "Look at him. This drunk does not deserve to live. Why is he alive yet your wife is dead? Restore order to your world."

Haagen's words sank into Ray. He lowered the gun back to Norton, who closed his eyes in trembling fear and whimpered. Ray didn't look at Norton, but looked away at the floor beside him, considering the past years of pain, emptiness, and grief that led him to this decisive moment. He thought about the rationale of retribution as a form of justice. Would it grant him peace? Ray gripped the gun so tightly his knuckles whitened. He couldn't feel the tips of his fingers.

Haagen watched Ray intently. "Ray, let me help you finalize your decision. Didn't you always wrestle with Melanie's last words to you?" Again, Haagen shocked Ray with another revelation. "Let me play this surveillance video for you."

It was the video of Melanie on the stretcher just before she was carted into the ambulance. "No crates," Ray heard Mel say again, which he interpreted as, "No craze." *Keep it together. Stay in control.* That's what he thought Melanie meant.

"We cleaned up the audio for you and enhanced it," Haagen said. "Here." He clicked play again.

The video replayed, and this time he heard Melanie say, "No grace." It was clear! There was no difficulty making out the sounds.

"You see?" Haagen concluded. "No grace. Your wife's dying words were for you to do what you must: show no grace to the one who did this to her—avenge her! She wanted you to take retribution. She was a strong woman. She knew what needed to be done to restore order. I'm helping you fulfill your precious Melanie's dying wish. Do not disappoint her. Seize this."

Those two words played and played in Ray's mind.

Then a vivid image of Deon's unwarranted sacrifice blazed into his mind, like a scene being replayed before his eyes. He saw him sitting in the chair. He committed himself to die in order to save someone he didn't know. This act of unexpected self-sacrifice at the expense of his life began to materialize an understanding of mercy and redemption. It was a sacrifice that had not made sense to him until now. Suddenly, in this situation in which he held the power to destroy this murderer, he began to know wholeness that comes not by destruction. It all became clear. Ray clearly heard Melanie's last words, and they made sense to him. They summarized the lessons he had been shown.

Ray answered, "My wife's last words were not 'no grace' but '*know* grace.'"

Haagen's face distorted.

"You want triumph over the broken things of life? It will not come by the means you employ. It will not come by coercion, retribution, or force. It comes by a truth you have yet to grasp." He took a deep breath. He declared the final verdict, "I will right the wrong committed against my wife and my family by giving this man what he does not deserve from me—my forgiveness."

Norton opened his eyes, and Ray met his gaze. Ray lowered the gun to his side, which felt lighter. He also experienced a covering of peace. He thought of Melanie and believed that his action dignified the life and person she was. A tear streamed from his eye as he smiled. An understanding about justice accomplished by mercy flooded him.

He looked at Jeremy who returned an approving expression.

With a disappointed look and folded hands, Haagen replied, "Perhaps you are not the man we thought you were. You are weak-willed."

"You asked," Ray said, "where does wholeness come from. It comes from redemption bought by sacrifice. I sacrifice my right to take this man's life."

"Pathetic!" Haagen spewed, losing his composure. He shifted in his chair and looked from side to side, at a loss for words. He seemed taken off-guard. The two agents at Haagen's sides moved in front of the desk to block Ray's line of fire. "You made your choice. But," he said pretentiously, "we calculated that you might choose this foolish route. It was not unanticipated. We plan for all contingencies."

All the assailants tightened the circle around Ray.

"Now you must see the folly of your choice," Haagen declared. "You have one bullet. Whichever agent you shoot will still leave you with the others to combat in your injured state. You have not thought this through. You and your son will now die here. What folly."

Ray looked at Jeremy. They connected. He said, "Jer, not by sight."

"Okay," Jeremy replied with a nod. "Dad, you're right."

"Right about what?" Haagen questioned. "Folly. Terminate these two weaklings! Good-bye, Ray Lee."

Ray smiled at his son in acknowledgement. The two of them had an understanding that eluded everyone else in the chamber. He said to the professor, "Haagen, I bet you didn't anticipate this."

As the agents moved in, Ray raised the gun towards the massive dome light. He fired. There was a bright flash followed by a rain of glass. All was dark.

Chapter 31
Rise

When Jeremy said, "Dad, you're right," it was not a reference to Ray being correct but was a designation of direction. He called for his father to take the right side while he took the left. The strategy of combating in total darkness was simply a matter of designating right side versus left side so that the father and son would not run into each other. But anyone else they ran into was an open target.

Commotion came from their enemies. "I can't see." "Where are they?" "Turn on the lights." "It's pitch dark!"

Ray heard a couple of grunts followed by moans from Jeremy's position. *Good boy*, he mentally praised Jeremy.

"Lie on your stomach," Ray whispered to Norton, "and be quiet." He heard Norton comply.

"Who's that?" he heard about two feet in front of him. He kicked and punched in that direction. After the first couple of hits, he mentally mapped where his target's body parts were and then struck the knees, solar plexus, and throat. The person dropped.

"Jim?" he heard three feet to his right. He swiftly moved in that direction and again overtook his opponent with several deadly and swift moves.

"No, wait. It's me!" he heard directly ahead of him towards the right side of Haagen's desk and maneuvered in that direction. He positioned himself right between two assailants. Neither of them knew he was there, but he sensed them with the lightest touch. Then, with lightning speed and pinpoint accuracy, he dispatched them.

He maneuvered around the right side of the room with his left hand extended out as a feeler, like the antenna of an ant. He lightly touched someone else. The fabric was definitely some kind of expensive suit material.

"Who's that?" the person asked.

Ray struck. After eight hits, the person went down.

He heard a gagging sound and a thud on the floor come from Jeremy's side. Shortly after, there was a painful yelp and another thump. *He's aiming for the knees and groin*, Ray ascertained by the yelps and thumps.

Good job, Jer.

"We need to get out of here, Professor," Ray heard someone say. That was Tracy's voice!

"Quiet!" he heard Haagen rebuke.

Hearing their footsteps, he estimated how far away they were. Ray took ten steps, silently gliding across the floor and slicing through the darkness, taking down another agent on the way. He smelled fragrant hair conditioner. Tracy must be near. He also smelled ointment for bruises and antiseptic for cuts. Marvin was nearby too.

When he felt the draft of someone moving in front of him, he unleashed a flurry of menacing punches and chops. He felt fair skin and long hair. It was Tracy. He sensed her falling. The smell of ointment and antiseptics was stronger. He struck out to his right. Feeling his target's scrawny physique, he could tell it was Marvin.

"Professor!" Marvin yelled. "Get out!"

Ray found Marvin's ribs and capitalized on them with punches and palm strikes. With the wind pummeled out of his lungs, Marvin fell quietly.

A person bumped into Ray from the side. "Marvin?" the voice asked. It was Gordon! "Marvin," he repeated.

Ray quietly reached out and placed one, gentle hand on Gordon's chest. He now knew where his face was. Ray struck Gordon's eyes, throat, groin, and knees. He struck hard and true, not leaving any room for error with this child-trafficker. He felt Gordon drop to his knees.

"Good night, *Uncle* Gordon," Ray said mockingly before punching him across the jaw and delivering a puncturing elbow strike into the temple.

A voice from the entrance whispered, "Why don't we use our flashlights?"

"No," replied a commanding voice—it was Sergeant Pierce. "Don't."

Dismissing the command, Bohr turned on his flashlight and a beam of light shone on Haagen, revealing his position and movement towards the side door.

"Professor!" Bohr exclaimed. "Let's get you out of here."

"Get that light off of me," Haagen snapped with his hand shielding his eyes.

Ray stood just outside of the beam of light. Haagen was only ten feet from him.

Suddenly, Officer Bohr let out an angry holler. "My eye! Punk got me in the eye!" He waved his light around erratically but could not find his attacker.

"That's why I said not to turn on your flashlight, idiot!" Sergeant Pierce reproved.

"I think I'm bleeding," Officer Bohr said. "Where's the door?"

"We need to get to the Professor first," Sergeant Pierce said.

Officer Bohr yelped and his light abruptly dipped down two feet. *Jeremy got him in the back of the knee!* Ray ascertained.

"The little punk is taking shots at me! Where are you? I'm going to wring your little neck!" Bohr threatened. "Give me the key to the main door," he told his commanding officer.

"Get the Professor first," Sergeant Pierce reiterated.

"Ah!" Officer Bohr yelped again. "He just punched me in the back of the head! You runt! Come here!"

Ray heard the repeated swishing of a nightstick in the air and then a thump.

Bohr cheered, "Got you, little punk!" He kept swinging his nightstick.

Jeremy got hit, but he toughed it out and stayed silent and hidden in the dark. Ray had to trust Jeremy to take care of himself, and he made the decision to go after Haagen. He took five steps in that direction before running into the professor. Instinctively, Ray struck him in the face with his palm and pummeled two punches into his chest. Ray felt how unbelievably strapping the old professor was. He felt strong bones and firm muscles. The professor did not fall but swung his fist in retaliation, managing to hit Ray in the chin. Ray shifted to the side. He sensed the professor swinging at Ray's previous position as he felt drafts from the professor's swings.

Ray heard Haagen's leg bump into the stone desk and immediately threw a kick in that direction. Connecting with Haagen's knee, Ray mentally mapped the professor's body and struck several vital points. Always keeping a hand on Haagen, he was able to sense where the professor's body was. Ray kicked him against the desk and lashed out relentlessly, beating on every part of Haagen's head, arms, legs, and torso with his punches and kicks.

Ray's own body ached from the previous melees, but he knew that taking down the head of the snake was the key to his and Jeremy's escape. If he could wound him enough, they would be too concerned with their precious leader to worry about pursuing him and Jeremy. But to his astonishment, the old man was built better than a twenty-two year old athlete! Ray struck and struck, keeping Haagen pinned against the desk, but the professor did not diminish in resilience.

"Over here!" Haagen finally summoned while he fought back, managing to land a couple of punches in Ray's abdomen and claw the side of Ray's neck. "Over here!"

Ray clasped Haagen's face with his hand to silence him and then found the Professor's throat and struck it twice. Haagen gagged and bent forward, allowing Ray to rain down punches on top of his head.

Haagen covered his head with his forearms and let out a pitifully unsuccessful shriek through his damaged throat. He gasped for air while being pelted by a hailstorm of fists. Knuckles repetitively collided with the top and back of his skull. Ray concluded the barrage with a kick to Haagen's kneecap. He felt the old man fall to his side. The old man was no longer fighting. He hardly moved.

Ray bent down and said softly, "Your evolved state didn't save you from me."

"Then kill me to prove that you are the better human being," Haagen scoffed, followed by moist, hacking coughs. Ray could tell by the coughing sounds bouncing off the stone floor that the professor's face was down against the floor. He was in bad shape.

Ray relaxed his hands and squatted by Haagen. He couldn't see him, but he could hear him labor with each exhale and choke on each inhale. Even in this moment, Ray wished he could change his old professor. He felt a kindred connection with his former teacher who had also tragically lost a soul mate, but he realized that he and his old mentor were valleys apart from each other. Though they shared the same pain, they did not share the same path.

It saddened Ray. He felt pity for this man, who could have been a blessing to the world and not a curse. *But what good is a brilliant mind with a corrupted soul?* he thought. He wished there was a way to help him.

Ray suddenly felt a large, fist batter him on the shoulder, knocking him onto his side. A large man immediately rolled Ray onto his back and mounted his stomach.

"Cockroach!" Ray's attacker insulted.

It was Sergeant Pierce. The talking between Haagen and Ray gave away his position. While the sergeant sat on top of Ray's abdomen, the policeman pounded Ray into the hard floor. Ray blocked the punches, but Sergeant Pierce's rock-like knuckles and club-like arms mercilessly bludgeoned Ray. It felt like Ray was defending himself against a bear. Ray fired a few punches at the sergeant's body, but they hit a bulletproof vest. Pierce's torso was long, rendering Ray unable to reach his face. Ray could only block. The clobbering tenderized his arms. He wouldn't be able to withstand this beating for much longer. He wiggled and shifted to heave Pierce off of his stomach, but Pierce's weight pinned him firmly.

While Pierce punched and pounded Ray, he cursed him with

every profane term he could pull out in the heat of rage. But while he threatened and insulted Ray, he didn't realize he was giving away his own position.

Just when Ray thought his arms would give out, he heard a loud pinging of metal against skull. The punches stopped. Then there was a bong, like the sound of a pipe hitting concrete. Pierce's body became dead weight on top of Ray. Pierce slumped and fell over to the side.

A blinding light shone into Ray's face, seeing only the radiating concentric circles of light from a flashlight.

"Dad!" Jeremy called, stepping forward into the periphery of the flashlight's beam. He gripped a metal billy club in his other hand. The club looked like it was still vibrating in the light. "Are you okay?"

"Jer," Ray acknowledged. "I'm all right." He sat up, rubbed his numb arms, and shook his hands to make the blood circulate again. "Thank you."

Jeremy shone the flashlight at Sergeant Pierce lying on the floor to make sure the massive gladiator was down for good. "Crooked cops," the teenager sneered.

Ray removed the flashlight from Pierce's belt. "Are we good here?"

"I think everyone's down," Jeremy affirmed.

"Come on. Grab Norton and let's get out of here."

"Norton?"

"He's a kidnapped victim. He's getting out with us."

Jeremy nodded and went to help Norton up.

"Leave us today," Haagen gurgled through the fluid in his mouth, "but you won't be rid of us tomorrow."

Ray shone his flashlight on Haagen. He scrutinized the beaten old man. His previously finely-combed grey hair looked like a patch of weeds. His face had cuts and welts. His left hand contorted in a seizure-like manner. Ray must've punched that hand while Haagen was shielding his head. Blood drooled out of his nostrils and the side of his mouth. The once distinguished man who sat on the glorious, wooden throne was pathetically lying on his side like an invalid.

"You come near my family again," Ray warned, "and I will beat you into the ground again. I don't care how many of your mindless henchmen I have to get through. If you touch me, my family, or my friends, I will come after you. And I will get to you."

Haagen's bloody smile wormed its way up his cheeks. "We will be watching you. You will hear from us again."

"Dad." Jeremy appeared with Norton beside him. "Let's get out of here."

Ray turned from Haagen and went to his son. He shined his light at Norton to quickly examine him. "You're fine?" he asked. "Can you run?"

"Yes," Norton answered peevishly.

"Let me see my phone," he told Jeremy.

Jeremy patted his back pockets and found his dad's phone where Jamie slipped it. He took it out and looked at it in puzzlement.

"It was a gift from your sister," Ray said.

Jeremy smiled and handed it to his dad.

Ray checked the satellite tracking app on his phone. He saw where they were on the schematics of ApexGen's subterranean structure and determined the best exit route. "Let's go." Shining his light toward the side door, he led the way.

As they ran to the exit, Jeremy scanned the room with his flashlight to probe for danger. A few of the assailants tried to slowly get up, including Officer Bohr, who still held one hand over the eye Jeremy jabbed with his fingers.

Ray grabbed the handle of the side, metal door. According to the schematics, beyond this door should be another hallway leading to four large rooms, two on each side. At the other end of the hall was the stairwell. Considering the other sort of rooms nestled on the 63rd floor next to the medieval, mythological chamber made him nervous.

He opened the door and led them into a modern hallway, where the floor was made of finished concrete and the walls were made of stainless steel. There was no artwork on the walls, but the sheen of the steel exhibited an attractive refraction. The rooms on either side did not have doors. There were glass windows to see into the room and a doorway for a person to enter. Recessed lights in the fourteen-foot ceiling dimly lit the modern hallway.

Ray led them into the hallway slowly. Norton hugged against Ray's left side, practically hanging off of his arm. As they passed the first room on the right side, the three of them looked in. It was a control room, similar to that of a command center with multiple monitors, giant screens, rows of computers, radar tracking images, and real time surveillance videos of various places around the world.

Fifteen employees dressed in casual business attire occupied this room. They stared at Ray, examining the intruder and watching to see what he would do. None of them moved. They weren't fighters. Ray could tell by their puzzled and apprehensive expressions and lack of initiative to confront Ray. He kept his company moving forward.

The second room, on their left, was an eloquent office. The doorway had a switch for a metal door to drop down from the ceiling and seal its occupant inside. It was a panic room. Dark wood panels lined the walls, a commanding desk sat in the center of the room on top of a red area rug, and trophies, awards, and plaques from M.I.T. adorned the walls. This could be none other than Haagen's private office. Ray was tempted to ransack it to obtain important information on ApexGen, but the room was immaculate. Nothing lay around for convenient swiping, and there was no time for pillaging.

Coming to the third room on the right, they saw an impressive meeting room with a long, thick wooden table and large leather chairs surrounding it. A half a dozen people in casual business attire were in this room.

Moving on they approached the fourth room on the left side. Ray heard voices coming from inside of it—male voices. Ray appeared in the window of the room and saw a dozen old men sitting around a circular, bronze table. The old men were dressed in expensive suits. They each had files, electronic tablets, and cell phones in front of them. In the center of the table was an impressive three-dimensional map of Los Angeles. Small red flags marked particular points on the map.

"Who are you?" a bald, old man demanded with a rough, commanding voice, as if he was the captain of a freight ship.

Ray stepped into the opening between the glass windows.

"This must be Ray Lee," said a wrinkly man with hair only on the sides of his head.

Ray, Jeremy, and Norton stood in the entryway silently. If Haagen was the leader of ApexGen, this group appeared to be the governing board. Ray mentally sized them up.

"If Ray Lee is here," an old man with a leathery face scoffed, "that must mean Haagen was unsuccessful."

"I knew that haughty professor would get in over his head sooner or later," said another old man with a flapping bag of skin under his chin.

"By your appearance, Ray," an old man with short, white hair spoke, "you must not have accepted Haagen's offer. Shame. You know you and your family will suffer for this once you leave this structure."

"Perhaps," a bald, old man with a perfectly trimmed grey beard said in a captivatingly suave manner, "you and Haagen had too much history for you to pledge your allegiance to him, but you might accept the offer to join ApexGen if it came from us." He spoke in a grandfatherly tone, but his expression was that of a CEO. He appeared wise, confident, and unwavering. "You don't have to agree with Haagen. Just agree with us. We keep Haagen in line. Now think about this young man, before you complete your intention of going into that stairwell. Even if you leave our subterranean structure, you know we cannot allow you to roam free with all that you have witnessed here. Your awareness is now your curse."

Ray thought carefully.

"Why don't you come here, Ray?" the bald, old man invited in a commanding tone. "Let us talk. You and I."

Suddenly, Ray concluded his mental consideration. He slowly walked toward the bald, old man with the beard. This silently approaching Asian man stimulated the curiosity of all the old men. Ray stopped right in front of the bald, bearded man and examined him.

The man looked up at Ray with a rock-solid composure. Ray silently stood before this old man, like he was standing at attention, but he was really examining his opponent.

The bald man said, "Good. Now, let us talk like men, Ray Lee. Listen to me—"

Ray's unexpected movement interrupted him. He bent over, blatantly reached across the bald, bearded man and took his electronic tablet off the bronze table. "My awareness will be *your* curse." He stood straight up with the tablet in one hand and the flashlight in the other.

The man's face hardened like a gargoyle.

Ray backed away. "If you want to stop me, you can try. My son and I won't hesitate to take out all twelve of you old farts."

Jeremy restrained himself from erupting into a childish laughter.

"Stay seated." Ray steadily backed up towards the door. He startled when the door slammed behind him. Whipping around, he saw one of the old men standing in front of the door with his hand on the handle. How did this old man move so stealthily that it escaped Ray's notice? It must've been during his fixed interaction with the bald, bearded man.

Before Ray could confront the man blocking his exit, a hand firmly gripped his right shoulder while another grabbed his left arm. Simultaneously, two old men jerked him backwards while a third came in front of him and clutched Ray's throat with his flaky, dry fingers. Being choked and having his left arm twisted, his right arm clung to the tablet. Another began hitting him in the back. His tender body felt every bony blow.

He twirled his left arm to loosen himself and kicked furiously in every direction, knocking the men back. He punched, hitting flabby skin and muscular bodies. He finally dropped the tablet and managed to execute several swift, deadly moves that took out three of them, but that only invigorated the other nine. Ray unleashed a second wave of strikes, but sensed that he could not exert his full force in his weakened state. One man blocked his punch and rotated his arm. Once Ray got free, another flipped him up and over, dropping Ray on his back. A couple of others swept his leg, causing Ray to fall on his butt. As soon as he rose, another tackled his waist and spun him hard onto the floor. Their efforts were coordinated and each one of them was a skilled grappler.

Finally, a man from behind clenched him in a headlock and flipped him around onto the floor on his stomach. The attacker tried choking Ray out. Ray smelled the old man's aftershave and felt the man's coarse stubble rubbing the back of his neck. Ray rolled onto his back and on top of his head-locking attacker. Others converged on him.

They relentlessly locked Ray's appendages, twisting and contorting his joints, straining his ligaments and almost popping his bones out of their sockets. They countered his strikes by blocking and grabbing. They cranked his shoulders back, rotated his wrists, and bent his elbows in the wrong direction. They pinched his jugular veins and clawed his throat. Every time Ray escaped a hold, someone else grappled him. The dozens of wrinkly, leathery hands grabbing him were overwhelming. His joints weakened and muscles fatigued as the elderly mob pressed in.

Ray heard Jeremy banging on the door from outside the room, calling for his dad and trying to open the locked door.

While he lay on his back and the man beneath him choked him, a different man arm-barred his left arm, bending his elbow backwards. Another did the same to his right leg, bending his knee backwards. Another twisted his left ankle. Someone bent his right fingers and elbow backwards while also twisting his wrist. Someone else mounted him and began slapping him. Dry, leathery hands stung his face. The others stood around, kicking him.

He feared that he faced death by geriatrics! He couldn't move. Every part of his body was about to snap. His vision blurred, and his consciousness started to fade.

He stopped hearing Jeremy outside of the door. Perhaps he and Norton fled. *Good.* At least, he accomplished saving his children. *But what family would they have? They would be orphans if he couldn't figure a way out. No, it can't end like this!*

Just when he was about to pass out and his ligaments were about to tear, he heard a loud bang on the door. He saw a blurry image of someone bludgeoning the old men on the back of their heads with a large fire extinguisher and then hosing them with it. It was Norton. He saw Jeremy swinging a tazer-baton. He felt his joints freed and the man slapping him roll off. Instinctually, he head butted backwards, knocking out the man beneath him, whose chokehold went limp.

As Ray rose to a wobbly stance, Norton continued to hose the old men and Jeremy waved his tazer-baton, igniting sparks in the white mist drifting in the air. Ray picked up the tablet off the floor and stumbled out of the door.

"Dad!" Jeremy followed his father out of the room. "Are you okay?"

Still gasping for air, Ray muttered, "We need to get out now. Who knows what else we'll run into." He saw one of the techs from the operations room standing by him with his keycard shaking in his hand.

"I made him open the door," Jeremy said, pointing the tazer-baton at him.

The young tech backed away frightened and returned to the operations room.

"Ray," the bald, bearded man called to him as he got up from the floor, "you're not leaving with my tablet."

Ray looked back into the room through the doorway one last time at the six old men still standing. He nudged Jeremy towards the stairwell, and Norton released a few more foamy blasts into the room for good measures. As they entered the stairwell, Ray heard the bald man contacting someone and giving orders to stop Ray.

Upon entering the stairwell, they saw five security guards lying on the floor with concrete debris around them.

"What happened here?" Jeremy asked quizzically, looking around for clues. "No one but us have come through here, right?"

"I don't know," Ray said. "We might find out soon enough. Let's go."

They began their ascent of the 63 flights.

. . . .

"Dad, you sure you want to take that? They won't let us out with it," Jeremy said.

"They weren't going to let us out anyways," Ray answered. "I'm guessing since this tablet belonged to one of those men, it contains crucial evidence about ApexGen. Whatever is on here has to be information from the highest level. This is our ammunition against them."

Ray started typing and sliding his fingers on the stolen tablet as he went up the stairs, but his distraction with the tablet slowed down his pace.

"What are you doing?" Jeremy asked. "We should hurry."

"Miranda," Ray called to Miranda with her still on speakerphone, "I need you to link me to one of our satellites. I'm transferring data. Stream it through our satellite to these destinations."

"I'm opening a streaming channel," Miranda responded.

"Dad, I think I hear people gathering outside the stairwell. Sounds like they're posse-ing up before they come in. We have to hurry," Jeremy insisted, looking over the railing from four flights above the bottom.

"It'll stream for the next seven minutes. Monitor that channel to be sure it stays open and live."

"Got it. You just get yourselves out of that hole, Ray," she ordered.

"Are you some kind of special agent?" Norton asked.

"No," Ray answered. "Just a father trying to protect his family." He shoved the tablet into the back of his pants while leaving it running. "Let's hustle."

"Yes!" Jeremy concurred.

"I can't tell you enough, thank you for helping me," Norton said as his panting grew heavier.

"Thank you for helping me back there when I got jumped by the elderly and not leaving us," Ray replied.

"Well, thank you for not shooting me back there," Norton responded through shortness of breath. "Listen, I don't know who you guys are, and I don't know what I did to you, but I'm sure I owe you an apology." He heaved in a strained breath. "Whatever I did, I'm truly sorry to you both."

On one hand, the apology didn't mean a lot since Norton didn't know what he was apologizing for. On the other hand, hearing the apology meant the world to Ray and Jeremy.

"Save your breath," Ray told him. "We'll have time to talk if and when we get out of here."

"Yeah, yeah. Good idea." Norton was already dripping with sweat.

They arrived at the 57th floor and kept ascending at a brisk pace, when suddenly the door on the 63rd floor burst open. Ray looked down the stairwell to see a dozen technicians in their white shirts and ties armed with tazer-batons stream up the stairs. A couple of agents and a couple of security officers followed the train. The bald, bearded man stepped through the door, pointed up the stairwell and announced sizable bonuses for every personnel who would take part in apprehending the escapees and retrieving the tablet.

Ray and Jeremy couldn't move much faster in their wounded conditions, and Norton struggled to catch his breath.

"Looks like they're unloading whatever people they have left at us," Jeremy said, peeking over the railing at the pursuing band. "Looks like a hodge-podge group, but there's still at least 15 of them!"

Ray paused at the entrance to the 53rd floor.

"Oh, are we taking a break?" Norton asked, panting. "They're still coming!" He saw both Ray and Jeremy looking at the door with a large "53" painted on it. "What's the matter? Did you leave something behind on this floor?"

Jeremy said, "A friend."

"So do we have to go get your friend?" Norton asked impatiently.

Ray seriously contemplated going back for Deon, feeling he couldn't leave him as he passed the floor he was on, but he recognized they had no way of freeing him from the machine. "We can't," Ray struggled to say. "I'll come back for you, my friend. Thank you." He touched the "53."

"Dad!" Jeremy yelled while peering over the railing. "They're on the 57th floor!"

"Let's go!" Ray pulled his hand from the "53" and went up the stairs.

The rumbling of footsteps beneath them sounded like a stampede.

"Does it sound like there's more of them?" Ray asked.

"Yeah, there's about 20 of them now," Jeremy answered, looking over the railing. "I saw a few more white-collars from the other floors join them. I think they all want the bonus."

They continued their journey to the surface in haste. Three employees, appearing to be accountants, stood in the stairwell of the 39th floor. But as Ray approached, they retreated back through the doorway. By their fearful expressions, Ray guessed that his reputation had become viral in ApexGen. They weren't going to engage him without the numbers. The three accountants ended up joining the pursuing band of 20.

Jeremy commented, "Are they going to start throwing secretaries and custodians at us?"

Ray smirked at the mention of custodians, triggering his recollection of the MiraCom battle. "I wouldn't be surprised if they did."

The absence of a substantial resistance validated Lieutenant Ashford's claim that he had emptied his entire security force into the generator room. Although, the pack of 23 closing in on them were still enough to overwhelm Ray and Jeremy in their wounded and fatigued states.

After climbing 1248 steps, Ray's legs felt like lead.

Passing the 18th floor, Jeremy peeked over the railing again. "They're at the 21st floor. They're gaining on us."

"I don't think I can make it," Norton announced, panting and dripping a trail of sweat on the stairs. His knees quivered as he leaned on the railing. "My legs. Can't move anymore."

"Come on," Ray grabbed Norton by the collar and dragged him up the next several steps until he ascended on his own again.

When they came to the 12th floor, Ray stopped.

"Why are we stopping?" Jeremy asked.

"I know where the five bodies at the bottom of the stairwell came from," said Ray, looking at a missing flight of stairs in front of him. Rebar protruded out of broken concrete. Black char covered the walls and the remaining steps.

"What happened here?" Norton asked.

"It must've been Abby. She blew the stairs to cut off her pursuers. She must've dropped a tube right on top of those five guys down there, blowing them off the steps."

"She is sick!" Jeremy praised. "Now what do we do?"

Ray phoned Miranda as he entered the 12th floor and asked her to guide him to the ventilation shaft. She directed him through halls and across office rooms. They passed by several non-threatening staff workers phoning in to report Ray's position. Ray heard the entourage of 23 ambitious employees rumbling into the 12th floor. Five more white-collared employees joined the band.

Ray and the others entered a lunchroom with a kitchenette. On the far wall was a metallic hatch, the size of a trash shoot. Ray forced the two employees out of the lunchroom and locked the door behind him. He searched the cupboards and under the sink to find a pack of rubber dishwashing gloves.

"Ray," Miranda said, "I lost contact with our satellite. But you're close enough to the surface where you have a signal."

"ApexGen got into our main server. I'm sorry, but I gave them Miracom."

"We'll talk about that later," Miranda stated. "Keep moving."

Jeremy pulled open the metal hatch and poked his head in. It was a tight space. There was a draft flowing down from the top. He looked down and saw, just as Stanley had said, a straight drop to the bottom, which he could not see. There was an iron ladder to his right that ran continuously up and down the entire shaft.

The pack of 27, some armed with tazer-batons, banged against the locked door.

"We have to go!" Jeremy shouted.

"Put these on," Ray said, tossing the pack of gloves to Jeremy. "Climb up the shaft."

Norton looked in the shaft. "In there? No way. I'll die!"

"You'll die here! Now go!" Ray shoved Norton in, forcing him to take hold of the ladder.

The locked door to the lunchroom loosened.

Ray went in after Norton. He nudged Norton's foot to make him climb faster. After they climbed to the 11th floor, they heard the hatch to the ventilation shaft on the 12th floor open. As Ray expected, they debated about climbing into the treacherous ventilation shaft. By the time, Ray and the others reached the 10th floor, one of the guards announced he was going to electrocute them. The guard tazed the metal ladder. Deathly zapping sounds echoed in the shaft, but Ray and the others were protected by their rubber gloves and shoe soles. The 27 did not pursue. Instead, Ray heard them say that they were taking the elevator up to the ground floor to cut them off.

"Why couldn't we take the elevator?" Norton complained.

"They control the elevators. They would trap us," Ray answered.

"What will we do when we get to the ground floor and they're waiting for us?" Jeremy asked.

"We'll figure it out when we get up there. Let's hope their elevator is delayed," Ray answered.

They ascended up the shaft to the ground floor.

. . . .

Jeremy emerged out of the ventilation shaft with his tazer-baton waving in front of him. Ray stepped into the lobby of the ground floor.

The lobby security staff, about eight of them, stood ready and waiting for Ray to emerge from the ventilation shaft. Only half the group of the 27 came out of the elevator just as Ray entered the lobby. The ApexGen personnel staggered around Ray and maintained a distance.

"You can't leave this lobby with the tablet," said a six-foot tall security officer with a receding hairline.

The confrontation between the security guards and Ray with his tattered, bloodied shirt drew the attention of many AmeriBank employees going up and down the escalators and walking across the lobby.

He suspected what they were doing. They didn't seal off the area but permitted the normal traffic of regular bank employees. They would use them as collateral damage and pin the blame on Ray who was the obvious thief!

"Set the tablet on the floor," the guard reiterated. "Or we will use force to take it from you in front of all of these people. Don't try to fight. You won't make it to the sidewalk before we shoot you." The lobby guards, unlike the subterranean ApexGen officers, were armed with guns.

By now, Ray was definitely feeling too weak to fight any more. His weary body wanted to collapse. He glanced behind him. Norton froze like a terrified rabbit. Jeremy was also injured and too battered to sustain another serious battle. The exit to their freedom was only 30 feet away. He could see the outside world through the glass walls. The street never looked so appealing before.

He couldn't leave the hellhole empty-handed and without evidence of this terrorist organization that threatened his family. ApexGen had to be shut down for not only his family's sake but also society's. He slipped the tablet out from the back of his pants.

"Come and pry it out of my hands," Ray invited with a piercing, cold tone as he narrowed his eyes at them. He shifted one of his feet back to assume a fighting stance.

Jeremy snapped his tazer-baton on and the crackle of electricity echoed in the lobby. He stepped up to his father's side.

The father and son squared off side-by-side for one last fight.

Ray felt the sores and cuts on his body. The taste of blood in his mouth was bitter. His hands trembled from fatigue.

"Dad?" Jeremy asked.

"We're going to get out of this," Ray assured.

"Those two back there have guns."

"I know."

"They're far away."

"I see that."

"How will we get to them before they shoot us?"

"I'm working on it."

The guards shifted their formation. The two guards with the guns remained stationed as sentries by the exit. They lifted their sidearms out of their holsters and raised them when suddenly pepper spray canisters appeared in front of their faces. They each received a full shower of burning pepper spray into their eyes, nose, and mouth. They spiraled down toward the floor but the pepper sprays followed them.

"Back off!" Miranda shouted. The terrifying echo of the Thunder Queen's voice in the lobby was music to Ray's ears. She grabbed the gun from the officer she dispatched.

Miranda and Abby stood over their victims. While Abby held the pepper spray in one hand, she held one more test tube in the other.

Before the six-foot tall security guard could respond, 30 individuals dressed in a familiar black uniform flooded through the entrance and into the lobby, disregarding security checkpoints. The band in black was his Wing Chun students led by Miguel!

"What's up, Sifu?" Miguel greeted from across the lobby. "Now all you chumps better back down or we're gonna have an old school throw-down!"

Ray proudly admired his students who were poised to fight.

The security guards looked to the six-foot tall guard. Ray saw him take notice of the notorious test tube in Abby's hand, Miranda claiming the gun of her victim, and the 30 martial artists invading his lobby. He shook his head at his fellow guards and the pack of eager accountants in resignation.

Ray internally sighed with relief.

"Let's go, Ray!" Miranda yelled. "This isn't a parade!"

Ray, Jeremy, and Norton hobbled to the exit. Ray passed Miguel and a dozen of his students, affirming them with head nods. As he approached Miranda and Abby, a smile beamed across his face.

"So good to see you," Ray said tenderly to Abby as they went. "I'm glad you're safe. And Jamie?"

"She's safe. Who's this?" Abby asked, looking at Norton.

"You'll never believe it," Ray responded while exiting through the large double glass doors. Miguel brought up the rear with the others.

In front of Ray was a caravan of seven getaway vehicles double-parked on the street, each with one of his students at the wheel ready for a fast break. He saw Fred riding shotgun in a blue van. The side door of the van slid open and there was Jamie welcoming them with a perky grin!

Ray jumped into the van with Jamie. Jeremy, Abby, Norton, and Miranda followed. The getaway vehicles sped away.

Chapter 32
Offensive

As Ray sat on the floor of the industrial van with no seats, the sight of Jamie, Jeremy, Abby, Miranda, and Fred gradually allayed his fighting spirit. His breathing calmed. Dried blood moistened by sweat covered the sides of his head. His sweat-soiled shirt was torn at the shoulder and missing a few buttons. His dirty hands appeared aged and roughened, and his knuckles were bruised and cut.

Jamie slowly got up and approached Ray. "Daddy," she said softly with outstretched arms.

Ray, filled with affection, got on his knees and received his daughter tenderly. Her little arms pressed into the wounds on his back, but he felt soothed. He hugged her soft, warm body with all the energy he could muster. He buried his bloodied nose into her small shoulder and began to cry.

He reached out toward his side for Jeremy. Jeremy immediately accepted the invitation and scooted over on his knees to hug his dad with one arm and Jamie with the other. Ray moved his head from Jamie's shoulder pressing his face against the side of Jeremy's head. His crying turned into weeping.

Everyone else in the van watched the emotional family reunion. Abby placed her hand over her heart. Miranda's usual stern face softened with compassion. Even Norton appeared moved.

"Daddy, are you okay?" Jamie asked.

Ray pulled his face away from Jeremy to look at the two of them without loosening his embrace. His tears washed some of the dried blood down his cheek. With Jamie practically sandwiched in the middle, he answered her, "Yes, princess, I am more than okay. I am the happiest father right now."

"You're hurt," Jamie said, inspecting the blood on Ray's face.

"I know, but I am happy. I am so glad I have my family."

The Lee family remained absorbed in their three-fold embrace, until Miranda asked, "Where is Deon?"

The three released each other. Ray replied, "He stayed behind, so Jamie could be free."

Miranda appeared emotionally bothered but was shaking it off. "I knew I saw something in that kid the night I found him searching for you outside Miracom."

"We're not going to leave him, are we, Dad?" Jeremy asked.

"No," Ray answered. "We'll be back for him, but we need to regroup and devise a plan."

"Where to now?" Fred was turned around in his seat.

"Back to the church first to retrieve all of our belongings."

"Could the ApexGen guys be heading there too?" Fred asked.

"Possibly. But they barely had anything to throw at us during our escape, so I'm betting they won't be responding too quickly in coming after us. Fred, you have my—"

"Right here, buddy." Fred lifted up the black canvas bag with the Harvester inside of it. "What are you going to do next? Knowing you, you have the next step already planned."

"The next step is to start sifting through the data I stole from one of ApexGen's chief executives."

Abby picked up the tablet, which had fallen out of Ray's back pants while he climbed into the van. "Sifu," she said with concern, "there's nothing on here. It's blank."

"Of course they would activate remote wipe once the tablet was stolen," Fred said. "All the data is gone then."

"I knew they would use the remote wipe once we got into the stairwell, but it doesn't matter."

Miranda smiled in one side of her mouth. "Because you transferred the data."

"Some of it at least. When I sized up the CEO guy, I figured he wouldn't be the one to activate the remote wipe, but he would order one of the IT to do it," Ray replied. "I guessed I had a couple of minutes, especially since he needed to recover from the fire extinguisher beating Norton gave him. Once we got into the stairwell I started transferring the data through our satellite before ApexGen took over Miracom's main server. While we escaped up the stairwell, I let the data transfer. I got very little, but I selectively transferred personal files and data about his cloud storage."

"Brilliant, Dad," Jeremy praised.

"Who's Norton?" Miranda asked.

Norton sheepishly raised his hand.

Before Miranda could follow up her question, Abby asked, "The tablet wasn't password protected?"

"That's the beauty of walking into the middle of a meeting and taking the tablet hot off the executive's hands. The tablet was open and in use," Ray answered.

"How will knowing about his cloud storage help us?" Abby asked.

"Don't tell me you're one of those who still backs everything up on a hard drive?" Jeremy teased. "The cloud storage is an internet storage space. Data from his mobile devices automatically back up information to the cloud."

"So, where did you transfer the data?" Fred asked.

"Five locations, including your personal email account and dropbox."

"Mine?" Fred said with surprise. "Why mine?"

"Because I need someone I trust and you were the first person I thought of in the spur of the moment. I need you to start hacking into his cloud storage. Use the data I siphoned from his tablet to crack his account. Download whatever you can. Back it up onto an external hard drive. I'm aiming to gather enough info to incriminate ApexGen."

"You really want to go down this road?" Miranda asked critically.

"I know it looks like I'm digging a deeper grave for myself." Ray looked at each of them. "But I've been in the belly of this organization. I've seen who they are. I've seen how they think and what they do. They will not stop coming after my family." He looked at Jeremy. "Jer, what is the best defense in Wing Chun?"

Jeremy smiled. "An aggressive offense."

"I'm defending my family," Ray explained.

Fred nodded. "I'm on it, then." He pulled out his phone and began checking for the content, and then he forwarded it to another undisclosed account.

"I'll help once I get my family situated," Ray added. "The CEO I stole this from likely thinks we don't have anything because he would've received a confirmation that his tablet was wiped. If we work fast and quietly, we can get what we need before he or his techs suspect anything."

"Do you have a plan for what you'll do with the information?" Miranda inquired.

"Not specifically, but I know I need to get it into the hands of people high up in law enforcement or the military. The question is finding someone I can be sure is not an ApexGen operative."

"I could help in this area," Miranda offered. "I have a trusted contact in Homeland Security. If the information is good, she'll know what to do."

"You sure you can trust her?" Ray questioned. "I've made the mistake of trusting the wrong people one too many times already."

"She and I have a lot of history. Much like you and Fred. I can trust her," Miranda assured. "Plus, she's high up enough where she can make something happen."

"That's perfect. From what I've seen, I think ApexGen easily falls under the category of terrorists."

"Let's hope we can show that. If the info we get off this CEO is insufficient, do you have a Plan B?"

"Does Ray have a Plan B?" Fred repeated with a laugh. "Do you know this man?"

"No, I don't," Ray replied.

"Wait. You don't?" Fred repeated with surprise. "That's impossible. You're Ray Lee. Ray Lee always has a Plan B."

"Not this time. At least, not at the moment. As of now, this is the only card I have to play. I'm hoping it's an ace."

"It will be an ace," Abby encouraged.

"Once we reach the church, you all should get back to your homes. You've all done more than I could ever ask for my family and me. Please know that I am truly grateful."

Ray asked Norton, "Do you have a way to get home?"

Norton replied, "Yeah, I can take the Metro. But, honestly, I can't leave without finding out what all of this was about. I feel like I owe you a real apology for something, man. I was kidnapped out of my living room. You had a gun to my head."

"What?" Abby asked.

Norton continued, "But you let me live. Then you saved me out of there. Look, I know we just went through a lot, so we don't have to do this now, but would you mind if we met up sometime?"

Ray examined Norton's face carefully and honestly for the first time. He saw passed the drunkard. He saw a trapped man.

Norton added, "You know, that's just what they keep talking about in Twelve Step—just got to be honest about things and reconcile with people. I'm guessing there's more going on between us than I know."

Ray said, "Yes, when the time is right—when I know my family is safe. Give me your number and address. I'll call you."

The van parked in front of the church.

After the others departed, Ray, Jeremy, and Jamie greeted Mr. Mills and entered the church. They got the lowdown from Cheryl about a bunch of Ray's associates making a mess of the place and treating the old, grey-haired lady rudely. She also told them about how a young police officer came but seemed to dismiss the matter and merely took a report. Ray was not surprised by the police's non-response and suspected the officer was a low level ApexGen agent. Her report ended when Elder

Nathan came out of the kitchen with a broom and dustpan.

"Ray, Jeremy, you're badly hurt. What happened to you?" Nathan said with concern. He peered around Ray, noticing the little girl behind him. "And there's Jamie! Are you okay?"

"Yes, mister," she answered. "Thank you. But could you help my dad and brother? They're not okay. I'm just a little hungry."

He squatted in front of Jamie. "I think we have some snacks in the kitchen. I'll get them for you and a first aid kit for your father and brother. Okay?"

"Okay," she said.

While Ray and Jeremy gathered their belongings in the old conference room, Nathan returned with food and a first aid kit.

Nathan said, "Pastor James wanted me to communicate to you that your lodging at the church has expired. I tried to stretch your original two-night stay to as many nights as I could. I got you the max. Pastor James started to ask if we needed to amend a lodging clause to our by-laws! He's a by-the-book man."

"We appreciate what you've done for us. I think we can go home," Ray said.

"Are you sure? Will you and your family be safe?" Nathan asked inspecting his injuries.

"I hope so." Ray placed his hand on the stolen tablet and file folder. "We can't be chased out of our home. The line has to be drawn. I'll implement some new safety measures, like extra locks, an iron fence with a gate, security cameras, and a big, ferocious dog."

"Yay!" Jamie beamed. "I want to name him 'Fluffy!'"

Nathan said, "Would you like help with getting your home in order? We have folks at the church who are skilled with installing those things and would likely be willing to help you for free or at a discounted rate."

"I'd like to get in touch with them," Ray replied.

Nathan scanned the apparent injuries on Ray. "I'll bet safety for your home and family is a top priority right now." He took out his phone, scrolled through his contact list, and scribbled down a set of names and numbers on a piece of paper. "The last contact on the list runs her own private security business. She might be of help to you while you get your house secured. Give them a call. These are good people who are great at what they do."

"That's quite a list of people in this church." Ray took the slip of paper.

"There's all kinds of people in God's house."

"Thank you for the help. My family and I can use it."

"You have a great family, Ray."

"Yes, I do," Ray rubbed both Jeremy's and Jamie's heads.

"And you're a good father," Nathan added.

Ray tilted his head and curled his lips as if to analyze the assessment of him.

"I know Melanie was proud of you for being a father and a husband. You were her best friend and her one and only soul mate. You should've heard the things she said about you to our ladies. 'He is a good man,' she would say."

Ray felt the warmth of those words. He could actually hear Melanie say that to him.

"Ray, whatever you and your family have gone through, whatever you are going through," Nathan said, "Melanie was proud of you. You should know that."

Jeremy lightly punched his dad on the shoulder.

Ray winced when Jeremy struck the bruise on his shoulder, but he gladly welcomed the affirmation from his son.

Nathan saw them to the door. They expressed their thanks one last time and gave their parting salutations. Ray and his children loaded into his SUV that Miranda had brought back from Miracom. Ray took one last look at the church and Mr. Mills sitting on the porch. He felt like he was saying good-bye to an old friend at the train station, but he knew this was not the last time he would see this church.

As they drove home, Jeremy asked, "Are we really going back to our house?" The uncertainty in Jeremy's voice was unmistakable.

Ray asked, "Are you okay with that?"

"It's just." Jeremy didn't want to recount the specific violations to their home. "I wonder if it can still be our home after all the crap that's happened to it. It's trashed." He shifted in his seat. "They know where we live. What if the plan with the tablet doesn't work and they come for us? Would even gates and a big dog keep them out?"

"Daddy," Jamie said, "maybe we shouldn't go back home."

Ray drove at a leisurely speed with one hand relaxed on the wheel. "I know, guys. Yes, we had a psycho, child-abducting babysitter in that house for two years. Yes, we had two crooked cops visit the house."

"We did?" Jamie asked.

"Uh-huh," Ray continued, "Yes, our house got ransacked and trashed."

"It did?" Jamie was astonished.

"Uh-huh. And yes, we had some tough times in there—fights, arguments. But this home is part of our story, guys. We will make new memories in it and cherish the old ones when your mom was there. We will make it safe again."

"The way you beat up Haagen and threatened him was pretty good," Jeremy said with a laugh. "That was awesome, Dad."

"You did?" Jamie asked.

"Uh-huh."

Jeremy with a revived posture of solidarity said, "I'm down to do this. Let's make this happen."

For the rest of the fifteen-minute drive to their house, they couldn't avoid reviewing their experiences at ApexGen with each other. Ray avoided the details to the fights and what they saw to not frighten Jamie. He also avoided discussing Jamie's confinement to the diabolical machinery. He did allow for Jamie to talk about how Tracy abducted her. She was very eager to tell her story to her father and brother. She freely shared about how she felt being held against her will and then taken to a suspicious house with strangers. She recounted her feelings of fear. Ray continuously reassured her that she was safe now. Jeremy did too.

Jeremy asked Ray what he intended to do about Deon. "We're not just going to leave him there, are we?" Jeremy asked, but Ray had no immediate response. The answer was "no," of course, but without having come up with a solid plan, he couldn't give an answer. "We'll have to plan this out," was all Ray would say. Jamie enjoyed hearing them talk about Deon. She was curious about the large man sitting by the bed she once lay in.

"I'd like to see Deon again," she said.

"Me too. We'll find a way," Ray said. "I'll talk with Miranda. I think she can help us get Deon."

"I hope he's okay," Jeremy said. "I still can't believe what he did."

"Me too."

Pulling up to the driveway, Ray felt the comfort of home although it had been trespassed and violated. He felt a surge to restore his home.

As they walked to the front door, he caught himself looking down the perpendicular street at Stanley's former parking spot under the canopy of trees. The thought of Stanley still made Ray's blood boil. He couldn't help inspecting the street to make sure Stanley and his grey sedan weren't around. He looked for Tracy's blue car, suspicious white vans, and creepy black SUVs.

"Dad, you see something?" Jeremy asked.

"No, no. Just me being paranoid now," Ray answered.

"I think we'll all be a bit paranoid for a while," Jeremy said.

They walked through the front door and found the home to be just as they had left it – a pillaged mess.

"Whoa," Jamie shuddered.

"It's okay, princess." Ray placed his hands on her shoulders. "We'll get this place cleaned up. It'll be our home again, but better."

"Where do we start?" Jeremy asked.

"Before we clean up the house, let's clean ourselves off. Hop in the showers and put on a clean set of clothes," Ray said, picking off a crusty scab of blood and gunk on his arm.

"Good idea," Jamie affirmed, "because you two are gross!"

"You don't smell too good yourself, little princess," Jeremy replied.

"Then you can start with your rooms. I want you to feel at ease again in your own rooms. Use the vacuum cleaner and trash bags. I'll start calling these contract workers from the church. But, first, wash up."

Ray walked past the scattered belongings littered on his bedroom floor and hopped into his shower. The pattering of hot water on his wounded back and shoulders felt therapeutic. The water rained down his face and dripped off his chin like a waterfall. He tasted some of his blood rinsing off of his face and running into his mouth. He watched the grey dirt swirl around the drain on the shower floor.

As he stood there allowing the water to cleanse him, he reflected on recent events. It felt too much for him to take in all at once—the battles he fought, the truths uncovered, the insights gained, the sacrifice he accepted. He thought about Abby's calculations and conclusions from the accident. The talk with Nathan echoed in his mind. He recalled the conversation of Deon offering himself to save his daughter. He clearly replayed Melanie's last words to him. He was overwhelmed. As the dirt and blood washed off of him layer by layer, he felt he had emerged anew somehow. He perceived himself, his loss of Melanie, and his present life differently. There were new meanings to his past and present. The new meanings left him with answers he had yet to fully realize but knew they were there. He had a new understanding of wholeness achieved by grace. He thought it was ironic that he was only getting this now, since he taught his students that in Wing Chun power came not from brute force but grace.

The new perspective posed some additional questions for him for the future. Would he return to his old career at Miracom? He didn't know. Seeing the Harvester at work rekindled an interest for inventing and patenting his ideas. The most important question looming in his mind was how he would be different as a single father. The break-through with Jeremy was the beginning of a different kind of relationship. He rescued both of his children but he knew in some way he himself was rescued as well.

After he put on a clean shirt and jeans, he checked on Jamie who was in her room placing scattered objects from the floor back on her desk. She looked behind her at her dad and said, "I'm rearranging."

"It's looking good," Ray encouraged as he examined the holes on her walls.

"I meant to give this to you." Jamie handed him the Post-It note that read, "I'm glad you're my daddy. Thank you for loving me and taking care of me."

Ray pretended to be surprised. Although he wasn't, his daughter handing the note to him genuinely warmed his heart. "Thank you, princess. This means a lot to me." He relished in having his daughter back home with him. He wished Deon could experience the comfort of being back with his grandmother. "You're doing a great job. I want your room to feel like it's yours again."

"It will, Dad. Don't worry."

She always made him smile even when they were in a mess. He said, "I need to call the people from the church. I'll come help you in a bit."

She replied, "Okay. I'll be here."

Ray saw Jeremy sitting on the floor, examining the torn pieces of his artworks.

"I'm sorry about your art." Ray stepped into the room.

Jeremy sighed, holding a large fragment of a pencil drawing of a raging beast. "I'll still keep these, because they were a part of who I was—part of my story."

"I know. You should keep them. Is there anything I could do to help?"

"No," Jeremy replied in a soft voice, "but thanks. I need to sort through everything. Going through this stuff is making me think, so it's slowing me down."

"I know what you mean. If you need me, I could help you with your room, and then you can help me with mine, because it's a mess."

"I'm sure I'll take you up on that."

"I'll be in the dining room."

Ray went to the dining room and called the dozen names Nathan gave him, which included a locksmith, a contractor who specialized in installing fences and gates, a technician who installed security cameras, and a director of a private security agency. Ray explained to them the trouble his family faced beginning with the abduction of Jamie. He told them the generic version of the story, leaving out details about ApexGen. At first, he felt awkward about giving his sob story to strangers, but when he mentioned Melanie, they surprised him with their warm responses and willingness to help him. Either they knew Melanie or their wives knew her. They praised her for the wonderful person she was or the positive impact she had on them. They talked with Ray about Melanie for several minutes and suddenly they were no longer strangers to him. Most offered Ray a generous discount for their services and others insisted on donating their services.

He scheduled workers to come to his house over the next week. An hour later, the locksmith came and put new locks on all of their doors. The director of the private security agency personally came for Ray to sign a contract for their services that included a private security guard keeping watch over the house from evening until morning beginning that day. Ray knew he needed the help. The overwhelming generosity was like a foreign breath of fresh air. He must've thanked each person he talked to five times.

It was a befuddling feeling. Even now from the grave, Melanie was blessing him and his children. A principle imprinted onto Ray's heart. The ripples of a good person echoes timelessly.

After these calls were completed, there was one last important call he had to make—a call to Miranda about Miracom.

. . . .

"Yes," Miranda answered the phone.

"Miranda, I need your help with one more thing—something very important," Ray said. "I know Miracom is compromised." He felt the urge to apologize and explain himself before continuing. "I'm sorry about that. I'm sorry I gave them the decryption code. I was down there, and they had Jeremy—"

"Ray," she interrupted, "I understand. You did what you had to do. We'll get Miracom back, and you'll make it up to me by helping me do that." She had the skill of conveying sympathy while speaking sternly.

"I know you have contacts with surveillance."

"I've already been on it. Once I saw that Deon didn't come out with you and heard you say he was trapped in there, I made a call."

"To whom?"

"Richard Pendleton at Verico. After what we've been through, there are not many I trust, but Richard is an old friend and colleague. He's another one of my few trusted contacts. Verico has two satellites in space and has the capability of accessing surveillance feeds from cameras throughout the city."

"Is he willing to help us?"

"Yes. Once I told him what's happened with you, Miracom, and Deon, he got on it right away. We'll have eyes on ApexGen soon enough. But he wants to meet with the two of us this afternoon, though, to hear in person about the details of our situation and whom we're up against in person. Can you do that?"

"Could we meet in a couple of hours? By then, a security officer will be coming to watch my house. I'll feel safer leaving the kids at home then."

"I know you should be with your children now. So taking you away from them is not the best idea, but a face-to-face meeting for what we're asking of Richard is minimal and standard."

"I understand. This is important enough. We need to figure out a way to get Deon out. I don't know how long it will take for us to crack the cloud account, sift through the data, and get Homeland Security to respond. So whatever we can do to take the initiative, I'm willing to do it. I can't just leave him in there."

"I'm texting you an address. It's 6:08 PM. We'll meet in two hours."

. . . .

"Daddy, do you have to leave again?" Jamie asked.

"Just for a little bit. Outside there's a security officer watching over you, and I've asked Abby to come and keep you company. She can play board games or watch a movie with you."

"She's not like Tracy?"

Ray felt his heart sink as he let out a big sigh. "No, dear. She's not. You can trust her."

The doorbell rang. Abby entered with a warm smile. "I brought burgers, fries, drinks and a coffee for you." She handed Ray a cup.

"You've barely been home and now you're here watching my kids. I know Jeremy could take care of things here, but I just felt better having you here with them. I should only be out for a couple of hours."

"Don't worry about it." She stroked his arm. "After the kids eat, I can help them clean up. Where's Jeremy?"

"He's cleaning in his room."

"I'll go get him." Abby walked to his room. "Hey Jeremy, want a burger?" She looked at the broken doorframe to Jeremy's room. "Wow, looks like they really busted down your door."

"Um," Jeremy replied as he came out of the room, "my dad did that."

"Oh."

"But it can be fixed." He took a seat at the dining table. "Burgers! Why does it feel like ages since I had a burger?"

"All right, you guys. I'll be back in a couple of hours. There's a security guard parked outside. Abby will be here with you. You'll be fine," Ray said.

"Don't worry, Dad. If anything happens, I'm sure Abby can whip up a weapon out of our glass cleaner and baking soda," Jeremy jested.

Abby chuckled. "Be safe out there," she said to Ray.

"I will."

. . . .

Ray followed Miranda's directions to an elegant condominium high rise in downtown Los Angeles. The directions instructed him to take the elevator up to the roof. Ray walked onto a large patio furnished with expensive furniture and stone fire pits. Ray saw the city lights and breathed in the cool night air. The patio was empty except for the two people in the center.

"Over here," Ray heard Miranda call to him.

"Mr. Pendleton," Ray walked up and greeted Richard Pendleton. "Good to finally meet you. I've heard much about Verico and I'm well aware of your leadership of it. I didn't know you and Miranda knew each other well."

"I have heard much about you too, Ray Lee," Richard replied.

"Thank you for what you're doing. Your help means the world to me."

"Well, let me show you what we've found before you thank me. I'll get straight to the point."

"Ray, have a seat," Miranda instructed. "In the last couple of hours, Verico's satellites already found something."

Richard pulled out several eight-by-ten photo images from his locked briefcase.

"What is it?" Ray asked. "What did you find?"

Richard laid the images out on the coffee table. "These were captured with high resolution infrared imaging by our satellite. You're looking at a van and a group of people in a subterranean parking structure. Someone was being taken out of the building an hour ago. His hands were bound behind him and his head was covered with a sack, so we can't see who he was. The van was unmarked and had no plates."

Ray examined the red, yellow, and blue images. The quality of the pictures was detailed. A few of the images were close-up shots of the bound person.

"Ray, I think that's Deon," Miranda said. "The build, frame, and size of that person matches Deon."

"What does this mean?" Ray asked.

"It looks like they moved your friend out of the building," Richard said. "We tried tracking the van but it suddenly disappeared. My guess is the van was equipped with electromagnetic deflection technology, where it could travel in stealth. The last image we received showed it heading east."

"We have no idea where this van went?" Ray asked.

"No," Richard answered.

"We have to find him, no matter what!"

"We'll keep our eyes on the building and the surrounding area, but I thought you should know."

Miranda said, "They didn't waste time relocating Deon."

"We have to keep looking," Ray insisted. "We have to tap into every surveillance camera feed in the city. We should have the satellite scan a wider area. He has to turn up. We can't lose him. Miranda, when we get the information of the cloud storage, we should let your contact at Homeland Security know about Deon. A rescue operation needs to happen ASAP."

"I know, Ray. I know," Miranda said. "Richard is doing all he can. We have the top of the line eyes on ApexGen. But as of right now, we can reasonably conclude that Deon is no longer at the ApexGen building and we don't know where he is."

"Why would they move him? Where would they take him to?" The questions disturbed Ray.

"Those are the main questions we don't have answers for yet," Miranda replied.

"Then I need to get ready for a painful encounter."

Not Easily Broken

Chapter 33
Whole

It felt like a Saturday morning with the sounds of children playing in the street. The first thing Ray did was take Jeremy and Jamie to Urgent Care outside of the city to have their wounds examined. He insisted that Jamie have blood work done and have the results sent to her pediatrician. Ray wanted to make sure that ApexGen did not place any malicious agents inside of her.

"Where to now? Are we going back to do more house cleaning?" Jeremy asked.

"Not yet. First we have a very important and difficult visit," Ray said.

They got in the SUV. Ray handed a piece of paper to Jeremy. "Could you punch this address into the GPS?"

"Sure," Jeremy responded. "What is this place?"

"You'll see," Ray replied.

"Is this a surprise?" Jamie asked.

"Sort of," Ray answered.

"Disneyland?" Jamie glowed with excitement.

"Not quite."

They drove into a neighborhood with devastating potholes, shady liquor stores, adult video stores, and loiterers leering at them. Graffiti marked gang turfs. Warning signs reading, "cop killers," decorated the sides of rundown buildings. Homeless people lay on the pavement next to their shopping carts. Sketchy individuals in black, puffy jackets monitored the street corners.

"This is definitely not Disneyland," Jeremy stated.

"How much further?" Ray asked.

"Not much. Take a right at the next street. Honestly, I thought we had our fill of dangerous places? You must think we toughened up, huh?"

"This is different."

"That's the address up ahead."

They parked in front of a small, white house with a yard invaded by knee-high weeds.

"Come on," Ray invited.

They walked up a cracked cement pathway and then up three

warped, wooden steps with flaking paint chips. Ray pulled open the torn screen door and knocked on the hollow door behind it.

"This is creepy," Jamie said.

"I agree with the princess," Jeremy concurred. "I think we've been in enough scary places to last us forever. Who are we here to see?"

A couple of locks on the door unlocked. Then, a chain was unhitched. The doorknob turned and the door opened. An old, African-American lady stood in the doorway. She had pearly white hair with some stripes of black. She wore thick glasses with a broad, clear frame. Deep wrinkles and jutting moles garnished her plump, saggy cheeks.

"Yes?" she said loudly, looking up at Ray over her thick lenses. "What is it?" She looked at Jamie. "I can't buy no more girl scout cookies. I'm tapped out, you hear?"

"Grandma G, it's me, Sifu Ray," Ray said.

She leaned forward for a closer look. "Seafood Ray!" she said boisterously. "Why yes, of course, it is. Come on in."

They stepped onto a thin, stained carpet. It was a meek living room, well-kept and modest. She dipped her head slightly and looked at Ray from under her bushy eyebrows. "Where's Deon? He didn't come home the last couple of nights. Said he was helping you."

"Yes, he did."

She raised her face toward Ray to examine him through her glasses. Her saggy cheeks drooped some more. "Well, y'all have a seat. Looks like you have something to tell me." She shuffled her feet to the kitchen, which was only several steps away. "You want some tea?"

"No, thank you, Grandma G." Ray and his children sat on a small sofa with a floral cover. The sofa was low, allowing Jamie's feet to touch the floor and making Ray's knees prop up.

"Don't be all polite like you don't want to bother me. Sure, you want some tea! I have a fresh pot on the stove. Made it this morning. You should drink more tea. It's good for you as you get older."

She came back into the living room with a tray of teacups, a container of sugar and a grey teapot. "This tea here is freshly brewed straight from the tea leaves. None of that cheap stuff in them tea bags." She placed a teacup in front of each of them on a small, oval coffee table and poured the tea. A thick Bible with a tattered, brown leather cover was on one edge of the table. "Now the question is whether you want some sugar."

"Yes, Grandma G," Jamie answered with a big smile, showing all of her teeth, obviously enjoying the teatime.

"Oh, child, aren't you a doll. Here you go, baby. Just one little spoon of sugar for you, 'cause we don't want you bouncing off my walls."

"Thanks," Jamie said.

"You boys want some sugar?" Grandma G asked.

"Sure, please," Ray agreed.

"There you go," she said as she spooned some sugar into their teacups. "The sugar takes away some of the bitter taste." She sat down on an old, faded-green, cushy, armchair and picked up her cup of tea to sip it. "Mmm. That's good tea, isn't it?"

Ray and Jeremy took their cues to sip their tea. Jamie had already been drinking hers with pleasure.

"Well, tell me about my Deon, Mr. Lee. What trouble has my boy gotten into now? Or, do you prefer to be called Seafood Ray?"

"Just 'Ray' is perfectly fine, Grandma G."

"Well, I'm glad you know my nickname around here. I take it that means Deon has been talking about me."

"Yes, he has talked about you. He spoke extremely fondly of you. He has a lot of respect for you. And in the recent days, he has meant more to my family and me than you know. That's what I've come here to talk to you about—"

"That is good to hear! He wanted to quit your school because you gave him a whoopin'. I told him he best not give up on your school or *I* would give him a whoopin'. You see, that boy is used to being the toughest, biggest cat in the hood. I told him he got humbled is what it was, and he needed it. It's tough though for a young black man to grow up 'round here. They grow up thinking they got to hold their own or they going to get owned. But I try to teach my Deon differently. I don't want him to be shaped by these streets. I seen a lot of these young men jaded by power, money, and sex." She startled herself and looked at Jamie with concern. "Sorry, baby. I didn't mean for you to hear that 's' word."

Jamie kept drinking her tea as if nothing unusual happened.

Grandma G continued, "They think if they gots the bling then they somebody. I don't have much schooling, but I know what it mean to be a good person and have a good life. My D is a good boy. I just gots to make sure his soul gets the right nourishment."

"You did a wonderful job of raising him," Ray said.

"He's the best guy I know," Jeremy added.

"Oh, that's good for me to hear," she responded warmly. "So, what's goin' on? Where is Deon? He didn't call home yesterday. Said he was still helpin' you. Did you all get everything taken care of?"

"Yes. Yes, we did." Ray's eyes automatically dropped. He saw his dark reflection in his tea. He glanced at Jeremy who answered his dad with a nod. Then he looked at Jamie endearingly before re-engaging Grandma G. He searched for the words. "Deon—" He realized how fresh the emotions still were. It was incredible that all of this happened just yesterday. The image of Deon sitting in that chair hooked up to the diabolical machines with the dozen tubes and wires inserted into him was so viscerally imprinted in Ray's mind, as if Ray could reach out and touch him.

Grandma G interjected during Ray's pause, "You all look like you been in some fights. Did you all run into some no-good folks?"

"We did."

"Oh please, baby, just tell me. What's happened to my D?" Grandma G's heightened concern was evident in her tone.

"Deon did something incredible for my family. And for me. He sacrificed himself."

"What do you mean?"

"My daughter, Jamie," Ray said and placed his arm around Jamie's shoulders, "was abducted by some very bad people. Deon helped me get her back. In order to save Jamie, he took her place. The abductors have him now."

"What? Who are these *abductors*? Where are they? Did you call the police?" Her voice grew in pitch and volume.

"It's better you don't know who these people are or it could bring trouble on you. In fact, there are members of the police who are a part of this criminal organization and that's why we can't go to the police."

"Is D's life in danger?" she asked.

Ray looked down and nodded. "Yes, it is."

She shook her head. A curtain of sadness and concern dropped over her face. "Ray, you tell me where he is right now and I'll go get him myself! Ain't nobody goin' to hold my baby!"

"We don't know where he is right now. The kidnappers moved him the same night the rest of us escaped from there."

"Moved him? To where?"

"I don't know yet."

"Oh, dear Lord!" Grandma G started to cry. "Ray, you best not be joking with me. I can't believe this. Oh, poor D. My baby."

"I'm so sorry."

"This ain't your fault," she replied, while wiping the tears from her face. "I can tell the difference between a good person and a bad person and the folks sitting on my couch are not my D's kidnappers. From what I can tell, you all are his friends. So, you don't be apologizing for what others have done to him. But his friends will work to get him back. If we

Whole

can't go to the police and we don't know where he is, what can we do?"

"A communications company is providing us with satellite surveillance of the organization that has him. I also obtained evidence against the organization that could shut them down. Someone who's helping me has a contact at Homeland Security. Once we sort through the evidence I found, we present it to this contact."

Her breathing stuttered and tears rolled again from the corner of her eyes. She sat back in her chair. Her teacup chattered in her shaking hands.

Ray motioned for Jeremy to help her. Jeremy got up and kindly reached to take the clattering teacup and plate from her hands, but she refused the gesture.

"No, I need my tea." She sipped it again. "I want you to tell me *everything* that happened. Tell me who these people are. Tell how they got Deon."

Ray started to object, "Grandma G, it is for your safety that—"

"Don't protect me, Ray. You don't know me. I raised six of my own children and two grandchildren in this house. I dodged bullets from a drive-by shootin'. I chased a drug dealer off of my property with a shovel. Got hit by a car once right down the street from here. Had to have three hip surgeries, and I'm still walking. I am 83 years old, and I have survived more than you know. I don't need your protection. I can protect myself. What I need is for you to tell me everything that happened to my grandson."

Ray's sympathy for Grandma G showed in his sloping eyebrows, as he looked at this small woman with utter respect. "It started with my daughter's babysitter kidnapping my daughter." For the next two hours, Ray told the entire story, recapturing every harrowing challenge. He described the battle at Gordon's house in detail, about how he and Deon coordinated with each other.

Grandma G silently listened during the whole two hours, not losing attention for even a second. Her eyes tuned into Ray, seizing every word. Even her tea went cold.

Ray highlighted the moment when Deon volunteered to take Jamie's place. He told her about the conversation between Deon and him. He repeated his reaction of disbelief, and how he was still trying to wrap his mind around what Deon did. Ray told her about the machine that at first held Jamie hostage and then Deon. "Your grandson saved my daughter," Ray concluded.

She sighed. Tears seeped into the web of wrinkles by her eyes. "I worried for him. I knew something was wrong when he didn't call last night. I felt it. I prayed and prayed for him."

"I feel responsible." Ray held back his tears, but Jeremy was already crying. "I don't want to assume the worse about what's happened to him. I'm holding out hope that he's okay. I'm hoping we can get him out when the right authorities get involved."

Her breathing leveled. "Everything you told me is unbelievable."

"He did what he did to save my daughter, Jamie," Ray said gratefully.

Jamie cradled her teacup in her little hands. "Thank you."

She looked at Ray through her grief. "This is the beautiful little girl my Deon saved?"

"Yes, this is Jamie." Ray continued, "I never met a person more loving, more sacrificial and more humble than Deon."

"I am terrified, you hear me? Terrified for my Deon," Grandma G said. "But my heart is also so proud of him. So proud." She looked at Jamie. "He rose to be the better man that I always knew he could be." While she sobbed, Ray allowed her words to seep into him like yeast percolating through dough. "He understood the sacrifice made for him, something I always taught him from the Good Book," she said, touching the Bible on the coffee table. "He learned the meaning of redemption. There's a word we don't hear often enough!"

Jamie said, "I like Deon. I'm very sorry you lost him. If you want, you can be my grandma."

"Oh, child, come here." Grandma G stretched out her arms to Jamie. Jamie put the teacup down and went to her. Grandma G embraced Jamie, pressing her face against Jamie's, squishing more tears out of Grandma G's eyes.

Ray and Jeremy watched the beautiful moment between the six-year-old girl and the eighty-three-year-old lady.

When Grandma G released Jamie, she said, "We have to get him back. Ray, I don't care what it takes. If the police don't help, then we have to find some other way to get him back." She had her arms loosely around Jamie's little waist. "The surrendering of one life to save another is no loss. I'm just not giving up on Deon."

"We're not either," Ray answered. "I'm going to do whatever I can and pull from whatever resources I have to fight for him."

Grandma G said, "It was no mistake that he met you. I don't believe in random chances. Deon was meant to meet you."

Ray replied, "I believe that too."

Grandma G started to refill their cups, but stopped. "Oh, dear. The tea has gone cold."

"It's okay. We better be going. I will call you everyday to give you an update about our progress with rescuing Deon."

"I'm an old lady. I don't know much about computers or internet. But if there's anything you think I can do to help get Deon back, you don't hesitate to tell me. You hear, Ray?"

"Absolutely."

They parted with exchanges of warm hugs and vows to hope for Deon's return.

. . . .

As they drove away, Jeremy kept looking at the little, white house. "I can't imagine what Grandma G must be going through. I mean, I guess I can because we lost Mom and almost lost Jamie."

"You didn't lose me, Jer. You found me," Jamie said. "Thanks."

"We did find you," Jeremy replied, "but going through all of that was like the feeling of losing Mom all over again. I was really afraid we would lose you, Jamie." He glanced back at Jamie and then faced forward to look at the road. "When I was scared we were going to lose Jamie, I wondered whether I wasted too much time being pissed off."

"You had the right to be angry," Ray affirmed.

"Yeah, I get that. You can give yourself that right to be angry. My school counselor told me that. Our family counselor told us that. But does anyone ever tell you that you can be angry too much or for too long? Aren't there people in the world who are angry their whole lives and their whole life is wasted? I mean if I could choose, I'd rather spend my time with you and Jamie instead of being caught up with giving the finger to the world. You know? When I thought I was going to lose Jamie, I wanted so badly to take back some of the time I spent being angry and not spending it with her. Having that feeling of losing someone all over again just made me think about that."

"What's the finger?" Jamie asked.

Ray and Jeremy were silent while Jamie waited patiently for an answer. They both restrained themselves from smiling and laughing.

"It's an expression," Jeremy explained, "but it's not an expression you should say."

"Oh, it's one of those things that you do, but I shouldn't copy," she specified.

"Uh, yes. There are a lot of things I do that you shouldn't copy." Jeremy looked to his father. "Dad, I'm sorry."

Ray drove at an even, moderate speed. No rushing. "Jer, I probably don't show this, and I know I haven't said it. So, you probably don't know this." He paused before saying the words, contemplating the weight of the words. "I'm proud of you."

Jeremy looked at Ray with puzzlement, revealing that he truly was caught off guard.

"You're a teenage boy who had to deal with the loss of his mother. You wrestled through the guilt and anger of that loss. You fought hard to save your little sister. You showed me how I could be a better father. You make me proud."

. . . .

Four weeks later. While Ray prepared the barbeque grill, he kept looking up at the elegant black, iron fence, equipped with an automated gate, surrounding his house. Security cameras mounted the fence, hidden cameras were installed throughout the house, and a top of the line alarm system with motion sensors monitoring the perimeter protected the newly renovated home. The reinforced doors and windows added a feel of impenetrability to the home that Ray needed. Their new rottweiler Fluffy played and slept on the front yard, ever keeping watch.

Ray tossed a hotdog to Fluffy, who happily ate it while lying on his belly at Ray's feet. He had mixed feelings about hosting a barbeque party, while Deon was still missing. Everyday, he checked on the surveillance data gathered by Verico's satellite. For eleven days, there was no news of Deon's whereabouts. The signal from Deon's cellphone, which he had on him, went dead the day he was moved. Then on the twelfth day of surveillance, debris or shrapnel struck one of Verico's satellites, damaging it so that most of its functions were inoperable. It would take at least a year to complete the repairs. Was it accidental or deliberate? The investigation was being conducted, but the incident seemed too timely to be coincidental. Richard and Miranda suspected that ApexGen did not like Verico having eyes on them, so they did not risk using Verico's other satellite to continue surveillance on ApexGen. The stellar attack demonstrated the capability ApexGen possessed.

Ray hired a private detective to investigate Deon's capture. He also did his own research, examining the infrared images captured on that first day and the images from the majority of the surveillance cameras in the city to which Verico had access. He even was brazen enough to make daily drive-bys of the AmeriBank building, hoping he would be fortunate enough to stumble on a clue. But any news of Deon's whereabouts or condition remained hidden. Every night, his heart wrenched at having to call Grandma G to give her a report of all their efforts but with no results.

Miracom's main server had not been recovered from the virus. Ray went back to work after being off for two weeks to help with the effort in restoring Miracom's systems. The system still ran, but ApexGen's malware interfered with operations by siphoning information received or transmitted through the radars and satellites. On top of Miracom's troubles, comb-over Thornton filed a lawsuit against the company to try and cash out on injuries and damages he suffered on the job.

Fred gathered an ample amount of information from the stolen tablet's cloud, having downloaded 43 percent of the data before the cloud was completely wiped. As Ray and Fred sifted through the data around the clock for 24 hours, they found that much of the data was significant enough to incriminate ApexGen. They sorted the data and compiled it to form a case. By the third week since Jamie's rescue, Miranda personally took the data to her contact in Washington, D.C., explaining the situation over a face-to-face meeting at an undisclosed location designated for such sensitive meetings. When Ray heard from Miranda upon her return that it looked like Homeland Security will treat ApexGen as a multi-cell terrorist organization and dismantle the Los Angeles cell as the priority, he felt a substantial hope in protecting his family and in retrieving Deon. So this barbeque seemed appropriate and strange at the same time.

Abby reminded Ray that, yes, there was much to still be worried and angry about with Deon missing, but there was also much—very much— to be celebrated with the rescue of his daughter, renovation of his home, and renewal of his family. "Life deals you both," Abby said to him, "and that's when you have to know how to grieve and celebrate at the same time."

He knew that she was right. He had to celebrate all the good that was happening. He also knew the celebration was an expression of gratitude to the tremendous amount of help he received. He was humbled by everyone's grace. If it were not for these people and the parts they played, his life would be in shambles. Those coming to his party were all of his Wing Chun students and all the professionals from the church who worked on his home for free or extremely discounted prices. Ray invited Grandma G with great hesitation. He didn't know if he was insensitive for inviting her because her grandson was still missing, but she wanted to come because she said it was a celebration of Deon. Ray knew she was right.

Fifty-three people celebrated on the front yard, backyard, and inside the house. Laughter and chatter filled the home. Grandma G played with Jamie and her friends on the front yard. Jeremy played on the gaming system with his friends inside the house. Ray mastered the brick grill, cooking hot dogs, burgers, ribeye steaks, and chicken.

Fred walked over and stood by Ray with a drink in his hand. "You're working too hard at your own party. Let me take over."

"I'm fine. I just want everyone to have a good time."

"Your home looks incredible now."

"All due to these folks here."

"Hey, I don't mean to talk business at your party but—"

"But you're going to anyway."

"Yeah. Anymore development since we leaked the top secret data?"

Ray said in a quieter voice, "Homeland Security wants to interview me. I have a secure video meeting with them next week. They know about my level of involvement with ApexGen, so they want to get as much information from me as possible."

"You stirred a big pot."

"We stirred it," Ray clarified. "I hope Deon is okay. I'm banking on dismantling ApexGen to enable us to get him back."

"I still don't understand why they would move him and what they would want with him."

"That is one of the disturbing mysteries. I think about it every night and it eats away at me."

Fred examined his friend for a second, and then took the tongs and spatula from Ray. "Hey, it's time for you to go mingle. I'll take over. Go get a Mai Tai."

"I'm fine doing this." Ray resisted.

"I mean it. Besides, I think there's a beautiful biologist who has been waiting all afternoon to spend some time with you. This is the first free moment you've had since we got out of that giant hole in the ground. I'm not going to let you hide behind this grill. Go."

Ray relinquished his role as chef to his best friend. "All right." As soon as he turned away from the grill, he saw Abby sitting at the nearest table talking to Fred's wife.

He moseyed to her table.

Once Fred's wife saw Ray approach, she excused herself. "I should go check on the kids. It was nice talking with you."

"Hey," Ray greeted casually.

"Hey," Abby greeted back.

He sat down across from her. "Enjoying the party?"

"Yeah. A lot of people. Tons of food. Your place looks great. I didn't know Miguel made Mai Tais!" She raised her drink. "They're good."

Ray chuckled. "We've all been learning a lot about each other

Whole

recently."

"How about you? Are you having a good time?"

"I couldn't be happier about Jeremy and Jamie. Jer and I still have some bumps, but there's a different understanding between us now. We fight but we recover." Ray watched Jamie running around with her friends while Grandma G played with them, although her version of running was rapidly shuffling her feet. He smiled with a glint in his eyes.

"It's good to see you at peace," she said.

"For once, I feel more whole, if that makes sense." He quickly edited his statement, "I don't think I have it all together, but there's something growing inside of me I can't explain yet. I'm still figuring it out."

Abby observed him caringly. "It's cliché to say, but it does take time."

"No, you're right. Cliché but right. I haven't had much time to process since we've been back. I might need to take a personal getaway to the mountains like I used to when I was in my early twenties and searching."

"If you need a babysitter while you do that, I guarantee that I'm legit," Abby said tongue-in-cheek.

Ray laughed. "I think I'll take you up on that offer, because I may never again hire babysitters I don't personally know."

"Just say the word."

"Thank you, Abby. What you and others have done for me means a lot. I'm very grateful. *You* in particular did so much for my family and me. I couldn't have made it without you being there."

She smiled and shook her head.

"I mean test tube bombs?" Ray said with a childish chuckle. "Really?"

"Well, you know…" she said. "Wait until you see what I can concoct with a blender!"

"You're amazing, you know that? And, I appreciated our talks."

Abby reached across the table and placed her hand on top of Ray's. She held his hand warmly and gently. "Ray, I'm here for you. I want you to know how much I care about you and your children. I *want* to be here for you." She caressed his hand gently with her fingertips.

Ray enjoyed her caress. "You've become close to me, and it has felt very good."

She smiled sweetly and continued caressing.

"I am attracted to you." He reached over with his other hand and placed it warmly on top of hers.

She couldn't caress his hand anymore but welcomed her hand being snuggled between his two strong hands.

He sighed. "But I am not able to love yet."

Her countenance slowly changed to sadness and sympathy.

"I want to, but I'm not able right now. I think I'm just beginning to heal, and, it sounds crazy, but I think I'm just starting to say good-bye to Melanie. Jeremy's still working through his hurts too, and I'm just now figuring out how to be here for him."

He read her emotions. She didn't appear dashed or crushed but softly hurt, like the lyrics of a sad song were playing in her heart.

"I know this is not what you want to hear. I think you're a wonderful, beautiful woman. You're brilliant. You're courageous. You're fun. You have a huge heart. You are as attractive on the inside as you are on the outside. I connect with you. But I also know that my spirit is in no condition to offer the kind of love that a relationship deserves."

Abby still didn't respond yet. She appeared at a loss for words.

"You could get any guy out there," Ray complimented. "I think you *should* go date and find the love of your life. I couldn't—I wouldn't—ask you to wait for me. If you meet someone—"

"I'll be here," she blurted. She squeezed his hand and then retrieved it back to herself. She said it again slower and softer, "I'll be here." She took a deep breath before saying, "I know a broken heart takes time to heal. Because I've seen your broken heart, I know what kind of a man you are, Ray Lee. You're the kind of man I will wait for."

Ray couldn't describe what he felt. He had a thousand words to say to her, but he didn't want to ruin the contentment of them simply looking at each other. He nodded, accepting her offer to wait for him.

"Daddy!" Jamie ran to Ray's side. "You're not cooking anymore! Come play with us! We're having a water balloon fight! Grandma G said we're going to get served!" She grabbed his hand on the table.

"Oh, is that what she said?" Ray asked.

"Yeah, come on, Dad! I don't know what she's serving us, but I bet it's going to be good!"

"Let's go, Dad," Jeremy shouted from the lawn, holding a water balloon in each hand. "Let's see you Wing Chun your way through this!"

The rest of the crowd cheered Ray on.

Ray said, "Well, I think Abby has to play too!"

"Oh no," Abby protested.

"Yeah!" Jamie replied excitedly. "Come on, come on."

"I don't do water balloon fights," she declared.

Ray grabbed Abby's hand and pulled her out of her chair.

"Wait," she protested again.

Jamie led them into an assembly of laughing people from ages 3 to

Whole

83, who armed themselves with water balloons for an all-out-battle. They were just waiting for Ray.

Brian S. Chan is a pastor, professor, painter, writer, husband, and father. A graduate from Dallas Theological Seminary with a Th.M. and an M.A. and a graduate of Talbot School of Theology with a D.Min., he teaches classes on a theology of beauty, faith and film, and a theology of heroes and villains at Biola University. He is a first generation American-born Chinese, a Wing Chun kung fu champion, and Northern Shaolin kung fu practitioner. He is also a visual artist who has exhibited his work in shows in the San Francisco Bay Area, Chicago, Dallas, Beverly Hills, Pasadena, Burbank, and New York City.

www.ingramcontent.com/pod-product-compliance
Lightning Source LLC
Chambersburg PA
CBHW051415290426
44109CB00016B/1312